INTEGRATING MAN AND NATURE IN THE METROPOLITAN ENVIRONMENT

Proceedings of a National Symposium on Urban Wildlife

National Symposium on Urban Wildlife

Organized by:

National Institute for Urban Wildlife
Gomer E. Jones, President

Sponsors:

Atlantic Richfield Foundation
National Institute for Urban Wildlife
National Wildlife Rehabilitators Association
The Wildlife Society
U.S. Fish and Wildlife Service
U.S. Forest Service

In Cooperation With:

American Planning Association
American Society of Landscape Architects
Maryland Chapter, The Wildlife Society
Society of American Foresters
Southeastern Section, The Wildlife Society

Symposium Chairman:

Keith G. Hay
National Institute for Urban Wildlife

Steering Committee:

Keith G. Hay, Chairman
Lowell W. Adams, National Institute for Urban Wildlife
Richard W. Atwater, Jr., American Planning Association
Hugh C. Black, U.S. Forest Service
Allen Brohn, Missouri Department of Conservation
Thomas M. Franklin, The Wildlife Society
Raymond L. Freeman, American Society of Landscape Architects
Frederick F. Gilbert, Washington State University
Don Green, U.S. Forest Service
Laurence R. Jahn, Wildlife Management Institute
Stephen R. Kellert, Yale University
Daniel L. Leedy, National Institute for Urban Wildlife
James R. Lyons, Committee on Agriculture, U.S. House of Representatives
Gary A. Moll, American Forestry Association
James L. Ruos, U.S. Fish and Wildlife Service
William W. Shaw, University of Arizona
Carl R. Sullivan, American Fisheries Society
Richard S. Thorsell, Edison Electric Institute
Larry W. VanDruff, State University of New York

Program Committee:

Lowell W. Adams, Chairman
Vagn Flyger
Aelred D. Geis
Clyde M. Hunt
E M Risse
Jon Rodiek
David Tylka
Joe Werner

Arrangements Committee:

Louise E. Dove, Chairman
Barbara L. Mc Falls
Michael Saunders

INTEGRATING MAN AND NATURE IN THE METROPOLITAN ENVIRONMENT

Proceedings of a National Symposium on Urban Wildlife

4–7 November 1986
Chevy Chase, Maryland

Edited by

Lowell W. Adams
and
Daniel L. Leedy

Published by
National Institute for Urban Wildlife
10921 Trotting Ridge Way
Columbia, Maryland 21044

ISBN 0-942015-00-2
Library of Congress Catalog Card Number: 87-50323

Published by the National Institute for Urban Wildlife, 10921 Trotting Ridge Way, Columbia, Maryland 21044.

Typeset and printed in the United States of America by Automated Graphic Systems, White Plains, Md.

Contents

Man and Nature in the Metropolitan Environment: A Challenge in Creative Conservation

Chairman: KEITH G. HAY, *Chairman of the Board, National Institute for Urban Wildlife, Columbia, Maryland*

Welcome

GOMER E. JONES, *President, National Institute for Urban Wildlife*

On behalf of the officers, directors, members, and staff of the National Institute for Urban Wildlife, I extend a sincere welcome to you all. I especially thank our symposium committees and session chairmen and cochairmen for all of the effort and expertise they have contributed. I believe their hard work will result in a most informative and inspirational program. This conference would not have been convened today without the support of our cosponsors: the Atlantic Richfield Foundation, The Wildlife Society, U.S. Fish and Wildlife Service, U.S. Forest Service, and the National Wildlife Rehabilitators Association. Thanks to you all!

NATIONAL INSTITUTE FOR URBAN WILDLIFE

I would be remiss if I did not take this opportunity to tell you a little bit about the National Institute for Urban Wildlife:

> "The purpose of the National Institute for Urban Wildlife is to be a responsible and effective scientific and educational organization advocating the enhancement of Urban Wildlife values and habitat and the wise use of all Natural Resources for the benefit of people in cities, suburbs, and developing areas."
>
> Mission Statement of NIUW
> Adopted 4 August 1983

To do this, we must communicate. Too often, I believe, we talk mostly to ourselves—biologist to biologist, planner to planner, architect to architect. When we do communicate to the public, we use words and phrases they do not understand. How many folks, after mentioning "urban wildlife" to them, looked at you with an incredulous stare and exclaimed—"URBAN WHAT?"

Time will not permit a full summary of Institute activities, past and present. However, I would like to briefly outline one of our most recent endeavors, an "Urban Wildlife Sanctuary Program."

URBAN WILDLIFE SANCTUARY PROGRAM

I. Purpose

To establish and certify a network of Urban Wildlife Sanctuaries on public and privately-owned lands across the nation to:

1. enhance urban wildlife habitat,
2. promote an appreciation and understanding of urban wildlife and its habitat needs, and
3. recognize private and public landowners who dedicate their properties to wildlife.

II. Who

The program is primarily directed to individuals, neighborhood associations, community organizations, cities and towns, corporate property owners, and developers.

III. What

Some of the features of the program include:

- recognition—certificate, signs, decals, publicity;
- publications—"how-to" materials;
- "hot line"—staff of qualified biologists to advise and counsel; and
- certification—sanctuaries must meet at least minimum criteria.

Integrating Man and Nature in the Metropolitan Environment. Proc. Natl. Symp. on Urban Wildl., Chevy Chase, Md., 4–7 November 1986, L.W. Adams and D.L. Leedy, eds. Published by Natl. Inst. for Urban Wildl., 10921 Trotting Ridge Way, Columbia, MD 21044, 1987.

IV. How You Can Help

You can help by:

1. promoting the program through your agency or organization, and
2. recommending local conservation clubs or agencies to be invited to become Affiliates of the Institute and assist in the promotion and administration of the program in their areas.

CONCLUDING REMARKS

The success of a meeting can only be measured by what happens AFTER the meeting is over. I hope each of you will leave this conference with a new resolve and commitment to promote an appreciation and understanding of urban wildlife. Follow up IS important. I suggest we all convene again in 2 years to see how well we are doing, and what remains to be done.

Opening Remarks

KEITH G. HAY, *Chairman of the Board, National Institute for Urban Wildlife*

On behalf of the National Institute for Urban Wildlife, I join with President Gomer Jones in bidding you all welcome. You represent a great mixture of interests, professions, and geographical areas, from the United States, Canada, Japan, and England. But more importantly, you also represent the growing concern throughout our nations for "Integrating Man and Nature in the Metropolitan Environment." The beaming of intellectual energy to a limited subject is one of the prime conditions of every advance in knowledge. I hope this rich mix will generate a synergistic stimulation of new thoughts, and I urge you all to actively participate in the discussions and offer your ideas and suggestions.

For me, this conference marks a very meaningful anniversary. It was 18 years ago last month, 21–22 October 1968, that the first national conference took place in Washington, D.C., addressing "Man and Nature in the City." The 1968 conference was sponsored not by HUD, HEW, the League of Cities, or the APA, but by the Bureau of Sport Fisheries and Wildlife. Dr. John Gottschalk, the Bureau Director at that time, who authorized and encouraged the conference, stated, "If our Bureau were to focus, as we have in the past, on the wide open spaces and neglect the people in the city, I believe it would soon find itself in a very questionable orientation with society." I was proud to have been a part of that early effort, and I am proud to say that the Fish and Wildlife Service again has been the major sponsor of the present symposium.

Eighteen years ago there was no National Institute for Urban Wildlife; we did not have a Fish and Wildlife Conservation Act (the nongame legislation that still awaits funding); nor did we have state income tax checkoff programs enabling the public to contribute directly to nongame enhancement. Urban ecology, urban wildlife, and urban forestry programs were unheard of in federal agencies. Today, some twenty states have urban fishing programs and several employ full-time urban wildlife biologists. The University of Arizona, Utah State University, the State University of New York (Syracuse campus), and West Virginia University now offer courses in urban wildlife. Colorado State University plans to offer a course in urban fish and wildlife management in the spring of 1987. Since 1973, several universities have sponsored conferences addressing wildlife in urban environments. Thus, much has been accomplished over these nearly two decades, but much remains to be done.

Historically, little attention has been paid to the need to retain a developing region's natural systems, resulting in urban geographic barriers that often inhibit the movement of wildlife or isolate it in bio-enclaves. High on our future agenda, therefore, must be the intentional design, preservation, and protection of a varied network of natural areas, especially riparian habitats, throughout America's cities, towns, and villages. Such an interconnected system of open space corridors would link metropolitan areas with rural communities and state and federal recreation areas to form a vast interstate ecosystem for wildlife conservation and outdoor recreation. The Institute's "Urban Wildlife Sanctuary Program" is a part of such an effort.

Dr. Gottschalk stated in 1968 that, "Seventy percent of the entire population of the U.S. will live in metropolitan areas by 1985." The figure turned out to be closer to 80%. Today's urbanites are certainly concerned about saving the grizzly bear, the condor, and the bowhead whale, but far more meaningful to the quality of their everyday lives is the presence of nature and wildlife where they live and work. This conference is dedicated to the preservation and enhancement of that natural presence and a better understanding of urban ecosystem management.

We have tried to enlist the support, cooperation, and advice of all the involved constituencies that guide and mold the urban mosaic today. I think that we have designed an excellent and diversified program for you and now let's begin with our first speaker.

Integrating Man and Nature in the Metropolitan Environment. Proc. Natl. Symp. on Urban Wildl., Chevy Chase, Md., 4–7 November 1986, L.W. Adams and D.L. Leedy, eds. Published by Natl. Inst. for Urban Wildl., 10921 Trotting Ridge Way, Columbia, MD 21044, 1987.

Urban Wildlife and the Fish and Wildlife Service: Meeting a Growing Challenge

FRANK H. DUNKLE, *Director, U.S. Fish and Wildlife Service, U.S. Department of the Interior, 18th and C Streets N.W., Washington, DC 20240*

I want to thank Gomer Jones for inviting me to speak with you this morning. Gomer was among the very first visitors to stop by when I became Director of the Fish and Wildlife Service. In such a visit, he was not just interested in demonstrating what an upstanding and accomplished group the National Institute for Urban Wildlife is, he came to check out the new guy in town and find out where he stood on urban wildlife matters.

I will share with you briefly what I shared with Gomer that morning some months ago.

My wildlife career in Montana did not prepare me to be an expert on urban wildlife. But even in the Big Sky State, our wildlife didn't stop at the city limits. Montana's cities and new suburban areas were host to a great diversity of wildlife species, including an occasional bear or moose. When I moved to Denver with its extensive park system, I found the same to be true. To my amazement, I have also found our Nation's Capital and its beautiful open space and riparian habitats to be home to most of the original species, although not in the same numbers, as were present when our Founding Fathers decided to make this area the seat of government.

Wildlife, thus, continues to be an integral part of the cities, towns, and villages in America. Is the Fish and Wildlife Service concerned and involved with these "metropolitan" critters? You bet we are.

The Service has a mission: ". . . to conserve, protect, and enhance fish, wildlife, and their habitats for the *continuing benefit of the American people.*" Noting that three-quarters of our citizens live in urban areas, what is more fitting than a mission that recognizes urban wildlife and their habitats?

Your conference theme virtually paraphrases the job description of several managers of national wildlife refuges across the country. From Tinicum Refuge in Philadelphia to Parker River near Boston to the Minnesota Valley National Wildlife Refuge practically in the heart of the Twin Cities to the San Francisco Bay Refuge, the Fish and Wildlife Service has been doing its very best to integrate "man and nature in the metropolitan environment." It has not always been an easy or harmonious process. We are still learning. We are still trying to spread the word of productive coexistence with wildlife and, at the same time, make the world a more hospitable place for wild species and a richer place for people.

The Great Swamp National Wildlife Refuge in New Jersey is within the New York City metropolitan area. In a way, it typifies much of the conflict that can accompany the presence of wildlife in man's modern cities. Early on, the refuge experienced confrontational protests between white-tail deer hunters and those who wanted the hunt halted. Those protests continue, almost as a ritual now, nearly every year. And year in and year out, the deer wander about and off the refuge and into the suburban neighborhoods where some people love them and others view them as destructive pests. But over and beyond all the ruckus, there is a natural urban ecosystem that still survives and remains a source of wildlife-oriented recreation. The Great Swamp National Wildlife Refuge has gained many friends and supporters over the years despite, not because of, its controversial deer herd. People support it and respond to it because it offers them a rare and much-needed glimpse of the natural world in the midst of one of the most densely populated regions of the Nation.

Urban refuges are unofficial labs, if you will, for the continuing study of urban and suburban wildlife matters. Most of the urban management areas include extensive wetland habitats. These offer a chance to tell the public: "No, wetlands are not wastelands—look for yourself, they're teeming with all kinds of life: birds, reptiles, amphibians,

Integrating Man and Nature in the Metropolitan Environment. Proc. Natl. Symp. on Urban Wildl., Chevy Chase, Md., 4–7 November 1986, L.W. Adams and D.L. Leedy, eds. Published by Natl. Inst. for Urban Wildl., 10921 Trotting Ridge Way, Columbia, MD 21044, 1987.

mammals, and a great variety of interesting plants." And there is a chance to say that without habitat, wildlife will no longer exist and the quality of the human environment will diminish.

Although urban wetlands are of undeniable importance, it is unlikely that the Service will expand its urban refuge system in the foreseeable future. Those areas must be kept in perspective with our highest priority to protect wetlands of national significance, for once these are lost, they may never be returned. In some cases, urban habitats will be considered, but to a large extent, these will need to be protected by non-Service efforts. The Service will lend technical assistance and advice to citizens or government agencies for the protection of wetlands in urban or rural locales. In fact, all Service field project leaders are urged to be available to help in this area. Although urban wetlands usually are not of national significance from the wildlife resource perspective, urbanites should know they have not been forgotten and the Service can be expected to consider their needs in coming years.

Service managers have been asked to accelerate identification and evaluation of the impacts of environmental contaminants on fish and wildlife resources. This year, the Service issued a report on the health of the national wildlife refuges and found that several showed potential problems from contaminants. Not surprisingly, some of these indicators occurred in association with urban refuge settings.

It has been a quarter of a century since Rachel Carson published *Silent Spring*. When it first came out, it engendered a great wave of environmental concern. Later on, in the 60's and 70's, we witnessed countless groups and individuals in spin-off attempts to catch the public's eye or to whip up a public frenzy over the hazards of pesticides. Throughout these years, there have been sustained efforts by scientists to understand better the complex relationships and impacts of new chemical compounds on wildlife. But is has been a continuing game of catch-up and we have not caught up. The Service is about 3 years behind in analyzing tissue samples sent in from field staffs. Let me emphasize—it is not that our scientists are slow, it is simply the relentless surfeit of new samples.

The American public cannot afford to drop its guard against environmental contamination. The topic is not a fad, like hula-hoops, something for one generation to indulge in and feel nostalgic about and the next to drop as irrelevant. It is a topic that commands serious attention and vigilance at all times, by all generations.

The new effort required to accelerate work on environmental contaminants will help, will be a public service, and will benefit materially the long-term prospects of urban and suburban wildlife.

Urban wildlife has become a bigger concern each year, virtually by default, what with steady increases in urban sprawl and ever-expanding suburban areas. Some scientists have projected that within the next 30 years, nearly 20 million acres (8.1 million ha) will be lost to urban sprawl. That's equivalent to the loss of an area greater than the State of New Jersey each decade!

Obviously, urban wildlife is an important area of opportunity for now and for the future. Some excellent pioneering work has been done. Within the Service, Al Geis of the Patuxent Wildlife Research Center has completed songbird food preference studies. Birdfeeding is a major wildlife recreational activity in urban areas. Throughout the country, as many people feed birds as there are hunters and fishermen combined—more than 60 million Americans. They are all wildlife users. Dr. Geis' work also has demonstrated the value of shallow marshes for urban stormwater management as well as water quality improvement and wildlife enhancement. The Service can continue to make important contributions.

Prior to Dr. Geis' research, the Service sponsored one of the very first conferences in urban wildlife—the "Man and Nature in the City" symposium back in 1968. Also during the 60's, the Service began a long-range effort that was to provide an important benchmark for studies on non-game birds. The Breeding Bird Survey, begun in 1965, has afforded the Service the opportunity to compile a very useful database on nearly half the non-game bird species for which we have responsibility. A report on the first 15 years of that study was recently issued by the Service and already is quite a highly-requested item. An update of the report, covering the period from 1979–1985, is expected late next year. The authors of the Breeding Bird Study, Chandler Robbins, Danny Bystrak, and Paul Geissler, have provided the wildlife manager with a valuable tool. The Breeding Bird Survey relies on the efforts of hundreds of highly qualified volunteers. Without their cooperation, no report of this magnitude could have been possible. The Breeding Bird Survey was not intended at the outset to be an urban-oriented text, but from the mid-1960's onward, so many of the once-rural counting routes became suburban and even urban in character that nearly 16% of the routes are now run in suburban areas.

Our primary resource interest in urban wildlife relates to migratory birds where the Federal government has a clear statutory responsibility for the continued welfare of 832 species covered under international agreements. Traditionally, the Service has emphasized programs for endangered species and migratory game birds as these now must be managed intensively. Under present fiscal restraints, I see no significant new commitments for urban wildlife and some 750 species of non-game birds.

Is this another of those "gloom-and-doom" stories? No. This is an opportunity to pool collective efforts. One of the Service's primary functions is to serve as facilitator and catalyst for other government agencies at all levels—scientists, conservation organizations, industry, and the interested public. For non-game birds and urban wildlife, there is a real need for better national guidance and coordination.

What I envision the Service having is a small, specialized staff to serve in a cooperative advisory capacity to persons like yourselves.

Public interest in wildlife, especially non-game birds in urban habitats, has grown markedly in the past two decades. This led in part to enactment of the Fish and Wildlife Conservation Act of 1980, more popularly known as the Non-Game Act. As yet, this Act has not been funded although the Service provided a study on potential revenue sources. It likely will be awhile before Congress creates a new funding source with which to implement this Act.

I already mentioned that urban issues in wildlife will be an area of increased concern in the years ahead. The management of many urban birds is a multi-national responsibility. Three hundred thirty-two of the 650 species of birds that make up the avifauna of the Continental United States are dependent upon winter habitats in Latin America and the Caribbean Region. As efforts continue at the federal, state, and local levels in this country to clean up and enhance the environment, some species may actually face an improved habitat base ***here.*** Their continued welfare then will become more dependent upon the success of the conservation efforts in Central and South America where they visit in migration and during the winter. There is an accelerating loss of tropical forest cover. Likewise, wetlands in other countries are being lost at an alarming rate and environmental contamination, perhaps less severe than formerly, knows no political boundary.

The Service, through its Office of International Affairs, currently is working with scientists and agency staffs in a number of Latin American countries. Although modest compared to some other Service programs, we think it has helped to stimulate national conservation interests there.

In closing, I offer an invitation to any metropolitan mayors or their representatives who may be present today. No, the offer is not urban wildlife grants. But I extend the opportunity to participate in a significant and potentially far-reaching resource renewal effort—the "Take Pride in America" campaign. This grass-roots effort to heighten citizen involvement in safeguarding the public land was initiated by President Reagan in his last State-of-the-Union address and has begun to pick up steam. To those of you involved in city government, I suggest that if you have any city parkland in need of rehabilitation and repairs, if you have one or several parks suitable to wildlife enhancement, why not turn these into Take Pride in America projects? Get your citizens involved and let the Department of the Interior know about it. Not only could you receive a national award, you could also hit upon a dynamic, cost-effective, novel idea that can serve as a model to park and recreation people in other city and county governments.

Take Pride in America appeals to the best in our fellow citizens. The concept already has reaped the Fish and Wildlife Service countless hours of volunteer support from people who really care about wildlife. If you want to know more about Take Pride, we can provide the details. I will even give you a telephone number: (202) 343-4034.

Thank you for the opportunity to be with you today. Let me reaffirm that the Service, under my tenure, will be genuinely committed to the protection and enhancement of wildlife in our Nation's urban and suburban environments. This is an important and fascinating frontier for the wildlife profession and I want the Fish and Wildlife Service to be an active partner in the future progress you are pioneering.

Planning with Nature: Alternative Approaches

MELVIN R. LEVIN, *President, American Institute of Certified Planners, 8427 Greenbelt Rd., Greenbelt, MD 20770*

INTRODUCTION

The planner who attempts to integrate urban development with nature is faced with opportunities and paradoxes. Urbanization by its very nature implies subjugation of the natural surroundings. This can be achieved with sensitivity by leaving much untouched as for example trees, ravines, hills, and wetlands. Or it can be done brutally with bulldozers, chainsaws and fill, and paving nature over. In either event, urban areas represent a controlled artificial environment, which can range from much greenery to mostly asphalt. Fortunately, the trend seems to be in the direction of sensitivity thanks to heightened public awareness as reflected in legislation, litigation, funding, and not least, to the growing realization on the part of developers that nature as preserved and enhanced represents a salable commodity.

THE URBAN CHALLENGE

Urban development requires a basic infrastructure of roads and other transportation facilities, numerous buildings, utilities, and services. Over this framework is superimposed housing tracts, shopping malls, and other development. The basic investment decisions are made with primary attention to finance, engineering, and efficiency with, in comparison, cursory attention to natural features—unless these are protected by serious legislation or are considered central to marketing as, for example, in the case of waterfront development. Fitting new urban development in open rural or suburban areas is difficult enough. The challenge is multiplied when new or recycled development takes place in built up areas and attention to nature has to be fitted into the equation. In any event, master plans make formal provision for nature, but in suburb or city it is often difficult to give adequate weight in the decision process to natural preservation and enhancement, partly because these annot be readily valued in financial balance sheets.

Two factors have influenced attitudes to nature regarding urbanization in the past two decades: the first, as noted, is the growing sophistication and awareness on the part of developers and purchasers that attractive natural features are indeed marketable even though their value cannot be precisely measured. The second is that nature is forgiving. Polluted rivers can be restored to life, decaying waterfronts reclaimed, vacant lots converted into parks, and appropriate street trees replanted. But we must recognize several threats to this generally upbeat assessment.

Many municipal engineers and other officials are indifferent or even hostile to even modestly unpredictable natural features. Some officials are concerned about liability; insurance coverage for parks, waterfronts, and stray animals is expensive or non-existent, and rigid control—paving, fencing, and restricted access—is thought to limit the danger of litigation. From the developers' and the municipal view, conventional gridiron streets and parcel development are usually cheaper and easier to fit into street and utility systems—substantial set asides for woods, parks served by curving roads, rambles, and trails raise problems.

On even so simple and apparently a noncontroversial amenity as providing street shade trees, there is room for concern. One city engineer pointed out that street trees raised parts of sidewalks, dripped sap on automobiles, obscured street signs, clogged sewers, and offered a standing invitation to small children and small animals to get into trouble. In the case of dense shrubbery near urban development, there is a school of defensive architects that calls for unimpeded visual access in high crime areas because undergrowth provides cover for muggers.

There is a special problem in adjusting urban development to open beach areas. Flooding, hurricanes, and erosion often threaten waterfronts, and there are difficult and so far unresolved problems in (a) public purchase of remaining vulnerable areas, (b) limiting urban development in such areas, (c) government decisions to insure or not insure vulnerable developments or, (d) government engineering decisions to construct groins or seawalls, or to replenish sand. And there is one critical area of adjustment—evacuation of thickly settled beach areas reached by narrow cause-

Integrating Man and Nature in the Metropolitan Environment. Proc. Natl. Symp. on Urban Wildl., Chevy Chase, Md., 4–7 November 1986, L.W. Adams and D.L. Leedy, eds. Published by Natl. Inst. for Urban Wildl., 10921 Trotting Ridge Way, Columbia, MD 21044, 1987.

ways in the event of severe storms. A major (e.g., 1938-size) hurricane could create a disaster because we have discounted potential natural hazards. Moreover, in the case of beachfront, there is the special problem of ensuring public access to natural amenities.

Another approach toward ease of access is the vest pocket park. Unfortunately this promising approach has been adversely affected by municipal funding problems, i.e., costly maintenance and supervision as compounded by the threat of litigation.

Another promising approach is reflected in changes in subdivision design and other land use planning. Cluster zoning that groups housing in a portion of a site to leave the remaining land open is one possibility. Use of nature preserves, trusts, foundations, and easements has become more widespread. Reclamation of decaying riverfront and waterfronts, with some attention to nature, has become a centerpiece of city redevelopment. Overhead wires have been put underground, some billboards have been removed, and in some areas slagheaps and trash mountains have been converted into parks. Equally important, it is now recognized that acquisition or other legal control is the way to preserve open space, not reliance on preservation by default in the hope and expectation that major privately owned tracts will remain unbuilt.

PEOPLE PROBLEMS

Given a little encouragement, planners, like other executives and professionals, will admit or volunteer that our real problems involve people, not engineering. We know how to build good housing, roads, and parks. We do not know how to ensure that people living in close proximity will share living space with some degree of civility. This mutual accommodation involves intricate issues of race, class, ethnicity, life styles, crime, voluntary and involuntary segregation, and specifically, the role of governments as it impacts on people's lives. Some of these problems have been alluded to in the reference to the relationship between shrubbery and crime. This may involve the free, safe use by all sectors of the population of public parks. On a different level, there is the harm to natural areas posed by off-the-road vehicle operators in forest and beach areas. In its simplest terms, there may be special hazards to vulnerable population groups such as the elderly, young children, women, and the handicapped posed by social aberrants who use secluded public places for pathological activities.

The popular reaction to the threat of rowdies, thugs, and such minor offenders as lovers of loud music or aromatic food is secession. On a personal level, there is the household mini playground, the VCR, and the wet bar. On a larger scale, there are the increasingly numerous high density urban developments that provide private swimming pools, tennis courts, indoor recreational centers, and wooded areas. In both cases, private secession offers a time tested method of restricting access to reasonably compatible fellow users.

There also is the commercial predator who poses an even greater threat to nature. A century's experience in preserving New York's Central Park is illustrative. There have been recurring recommendations and proposals to nibble away at the park to convert part of it to a casino or other commercial use. And in cases where the decision has clearly come down on the side of public acquisition, there are also recurring pleas for slowing the pace and retaining nonconforming uses. There are recurring proposals for high density development in areas set aside for open space and low density growth. In effect, the developer is a freeloader who capitalizes on surrounding open space. Too many jurisdictions issue ringing declarations in favor of public natural preservation in theory only to accede to developer applications in practice. They are much like the public official immune to ethical flexibility—except when someone makes him an offer.

In short, we must recognize that this is an area in which there are no single, permanent sweeping victories; triumph is a ticket of admission to permanent guerilla wars to protect, preserve, maintain, and extend. Demobilization is not advisable.

CONCLUSIONS

Given the progress in the last 20 years, it is not difficult to be reasonably optimistic about the prospects of harmonizing urban development with a sensitive treatment of the natural environment. The brutal rape of the landscape characteristic of earlier generations has been slowed or halted, and in some cases reversed. There is a growing recognition of the crucial role of nature in developing small scale, humane, and livable environments. Better travelled, more sophisticated electorates are asking why rich America cannot plan for people and nature as effectively as in poorer countries elsewhere in the world.

A major unresolved problem concerns the reality and perception of elitism. Planners are charged with the duty of widening the range of informed and intelligent choices. In a direct sense, we, like other professionals, are public educators, conducting perpetual adult education seminars in a variety of settings and for a variety of audiences. We have made mistakes, as in overdesigning parks that remain half used, in skewing our programs to yachtsmen and tennis players, often neglecting the needs of the ethnics, the poor, the elderly, and other groups. We reflect in our plans and our behavior the conflict between heterogeneity through open access—even subsidized access—and the realization that substantial homogeneity may be needed to preserve harmony at close quarters. But while problems remain, progress has been real and tangible. Barring such external disasters as meltdown and inundation by oil spills or nuclear waste, we can look forward to the future with some confidence. We have learned the hard way, at great cost, but we have learned.

Conservation Partnerships: The Challenge Ahead

PATRICK F. NOONAN, *President, The Conservation Fund, 1800 North Kent St., Suite 1120, Arlington, VA 22209*

Good morning. For 15 or 20 minutes this morning, I would like to share with you a perspective on where the conservation movement has been, and, most importantly, where I believe we are going in this country, and why it is incumbent upon all of us to become very much involved over the next 3-year period. I would like to say first, Keith, thank you very much for inviting me. This is really a very great day for wildlife if you think about it. The rain outside; the elections that are going to be very interesting, especially the Senate races, which I am going to comment on because I think they are a window—a microcosm of what America is saying; and thirdly, the fact that you are here addressing this important issue of urban wildlife.

In 1907, the conservation movement formally began when President Theodore Roosevelt called together the governors, here in Washington, for the historic Conference of State Governors. Roosevelt said that the conservation of natural resources was the fundamental problem facing America. He went on to say that, unless all citizens involve themselves in that issue, through their elected officials, it would avail us little to solve all other problems. That was some 80 years ago.

We are still a very young movement. We have made some progress. Frankly, I think we have not made enough progress. In 1962–63, Laurance Rockefeller put together the Outdoor Recreation Resources Review Commission (ORRRC). That commission was a hallmark in our conservation movement. It led to the creation of the Land and Water Fund, the Bureau of Outdoor Recreation, clean air, clean water, scenic trails, wilderness systems—we could go on and on. Twenty-five years have now passed since that report was published.

Laurance, in 1982–83, 20 years after his earlier effort, put together a small group to revisit ORRRC to see if conditions had changed in America and what was needed for the future. When that report was submitted, he called for a bipartisan congressionally-established new commission. For a variety of political reasons, it did not become congressionally established, but President Reagan, on his own, took initiative to establish a 15-member commission known as the President's Commission on Americans Outdoors.

I am privileged to be one the members of that commission. I am a registered independent and I think conservation is a bipartisan issue. It has always been a bipartisan issue, and hopefully, based upon the elections today and decisions we have seen in the last 24 hours, it will remain a bipartisan issue. We do have some very important officials on our commission. Morris Udall in the House and Bennett Johnston in the Senate are Democrats. Bennett Johnston is going to be a key player for us for the next 6 years. On the Republican side, we have Wallop in the Senate, and Vucanovich from Nevada in the House. The chairman is Governor Lamar Alexander of Tennessee, an outdoorsman and conservationist. The vice chairman is Gil Grosvenor, President of the National Geographic Society.

For the past 15 months, our commission has traveled across the face of America. We have held 18 public hearings; 1,200 individuals testified, including many in this room; 800 individuals wrote position papers or new ideas papers; and we have really done an outreach program that has been very well accepted. In addition, 42 states responded to Governor Alexander, who was then chairman of the Governor's Conference, and provided state plans from their perspective, on where they felt conservation was going. We created a climate of interest.

The commission's report will go to the printer on 1 February 1987. Two documents will be published. One will be a professional document, written for many of the people in this room who are professionals, as well as citizens. It primarily will focus on new ideas, new techniques, and new programs for the next 25 years that we need to put in place. The second document, which I believe is even more important, will be a 28- to 30-page marketing document contributed by National Geographic, the best in their field. One hundred thousand copies will be distributed to elected officials across the country, to citizen groups, and to major private corporations. In addition, it will be the focus of a

Integrating Man and Nature in the Metropolitan Environment. Proc. Natl. Symp. on Urban Wildl., Chevy Chase, Md., 4–7 November 1986, L.W. Adams and D.L. Leedy, eds. Published by Natl. Inst. for Urban Wildl., 10921 Trotting Ridge Way, Columbia, MD 21044, 1987.

follow-up in National Geographic, which goes to millions of Americans. It will be a bold report. It will have pictures, and it will have language that will excite us and compel us to act. Why? Because we are still in the dark ages in this country in terms of land use and how we approach natural resources, especially in our urban areas. I speak somewhat from experience: I am a member of the American Institute of Certified Planners, I am a licensed professional appraiser, and I have dealt with some 3,000 real estate transactions affecting conservation in the last 20 years. We are still in the dark ages, and I will explain why in a moment.

We found in our commission's work that 75% to 80% of the people by the year 2000 are going to be living in metropolitan areas. We have to change our orientation from a rural park system, in terms of national parks, refuges and forests, which were great in the 1930's, '40's, '50's, and '60's, to more emphasis on urban issues. We lost the Bureau of Outdoor Recreation. We have lost most of the Land and Water Fund. The reason we lost them is ourselves. We have a very weak constituency. We have a very weak power base. We are not organized in Congress. We did not lose the Small Business Administration or the Small Business Investment Corporation, under this Administration. Yet we have lost the bureau succeeded by the Heritage Conservation and Recreation Service, and the Land and Water Fund is at a pittance.

The Land and Water Fund was created in the mid-1960's and today is authorized at $900 million. This year we will be lucky if we get $100 million. We have never rung the bell once, at $900 million. The best was in the Carter era when we got to $750 million under Secretary Andrus when he was Secretary of the Interior, and that was only once.

We have an in-holding problem in this country—an authorized backlog that we have created, Congress created, of $3 billion. These are areas that Congress authorized for purchase in parks, refuges, and forests, for which there is no funding in sight. There are in-holders across this country, who wish to sell, and have a cloud on their title, because of this situation. Frankly, that is something we cannot allow to continue. The President's Commission on Americans Outdoors found that the problem is a lack of an organized constituency, and I mean a broad-based constituency, I mean citizens. The thrust that you are going to see, in terms of our recommendations, is going to be some new perspectives for the conservation and environmental movement, and for land-use decision makers in this country. As we all know, there is a new tide of interest in land use. I am a professional appraiser. Recently the president of our largest society said to the appraisers, you must now have an ecological conscience because it can mean the difference between profit and loss and in many cases avert financial ruin. That is an amazing decision for the appraisal profession, because frankly, none of us was trained in ecology or in environmental standards. When I got my Master's in land use planning, none of us had any ecological principle courses. Planners, unfortunately, do not speak the same language as ecologists and environmentalists, and we need to build those bridges. It does us no good to talk to ourselves. We need to broaden our constituency and our power base. The conservation and environmental movement of this country is booming. There are 10,000 nonprofit conservation and environmental groups in this country. They are still being formed at the rate of 300 a year, and yet we get less than 1% of the charitable dollar. Eighty billion dollars were given away in this country last year, and $75 billion were given in volunteer time. Broadly speaking, our field of recreation and conservation got less than 1% in both areas. That is tragic. We need to find ways to address the public and private sector funding, and also to build bridges and broaden our constituency.

We have a clean air act, a clean water act, and some great federal programs. Yes, they need to be strengthened, and we are going to continue to be vigilant, but now we need to go back to the grassroots, to the local level, to the power bases, and get citizen involvement at the local level. We need challenge grants, which I am going to talk about later. Most importantly, perhaps, we need an ethic. We need what Leopold wrote about in *Sand County Almanac,* when he said that we need to treat land as a resource, not as a commodity to be bartered and sold. We need environmental education. We need adult education courses. We need an American Conservation Corps. Those programs will all be called for in our commission's report. And hopefully, our report will be implemented over the next 3–5 years. We need to strengthen and continue to be vigilant with our clean air and clean water acts. We need to resolve the in-holding problems. That was an agenda of the 1960's and 1970's. We need to just buy out the backlog and resolve that issue and go on.

The Land and Water Fund will be critically important in the years ahead, and we must revitalize it and change its mission. We need to change it in two or three ways. First, as you know, the Land and Water Fund primarily comes from offshore oil and gas revenues. We are going to expand the sources of revenue that go into that fund. Secondly, we are going to increase eligibility to urban areas and to states. Unfortunately, we are going to cut back a little bit on the federal side, after we do complete the in-holding backlog. There is a simple reason why. We have acquired most of the great national parks, refuges, and forests. Most of those areas, except for endangered species of national significance, and river systems, have been identified. Land-use decision-making is a state and local effort, and we need to integrate better with it and to tie in incentive grants.

Working with Keith Hay, your very good chairman, who has served as an advisor to us, to our staff, we are going to be recommending a national system of greenways. You know, the good Lord planned this earth. It is really pretty simple. There are fragile areas—rivers and streams and wetlands, and slopes over 20%. Those are fragile, unique, and generally the highest biological-value areas.

Conservation needs to come first, not last. When I was a professional planner, here in Montgomery County, with a planning school background, we used to color the maps orange and blue and hope that everything would take place, but it did not. And what was left over, we colored in green, because that is the way we approached it. Land use was economic, highest and best-use driven.

We want to reverse that approach and make conservation first. We want to map the 3.2 million miles (53.4 million km) of rivers and streams in this country. We want to put them on the map as an interstate conservation system, a national system of critical resources. They provide the backbone, the fabric, of a national network for wildlife, recreation, trail users, and fishing. The rivers and streams permeate every community in this country.

Our greenway program that we will call for will be based primarily on water, the issue of the 1990's and the 21st century. It will be calling for funding and voluntary incentives; it will be calling for some regulatory disincentives, because we are going to have to put teeth in this; and we are going to call for it to be implemented at local and state levels. We also are going to call for the Land and Water Fund to be a block grant program, benefitting states and local government. Local planning is very important, and we are pretty professional now. We know enough about what we want to go after. We hope to require state and local data centers to identify greenways and endangered species, so we know first what we want to protect, and can direct growth away from sensitive areas. We cannot stop growth. There are more people coming. There is a new Los Angeles every year in America. But we need to set the priorities and create the inventory. The greenways and those wildlife corridors are logical and are best left in their natural state.

The constituency is going to be critical, and we need to find a way to build a broad base. How are we going to do it? We believe in calling for a new institution to establish a National Partnership for Conservation. We have a National Endowment for the Arts (NEA), and a National Endowment for Humanities (NEH). If you look at our field of interest, our funding has gone down, and funding for NEA and NEH has gone up. Why? Because they have a power base, they have an organized constituency, they care, and they get involved. They fight for their appropriations first, and then they split it up. We fight with each other going in, and never get the total pot. The NEA-NEH model is a very interesting model. It is a quasi-public model fostering partnerships. Five thousand grants a year—matching grants, challenge grants—and loans and incentives from NEA for local action. The real agenda is to create that constituency, to create that interest, and to create the broad base of individuals to work with their elected officials, as Roosevelt said 80 years ago.

We hope to recommend the funding of $1 billion/year. Frankly, we are still divided on the commission, on what the level of need is. To me it is obvious. We conducted our hearings across the country, and 43 governors responded to us, saying a minimum of $1 billion is critical in authorized funding for Land and Water. Moreover, they want an endowed trust fund. They want a commitment that provides a source of money for future generations, so they do not have to fight each year in the appropriation process. Allocations from the fund may be 30% federal, 30% state, 30% local government, and 10% to the new institution. Why 10% to the new institution? Because that will create citizen action in communities across the nation. That is the potential 5,000 grants to local nonprofits and local government, for innovation to move us forward. We hope President Reagan will sign the wetlands bill. We think that to bring in the wetland interests and the duck hunters, who are interested in habitat, will create a broader base of support.

Partnerships. You know, the private sector is very important to us. Yes, we need to disagree on occasion, but we also need to cooperate on occasion. We need to seek new partnerships, and set examples for others, and we need to compliment each other where appropriate. We are going to be calling for a habitat enhancement program across the country on private lands. As you know, one-third of the land in America is owned by the Government, one-third by corporate enterprise, and one-third by individuals. The two-thirds in private ownership is critical to us. We want a complete and thorough review of all programs affecting habitat in this country, in terms of providing incentives and disincentives for habitat enhancement. We want a special recognition program for corporate enterprise, where they will work with us to develop habitat enhancement programs on private lands and in urban and rural areas, both needs working off the same funding source. No longer can we pit the National Park interest against local parks. We have to work together off the same funding program.

New dollar sources will be critical. In addition to offshore oil and gas, you may see us call for onshore oil and gas revenues and transfer taxes. More and more governments are passing transfer taxes. We are looking at a national real estate transfer tax. We have had one some seven times in our history, a national real estate transfer tax, with portions of the funds linked to local, state, and federal needs.

The future is really up to each of us. We are part of the problem because our constituency of urban wildlife interest is not well organized. We have 10,000 nonprofit organizations. We do not talk enough with each other and do not have a common meeting ground to build coalitions of interest. So maybe 1987, when our report is submitted, will be the beginning of a new conservation era in this country. It will take the 1990's to get it implemented. Do not look for overnight successes. You are going to be the key, as individuals, and the groups you represent, whether private or public, to work to create a new level of interest in conservation, and a new level of interest in local and state conservation and recreation efforts. By the way, we do not mention the term land use in our report at all. I think that is unfortunate, but it is still an anathema to many local jurisdictions across the country.

Finally, let me return to the elections today. The elections today are very important for us. Forget partisan politics for a minute. If you look at who was reelected, and newly elected, a great number of them have strong interest in the outdoors, and I use that word very deliberately, the outdoors. It is a broad term. It ties into habitat. It does not lock us into endangered species, or ball fields. We need to serve both with our new program. We should be very excited with the elections. Bennett Johnston, who is on our commission, will play a key role in the future, as head of the Energy Committee. Bumpers will play a key role in the Interior Subcommittee on Lands and Minerals. He is a key individual interested in our issues. A number of strong Republicans are coming back. Again, conservation has to be a bipartisan issue. We need to raise our interests above partisan politics.

The commission's work will close 31 January 1987. The report will come out and then the challenge will be up to you. Individually, you can do something. You can focus on your own community, or your own state, or your own organization. But if we are really going to accomplish what I think Leopold was telling us, in terms of land being a resource—a community of biological diversity—and if we are really going to perform as we should for ourselves, and more importantly for our children, we have an obligation to be involved as never before.

Thank you very much.

The Public-Private Partnership for Park Preservation: The Massachusetts Model

PAUL A. FARACA, *Boylston Properties, 120 Boylston St., Boston, MA 02116*[1]

I stand before you as a newcomer to the movement of conserving nature and wildlife in the urban setting. Until 1981, my consciousness was totally consumed by my chosen occupation of developing profitable real estate. In 1981, we purchased a hospital complex, The Women's Free Hospital, for adaptation to luxury housing. These magnificent old buildings, some over 100 years old, are located on a 4-acre (1.6 ha) parcel whose grounds were planned and designed by Frederick Law Olmsted. The site, in Brookline, Massachusetts, abuts the famed Olmsted's Emerald Necklace.

I am reluctant to publicly admit that, although Olmsted's name was familiar to me in 1981, I was not sure if he was the third baseman for the Red Sox, or a tight end for the Patriots, or, perhaps, the First Violinist of the Boston Symphony. I share this embarrassing fact because I believe that my process of growth, of awareness, is an encouraging metaphor for what is possible, and for what is wanted and needed for the survival of nature in our metropolitan areas.

In the past 5 years, I have participated in the incorporation of the Massachusetts Association for Olmsted Parks, in the creation of the funding of a $15,000,000 capital (a state grant program) to restore and preserve 12 historical Olmsted Parks in eight Massachusetts cities, in the creation of the successful Boston Park Ranger Program, and in the creation of several public private partnerships bringing private-sector dollars to areas of traditional public responsibility. And now, in 1986, the great and general court of Massachusetts has in committee an $8,000,000 capital expenditure bill that has better than a 50-50 probability of passage before 31 December 1986. This bill will provide money for acquisition, as well as rehabilitation, of many parks beyond Olmsted and beyond historic. The past 5 years have been very exciting and very rewarding. However, my drama is worth speaking about, only if you can take from it ways of forwarding your particular wish list.

The acquisition of the Parkway Hospital started it all; for at each planning board, zoning board, conservation commission, historic commission, and the many neighborhood informal pre-hearing meetings, two neighborhood women would always speak out about the importance of the historic Olmsted landscape, that I, of course, was proposing to rearrange, to facilitate the construction of more housing units.

The short version of this tale of my conversion is simply: they convinced me that I could make more *profit* by restoring the original landscape plan; their strong belief was that the marketplace contained many condominium buyers who would see the restoration as an asset. This turned out to be very valid. Not only valid in that many people would prefer to live in this special setting, but it also was viewed as protecting their high resale probability, and in a very important urban political sense, it stabilized the immediate neighborhood. Thus, the concept of "Enlightened Greed" came to life for me.

This magnificent hospital was built adjacent to Olmsted's famous Emerald Necklace, a winding greensward that follows rivers and ponds, wandering through several cities and towns surrounding and penetrating the City of Boston.

This portion of the Muddy River Riverbank and Parkway was badly neglected and grossly overgrown. We entered into an agreement to restore, and then to maintain the portion of the public land directly in front of the new development. What a transformation! For very few dollars, we were able to recreate the grace of the past for the neighborhood. It got me named the Environmentalist of the Year, and not so incidentally, helped the project's marketing and ultimately profit, immensely.

Why am I here? Why am I addressing this symposium with a speech that is laced with words such as profit, mar-

[1]A real estate developer by occupation, the author is chairman, Massachusetts Association for Olmsted Parks, and chairman, Advisory Committee for the Massachusetts Statewide Comprehensive Outdoor Recreation Plan (SCORP).

Integrating Man and Nature in the Metropolitan Environment. Proc. Natl. Symp. on Urban Wildl., Chevy Chase, Md., 4–7 November 1986, L.W. Adams and D.L. Leedy, eds. Published by Natl. Inst. for Urban Wildl., 10921 Trotting Ridge Way, Columbia, MD 21044, 1987.

keting, real estate development, Enlightened Greed? Why—because I strongly believe that the age of bake sales, wealthy patrons, and benefit dances has passed. There is not enough time left. We must act now, together, private sector with public agency with non-profit, to protect and expand the precious few parks and riverbanks and other natural systems that do and can exist in our expanding metropolitan areas.

In the printed announcement of this symposium, the opening sentence contained these sobering facts, from Dr. Lowell Adams and I quote: "By the year 2000, the United States population will rise to over 300 million people, 90 percent of whom will live or work in cities." For those of us with our shoes on, that is less than 15 years.

As conservationists, naturalists, planners, and other park professionals who have a specific focus on urban areas, you must expand your energy, your communications, beyond your traditional cultural subgroups. Dialogues with the development community and with the political leadership are essential to providing the means to succeed. To succeed with your particular wish list, in your particular "territory," remember my earlier phrase, *Enlightened Greed!* Keep in mind, I spoke earlier of participating in the raising of $15,000,000 for park preservation and restoration. Allow me to put forth the specifics.

Our Olmsted non-profit organization put together a very professional inventory publication. We chose 12 parks in eight cities, not necessarily because they were the most historic or because they were in the worst physical condition, but with these factors as guidelines, we chose those Olmsted Parks that were located in key political districts (Senate and House Ways and Means, Environmental Affairs, etc.), and an actual statewide political overlay map was prepared!

This inventory publication, with instruction of how to create your own professional inventory for other local parks, was mailed to every member of each conservation commission, each historical commission, statewide. Also, it was mailed to all members of city councils, community activists, to aligned non-profits, to all members of the Massachusetts House and Senate, and to mayors, aldermen, etc.

We set out to create a political base—to create an awareness that Olmsted was special and his work worth saving.

From this growing awareness, the State Department of Environmental Management was convinced that an Olmsted capital outlay bill could be politically successful.

Then we went to the telephones and the lobbying began. Letters and calls and visits from the Conservation Commissions, etc. started to bombard the Governor (who has been a great supporter for quite some time). All key committee chairmen and staffers (informed staff people are crucial for success) also were lobbied. As a result: (1) the politicians got highly visible construction projects in their home towns (work commenced this summer, an election year!); (2) the park-using public will get attractive new facilities that reflect the original design intent, fully accessible to the handicapped; and (3) the municipalities, all in old urban areas, will renew, in old neighborhoods, that needed help. Property values increased as fix-ups spread, thus producing more tax revenue.

My definition of Enlightened Greed is when all participants in the process get to divide the spoils.

ENLIGHTENED GREED IN A WORLD THAT WORKS FOR EVERYONE

The idea is not a new one. In 1865, Frederick Law Olmsted was lobbying real estate owners in Brooklyn, New York for support for his vision of Prospect Park, based upon the concept that their properties would increase in value. He was right. The concept worked for 75 years. Prospect Park has recently been renewed and the concept is once again working. The public-private partnership takes many forms. You must be open to create the form that works in your territory. For example, the Boston Redevelopment Authority (BRA) recently awarded the designation to develop the prime corner across from the Boston Public Gardens to the developer who had the creativity to publicly promise that, if he was designated, in addition to the Linkage payments required by Boston's ordinances, he would donate $70,000 per year for several decades to the friends of the public garden for annual maintenance. You can bet a ride on the swan boats, that the friends immediately got to their phones and writing desks, and let the media, the BRA Board, and anyone else know who could influence the designation that we all would win if this developer was selected. *Enlightened Greed.*

I am honored to be here. I am grateful for the work you have chosen to accomplish. You will make our surroundings more liveable. We thrive as a nation because our individual lives work, and part of this is certainly due to the balance you work to create between man and nature. When I see this delicate balance in our cities, especially Boston, New York, Washington, and Chicago, I think of the genius, the vision of Frederick Law Olmsted. Allow me to share his thoughts of 25 February 1870 when he wrote a paper titled "Public Parks and the Enlargement of Towns" to be presented at a symposium being held at the Lowell Institute.

> "We want a ground to which people may easily go after their days work is done, and where they may stroll for an hour, seeing, learning, and feeling nothing of the bustle and jar of the streets, where they shall, in effect, find the city put far away from them.
>
> "We want the greatest possible contrast with the streets and the shops and the rooms of the town which will be consistent with convenience and the presentation of good order and neatness. We want, especially, the greatest possible contrast with the restraining and confining conditions which compel us to walk circumspectly, watchfully, jealously, which compel us to look

closely upon others without sympathy. Practically what we most want is a simple, broad, open space of clean greensward, with sufficient play or surface and a sufficient number of trees about it to supply a variety of light and shade. This we want as a central feature.

"We want depth of wood enough about it not only for comfort in hot weather, but to completely shut out the city from our landscapes."

This was 116 years ago!

Ladies and Gentlemen, thank you for the honor, the opportunity, to speak to you. I encourage you to use the concept of Enlightened Greed. I encourage you to conduct your programs, to attain your dreams, with the politics of Inclusion, rather than the old safe politics of Exclusion.

Thank you and God bless you.

Land Use Planning and Urban Wildlife

JOHN L. WACKER, *President, American Society of Landscape Architects, 1733 Connecticut Ave., N.W., Washington, DC 20009*

Mr. Chairman, distinguished speakers, officers of the National Institute for Urban Wildlife, members, and guests. It is a real honor to be here today, to share the thoughts of our profession, and to talk about a very timely subject. It is a real pleasure, too, to follow a Massachusetts resident. We do not get to do that too often—there are not that many of us! Massachusetts is a state that still calls itself a Commonwealth, by the way, where I would like to think we have more than "enlightened greed." We have "enlightened action." Enlightened greed motivates people to enlightened action, and that is really what Mr. Faraca was talking about. I will share some of my thoughts on that point a little later.

Whether involved in the planning and design of the natural or man-made environment, whether undeveloped land or recycled land, landscape architects are committed to providing a framework to promote proper land use decisions, which will benefit both man and nature. With ecologically-based natural resource analysis, we can protect and enhance those elements essential to the interrelated global system and the interconnected web of life to create an important improvement in the human bond with other species. It goes without saying, of course, at this conference, wildlife needs open space systems in the land. Man, too, needs those same open space systems for protection, health, scenic beauty—all of those things that the open space and corridor systems provide in the landscape.

In order to develop these for mutual benefit, though, we need the total commitment of all those who believe that wildlife and open space are essential to the proper balance. With ever-increasing population in our urban environment, nature most always relinquishes and recedes. I am not too optimistic about its ability right now to recover, as man consumes and develops the land. We are now able to recognize that we are in danger of losing the global garden. By education, information, and forceful community action and involvement, I believe we will ensure that the necessary elements in the public welfare can be protected. The very basic need for wildlife in our metropolitan environment is indeed a complex challenge, and I did not realize that until I began preparing the thoughts of our profession for what it really means.

Although all in this room are really committed to the whole concept of preservation and enhancement, we must ask ourselves if we have yet demonstrated the full range of urban wildlife to the decision makers. We have heard from the developers. But have we demonstrated those values to the dwellers on the land and, most importantly, to the young who will be all of the above? I believe that our primary challenge, therefore, is to inform and to educate about nature. I believe that we are in the business of education, and most importantly, in the elementary and secondary school systems. When you think back on a little bit of history, the litter bug—whether you like the litter bug or not—did a great deal for putting in the minds of the young people at the time what it means to the environment. Then along came "Woodsey Owl"—"Give a hoot, don't pollute!" Smokey the Bear was there, and had a lot to do with implanting ideals in the minds of our young people. These are strong images used to educate and inform our young, and our elders as well. Although we are not necessarily advocating gimmicks or slogans, the importance of visual images cannot be overlooked in the creation of knowledge, understanding, or ideals.

However, the mere mention of the term "urban wildlife" evokes a wide variety of responses in our fellow man. I tested that, and I do not have time to share all of the results with you, but I do want to share one. In the upper reaches of hunting and fishing country of New Hampshire, where zoning is not well-received at all, I saw a bumper sticker that said, "Support Wild Life—Throw a Party!" I could not believe that this is what is happening in our attitudes.

In any event, Edmund O. Wilson, in *Biophilia and The Human Bond with Other Species,* noted that the first step in any crisis in an historical movement in the history of man is almost invariably ethical. Then, as knowledge grows and information is developed, we move into the informational

Integrating Man and Nature in the Metropolitan Environment. Proc. Natl. Symp. on Urban Wildl., Chevy Chase, Md., 4–7 November 1986, L.W. Adams and D.L. Leedy, eds. Published by Natl. Inst. for Urban Wildl., 10921 Trotting Ridge Way, Columbia, MD 21044, 1987.

and more narrowly intellectual phase. Finally, as understanding becomes sufficiently complete, the question turns ethical again. Edmund Wilson believes we are entering the second stage in the environmental movement. It is comforting, however, to recall that in 1864 it was George Perkins Marsh who called for balance in nature with man and warned of the consequences of man's dominion over nature. I am young enough to think it started with Rachael Carson! There may be others who are younger and think of other people in the movement. It is equally comforting to learn, however, that we are moving away from the whole Cartesian thought that we have lived with the belief that there is a strict division between mind and body where the body is viewed simply as a machine. Frank Fritzoff Capra, in *The Turning Point,* says there emerges a systems view of life, a new vision of reality for cultural transformation, that is based upon essential interrelatedness and interdependence of all phenomena—not just the physical or biological, but also psychological, social, and cultural. What is preserved in a wilderness area is not individual trees or organisms or wildlife, but the complex web of relationships among them. Such a new vision is truly ecological and goes well beyond those immediate concerns for environmental protection.

There is no question that we are moving into a new era over all of the globe. As those in a profession of some 30,000 landscape architects trained in aspects of resource analysis, we are committed to the values of planning to improve the quality of our lives and our landscapes. This most certainly includes the wildlife in all of the urban, suburban, and regional environments. This year the American Society of Landscape Architects has focused new efforts in the management and understanding of our public lands with the creation of a National Committee for Public Lands. In addition, as you heard from Pat Noonan, we developed our own Americans Outdoors Task Force, to share the perspectives of landscape architects with the President's Commission on Americans Outdoors. A member of our staff, Ray Freeman, is here who participated with Pat Noonan in many of those programs that you heard about.

In reviewing the nearly 40 national policies of the American Society of Landscape Architects, 20 of which are devoted to environmental and larger issues of pollution and atmospheric elements, I found that we have no policy on wildlife. Perhaps it is time for us to join with you, and I suggest this as a challenge to landscape architects, to begin to develop a policy on wildlife that will, especially in the urban focus, help us to work with you in a more cohesive way.

We are involved, as landscape architects, in public practice, and in just three agencies alone in this country there are 400 million acres (162 million ha). Also, our private practice firms perform land planning, at all scales, from new town planning to resource analysis, to the very small pocket parks and community projects such as tree planting. We have an academic practice contingent who support and teach in our 55 schools around the country.

Now I would like to share with you a few local examples in Massachusetts that had to do with "enlightened action." Some 23 years ago, and this may help your corridor concept, four of us formed the Charles River Watershed Association, which eventually grew to include 30 cities and towns. That group still exists today. It was responsible for insisting on and eventually achieving with the Corps of Engineers, the notion of using the natural valley water storage capacity in the upper reaches of the river, and stopping the Corps from building a dam, which was the primary solution proposed for water management. Today, that group is concerned with public access and provides the proper political motivation to acquire lands along the river. The water quality has been raised so that we are now talking about swimming in certain parts of that river. It can be done.

There also exists in Massachusetts another example that I wanted to share with you. There are 350 cities and towns that have conservation commissions. Those conservation commissions' basic requirements and basic duties are to protect the wetlands of the state. They are involved with citizens who constantly are on the lookout for infringements of the wetlands from development. Just this year, our governor signed a new law to protect wildlife, and this was in addition to the Wetlands Protection Act in the Commonwealth. The new law closed a much-needed gap because the state did not have the wildlife provision to stop some of those developments. It is a very important new law in our state.

I believe we must see the solution to the enhancement of wildlife as part of the larger issue of open space in the environment, and work more with environmental scientists, where we aid in development of the indicators of environmental health, of which wildlife is an essential ingredient. We must expand and energize our existing organizations into coalitions with a greater force in the outcomes. We cannot expect the private sector to do it. As you heard, their motivations may be different, but they are coming around. We cannot expect the public sector to do it alone. Therefore, it falls to the nonprofit sector and this is reaffirmed in the 1985 Environmental Quality Report, which I call to your attention. That report mentions that the nonprofit coalitions can be the force that establishes the values for the true environmental quality. In these coalitions, there is a deep sense of mission and commitment. They tackle a wide range of problems and solve them. They proceed quickly and quietly, take action, and do not just leave wildlife and open space to the left-over planning documents that you heard about from an earlier speaker. I believe more must be done in each community. The local action is critical to interact, to identify, and in some cases, to develop new habitat needs of urban wildlife.

I wanted to say, when Paul Faraca was speaking, that there is nothing wrong with the politicians; all you have to do is to take them to lunch. In the early 1960's, in Massachusetts, we had involvement of young rebel legislators. One of those committed rebel legislators was Michael Dukakis. We took him to lunch. We invited him to urban design discussions. We invited him to discuss open space. It was with him that we stopped the Jamaica Way so that a hospital in the Brookline area could have the development that it has and not have the Jamaica Way and the Boston area lined with cars and roads, and have all the trees cut down and the habitat that was there destroyed. Mike Dukakis is now Governor of Massachusetts and it is no wonder that he cares about open space and wildlife habitat, and signed this new law.

Many of our private practice firms, with the support of city councils, develop plans that protect large amounts of land suitable for wildlife. I believe the town councils and boards and cities with their ever-changing members constantly need information and education about wildlife and open space. In Massachusetts recently, there was a 50-acre (20 ha) parcel that was ready to be developed. It was a wetland parcel. The proposal went all the way to the Corps of Engineers and the EPA and was finally overturned. Yet, you read other documents from around the country and learn that there are 300,000 acres (122,000 ha) of wetlands every year that are destroyed.

Our profession, though very young, is rich in historical roots, and in preservation and conservation. I am sure that most of you are familiar with Ian McHarg's *Design with Nature.* We have another book, *Earthscape,* written by John Simons, calling for environmental awareness in all aspects of land use planning. Although these books suggest large scale, great concern for the interconnected landscape, we must care about every small parcel of wetland and open space. I believe we must be "pro-active." Most of the town boards and agencies are "reactive." It is time to turn that around. Also, I believe we need to focus some of our development thoughts on state land use laws. To my knowledge, there are only two states in the country that have land use laws, Vermont and Oregon. I had the privilege of testifying as an expert witness in Vermont on "Aesthetic Value," which can be measured. We need to develop more direction in the states. We need to inventory and clearly delineate important natural resources. We need to get on with it and do it.

The global garden is at stake. The biosphere as a single organism may be more out of balance at this very moment than we realize.

Urban wildlife is essential to that balance. We landscape architects will accept whatever challenge necessary to change that balance and work to develop a conservation strategy for every bioregion in this country. The forests may all be cut, radiation slowly rise, and the winters grow steadily colder, but if the effects are unlikely to become decisive for a few generations, very few people will be stirred to revolt. Ecological and evolutional time spanning centuries or millenia can be conceived in an intellectual mode, but has no immediate emotional impact. Only through an unusual amount of education and reflective thought do people come to respond emotionally to far-off events, and hence place a high premium on posterity. These words are from Edmund Wilson, the great biologist.

We landscape architects are excited about your network concept. We stand ready to participate with you, both individually and collectively, in every corner of this land, to protect and enhance our fragile garden.

Thank you.

City Critters: A Cast of Millions[1]

DAVID M. BIRD, *Macdonald Raptor Research Centre of McGill University, 21,111 Lakeshore Road, Ste. Anne de Bellevue, QC H9X 1CO, Canada*

Virtually every urban or suburban dweller with eyes and ears cannot help but notice these days the impressive variety of wildlife species that have adapted to backyard life within our cities. It has become unnecessary to travel hundreds of miles into the country to be entertained by the antics of playful squirrels, the cool composed manner of a foraging raccoon, the colorful flashes of feeding birds and butterflies, or the purposeful flitting of a bat in the twilight. It is all there, right in our own backyards. Sometimes just a few alterations to your outdoor living space will not only provide more feeding and breeding habitats for wildlife, but also will serve to enrich your life.

Understandably though, we can all have too much of a good thing. Not everyone welcomes pigeons on the balcony, bats in the attic, snakes in the basement, or gophers in the garden. You need not reach for your guns or poison, however. There are less drastic and essentially harmless methods available for maintaining peace with most city critters. And whether you are cooperating or battling with backyard wildlife, there is always room for a little humor.

Having recently published a book entitled "City Critters: How to Live With Urban Wildlife," my objective is to briefly introduce you to the kinds of critters you will be reading about in these proceedings, literally a cast of millions.

I do not have to tell you that there are a lot of squirrels out there. On a stroll through many North American towns or cities, you might encounter, from smallest to largest and depending on its range, the diminutive, but gutsy flying squirrel (remember Rocky and Bullwinkle?), the ill-tempered red squirrel, the early-rising gray squirrel, and the indolent fox squirrel.

Generally, the gray squirrel's salt-and-pepper appearance results from alternating bands of white, black, and brown on the hair. So where do all those black squirrels come from? Well, they are simply a variation of the gray squirrel, sometimes popping up unexpectedly in a litter of grays. Some regions, especially in northern latitudes, contain whole populations of blacks.

Squirrels are thankfully devoid of anal musk glands, but like some people I know, they do have sweat glands between the pads on their feet.

And how about those fluffy tails!? Not only do they serve as a balance (and occasionally as a parachute) in their acrobatical branchwork and as a rudder during their infrequent swims, they act as a sunshade on hot days, a warm bodywrap on chilly days, and an extremely useful sensor for air currents. Best of all, they can be flicked about in various manners to warn everyone of the extent of your ill mood!

You might observe fox and gray squirrels feeding in the same tree; however, the crotchety old males generally keep to themselves. The red squirrel's range often overlaps with the fox, but ample evidence suggests that the former's aggressive nature seldom permits tolerance of the two bigger species in its territory. In short, when it comes down to food and den sites, the red is a tough competitor.

The grays are more agile in the trees than the stumble bum fox, but occasional spills from as high as 40 meters result in little or no injury. The flying squirrel (which does not actually fly) has been known to glide to another tree 45 meters away and turn at 90 degrees in mid-air. As for swimming, a gray squirrel can manage three kilometers in calm water, but the smarmy little red can even dive a half meter or so below!

Unlike the lazy fox squirrels, grays are up and at it before sunrise. However, they do spend much of the afternoon sleeping and sunning themselves.

Squirrels are renowned for caching food, too. Caches have no particular ownership and communal hoarding is common. Although some memory is used to locate stores, squirrels are capable of smelling them out, even under 30 centimeters of snow.

Few easterners with any interest in nature whatsoever

[1]Excerpted from *City Critters: How to Live With Urban Wildlife* published by Eden Press, Montreal, 1986.

Integrating Man and Nature in the Metropolitan Environment. Proc. Natl. Symp. on Urban Wildl., Chevy Chase, Md., 4–7 November 1986, L.W. Adams and D.L. Leedy, eds. Published by Natl. Inst. for Urban Wildl., 10921 Trotting Ridge Way, Columbia, MD 21044, 1987.

have not experienced the greedy but delightful antics of the tiny panhandling chipmunk as it scurries back and forth with booty begged from highly willing victims.

Most intriguing is the chipmunk's ability to stuff enormous quantities of food inside its mouth pouches. To give you an idea, consider these records from four different chipmunks: 31 corn kernels, 13 prune pits, 70 sunflower seeds, and 32 beechnuts, respectively.

Unlike bats and woodchucks, they are not true hibernators. The chipmunk lives off stored food and not accumulated fat deposits. Apparently when it awakens for either a snack or toilet duties (and they are very clean about this), the chipmunk stumbles around with its eyes closed, just like some humans I know!

Just about everybody recognizes the raccoon with its brownish-gray butterball body, ringed tail, and the Lone Ranger mask concealing a pair of beady black eyes. They are amazingly strong for their size; one raccoon with a good toehold in its den supported a 200-pound man by its tail!

Above all else, raccoons are well endowed with the smarts. Where food is concerned, they are very quick to learn how to open fastening devices of all kinds and will remember the techniques for up to a year without practice.

"Cute," "cuddly," "curious," "comical," and "lovable" are just a few of the words used by the public to describe the raccoon. Let me add a few more. . ."mischievous," "tough," "cantankerous," "bold," "tenacious," and "vicious." In other words, a split personality.

Do not be fooled into thinking that lack of entry will foil them either, as they are quite capable of enlarging existing holes and scraping out new ones.

Raccoons can motor along by bounding at about 25 kilometers per hour, but it is only a matter of time before these clever creatures catch onto buses and taxis.They are excellent swimmers, known to cross rivers and lakes up to three hundred meters wide.

They do not really have mates in the normal sense; the promiscuous males are polygamous and will breed with as many receptive females as possible. Copulations may last for 20 minutes to a whole hour per session, but the female, generally passive during the event, may terminate the session after a half-hour by turning her head and baring her teeth!

Everyone knows that raccoons wash their food before eating it. . .right? Wrong! Only captive animals exhibit this behavior and it has nothing whatsoever to do with cleaning or moistening food. This behavior is simply a substitute for "dabbling" or searching for aquatic prey by wild 'coons.

It is a lot easier to list what raccoons do not eat because they eat just about anything. They can open ice chests and tightly fitted lids, as well as unlatch doors. One thirsty devil even managed to uncork a whiskey bottle pilfered from a camper truck! As for your garbage, they love leftovers, but will ignore raw onions.

When taxonomists dished out the latin names for our wildlife, they sure gave the skunks a smelly deal. The two common urban varieties, the striped and spotted skunks, are called *Mephitis mephitis* and *Spilogale putorius*, which mean "bad odor, bad odor" and "stinking spotted weasel," respectively. But they come by their names honestly. On each side of the anus is a scent gland about 2.5 centimeters long, with a protuding nipple, capable of spraying up to 5 meters away. If it is any comfort to you, no urine is sprayed with the musk. The glands are good for about five to eight shots each, totalling roughly two tablespoons of musk. Replenishing a full load takes 2 days.

An adult male dens with his harem, fighting off other males. One fellow fertilized six females and they all gave birth the same day. Coitus can be quite forceful and violent with both partners biting and dragging one another around. Apparently, rabies may be transmitted to each other in this manner.

Skunks are omnivorous and so eat just about anything edible they can catch. Interestingly, skunks are clever enough to render some creatures harmless to them by rolling them across the ground; this removes poisonous bristles from fuzzy caterpillars, skin poison from toads, and expends the beetles' defensive secretions.

Cottontails thrive in towns and cities, frequenting vacant lots, gardens, shrub plantings, golf courses, parks, and heavily planted residential areas. A true rabbit, defined by its mostly naked, helpless young, the cottontail essentially derives its name from that cottonball of a tail. It is the deeply cleft upper lip that has given rise to the expression, "hare-lipped." They are fairly quick, too, covering up to 4.5 meters in the first few leaps and maintaining a speed of roughly 30 kilometers per hour in a short sprint.

The expression, "breeding like a rabbit" does have some basis in fact. With up to three litters per year in the north, and as many as six in the south, each of which contains between three and six young, it is not surprising that some females produce up to 29 young per year. The gestation period is only 28 to 29 days, but within a few hours of giving birth, the female is ready to start all over again.

Although it is not a fossil holdover from the dinosaurs as is commonly believed, the opossum is the only marsupial, i.e., bearing its young in a pouch, on the North American continent. Another myth is their so-called slow-wittedness. Far from stupid, the opossum has ranked above the dog and rivalled the pig in intelligence tests. They are not especially rapid or agile climbers in spite of having an opposable thumb and a prehensile tail, which acts as a fifth leg. They can indeed hang by that tail, too.

Although not a ploy unique to them, feigning death when faced with an unescapable threat is common to "possums."

Copulation lasts about 20 minutes, but notably, the mating pair tumble over on their right sides to achieve sperm transfer (the left side apparently does not work). Although one male was seen trying to copulate with a dead female in the middle of a highway, an opossum definitely does not copulate with his mate's nose, as is commonly believed.

After severe winters, many opossums are marked by excessive numbers of cuts, scratches, ripped ears, lost toes, and broken teeth and bones. They have a remarkable faculty for healing though.

The woodchuck or groundhog deserves a few words. Sure, I know they prefer open farmlands, but I also know I have seen them in golf courses, parks, ravines, and big, big backyards in suburban areas.

They can swim quite well with just their nose and top of head above the surface. They also can forage in trees. One startled 'chuck zipped 5 meters up a jack pine, and others have been seen lounging around 9 meters up in trees.

When not feeding their faces, woodchucks often squat in the mouth of their dens, sunning, scratching, and pulling their hair. Unlike many other four-legged mammals in North America, they do undergo true hibernation by entering torpor. Their heartbeat drops from 100 beats per minute to about 15, the body temperature from 35° to 8° Centigrade, and breathing rate decreases to less than one inhalation per 6 minutes.

And this is like telling children there is no Santa Claus, but Groundhog Day has no factual basis whatsoever. Woodchucks often emerge during spells of warm weather even in mid-winter.

Restricted to southern and western regions, particularly the plains and prairies, pocket gophers might be encountered any place where there is loose, soft soil and plenty of juicy, edible plants to munch on.

Gophers have large, prominent incisor teeth, which protrude from the front of the mouth and minimize the dirt eaten while cutting apart roots.

Apparently, gophers can run backward through their burrows, using their sensitive tails as probes. Except during the mating season, they are not likely to run into each other either, because these quarrelsome critters will even plug connecting holes to avoid meeting one another.

You may never see a mole, but if you do, you will recognize it by its long, naked snout that extends 12.7 millimeters beyond its mouth, large broad forefeet, soft velvety fur, and eyeballs reduced in size to the point of being useless.

The eastern mole, the most common invader of urban areas, has an insatiable appetite and will often eat 50% to 100% of their body weight daily. Moles need all that energy to accomplish the burrowing they do each day.

Second perhaps to the Norway rat, the ubiquitous house mouse is the most troublesome and economically important rodent in North America. It is certainly the most common mammal in man's cities, next to man himself. They are categorized as nibblers because they spoil more food by contamination than they eat; they eat about 3 grams daily.

With a year-round breeding season, a 19-day gestation period, an average of eight litters per year each consisting of four to seven young, and an age at first breeding of up to 2 months, we must be grateful that mice have an average lifespan of only 1 year.

This nocturnal "mighty mouse" can climb just about anywhere in any direction on any rough surface and can chew through wood, concrete, vinyl, rubber, and even aluminum.

And I would be remiss if I failed to include the undisputed king (the house mouse being the crown prince) of all city critters, the rat, both Norway and roof varieties. Being an excellent swimmer both above and below water, the Norway rat has been known to pop in uninvited out of a toilet or basement drain.

Rats have poor sight and are color-blind, but they more than make up for this with their excellent powers of smell, touch, hearing, and taste. For example, they can detect contaminants in their food as minute as 0.5 parts per million, a figure far below the threshold of humans.

Rats are also highly promiscuous; the rabbit's got nothing on them. To illustrate, one Norway rat and her young of the year produced another 1,500 rats in one year!

Next to humans, the Norway rat's biggest enemy is another Norway rat. In their social hierarchy, the larger rats and females with young are dominant. Hence, most rats die from cannibalism resulting from fighting among themselves.

What do we know about bats? Well, they are a public menace because they entangle themselves in hair, bring bedbugs into the house, and spread rabies. Wrong, wrong, wrong! Mankind could not be blessed with a greater friend in nature's circle; however some bats can have rabies.

There are basically two types found in urban environments: the colonial bats including the little brown (probably the most abundant), big brown, Mexican free-tailed, evening, pallid, and eastern pipistrelle; and the solitary types including the red, hoary, and silver-haired bats. The most remarkable feature of bats is their ability to echo-locate with sonar. Emitting ultrasonic sounds at roughly 10 per second, the whole process of detection, pursuit, and capture of an insect takes about 1 second.

They can compete easily with the fanciest electronic bug zappers. It has been estimated that a colony of 500 bats accounts for over five hundred thousand flying insects nightly; that is a lot of bugs!

Mating generally occurs in the roosts, but red bats have been observed attempting copulation on the wing. Clinging with a vice-like grip on their mother's teats, the sucklings have been known to take a ride with her during a change in roosts. One red bat was seen carrying three or four babies whose combined weight exceeded her own.

No other class of animals better illustrates our polarized views toward sharing our habitat with wildlife than do birds. The two extreme views are best shown by the case of the pigeon. If you stroll through any major city core, you will surely encounter a kind soul dumping bags of bread crumbs among a hungry horde of pigeons. The mere suggestion that pigeon numbers are in need of control is enough to rouse some of these gentle people to physical violence!

A pair takes 18 days to incubate a clutch of one or two eggs, and the young leave the nest between 4 and 6 weeks of age. Before they even leave though, Mom has laid another set of eggs. Pigeons breed virtually year-round, especially in spring and fall.

The pigeon is not the most numerous bird species in the city. That honor is bestowed upon the tiny house sparrow. And there is one more feathered rascal that has pitted itself against urban residents on many occasions. From less than two hundred individuals released in 1890 and 1891 by a man who wanted Central Park in New York City to contain all the species mentioned in Shakespeare's plays, the starling now numbers more than one hundred forty million birds in the U.S. alone!

It is hard to dislike the industrious woodpeckers, but as long as man uses wood as a building material and prizes his ornamental and fruit trees, not everyone will be a fan of theirs. The hairy, downy, and red-headed woodpeckers, as well as the yellow-bellied sapsucker and common flicker, are the most abundant in North America and most likely to be encountered in suburbia.

Even the beautiful and highly beneficial cliff swallow incurs the wrath of suburban man. A single nest might be composed of 900 to 1,400 mud pellets, each representing a trip, sometimes up to 0.8 km away.

Widely distributed across North America and one of the best-known birds, the clever crow naturally is a common sight in suburbia. These omnivorous critters will eat just about anything and over 600 different items have been logged on its menu. Gulping down about eight to ten meals per day, its daily intake might equal a quarter-pounder's worth.

In many towns and cities, herring and ring-billed gulls are attracted to land-fill sites and quarries. Some populations have developed interesting feeding patterns that coincide with the morning openings of fast food outlets!

So far I have only addressed those avian species that have been known to conflict with the interests of urban and suburban residents. There is another side to the coin and here I refer to the color, music, and life that birds add to our sometimes monotonous and desolate city landscapes.

Bird appreciation is second only to gardening as North America's favorite pastime. Let's face it—birds have wings and they can end up anywhere they darn well please! Mallard ducks cavort in ponds, lakes, and man-made reservoirs in city centers; screech owls frequent tangled vines in suburban areas; and their larger cousin, the great horned owl, hides and hunts among the wooded ravines. American kestrels, merlins, and peregrine falcons are three diurnal raptors that have adapted to nesting in man's cities.

Hummingbirds are among the most delightful of backyard guests. Weighing just over 3 grams, their wings beat an incredible 75 times a second!

For the most part, the reptiles and amphibians, collectively known as the herptiles, have gotten a raw deal from urbanization. In spite of it, a small number of them are either holding their own or even increasing their numbers within city boundaries. Increased food and cover, along with decreased numbers of predators, may lead to the latter.

Just the mention of the word "snake" to some people (like my Mom) is enough to cause heart palpitations. No matter what I say, Mom will never become a snake groupie, but at least she will not run around stomping and beating to death every snake she encounters, either. Among those snakes that do quite well in urban centers, we find the eastern garter, the northern brown, and the red-bellied.

Contrary to popular opinion, snakes do not swallow their young to protect them; if they did so, their strong digestive juices would probably kill them. Unfortunately, the northern brown snake, likely the most abundant snake in New York City, is sometimes mistaken for a baby Massasauga rattler and the red-bellied is often beaten to death as a copperhead. Obviously, the snakes are faced with a huge public relations problem.

Box turtles have really got to be one of the most harmless of all city critters. Interestingly, they are immune to poisonous mushrooms, but any animal feeding on a box turtle after the latter has eaten such fare, becomes ill. Often taken as pets, the box turtle's problem is that it is too harmless.

Another equally innocuous critter, the red-backed salamander, appears to show a high degree of urban tolerance. Of the toads, Fowler's toad seems to be able to "tough it out" in man's cities and is, in fact, increasing its population in some. Because of their diet and unobtrusive nature, I cannot think of a better animal to have around the yard.

Although the bullfrog can be heard bellowing in weedy areas along lakes and ponds within city limits, there are two better examples of city-dwelling frogs and they both originated from Cuba! Limited thus far to southeastern Florida and the Keys, the Cuban or giant tree frog has gained the reputation of causing power failures by scaling hydro poles and straddling two wires on the small transformers. The greenhouse frog takes well to human habitat, especially gardens and greenhouses.

Well, with the exception of umpteen million insect species and the fish lurking below the surfaces of ponds, lakes, streams, and reservoirs within towns and cities, that is a brief look at some of the slickest, wiliest critters ever to hop, slither, run, or fly across the face of the earth. We can fight nasty futile battles to eradicate them from our urban or suburban centers, or we can learn to co-exist with them peacefully by using preventive medicine and enhancing their natural habitat. You might ask yourself why you should take the latter route.

I can give you several reasons. From psychological and sociological points of view, it is my firm belief that whatever wildlife forms choose to reside with you actually reflect your personality and even your social status (if this is important to you). Enjoying urban wildlife can consist of simply feeding pigeons in the park, to taking a guided tour on a trail in a suburban park. Aesthetically, a neighborhood and backyard comprised of the flashing colors of cardinals, bluejays, tanagers, and goldfinches amid the greenery and flowers must surely be a more welcome sight than block after block of concrete and asphalt. Economically, it is a well known fact that property values are increased by trees, shrubs, and flowers—especially if in close proximity to a permanent water basin designed to enhance wildlife populations. Urban wildlife also serves as a useful barometer of a healthful human environment.

Most important of all, we must manage wildlife in urban areas not just for aesthetic, economic, and recreational reasons, but for its own sake. City critters are very interesting animals; they constitute an important part of our wild heritage.

Urban Planning to Benefit Wildlife and People

Chairman: ROBERT S. DORNEY, *Professor, School of Urban and Regional Planning, University of Waterloo, Ontario, Canada*

Cochairman: E M RISSE, *Consultant in Planning, Reston, Virginia*

Development of a Natural Resources Planning and Management Process

JOHN E. HENCH, *Department of Animal Sciences, University of Maryland, College Park, MD 20742, and the Maryland-National Capital Park and Planning Commission, 8787 Georgia Avenue, Silver Spring, MD 20910*[1]

KEITH VAN NESS, *Maryland and Washington, D.C. Breeding Bird Atlas Project, 14705 Sugarland Road, Poolesville, MD 20838*

ROB GIBBS, *The Maryland-National Capital Park and Planning Commission, 8787 Georgia Avenue, Silver Spring, MD 20910*

INTRODUCTION

The Montgomery County, Maryland, Department of Park's natural resource planning and management process is a valuable tool for the park system. It exemplifies Montgomery County Park's (MCP's) commitment to natural resources protection and conservation for present and future generations. As the conversion from rural to urban land-use continues, it will assure that some local natural and environmental educational resources are preserved.

This paper describes our considerations and efforts in developing the process. In so doing, we have attempted to: (1) address the issue of species diversity from the community level as well as a species-by-species approach, (2) discuss relevant ecological issues, and 3) illustrate the utility of natural resources modeling in land-use planning. Our efforts were not directed at developing a system of natural areas, but rather at a planning and management process that is dependent upon, and in turn conserves, natural resources in Montgomery County parks.

BACKGROUND

The Setting

Montgomery County, Maryland, covers 316,160 acres (128,000 ha), lies adjacent to Washington, D.C., and is within the Piedmont section of the oak-chestnut (now oak-hickory) forest region (Braun 1950). Elevations range from 229 to 702 feet (69.8 to 213.9 m). Long, narrow stream valleys drain the gently rolling topography. Ninety-two percent of the county's soils are classified as uplands. The remaining soils are on old, high terraces along the Potomac River, or on floodplains (Matthews et al. 1961). Approximately 620,000 people, with a median household income of $39,154, reside in the county.

The Montgomery County Park System

In 1927, the Maryland General Assembly passed a bill authorizing a Maryland-National Capital Park and Planning Commission (M-NCPPC) for the Montgomery County and Prince George's County suburbs. The bill directed that the new agency coordinate development in the bicounty area, acquire land for parks, pathways, and other public places, issue bonds and condemn land for this purpose, and levy taxes within the planning district (MacMaster and Hiebert 1976). Rogers, the Commission's first architect, noted (1931) that Montgomery County's stream valleys could be developed for parks "by using in almost every case only such land as is unfit for building purposes." Today, the Montgomery County Park System includes 26,416 acres (10,694.7 ha) of stream valleys and uplands. An additional 10,000 acres (about 4,048 ha) will be acquired in the near future. Stream valley parks and regional parks form the backbone of the park system. Smaller local parks, athletic parks, and historic farm parks also serve the county's open space and recreational needs.

The Preservation of Natural Diversity

Plant and animal species are not spread randomly across the landscape but are grouped into more or less distinct

[1]Statements made in this paper are our own and do not necessarily reflect current opinions or adopted policies of the Maryland-National Capital Park and Planning Commission.

Integrating Man and Nature in the Metropolitan Environment. Proc. Natl. Symp. on Urban Wildl., Chevy Chase, Md., 4–7 November 1986, L.W. Adams and D.L. Leedy, eds. Published by Natl. Inst. for Urban Wildl., 10921 Trotting Ridge Way, Columbia, MD 21044, 1987.

communities (Daubenmire 1968). In general, plant distributions are controlled by physical features of the environment—including underlying bedrock, soil type, soil pH, soil moisture, slope, aspect, and elevation—whereas animal distributions are controlled by the vegetation growing in an area. Persistent plant communities, and the animal species associated with them, are considered natural communities (D. Daniel Boone, pers. commun., 1986). In order to successfully protect and manage natural communities, it is important to understand how they develop, change through time, and are affected by human manipulation.

The Natural Heritage Program, Maryland Department of Natural Resources, is developing preliminary descriptions of Maryland's natural communities (D. Daniel Boone, pers. commun., 1986). The descriptions include comments on underlying bedrock, soils, slope, aspect, altitude, and characteristic plant species. Our preliminary field work has revealed that seven of these communities (i.e., mid-Atlantic flatrock, riverside outcrops of the Potomac basin, mid-Atlantic serpentine barrens, dry forest on acidic bedrock, mesic forest on acidic bedrock, central floodplain forest, and central swamp forest) occur in Montgomery County. The geologic map of Maryland (Cleaves et al. 1968), Montgomery County soils maps (Matthews et al. 1961), and National Wetlands Inventory maps, U.S. Department of the Interior, Fish and Wildlife Service, can be used to obtain approximate boundaries for most of these natural communities.

Natural communities occur in various stages of secondary succession. The physical environment and past land-use practices control succession's rate and limit. On Maryland's Piedmont, secondary succession proceeds through the following stages: (1) bare soil, (2) grass-herb-seedling, (3) scrub-shrub, (4) forest dominated by shade intolerant trees (often coniferous species), and (5) forest dominated by shade tolerant trees (always deciduous species) (Hench et al. 1985).

Chipley et al. (1984) estimated that by protecting adequate examples of Maryland's natural communities, at least 85% of the state's native species would be preserved. They refer to this community approach as the coarse filter for capturing and protecting elements of natural diversity. For example, by protecting adequate examples of mesic forest, jack-in-the-pulpit (*Arisaema atroubens*), yellow poplar (*Liriodendron tulipifera*), and red-eyed vireo (*Vireo olivaceus*) also may be protected because these species are usual components of this natural community type. However, some species are not found in most examples of natural communities that seem appropriate for them, or are restricted to rare natural community types. Boone (1984) developed a list of these rare and endangered plants and Brosnan (1984) did the same for animals. Chipley et al. (1984) referred to these lists as the fine filter for capturing and protecting elements of natural diversity, and recommended that species on these lists be given priority for research and protection efforts. As examples, a recent survey of fauna in a springhead in Rock Creek Park, Montgomery County, near the boundary between Maryland and the District of Columbia, revealed a previously undescribed harpacticoid copepod (Crustacea), *Attheyella* (Mrazekiella) *spinipes* (Reid 1986). And in the spring of 1986, one of us (JEH) and John Schmitt collected a pygmy shrew (*Microsorex hoyi*)—a species that is rare throughout its range and under review for federal listing as threatened or endangered (U.S. Fish and Wildlife Service 1985)—from each of two locations in Little Bennett Regional Park, Montgomery County. These two species would be given a higher priority for research and protection efforts than the red-backed salamander (*Plethodon cinereus*), a species that is common throughout eastern North America.

The Effects of Nonconsumptive Recreation on Wildlife

Planners must assess and provide for the public's recreational demands. In turn, ecologists must evaluate the effects of recreational activities on natural resources, including wildlife and their habitats. Boyle and Samson (1985) reviewed 163 original studies that examined the effects of nonconsumptive outdoor recreation on wildlife—including amphibians, reptiles, birds, and mammals—in order to bring attention to, and provide a better understanding of, the relationship between recreationists and members of these taxa. Of the studies that were reviewed, the original authors reported effects on wildlife from hiking and camping (52), boating (37), wildlife observation and photography (27), off-road vehicle use (20), snowmobile (12), swimming and shoreline recreation (8), and rock climbing (7). Birds were the most common subjects for investigation (61% of the studies), followed by mammals (42%), and amphibians and reptiles (4%). Negative effects were commonly reported for most all recreational activities and for all taxa (Boyle and Samson 1985).

The Question of On-site and Off-site Impacts

A frequently asked question in the park business is "What are the effects of land-use changes—including development and land management activities—on natural resources?" Roberts and O'Neil (1983) reviewed 28 different methods that could be used to answer this question. Hench et al. (1985) developed a method specifically for the Montgomery County Park System. These methods vary from qualitative to quantitative and many can be used for baseline assessments, monitoring, future predictions, mitigation, and species management. However, none can be used to accurately predict the effects of habitat fragmentation, the loss of habitat heterogeneity, edge, or reduced habitat space, on resources beyond the actual development or management site. As a result, off-site predictions are often clouded by qualifications and value judgments and remain a policy decision. A few of the ecological issues that should influence this decision are discussed below.

Forest fragmentation is associated with a number of factors that are detrimental to migratory songbirds (Wilcove

1985). These factors include cowbird (*Molothrus ater*) parasitism, the loss of habitat heterogeneity, potential barriers to dispersal between woodlots, and increased nest predation. Brittingham and Temple (1983) reported cowbirds parasitizing bird nests as far as 1,000 feet (304.8 m) in from forest edge. Freemark and Merriam (1986) determined that larger and more heterogeneous forests had more species and pairs of migratory and resident songbirds. Large forest size was more important for increasing the number of forest interior species, whereas habitat heterogeneity was more important to edge-related species. To maintain a diverse forest avifauna, Freemark and Merriam (1986) recommended maximizing both forest size and forest heterogeneity.

Whitcomb et al. (1981) and Lynch and Whigham (1984) examined the influence of forest fragmentation on central Maryland's breeding birds. Their research results are summarized below:

1. Seventeen neotropical migrant bird species typically account for 80 to 90% of the breeding individuals in extensive tracts of upland deciduous forest.
2. Ten neotropical migrant bird species that are restricted as breeders to the interior of these forests are rare in small (2-12 acre, 0.8–4.9 ha) forest patches, somewhat more common in patches of intermediate size (15–35 acres, 6–14 ha), and are most abundant in large (173+ acres, 70+ ha) forested tracts. Seven of the species that are capable of using forest edge as well as forest interior are equally abundant in forest patches of all sizes.
3. Only three of 11 permanent resident species are restricted as breeders to the interior of upland forests.

Robbins (1984) reported that approximately 85 acres (about 40 ha) of roughly circular habitat, in the interior of a woodland, may be the very minimum area that can maintain most of central Maryland's breeding bird species. Smaller woodlots, or larger forests with a low area to edge ratio (e.g., long, narrow stream valley parks), will support fewer numbers of forest interior species, and more of the species typically associated with forest edge, forest edge-scrub, and field-edge habitats. Not surprisingly, this latter group of edge species includes the typical breeding birds of central Maryland suburbs (Geis 1974, Whitcomb et al. 1981).

Wilcove (1985) noted that the long-term survival of migratory songbirds in large forested tacts should not be taken for granted. He measured rates of nest predation in central Maryland forests and in Great Smoky Mountain National Park, Tennessee. The rates were 70.5% in suburban woodlots, 47.5% in rural woodlots, 18.0% in a 2,235 acre (905 ha) forest (all Maryland habitats), and 2.0% in Great Smoky Mountain National Park. These observations suggested to him that forested tracts even as large as 2,223 acres (900 ha) may eventually experience declines in breeding populations of these species.

Edges are a universal phenomenon associated with forest fragmentation. Ranney et al. (1981) showed that forest edges are about 49 feet (15 m) wide and affect the species composition, structure, and dynamics of forests. In general, the creation of a new edge, or disturbance of a mature edge, causes a regression from mesic (mature) conditions to dry (pioneer) conditions in the forest interior. This regression occurs in response to increased light, which affects shade tolerant and intolerant species differently (Spurr and Barnes 1980:380–398), and increased wind. Wind buffets edge trees (Moen 1974), enhances seed dispersal (Crockett 1971), and changes soil moisture by increasing evapotranspiration (Ranney et al. 1981). The interaction of edges with interiors is a function of forest island size. Edges increase the proportion of shade intolerant species in the interior. When circular forest islands are reduced to less than 13 acres (about 5 ha), or forest corridors (e.g., stream valleys) are reduced to less than about 330 feet (101 m) wide, forest composition will shift towards less mesic and more shade intolerant species (Ranney et al. 1981).

Forest fragmentation frequently results in a reduction in habitat space. Space is an important life requisite need for animals, and this need varies among species. Stewart and Robbins (1958) reported that the average territory sizes for a pair of tufted titmice (*Parus bicolor*) and barred owls (*Strix varia*) were 10 acres (4 ha) and 200 acres (81 ha), respectively, in central Maryland floodplain forest. These data can be used to illustrate two points. First, a park cannot provide space for even a single pair of individuals if the available habitat area is less than the critical home range or territory size of the target species. And obviously, one pair does not constitute a minimum viable population (MVP). Scientists who have worked with real management situations suggest a minimum of several hundred genetically effective individuals (see Soulé and Simberloff 1986). This brings us to the second point. In order to maintain large herbivores or large predators in a community, along with the important regulatory functions that they perform, parks have to be big. Consider the fact that approximately 30,000 acres (12,146 ha) of mature forested stream valley is needed to support a MVP of 150 pairs of barred owls. On the other hand, some large species can be effectively managed with a system of smaller parks that are connected with suitable travel corridors (Harris 1984:141–144).

To summarize this section, habitat fragmentation, edge, the loss of habitat heterogeneity, and reduced habitat space are a few of the ecological issues associated with development. It is not realistic to consider their negative effects on all species beyond a development or management site, but staff should be aware of their effects on rare and endangered species, as well as on plants associated with mesic shaded sites, forest interior birds, large herbivores, and large predators. An effective development policy for dealing with these issues would be to site recreational facilities on the park's periphery, and thereby minimize impacts on the interior. Further, through careful landscape design, the peripheral areas could buffer the interior from effects of unhindered development outside of the park.

The Use of Overlays in Park Master Planning

McHarg (1969:31–41) presented a method of mapping physiographic factors so that the darker the tone, the greater the cost, and similarly mapping social and natural resource values so that the darker the tone, the higher the value. He demonstrated that when the maps (i.e., overlays) were made from transparent materials, and superimposed on a light table, areas providing the most benefit for the least cost were revealed by the lightest tone. We propose that MCP adopt this method of decision-making for use during its master planning process.

THE PROCESS

MCP's Mission

As an initial step in developing the process, we asked Donald K. Cochran, Director of Parks, to draft a preliminary statement of MCP's mission. In his opinion that mission is to:

> conserve and enhance the natural environment, to provide a wide variety of outdoor leisure time activities for the park user, and to ensure that the park system is convenient, safe, and enjoyable for all who use it.

We used this mission as a guide during the development of MCP's natural resource planning and management process.

M-NCPPC's Development Policy for Regional Parks

The primary land-use issue in planning and managing parks is one of impact on natural resources. This issue is central to MCP's mission and therefore deserves staff's full consideration. As our store of ecological knowledge increases, so does our appreciation of the many complex interrelationships occurring in nature. Some of these were discussed in the previous section as ecological issues. From these interrelationships, we can assume that impacts on one part of the environment will often affect other parts as well. With this assumption in mind, we asked the following questions: "How does a park's developed areas impact its undeveloped areas and vice versa?" and "How can staff successfully integrate developed areas with undeveloped areas for the betterment of both and the detriment of neither?"

M-NCPPC's 66/33 development policy, approved as a Commission resolution on 15 December 1968, provides a partial answer to our questions. Simply stated, the policy requires that at least 66% of each regional park (i.e., parks of at least 200 acres, 80.9 ha, that encompass uplands, and occasionally floodplains and wetlands), be maintained in *natural areas* or *conservation areas*. (However the resolution does not define these planning categories.) The remaining 33% of a regional park may be developed for recreational activities. Henceforth, we refer to the 33% as *active-use areas*. To clarify and standardize the meaning of these planning categories, we propose the following definitions:

- *natural areas*—the sum total of acres of land not developed for public use, and encompassing those natural resources being preserved to maintain a diversity of native natural communities as a legacy for future generations. Within these communities, natural processes and desirable ecological changes should be allowed to take place. Management activities should be limited to those necessary to mitigate the influence of humans and species that are both nonnative and undesirable (e.g., gypsy moth, *Lymantria dispar*).
- *conservation areas*—the sum total of acres of land not developed for public use, and encompassing those natural resources being managed to maintain select plant and/or animal species. For example, pink lady's slipper (*Cypripedium acaule*) and pine warbler (*Dendroica pinus*) are associated with stands of Virginia pine (*Pinus virginiana*) on dry, acidic soils. Because these stands do not usually represent a terminal stage of secondary succession in Montgomery County, the stands, as well as species associated with them, can be maintained only by removing more shade tolerant tree species from their understory.
- *active-use areas*—the sum total of acres of land developed for public use. These areas include trails, roads, nature centers, buildings, campgrounds, golf courses, ball fields, tennis courts, children's play areas, agricultural fields, horticultural gardens, lawns, stormwater management facilities, artificial ponds, artificial lakes, etc.

Although the Commission's development policy does not apply to stream valley parks, we recommend that the philosophy of the 66/33 ratio guide the planning and management of these parks as well.

Natural areas and conservation areas are an essential part of the park system. In addition to their significance as protected habitats, these areas contribute to the quality of the public's experience in each park. For it is the natural-conservation areas (N-CAs) that give each park its own special feel in terms of size, naturalness, isolation, solitude, and potential adventure. N-CAs positively impact the active-use areas (AUAs) by contributing to the character of AUAs, by serving as an outdoor classroom for nature study or an outdoor laboratory for scientific research, and by providing the tranquil environment that many park users seek. Staff can, and should, provide the public with opportunities to experience a park's natural areas and conservation areas. Carefully designed trails—including those for walking, jogging, and horseback riding—can penetrate the N-CAs. Observation platforms, study blinds, food and cover plots, and feeding stations can facilitate a safe and enjoyable interaction between people and wildlife. In turn, AUAs can positively impact N-CAs by providing a broad constituency of park users who can be called upon to support the department politically when alternative land-use proposals, originating in other County agencies, threaten a park's integrity.

Natural Resources Management Program

In support of MCP's mission, and to complement and balance existing departmental programs in planning, engineering, and design, we propose the creation of a natural resources management program with goals to:

- Restore, preserve, and manage natural resources in regional and stream valley parks. Efforts should be made to maintain a diversity of plant communities typical of Maryland's Piedmont, and viable, diverse, native animal populations characteristic of existing or created habitats.
- Manage natural resources in such a way as to provide an attractive, safe, and natural environment for the park user.

In order to achieve these goals, it will be necessary to systematically collect and compile natural resources data in each regional and stream valley park. Specifically this will require staff to:

- determine the location and extent of discernable natural communities,
- map all areas in each regional and stream valley park according to natural community type,
- identify specific plant community characteristics for each natural community unit including plant community structure (physiognomy) and plant species composition and abundance (floristics), and
- inventory animal species associated with each plant community unit.

Geologic, soils, and topographic maps; aerial photographs; knowledge of past land-use; and plant and animal species inventory data can be interpreted to create a natural resources concept plan for each park. While creating a plan, staff should be looking for answers to the following questions: "What are the sensitive ecological areas (e.g., wetlands) that must be protected?" and "What sites must be avoided during development in order to protect rare and endangered species?" When completed, a natural resources concept plan should illustrate staff's objectives for the restoration, preservation, and management of a park's natural resources, and provide the information needed to select the best N-CAs during the master planning process.

Building a Park Master Plan

Each regional and stream valley park represents a major public investment that affects the quality of human life, adjacent land values, and the survival of native plant and animal species within its sphere of influence. Within the context of this expanded role, the significance of the master planning process becomes clear. To be successful, the process must incorporate: (1) knowledge of Montgomery County's natural communities, and rare and endangered species; (2) relevant ecological issues; (3) aesthetic and recreational values; (4) design and engineering constraints; (5) public health and safety issues; and (6) adjacent land-use considerations. In addition, citizens should be given opportunities to participate actively in the planning of their parks.

During the master planning process, a park's natural resources concept plan should be compared to its recreation concept plan. (Concurrent with the preparation of the former plan, staff should develop a recreation concept plan. This plan should include a justification, conceptual design, and discussion of engineering constraints for each recreational facility that is proposed.) Trade-offs in natural resource and recreation values should be discussed within the context of any design and/or engineering constraints, and final details of the 66/33 ratio negotiated. A series of overlays—including bedrock, soils, topography, hydrology, natural communities, vegetation, known locations of rare and endangered species, existing development, historical sites, and adjacent land-use—should be assembled to facilitate decision-making. The end product of this process will be a viable park master plan that guarantees quality N-CAs as well as quality AUAs. Following review by senior management staff, and a period for public comment, the plan can be sent to the Montgomery County Planning Board for final endorsement.

Criteria for Calculating AUAs

Recently, staff has expressed concern about the impacts of AUAs—in particular recreational activities, trail corridors, and large forest openings—on N-CAs. These concerns have arisen along with an understanding that there will always be impacts associated with AUAs that go far beyond actual site dimensions. However, because it cannot be assumed that we can quantify, or even recognize, all of the variables contributing to off-site impacts, the delineation of impact zones beyond actual site dimensions is subjective, and therefore must be considered a policy issue.

In order to standardize the calculation of the 66/33 ratio, we propose that the following formula be used to determine a park's 33% AUA:

$$\text{AUA} = (\text{park acreage} - \text{wetland acreage}) \times 0.333$$

where:

Wetland acreage = total acres of naturally occurring wetlands (e.g., springs, intermittent and perennial streams, creeks, marshes, swamps).

Given knowledge of the effects of recreational activities and forest fragmentation on natural resources (see the BACKGROUND), we also propose the following rules for impact zones to be included in AUAs:

1. Apply a constant impact width of 20 feet (6.1 m), 10 feet (3.0 m) on either side of center, to all trails, and

2. Apply a constant impact width of 50 feet (15.2 m) from the mowed or maintained edge of all other AUAs.

A park's boundary should not be considered as an impact zone.

CONCLUSION

Rogers (1931) wrote "With small though significant beginnings behind them, but with a very ambitious program and the power to attain that program ahead of them, the Maryland-National Capital Park and Planning Commission . . . face[s] the future with the determination to develop a park system equal to the finest in the country." It was the vision, hard work, and dedication of Rogers and many other men and women through the years that have resulted in the Montgomery County Park System today. We hope that the planning and management process proposed herein will facilitate staff's efforts to attain the right balance between recreational development and natural resources preservation in regional and stream valley parks. Our success in this endeavor will no doubt be judged by generations yet to come.

Acknowledgments.—Park staff, including planners, engineers, designers and naturalists; Donald K. Cochran, Director, Montgomery County Parks; Vagn Flyger, Professor, University of Maryland; and David K. Weaver, Director of Natural Resources and Public Safety, Suburban Hennepin Regional Park District, Hennepin County, Minnesota, contributed significantly to our work. Kenneth W. Ernst and Piera Weiss reviewed an earlier draft of the manuscript.

REFERENCES CITED

Boone, D. D. 1984. The rare and endangered vascular plants of Maryland. Pages 75–110 *in* A. W. Norden, D. C. Forester, and G. H. Fenwick, eds. Threatened and endangered plants and animals of Maryland. Md. Nat. Heritage Program Spec. Publ. 84-1, Annapolis.

Boyle, S. A. and F. B. Samson. 1985. Effects of nonconsumptive recreation on wildlife: a review. Wildl. Soc. Bull. 13:110–116.

Braun, E. L. 1950. Deciduous forests of eastern North America. The Blakiston Co., Philadelphia. 596 pp.

Brittingham, M. C. and S. A. Temple. 1983. Have cowbirds caused forest songbirds to decline? BioScience 33:31–35.

Brosnan, M. C. 1984. The rare and endangered animals of Maryland. Pages 219–226 *in* A. W. Norden, D. C. Forester, and G. H. Fenwick, eds. Threatened and endangered plants and animals of Maryland. Md. Nat. Heritage Program Spec. Publ. 84-1, Annapolis.

Chipley, R. M., G. H. Fenwick, and D. D. Boone. 1984. The Maryland heritage program. Pages 33–42 *in* A. W. Norden, D. C. Forester, and G. H. Fenwick, eds. Threatened and endangered plants and animals of Maryland. Md. Nat. Heritage Program Spec. Publ. 84-1, Annapolis.

Cleaves, E. T., J. Edwards, Jr., and J. D. Glaser. 1968. Geologic map of Maryland. Md. Geol. Survey, Baltimore.

Crockett, J. V. 1971. Landscape gardening. Time-Life Books, New York. 160 pp.

Daubenmire, R. 1968. Plant communities, a textbook of plant synecology. Harper and Row, New York. 300 pp.

Freemark, K. E. and H. G. Merriam. 1986. Importance of area and habitat heterogeneity to bird assemblages in temperate forest fragments. Biol. Conserv. 36:115–141.

Geis, A. D. 1974. Effects of urbanization and type of urban environment on bird populations. Pages 97–105 *in* J. H. Noyes and D. R. Progulske, eds. A symposium on wildlife in an urbanizing environment. Univ. of Mass., Amherst.

Harris, L. D. 1984. The fragmented forest, island biogeography theory and the preservation of biotic diversity. Univ. of Chicago Press, Chicago. 211 pp.

Hench, J. E., V. Flyger, R. Gibbs, and K. Van Ness. 1985. Predicting the effects of land-use changes on wildlife. Trans. North Am. Wildl. and Nat. Resour. Conf. 50:345–351.

Lynch, J. F. and D. F. Whigham. 1984. Effects of forest fragmentation on breeding bird communities in Maryland, USA. Biol. Conserv. 28:287–324.

MacMaster, R. K. and R. E. Hiebert. 1976. A grateful remembrance, the story of Montgomery County, Maryland. Publ. of Montgomery County Government and the Montgomery County Historical Society, Rockville. 422 pp.

McHarg, I. L. 1969. Design with nature. Doubleday/Natural History Press, New York. 197 pp.

Matthews, E. D., E. Z. W. Compy, and J. C. Johnson. 1961. Soil survey of Montgomery County, Maryland. U.S. Dep. of Agric., Soil Conserv. Serv. and Md. Agric. Exp. Station. Series 1958, No. 7. 107 pp. + 54 plates.

Moen, A. N. 1974. Turbulence and the visualization of wind flow. Ecology 55:1420–1424.

Ranney, J. W., M. C. Bruner, and J. B. Levenson. 1981. The importance of edge in the structure and dynamics of forest islands. Pages 67–95 *in* R. L. Burgess and D. M. Sharpe, eds. Forest island dynamics in man-dominated landscapes. Springer-Verlag, New York.

Reid, J. M. 1986. *Attheyella* (Mrazekiella) *spinipes*, a new Harpacticoid copepod (Crustacea) from Rock Creek Regional Park, Maryland. Proc. Biol. Soc. Wash. In review.

Robbins, C. S. 1984. Management to conserve forest ecosystems. Pages 101–107 *in* W. C. McComb, ed. Proceedings—workshop on management of nongame species and ecological communities. Univ. of Ky., Lexington.

Roberts, T. H. and L. J. O'Neil. 1983. Habitat evaluation methods—examples and guidelines for selection. Pages 266–269 *in* J. F. Bell and T. Atterbury, eds. Renewable resource inventories for monitoring changes and trends. Proc. of an Int. Conf. Corvallis, Oregon.

Rogers, R. W. 1931. A park system for the Maryland-Washington metropolitan district. City Planning 4:15–23.

Soulé, M. E. and D. Simberloff. 1986. What do genetics and ecology tell us about the design of nature reserves? Biol. Conserv. 35:19–40.

Spurr, S. H. and B. V. Barnes. 1980. Forest ecology. John Wiley and Sons, New York. 687 pp.

Stewart, R. E. and C. S. Robbins. 1958. Birds of Maryland and the District of Columbia. North Am. Fauna No. 62. U.S. Dep. of the Inter., Fish and Wildl. Serv., Washington, D. C. 401 pp.

U.S. Fish and Wildlife Service. 1985. Endangered and threatened wildlife and plants; review of vertebrate wildlife. Fed. Reg. 50:37,958–37,967. (18 September)

Whitcomb, R. F., C. S. Robbins, J. F. Lynch, B. L. Whitcomb, M. K. Klimkiewicz, and D. L. Bystrak. 1981. Effects of forest fragmentation on avifauna of the eastern deciduous forest. Pages 125–205 *in* R. L. Burgess and D. M. Sharpe, eds. Forest island dynamics in man-dominated landscapes. Springer-Verlag, New York.

Wilcove, D. S. 1985. Nest predation in forest tracts and the decline of migratory songbirds. Ecology 66:1211–1214.

The Use of Zoning Ordinances in the Protection and Development of Wildlife Habitat

STEVEN J. BISSELL, KATHI DEMAREST, AND DONALD L. SCHRUPP, *Colorado Division of Wildlife, 6060 Broadway, Denver, CO 80216*

INTRODUCTION

When Prince John signed the Magna Carta (at the point of a sword, according to legend), he established the central premise of land use in English speaking countries for centuries to come. That document recognized that land was a commodity, and as such could be controlled, disposed of, inherited, traded, sold, and bought just like any other privately held property. This concept of land as private property, protected by law, was and is central to land use issues in the United States. Under this concept, the protection of private property is within the police power of the state and as such is delegated to counties and municipalities, in most cases (Dawson 1982).

Because of the variable nature of local government in the United States, local land use planning has tended to be highly variable. Until the early part of this century, there were few uniform rules and methodologies. However, since then the use of zoning has become a major tool of local governments, especially county governments. The types of zoning and the uses of zoning have become highly complex, to say the least (Babcock 1966, Abrams 1978, Smith 1983, Babcock and Siemon 1985), but the basic concept of local government protecting land from incompatible uses on adjoining land is more or less standard throughout the country.

Generally, zoning is viewed as the enactment of ordinances by local government to designate areas for certain uses, activities, architectural styles, building heights, housing densities, etc. The types and extent of zoning change yearly, and the applications of zoning ordinances are just as complex (Gailey 1985). This seeming lack of uniformity prompted the Presidential Commission on Housing (1982) to recommend a national zoning law that would, in essence, deregulate zoning of private property. Additionally, Delogu (1982), in a widely cited paper, called for the complete deregulation of land use.

We believe that local control of land use can be effectively utilized and that deregulation would likely result in poor management of natural resources, especially wildlife. In Colorado, we have made effective use of local ordinances and land use regulations. Zoning rules, in particular, are amenable to the protection of wildlife habitat and the development of broad areas in and near urban centers.

The critical element in our program is that it is implemented at the local level through and by local government or citizen groups. We believe that programs such as ours depend upon the concept of local control of land use for success. Programs designed at and directed from the state or federal level have not been successful, in our opinion, because they fail to recognize the very basic nature of private property in American political life. We believe that programs of land use control, even if fairly radical in nature, will succeed if they are viewed as local programs, administered by people living close to the land. For example, Weld, Saguache, and Baca Counties are all very rural, agricultural counties in Colorado. All have implemented local soil conservation programs that prohibit, in some cases, the plowing of fragile grasslands. Despite the seemingly controversial nature of these ordinances, none have been seriously tested in the several years they have been in place because, local authorities believe, the rules are designed and directed by local residents. Similar programs directed at the conservation of natural resources, such as wildlife, probably will succeed if they remain under the jurisdiction of local government.

METHODS

There are 674 species of terrestrial vertebrates in Colorado (Chase et al. 1982, Bissell 1982, Hammerson and Langlois 1981) that are used as the basis for the development of site specific species lists (Bissell and Graul 1981). These lists are used to designate 15 to 20 species as the basis for local planning efforts. These species generally fall into sev-

Integrating Man and Nature in the Metropolitan Environment. Proc. Natl. Symp. on Urban Wildl., Chevy Chase, Md., 4–7 November 1986, L.W. Adams and D.L. Leedy, eds. Published by Natl. Inst. for Urban Wildl., 10921 Trotting Ridge Way, Columbia, MD 21044, 1987.

eral categories that have different selection criteria. Economically important species, such as big game, are nearly always used as they are of importance to the local community and the state. Species with restricted distributions or highly specific habitat requirements are selected because they serve as barometers of restricted habitat types. Threatened or endangered species are used to meet legal requirements. The overriding consideration is that there must be adequate information available to positively describe the occurrence of the species in the county. For the purpose of this procedure, we make no assumptions or extrapolations concerning the species, but only consider primary data.

Local concerns may not only involve what animals are present, but their distributions as well. The goal of the Colorado Division of Wildlife (CDW) is to provide specific information about the distribution of species present in a county. Distribution maps are prepared by CDW personnel with the cooperation of biologists from other agencies. These maps depict the distribution for those wildlife species selected in the county. A distribution map for a particular species will show its seasonal needs and specific use areas. For example, the map for elk in Teller County (Fig. 1) shows their overall distribution, winter range, winter concentration areas, and severe winter range. Other areas that also

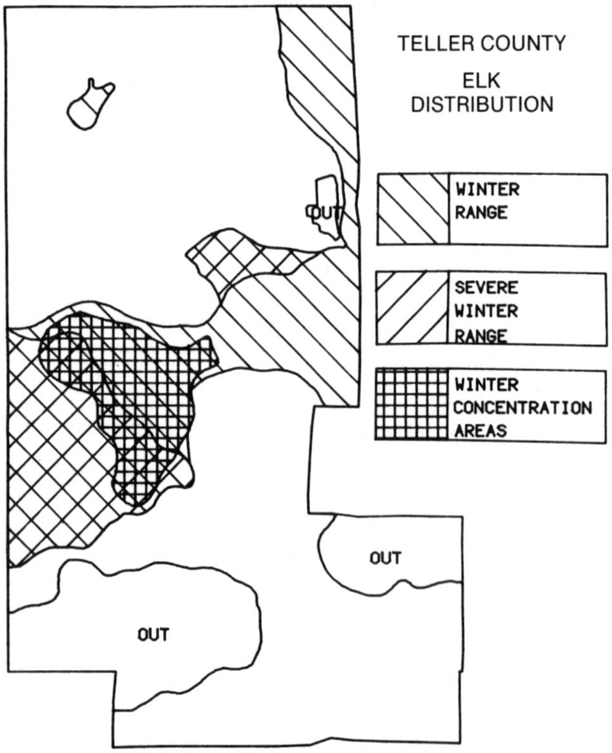

Fig. 1. The distribution of elk *(Cervus elaphus)* in Teller County, Colorado. The entire county, except for the areas labeled "out" is within the overall distribution.

can be mapped for elk include calving areas, highway crossings, and migration routes.

This information is mapped by CDW personnel on overlays to the United States Geological Survey Topographic Quadrangle Series of maps (1:24,000), or its sister series, the county format series (1:50,000). Some mapping is done using standard basemaps of the U.S. Forest Service and the U.S. Bureau of Land Management Public Lands Series (1:126,720). Division of Wildlife personnel convert the wildlife distribution maps to a computerized format using a Geographic Information System. This enables us to reproduce all the species distribution maps for one county to a common scale, as specified by the county.

To accompany the computer plotted maps, tabular summaries are available giving: (1) the area in square miles for each identified habitat feature (for example, there are 148 square miles (383.6 sq. km.) of elk winter range in Teller County); (2) base population estimates; and (3) estimated density (number of animals/square mile).

Aquatic resources in the county are identified by mapping all waters that support fisheries. Initial identification is done by searching compilations of CDW aquatic survey data. The resulting lists of waters are reviewed for accuracy by CDW field personnel. Relative fisheries values are assigned to each water. A summary is completed for the county, identifying waters of high, moderate, and low fisheries values. One of the final steps is mapping the relative fisheries values of rivers, streams, lakes, and reservoirs on a countywide basis. Waters with no fisheries value are omitted from the map.

Another piece of wildlife information provided to counties is the Wildlife Habitat Composite Map. This composite map is produced by "stacking" the individual species maps and calculating the cumulative value of overlap areas. The composite map summarizes the wildlife information in a subjective, yet easily understood format. Personnel from the CDW review the composited information and evaluate the potential for low, moderate, or high impact to wildlife habitat based on projected land use changes. For each county, the composite map shows the three zones of potential impact to wildlife habitat (Fig. 2).

The composite map enables a county to establish review procedures that address potential land use changes within the identified three impact zones. The composite map is often the only wildlife map used by the counties and developers in order to determine if potential benefits or conflicts regarding wildlife exist.

To aid in using the composite map, a worksheet is available for each county that shows specific wildlife species and the projected impact to each species. The worksheet generally is used for a proposed project located in the moderate or high potential impact zones. The worksheet is intended to be filled out by the planner and/or proponent of the project using a county base map and the individual species maps (Fig. 1). The proposed location of the devel-

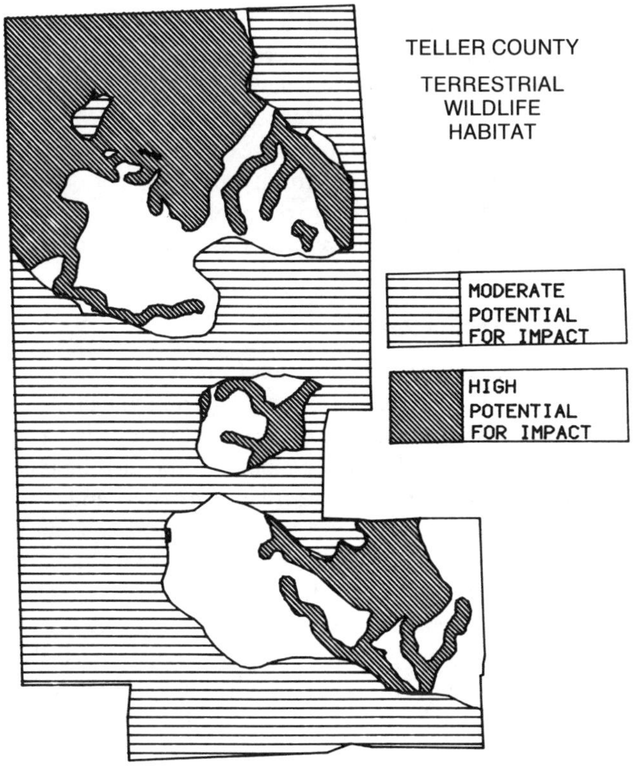

Fig. 2. The composite distribution of terrestrial wildlife in Teller County, Colorado, evaluated for high and moderate potential for impact to wildlife. The unstippled area is, by default, low potential for impact.

opment or land use change is drawn on a county base map. The base map is then overlaid on each of the individual species distribution maps. Areas of overlap of the development area and species distribution are then noted on the worksheet.

The worksheet provides the planner and project proponent a direct cause and effect perspective on the impacts of any proposed action. The worksheet also is a good method to initiate contact between planners, project proponents, and CDW personnel in order to discuss potential impacts and alternative approaches to lessen or eliminate the impacts.

APPLICATIONS

Teller County

Teller County is immediately adjacent to Colorado Springs and has experienced accelerated growth in recent years. It has become a non-industrialized suburb of Colorado Springs, with most of the private property becoming subdivided for single-family dwellings.

The three zones of potential impact have been used as the basis for a natural resource zoning ordinance in Teller County (Fig. 2). The ordinance requires that proponents who wish to undertake a project in the zone of high potential impact to wildlife file a conservation plan, as well as the project proposal, with the County Planning Commission. The conservation plan must address the impacts to wildlife, as identified on the species maps provided by the CDW. The proponent is encouraged to work with the Division in the development of this plan. The plan must, in some cases, include remedial measures to be implemented by the proponent and must be reviewed by the Division before submittal to the Planning Commission.

If a proposed project is in the zone of moderate potential for impact, the proponent must consult with the Division of Wildlife before submitting a proposal to the County Planning Commission. Projects in this area usually do not require design modification, but are mitigated by minor adjustments. Projects in the area of low potential for impact do not require any special measures by the proponent.

This natural resource zoning ordinance was designed by local government with consultation from the Division of Wildlife, but it was written entirely for local political realities. It has the same authority as any other zoning ordinance and would require formal action by the Board of County Commissioners to be bypassed, modified, or repealed. One aspect of the ordinance is that the species maps are a part of the ordinance and must, by law, be updated periodically.

Evergreen Planning District

The Evergreen area of Jefferson County, Colorado, is a highly developed mountain suburb of greater Denver. Development pressure is intense and development has proceeded without a great deal of consideration for wildlife resources. However, wildlife values have remained high due to undeveloped private lands, state and local public parks, and extensive U.S. Forest Service lands nearby. In recent years, the accelerated growth has threatened natural resources and created serious conflicts between development proponents, local residents, and management agencies. In 1984, the Jefferson County Board of County Commissioners appointed a Citizens Advisory Group, consisting of local residents, to review the developmental patterns and make recommendations to the Board for zoning rules within the planning district.

The group was given guidance and assistance by the county planning staff. A study area was agreed upon and mapped, basically representing the middle third of the mountainous portion of the county. Several major goals were identified before the group began its data collection. They met weekly, with subcommittees meeting almost as often to explore details of the group's designated areas of concern. They asked representatives of all the government agencies, homeowners' groups, and other significant interests to come and discuss their concerns, procedures, and roles in the land use process. Members of the group also set up "listening posts" for citizen input. Wildlife resources were repeatedly mentioned as amenities to the standard of living in the Evergreen area.

An ongoing part of the group's work was to map a number of important land uses and constraining or influencing factors. These included:

- geologic problem areas
- water districts, plus well permit information
- existing parks (federal, city, and county ownership)
- schools
- impact potential for elk, deer, turkeys, and raptors
- significant vegetation types (meadow, riparian wetland, and mountain shrub)
- fire hazard ratings
- current zoning

These maps were composited to identify major areas where development constraints existed. The group discussed, revised, and consolidated what the public told them and drafted a document outlining guidelines for development within the study area that they felt would address everyone's concerns. The document then underwent final public review with a formal public hearing before the County Commissioners.

To really appreciate the results, it is necessary to understand the difficulty in obtaining gains for wildlife in a rapidly developing, mostly urban, Front Range county. Much of the best wildlife habitat also is the most developable land. The community advisory group mapped density zones with lot size limitations in accordance with potential for wildlife impact. Some wildlife areas were recommended for no development. Although the plan is not yet approved, these recommendations are being considered by the county. It is certainly safe to say that the heavily developing portions of the study area will stay that way. Density reductions and protection of the most important habitat areas will require a major commitment by the county as requested by the county's residents.

An important part of the community advisory process is the ability to get significant community values considered in policy decisions. Because wildlife was shown to be an important "amenity" to a good portion of residents, the CDW was not alone in expressing the importance of making the most of wildlife habitat. One result of mountain development is often deleterious impacts to wildlife, and community support is critical in influencing ongoing policy.

This process is not without its drawbacks. It is expensive and requires staff commitment from the County Planning Office to keep it moving toward completion. The Evergreen group started out with a 6-month time frame—and ended up taking 15 months. It takes enormous commitment from the group members in terms of time and effort. It requires continual attention to the goal of avoiding conflict among the different interests represented within the group. Finally, as a local political issue, there is always the possibility it will further divide already polarized local interests.

If the County Commissioners adopt this plan as it is written, wildlife will gain through lower residential density and, possibly, protection of habitat and integrity of major movement corridors. It would certainly be an improvement over the current consideration given to wildlife in this area. This process resulted in three very important benefits. It provided: (1) the setting for positive community interaction with the CDW; (2) an opportunity for CDW personnel to present wildlife information to the public; and (3) an opportunity for the public to voice their concerns and support for wildlife.

Barr Lake State Park

The eastern portion of Adams County is dominated by the South Platte River and is essentially a highly urbanized portion of Denver. Barr Lake State Park is directly within this corridor and is becoming rapidly surrounded by urban sprawl. Lovell et al. (1986) described the history and recent biology of the park. The park is designated for low impact outdoor recreation with wildlife as the primary resource. There is a large heronry in the park occupied by great blue herons *(Ardea herodias)*, snowy egrets *(Egretta thula)*, cattle egrets *(Bubulcus ibis)*, and double-crested cormorants *(Phalacrocorax auritus)*. The park is a nationally recognized bird watching site and has more than 300 species recorded within the park boundaries.

In order to fully develop the wildlife resource within the park and to protect the wildlife-oriented recreation, the Division of Wildlife believes that it is necessary to influence land use decisions adjacent to the park. Adams County Planning Department, working with data from the Division of Wildlife, has used the three-tiered zones of potential impact to designate open space corridors in eastern Adams County. The area around Barr Lake State Park was mapped as high potential for impact to wildlife.

A proposal for a Planned Unit Development mobile home park to be located just south of Barr Lake State Park was submitted to the county. The design called for construction of a high-density mobile home community throughout an entire square mile section south of the park. Because the area was mapped as high potential impact to wildlife and the proposed project was situated so close to Barr Lake State Park, both the Colorado Division of Parks and Outdoor Recreation, and the CDW were asked to comment. With input from both agencies and with the support of the Adams County Planning Department and County Commissioners, the density of the development was reduced and construction was limited to the southern half of the section. The northern half was dedicated as open space, which created a half-mile (0.8 km) buffer zone between the development and the park.

Additionally, because of the location, an on-site sewage treatment plant was proposed by the developer. The proposal originally called for discharge of secondary effluent into a canal that runs adjacent to Barr Lake for approximately 4 miles (6.4 km) before exiting the park to the east. Effluent seepage into the lake was believed possible, which would accelerate an existing problem with eutrophication. Based upon advice from the Division of Parks and Outdoor Recreation, and the CDW, the developer is restricted to a non-discharging system and has yet to be granted a site permit from the Colorado Department of Health.

The CDW and the Division of Parks and Outdoor Recreation also are working with the developer through the Adams County Planning Department to improve the designated open space in order to provide better recreational opportunities to potential residents. The developer and Adams County have been advised by the Division of Parks and Outdoor Recreation that Barr Lake State Park is a day-use area with minimal recreational facilities, and that the park focuses on minimal impact recreation. Because of this, designated open space within the development area must provide recreational facilities for the residents, and the developers should not depend on Barr Lake State Park to supply these needs.

DISCUSSION

Much of the literature available concerning urban wildlife management is directed at species management or the management of small areas for specific reasons (see Noyes and Progulske 1974, for some excellent examples). In addition to those concerns, we have developed a methodology that allows for the effective management of wildlife resources over wide areas of privately held property, and for programs that have been described by Graul and Miller (1984) as "Ecosystem Management." The primary tool we have used is the authority of local government through the zoning ordinance.

We agree with Whyte (1959) that zoning is not a universally applicable technique and should not be viewed as a substitute for management programs, such as conservation easements or habitat acquisition. Rather, zoning is a function of local government and should express local concerns. Wildlife resources should not be viewed as obstructions to development, but as local amenities that may enhance or modify development. The critical element is that zoning or any rule or regulation of local government must be used within the context of local politics. Management agencies, be they state or federal, must assume the role of technical advisors to local government, which is a departure from the traditional role of regulatory agencies.

Delogu (1982) suggested that the deregulation of local controls of land use will allow the free market to operate and that economic controls alone will be sufficient to ensure adequate consideration of natural resources. We strongly disagree with that conclusion. Growth in urban areas will continue along economic patterns without any real environmental awareness unless it is mitigated by long-range, ecologically-sound planning.

The Presidential Commission on Housing (1982) called for a national zoning act that would establish standards along very narrow lines. We believe that this approach misses the point of local control of land use. People who live on the land are best able to determine proper use of the land. National standards cannot reflect local desires and conditions, either ecological or political, and seem to naively ignore the history of land use in America.

In addition to the above examples, we have effectively used the method outlined in this paper elsewhere in Colorado with some success. In our opinion, the basic necessary element is the close involvement of local government, citizens, and Division of Wildlife personnel. Programs originated at the state or federal level have not, in our opinion, been as successful in the protection of wildlife resources on private property or the full development of wildlife habitat in areas subject to more direct control.

Acknowledgments.—R. Zaccagnini and D. Lovell developed the data for Teller County and Barr Lake State Park, respectively. L. Sikorowski reviewed much of this material in a different form and J. Hekkers reviewed the manuscript and made many useful comments. County planning personnel throughout the state have materially contributed to the development of the methods described here and we thank them.

REFERENCES CITED

Abrams, S.D. 1978. How to win the zoning game. The Michie Co., Charlottesville. 384 pp.

Babcock, R.F. 1966. The zoning game. The University of Wisconsin Press, Madison. 202 pp.

Babcock, R.F., and C.L. Siemon. 1985. The zoning game revisited. Oelgeschlagen, Gunn and Hain, Publ., Inc., Boston. 304 pp.

Bissell, S.J. (ed.). 1982. Colorado mammal distribution latilong study. Colo. Div. of Wildl., Denver. 24 pp.

Bissell, S.J., and W.D. Graul. 1981. The latilong system of mapping wildlife distribution. Wildl. Soc. Bull. 9:185–189.

Chase, C.A., S.J. Bissell, H.E. Kingery, and W.D. Graul (eds.). 1982. Colorado bird distribution latilong study. Colo. Div. of Wildl., Denver. 78 pp.

Dawson, A.D. 1982. Land-use planning and the law. Garland STPM Press, New York. 246 pp.

Delogu, O.E. 1982. Local land use controls: an idea whose time has passed. Maine Law Rev., 36:261–310.

Gailey, J.B. (ed.). 1985. Zoning and planning law handbook. Clark Boardman Co., Ltd., New York. 407 pp.

Graul, W.D., and G.C. Miller. 1984. Strengthening ecosystem approaches. Wildl. Soc. Bull. 12:282–289.

Hammerson, G.A., and D. Langlois (eds.). 1981. Colorado reptile and amphibian distribution latilong study. Colo. Div. of Wildl., Denver. 24 pp.

Lovell, D.C., J.R. Choate, and S.J. Bissell. 1985. Succession of mammals in a disturbed area of the Great Plains. Southwest Nat. 30:335–342.

Noyes, J.H., and D.R. Progulske (eds.). 1974. Wildlife in an urbanizing environment. Planning and Resour. Development Ser., No. 28. Univ. Mass., Amherst. 182 pp.

President's Commission on Housing. 1982. The report of the President's Commission on Housing. Supt. Doc. 82-9780, Washington. 278 pp.

Smith, H.H. 1983. The citizens guide to zoning. Planners Press, Chicago. 242 pp.

Whyte, W. 1959. Securing open space for urban America: conservation easements. Urban Land Inst., Tech. Bull. No. 36, 67 pp.

St. Louis Vegetative Cover Study

David L. Tylka, *Missouri Department of Conservation, 1221 S. Brentwood Blvd., St. Louis, MO 63117*

Elizabeth A. Cook, *Illinois Natural History Survey, 607 E. Peabody, Champaign, IL 61820*

INTRODUCTION

Urban people enjoy wildlife. Ninety-three percent of the urbanites in the three major metropolitan areas of Missouri (St. Louis, Kansas City, and Springfield areas) view urban wildlife around their homes as "enjoyable" rather than "annoying." Approximately half of the people who live in the St. Louis area feed and watch birds, and 26% of this area's population photograph wild animals and plants (Witter et al. 1981).

The abundance and diversity of wildlife in an urban area are dependent upon the relative amount of wildlife habitat in the urban environment. Of the various components of urban wildlife habitat, vegetation and water are the most essential, as well as the most manageable (Leedy et al. 1978). The amount, diversity, and distribution of vegetation are major factors affecting the distribution and abundance of wild animals. Plants not only furnish food, but they also provide cover from the weather, protection from predators, and breeding and nesting sites. Therefore, vegetative management is the basic key to urban wildlife management.

Urban vegetation is not only important as wildlife habitat; it constitutes varying degrees of natural open spaces. The plants of these urban open spaces furnish biotic diversity; they also filter particulates and gases out of the air, reduce soil erosion, stabilize streambanks, increase surrounding property values, ameliorate temperature extremes, furnish relief from visual and noise pollution, and offer urbanites places for various forms of recreation.

To assess the status of urban wildlife habitat types and to document the number of different categories of urban open space, the Missouri Department of Conservation completed a vegetative cover study of St. Louis City and County in March, 1985.

STUDY AREA BACKGROUND

Located just below the confluence of the Mississippi and Missouri Rivers, the St. Louis City and County governments were officially recognized around 1810. In 1876, St. Louis City voted to separate itself from the 524 square miles (135, 716 ha) of St. Louis County and establish its present day boundary, which encompasses an area of 66 square miles (17,094 ha). Thus, St. Louis City chose to limit future city expansion and, as a result, 90 self-governing municipalities have now been incorporated in St. Louis County. These municipalities take up over two-fifths of the county land area and make up two-thirds of the county population (St. Louis County Dep. of Planning 1986).

The City of St. Louis grew from a population of about a thousand around 1800 to 310,854 by 1870, and to a high of 856,706 in 1950. Since around 1950, however, the population of St. Louis City has decreased significantly, with the 1980 census at 452,801. The population of St. Louis County rose from 40,325 in 1870 to 974,180 in 1980. The St. Louis Metropolitan Statistical Area (MSA) had a population of 2,354,378 in 1980 and is the twelfth largest MSA in the nation (St. Louis County Dep. of Planning 1986).

As late as 1954, most of the St. Louis Region's urban mass was contained in a relatively compact, high-density pattern in close proximity to St. Louis City. Between 1954 and 1975, however, there was a trend toward dispersion, correlating with a relatively large amount of highway construction and mortgage financing readily available at low interest rates. The demand for single-family residences on large lots, the abundant supply of low-cost gasoline for commuting, and the relocation of business and industry away from the St. Louis City core area all contributed to population dispersal and a decrease in development intensity. Industrial development outside the core area has gen-

Integrating Man and Nature in the Metropolitan Environment. Proc. Natl. Symp. on Urban Wildl., Chevy Chase, Md., 4–7 November 1986, L.W. Adams and D.L. Leedy, eds. Published by Natl. Inst. for Urban Wildl., 10921 Trotting Ridge Way, Columbia, MD 21044, 1987.

erally tended to occur within industrial parks located along major thoroughfares near major intersections. Commercial development has occurred in central business districts of cities, in strips along major corridors, and in shopping centers. Although commercial and industrial land uses are significant (26% in St. Louis City and 11% in St. Louis County), residential land is the largest of all developed land use categories, 47% in St. Louis City and 58% in St. Louis County (East-West Gateway Coordinating Council Staff 1977).

St. Louis City and County have over one hundred miles (161 km) of the Missouri, Mississippi, and Meramec Rivers flowing along their boundaries. Although floodplain acreage figures are unavailable, with this many miles of river surrounding the area, relatively flat floodplains make up a substantial portion of the City and County. Most of St. Louis City has a generally flat topography with slopes below 10% (St. Louis County Dep. of Planning 1973). The major portion of St. Louis County has slopes below 16%. Approximately the western fifth of St. Louis County has steep slopes of over 16% (East-West Gateway Coordinating Council Staff 1977). Thus, the topography of this area lends itself to development.

METHODS

Landsat Thematic Mapper (TM) satellite data in computer compatible digital format were used to interpret vegetative cover and inferred land use for the study area in St. Louis. TM data's 30 by 30 meters resolution is appropriate for analysis of the urban landscape. A 29 August 1982 TM scene was primarily selected because it was a cloud-free day during the growing season.

Processing digital satellite data into usable information requires several steps. Initially, the data were geographically referenced to the Universal Transverse Mercator map coordinate system via the selection of known-location ground control points. Georeferenced satellite data can be overlaid with other computer-stored map information and with output in representative map scales using computer graphics.

Unsupervised classification techniques applied to the data identified 79 spectrally-distinct classes. The theory behind unsupervised classifying is that the researcher does not "predefine" the classification scheme by selecting training fields, but rather the computer algorithm clusters the data according to their unique spectral characteristics. Locations of the spectral classes were studied on aerial photography and in the field in order to group and identify them as 16 significant land cover classes. During interpretation, the study area was divided into two subareas based on degree of urbanizaton. The stratification was implemented to avoid classification errors due to similar vegetative cover having different land use. For example, cemeteries and golf courses are sometimes not spectrally separable from pasture and hayland, although land use can be inferred from urbanization and location in the country. After a classification scheme was finalized, subareas were merged.

To facilitate public usage, the 16 land cover classes were aggregated into six general land cover classes, with special attention given to types of vegetative cover. Boundaries of selected municipalities, regions, watersheds, public lands, and significant urban transportation corridors were digitized from existing map sources. These boundaries were overlaid with the classified TM data to produce area land cover statistics and graphics.

RESULTS

The six general land cover classes aggregated were (1) developed land, (2) successional fields (with greater than one-third canopy closure), (3) agricultural land, (4) moderate to dense forestland with understory vegetation, (5) water, consisting specifically of open water, flowing and impounded water, and wetlands, and (6) manicured green space.

Manicured green spaces were discernible only within a core area of St. Louis City and County (an area within the Interstate 270 Highway Loop). These manicured green spaces were mowed and maintained grassy areas such as cemeteries and golf courses. Two specific categories of manicured green space were separable—those areas with less than one-third canopy cover and those areas with more.

Developed land was subclassified as primary residential, secondary residential, impervious surfaces, barren land, intensive urban land, and extensive urban land. The primary residential subclass was relatively new residential land with young, sparse vegetation and less than one-third canopy closure. Secondary residential was older and had over one-third canopy closure. Impervious surfaces were primarily asphalt and concrete areas, such as parking lots and large concrete buildings. Quarries and similar land uses made up the barren land subclass. Intensive urban land was typically a mixture of residential and commercial lands with impervious surfaces common. Extensive urban land was generally a low-intensity mixture of residential and commercial lands.

The agricultural class included row crops, pasture and idle cropland, and bare soil such as tilled lands.

The total study area of St. Louis City and County comprised 366,748 acres (148,533 ha) (Table 1).

Subunits of the study area were defined, and vegetative cover types, percentages, and areas were calculated for these subunits. St. Louis City and County was first divided into six smaller regions by using major transportation corridors. Each region generally ranged in size from about 52,000 acres (21,000 ha) to about 86,000 acres (34,800 ha), except for a small region in the southern tip of St. Louis County that was only about 20,000 acres (8,100 ha). As one might expect, regions close to the central core area were highly developed (about 64–69%) and had relatively small amounts of forestland (about 4–7%). Regions farthest away from the

Table 1. Land cover classification for St. Louis City and County, Missouri, 1982.

Cover type	Composition (%)	Size (acres)
Developed land	37.0	136,010
Successional fields	4.6	16,997
Agricultural land	28.8	105,759
Forestland	19.2	70,583
Water	2.9	10,466
Manicured green space[a]	7.3	26,933
Total	99.8	366,748

[a]Manicured green space was a cover type discernible only within the Interstate 270 Highway Loop Core Area.

core area in the western portion of St. Louis County, where the topography is steeper, had only about 10–14% of developed land but about 30–45% forestland.

Data also were collected on 27 municipalities in the study area that occupied the largest areas. Developed land in these selected municipalities ranged from a low of 15.6% in Valley Park to a high of 81.2% in Overland. Forestland ranged from 0.9% in St. Louis City to 32.7% in Valley Park and 31% in Ladue.

Lastly, data on eight large conservation areas or parks, ranging from about 300 acres (120 ha) to about 2,400 acres (970 ha), were tabulated. These tracts varied from St. Louis City's Forest Park, located in a highly urbanized area, to Rockwoods Range Conservation Area, located in a forested and hilly portion of St. Louis County. Forest Park contained 43.7% developed land, 44.4% manicured green space, and only 5.8% forestland. Rockwoods Range Conservation Area had only 0.1% developed and 98.1% forestland.

DISCUSSION

Through personal experience and events reported by the news media, most urban people can make generalizations about the effects of urbanization upon the land. However, quantifying changes taking place in the urban environment and specifically locating these changes are measures lacking in most urbanized areas. Without this specific information, most urban land management decisions and environmental quality considerations are being made primarily on generalizations about the urban landscape. Dorney (1974) stated, "We are too often left with environmental quality 'motherhood' statements, defensively trying to protect remnant ecosystems (albeit important) and winning a skirmish here and there, but essentially being overwhelmed by sophisticated information systems generated by other professionals from their specific viewpoints." The St. Louis Vegetative Cover Study provides a more sophisticated environmental information system that can be utilized not only by land managers and administrators, but also by conservation organizations and individuals.

Many of these urban land management decisions affect the quality of life for urban dwellers. Decisions about parkland management, natural open space acquisition, and maintenance of common grounds affect the lives of urbanites. When officials make decisions, more attention needs to be paid to urbanites' enjoyment of nature. According to a study by Shaw and Mangun (1984), 54% of the population of the United States (89 million people) enjoyed wildlife in residential settings, with most of these people observing, identifying, photographing, or feeding wildlife within a radius of 1 mile (1.6 km) from home. It also was revealed in this report that woodlands were the habitats most frequently used by these people. Ian Laurie (1979) stated, "Existing and future open spaces must be assessed in terms of their 'natural potential' (i.e. the recognition of an optimum level of natural form and character in relation to man's needs) and all new development must contain the opportunity for daily contact with nature for those who will use it." Apparently, the nature and pressures of urban living emphasize the need for natural open space and the recreational opportunities associated with these natural habitats.

People in St. Louis are utilizing the St. Louis Vegetative Cover Study to assist them in making parkland management decisions. A proposition to develop about 10 acres (4 ha) of forestland and manicured green space in Forest Park, St. Louis City, was denied. Proponents to keep this area of the park undeveloped pointed out that because Forest Park contained only 79.2 acres (32.1 ha) of woodland and because St. Louis City contained only 412 acres (166.9 ha) of woodlands, the loss of even 5 or 10 acres of woodlands would be unacceptable.

Municipal officials in Bridgeton, Ellisville, and Kirkwood have used the St. Louis Vegetative Cover Study to help justify the acquisition of natural open spaces in their cities. These open spaces are used not only for recreation, but they also offer opportunities for environmental education. Many urbanites have been removed or separated from the land by a generation or two. Natural open spaces present areas where the public (especially children) can develop a greater understanding of natural processes and life forms that exist in these natural vestiges. Acquiring and conserving these natural open spaces add to the ecological stability of the area and offer aesthetic benefits to nearby residents. Acquisition and conservation of these areas also have economic returns, such as increased property values to surrounding landowners and the possibility of attracting compatible development.

Not all of the usage of this study has been successful. It was used to try to convince (unsuccessfully to date) the regional agency for stormwater control to adopt a more natural approach to urban stormwater management. As urban stormwater control agencies develop a more holistic watershed approach to stormwater management, prospects of utilizing this vegetative cover study will increase.

Municipal officials have used the St. Louis Vegetative Cover Study to help justify stringent street tree ordinances and ordinances requiring businesses to make landscape plantings and to use vegetative screenings when adjacent to residential areas. These ordinances affect the quality of life now and also in the future. Individuals who value natural vegetation around their residences or potential residences have referred to the St. Louis Vegetative Cover Study to see how much vegetative open space exists in different communities where they are considering relocation.

POSSIBLE FUTURE APPLICATIONS

The St. Louis Vegetative Cover Study is one of the first urban applications of TM satellite data. Plans to utilize this system and conduct a similar study in Kansas City, Missouri, are underway. Besides being a pilot urban program, this study will become a benchmark for comparative studies that can document future changes and trends in vegetative cover.

This information could be used to assess the 1982 status of urban wildlife habitats and to generate lists of wildlife that could potentially use the habitats found in the study area. These data also could facilitate future studies on particular urban wildlife species. The St. Louis Vegetative Cover Study could be used to direct urbanites to sites where there would be opportunities to observe, photograph, or hunt (with certain restrictions) particular wildlife species. With further analysis, the study could facilitate identification and subsequent conservation of important wildlife corridors.

The applications of the St. Louis Vegetative Cover Study to other disciplines are just being realized. A further step to this study would be to integrate topography and soil moisture indexing with vegetative cover information to improve forecasting the chances of floods occurring in specific watersheds. Real estate companies and developers could use the study to convince people to locate in particularly attractive vegetated localities within the study area.

When the sciences of urban design, planning, and land management make future advances, a holistic ecosystem approach to future urban challenges will be developed utilizing information systems such as the St. Louis Vegetative Cover Study. Public acceptance and desirability of a more natural approach to urban land management (such as natural lawn ordinances) must evolve. However, fundamental value changes in our society concerning the interaction of man and nature will take time. The "back-to-nature" movement is attempting to combine advanced technology and ecological understanding with traditional life styles. The concept of a balanced, diverse, and stable urban ecosystem will be the goal of progressive cities of the future.

Acknowledgments.—The authors wish to express their sincere appreciation to the staff of the Geographic Resources Center at the University of Missouri, Columbia, for providing technical support. We especially want to thank Mr. Terry Barney for his suggestions and effort on all phases of the project.

REFERENCES CITED

Dorney, R.S. 1974. Incorporating ecological concepts into planning, with emphasis on the urban municipality. Pages 99–110 *in* G.B. McKeating, ed. Nature and urban man. Nature Fed., Ottawa.

East-West Gateway Coordinating Council Staff. 1977. Year 2000 land use plan, St. Louis metropolitan region. East-West Gateway Coordinating Council, 112 North 4th St., Suite 1200, St. Louis, MO. 215 pp.

Laurie, I.C. 1979. Introduction. Pages xv–xix *in* I.C. Laurie, ed. Nature in cities, the natural environment in the design and development of urban green space. John Wiley & Sons, Chichester, England. 430 pp.

Leedy, D.L., R.M. Maestro, and T.M. Franklin. 1978. Planning for wildlife in cities and suburbs. FWS/OBS-77/66, U.S. Dep. Inter., Fish and Wildl. Serv., Washington, D.C. 64 pp.

St. Louis County Dep. of Planning. 1973. Land element: general plan. St. Louis County Dep. of Planning, 41 S. Central, Clayton, MO. 55 pp.

St. Louis County Dep. of Planning. 1986. St. Louis County, Missouri fact book—1986. St. Louis County Dep. of Planning, 41 S. Central, Clayton, Mo. 132 pp.

Shaw, W.W. and W.R. Mangun. 1984. Nonconsumptive use of wildlife in the United States. Resour. Publ. 154, U.S. Dep. Inter., Fish and Wildl. Serv., Washington, D.C. 20 pp.

Witter, D.J., D.L. Tylka, and J.E. Werner. 1981. Values of urban wildlife in Missouri. Trans. North Am. Wildl. and Nat. Resour. Conf. 46:424–431.

Urban Wildlife Habitat Inventory: The Willamette River Greenway, Portland, Oregon

MICHAEL C. HOUCK, *Audubon Society of Portland, 5151 NW Cornell Road, Portland, OR 97210*

INTRODUCTION

"... rivers and the inhabitants of the watery element were made for wise men to contemplate, and fools to pass by without consideration."

Izaak Walton

The Willamette River is a significant natural resource of statewide importance in Oregon. Its 250 mile (402 km) course takes it from the high Cascades through the fertile Willamette Valley to its confluence with the Columbia River in Portland. The Willamette flows through nine counties and 19 cities.

The Portland segment of the river (Fig. 1) bears little resemblance to the shallow, braided system of sloughs, wetlands, and lakes that greeted the 1806 Lewis and Clark expedition. By 1851, much of the adjacent coniferous forests had been cleared for the newly established city and much of the river front had already been dedicated to port activities (Audubon Society of Portland 1986).

By the 1960's, not only had the river been transformed physically, but its quality had been degraded to the extent that it was a health hazard. This prompted a public effort, led in large part by the late Governor Tom McCall, to remedy both the pollution and natural resource issues that plagued the river in both rural and urban locations throughout the Willamette Valley.

Between 1967 and 1975, a statewide planning effort was initiated to address conflicts along the Willamette. The state legislature began the effort with an unsuccessful attempt to promote acquisition of land. Unfortunately, by 1971 little acquisition had taken place. In 1973, the state legislature enacted a Greenway Statute and directed the Oregon Department of Transportation, in cooperation with local jurisdictions, to prepare a plan for the Willamette River Greenway. Deficiencies in content and implementation ultimately led Oregon's statewide land use body, the Land Conservation and Development Commission to establish the WILLAMETTE RIVER GREENWAY: GOAL 15, which is now one of Oregon's 19 planning goals. These goals provide the framework for planning in all cities and counties.

Goal 15 directs county and urban jurisdictions to "... protect, conserve, enhance and maintain the natural, scenic, historical, agricultural, economic and recreational qualities of lands along the Willamette River as the Willamette River Greenway." It further directs that each juris-

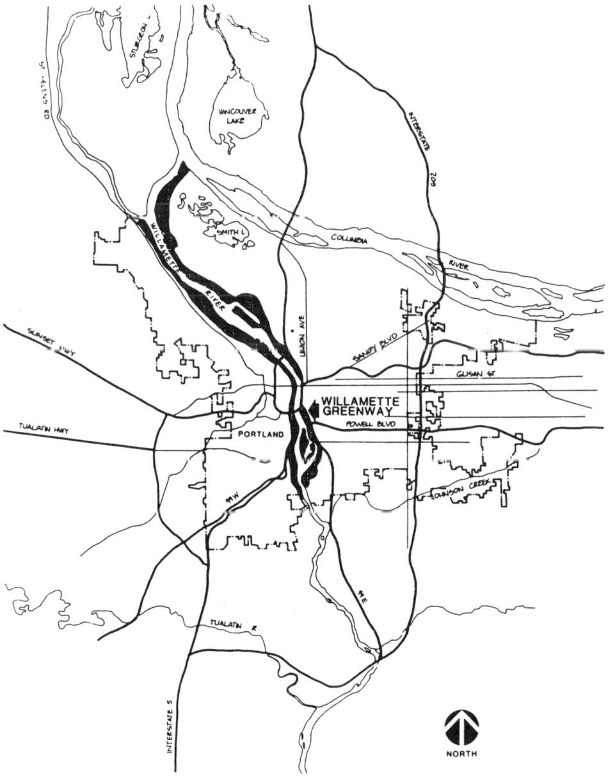

Fig. 1. The Willamette River and associated Greenway, Portland, Oregon.

Integrating Man and Nature in the Metropolitan Environment. Proc. Natl. Symp. on Urban Wildl., Chevy Chase, Md., 4–7 November 1986, L.W. Adams and D.L. Leedy, eds. Published by Natl. Inst. for Urban Wildl., 10921 Trotting Ridge Way, Columbia, MD 21044, 1987.

diction shall conduct inventories "to determine the nature and extent of the resources. . ." along the Greenway. Among the 15 resources to be inventoried are: significant natural and scenic areas, and vegetative cover; fish and wildlife habitats; ecologically fragile areas; and acquisition areas.

Cities and counties must take these inventoried resources into consideration when formulating their Comprehensive Plans and designating land uses along the Greenway.

In addition to the Willamette Greenway Goal 15, there is a Lower Willamette River Management Plan that is used by the Division of State Lands to manage submerged and submersible lands. Another of Oregon's land use goals, Goal 5 (Open Spaces, Scenic and Historic Areas, and Natural Resources), applies on a citywide basis, including the Willamette River.

The City of Portland adopted its Willamette River Greenway Plan in 1979 and incorporated this plan into its Comprehensive Plan in 1980. The Greenway Plan emphasizes water-dependent and river-related development. All other uses must be in keeping with the natural and scenic qualities of lands along the Willamette River.

This paper describes a wildlife habitat inventory update, which expands on the data available from the Fish and Wildlife Habitat Inventory that was conducted in 1973 as part of the Lower Willamette River Management Plan.

METHODOLOGY

The methodology for conducting this wildlife habitat inventory has evolved over the past 5 years from similar efforts in Washington County and the City of Beaverton. The first attempt, in urban Washington County, simply involved the use of large-scale maps (1:1000) with floodplain and forest overlays. The result was qualitative descriptions of sites that accompanied crudely drawn boundaries on planning bureau maps. Given a 2-week deadline for the work to be completed in nine Community Planning Areas, the information was the best that could be produced. One of several significant flaws in the statewide land use goals is that the jurisdictions need only use the "best information available." It is often the case that city and county jurisdictions fail to seek any information for the inventory of significant wetland and other wildlife habitat resources (Houck and Rogers 1984). Unless challenged by the public, no justification need be given for exclusion of significant natural resources from the inventory. This is a source of ongoing conflict in Oregon's land use arena.

The methodology improved in quality, consistency, and acceptance during the second inventory effort that grew out of a land use conflict in the City of Beaverton in 1984. City Council and the Planning Commission demanded a quantitative approach to wildlife habitat inventory. What resulted from this directive was a WILDLIFE HABITAT ASSESSMENT form (Fig. 2), which was developed cooperatively by Portland Audubon Society, U. S. Army Corps of Engineers, U. S. Fish and Wildlife Service, Oregon Department of Fish and Wildlife, The Wetlands Conservancy, and the City of Beaverton.

Wildlife Habitat Assessment

UNIT NO. ______ LOCATION ______ SQ. FT. ______ SCORE ______* ______**

COMMENTS ______

COMPONENT		DEGREE	SCORE *	**	COMMENTS
WATER	Quantity & Seasonality	NONE 0 .... SEASONAL 4 .... PERENNIAL 8			
	Quality	STAGNENT 0 .... SEASONALLY FLUSHED 3 .... CONTINUALLY FLUSHED 6			
	Proximity To Cover	NONE 0 .... NEARBY 4 .... IMMEDIATELY ADJACENT 8			
	Diversity (Streams, Ponds, Wetlands)	ONE PRESENT 2 .... TWO PRESENT 4 .... THREE PRESENT 8			
FOOD	Variety	LOW 0 .... MEDIUM 4 .... HIGH 8			
	Quantity & Seasonality	NONE 0 .... LIMITED 4 .... YEAR AROUND 8			
	Proximity To Cover	NONE 0 .... NEARBY 4 .... IMMEDIATELY ADJACENT 8			
COVER	Structural Diversity	LOW 0 .... MEDIUM 4 .... HIGH 8			
	Variety	LOW 0 .... MEDIUM 4 .... HIGH 8			
	Nesting	LOW 0 .... MEDIUM 2 .... HIGH 4			
	Escape	LOW 0 .... MEDIUM 2 .... HIGH 4			
	Seasonality	NONE 0 .... LIMITED 2 .... YEAR AROUND 4			

*Existing **Enhancement Potential

ADDITIONAL VALUE					
DISTURBANCE	PHYSICAL	PERMANENT 0 .... TEMPORARY 2 .... UNDISTURBED 4			
	HUMAN	HIGH 0 .... MEDIUM 2 .... LOW 4			
INTERSPERSION		LOW 0 .... MEDIUM 3 .... HIGH 6			
UNIQUE FEATURES 0 - 4		WILDLIFE ______ FLORA ______ SCENIC ______ RARITY OF HABITAT TYPE ______ EDUCATIONAL POTENTIAL ______			

Developed With the Assistance of:

Mike Houck-Audubon Society
Ralph Rogers-U.S. Army Corps of Engineers
Dennis Peters-U.S. Fish & Wildlife Service
Diana Hwang-U.S. Fish & Wildlife Service
Gene Herb-Oregon Dept. of Fish & Game
Jack Broome-Wetlands Conservancy

Fig. 2. The wildlife habitat assessment form developed for the Willamette River Greenway.

Wildlife Habitat Assessment Rating Sheet

The intent of a one-page rating sheet (Fig. 2) was to provide information easily understood by the public, policy makers, and landowners. Achieving that objective while simultaneously producing a useful tool for assessing relative wildlife habitat values was a challenge.

There are a multitude of techniques to a quantitative approach to habitat descriptions. For example, King County, Washington, has developed a detailed quantitative inventory for its wetland resources. King County's approach is exhaustive and, consequently, produces an inventory that will stand up to scrutiny. It also is complex, difficult for the layman to understand, and requires substantial staff expertise in natural resources.

Our one-page format attempts a compromise among agency representatives, planners, policy makers, landowners, and the public. It achieves the objectives of addressing wildlife needs recognized by all biologists as being critical (FOOD, WATER, and COVER); allows for recording of PHYSICAL and HUMAN DISTURBANCE; addresses the concept of INTERSPERSION; and provides for UNIQUE FEATURES (wildlife, flora, scenic, rarity of habitat type, and educational potential). The inventory sheet is heavily biased toward aquatic systems. We are particularly concerned about riparian and wetland habitats in the Portland metropolitan area.

The Willamette Greenway: Evolution of the Methodology

The City of Portland decided to take a similar approach to improving its data base for the Willamette Greenway Update. The data from the 1973 Lower Willamette Greenway study indicated on a percentage basis how different reaches of the Willamette rated for mammals, birds, and reptiles, and assigned classes of Excellent, Good, Fair, and Poor for the habitats that were inventoried. There was no detailed written document that accompanied this inventory. The data were not site specific.

Building on the Beaverton experience, the Portland Planning staff and I developed a habitat evaluation process that included the following elements.

- Filling out a Wildlife Habitat Assessment Sheet for each of 174 habitat sites (site boundaries were determined by natural breaks in vegetation, land use, and other features).
- Tape recording field observations of vegetation, animals, and comments concerning the potential for each site.
- Taking overlapping photographs (Kodachrome slides) of the sites to ensure that the entire inventory area had a photographic record.
- Field validating the Wildlife Habitat Assessment Sheets on selected sites by U. S. Environmental Protection Agency and Oregon Department of Fish and Wildlife biologists to ensure consistency of results.
- Placing final numerical scores for all sites on a large-scale aerial photograph and comparing all 174 final sites to determine whether there were obvious discrepancies among the data.
- Ordering the sites by scores (114 points being the highest possible and O being the lowest possible) and placing each site into one of five "classes" or "ranks," based on similarity of final scores.
- Involving major property owners in reviewing the results and giving them an opportunity to express concerns. The openness of the process resulted in little dispute over the inventory methodology or results.

RESULTS

The final product of the wildlife habitat inventory is a section-by-section map of the entire Willamette River within the City of Portland, with site-specific data on 174 sites. The number of sites per "Rank" (and their score range) were as follows:

RANK I SITES (114-91): 7
RANK II SITES (88-70): 21
RANK III SITES (68-40): 29
RANK IV SITES (39-30): 17
RANK V SITES (29-0): 100

It is not surprising that very few sites received high ratings in a highly industrialized port city. Four of the seven RANK I sites are in or adjacent to Oaks Bottom, a 160-acre (64.8 ha) city park at the extreme upstream end of the study area. The other three RANK I sites are located at the extreme downstream end of the Greenway, on the south bank, opposite intensive Port of Portland development. They are all relatively natural in character and all contain significant wetlands and riparian vegetation.

The 21 RANK II sites are comprised of "islands" of more or less disturbed habitat, but retaining much of their natural riparian character. These are spread throughout the study area. Not surprisingly, the remaining 146 sites are situated in the heart of the industrial district, adjacent to Port facilities and the downtown core.

Integration into the Willamette Greenway Plan

As a result of the inventory, the Planning Bureau now has site-specific information regarding relative significance of 174 sites with respect to wildlife habitat. This information will be used by planning staff and other government agencies (Division of State Lands, Oregon Department of Fish and Wildlife, U.S. Fish and Wildlife Service, and U.S. Environmental Protection Agency) in reviewing land use applications along the Willamette River. It also is being considered by the Planning Bureau in the current update of existing land use policies and regulations along the Willamette Greenway.

Discussion Draft

These data and other inventories were considered in the Bureau's newly released Discussion Draft, "WILLAMETTE GREENWAY UPDATE 1985/86" (Fig. 1). This update reviews existing regulations along the Willamette River with the goal of streamlining land use processes, eliminating ambiguity in the regulations, and improving access to the river.

RECOMMENDATIONS AFFECTING WILDLIFE HABITAT

Land Acquisition

Within the Planning Bureau's acquisition package are several sites that were identified through the inventory as highly significant wildlife habitat. These included lands adjacent to Oaks Bottom Wildlife Refuge (city park); Ross Island (currently being mined for aggregate resources); Hardtack Island; East Island, the riparian forest at the Harborton site; land necessary to construct and landscape the Greenway trail; and "shorelines where necessary to preserve the vegetative fringe, natural shoreline or public access to the river."

Greenway Trail

The 1979 Greenway Plan called for the construction of a combined bicycle and pedestrian recreation trail system along the Willamette River. Property owners were required by the Plan to construct the portion of trail on their property as development occurred.

It is noteworthy that a great deal of emphasis on improving public access to the Willamette River appears in the Planning Bureau's Discussion Draft. The recommendations include: expediting completion of the Greenway trail in planned phases; development of viewpoints and view corridors along the river; and a public awareness program consisting of signing along the route, and brochures depicting the Greenway trail and 40 Mile Loop Trail. The latter is a 100-mile (161 km) partially completed regional trail system originally proposed by the Olmsted brothers.

These two trail systems, when completed, will provide public access near all of Portland's significant habitat sites. It should be noted that the Bureau of Parks and Recreation is sensitive to overuse of natural areas. Feeder trails will be designed with the resource in mind.

Land Use Development Standards

New landscaping standards are proposed for the Greenway. Generally, lands along the river bank and upland properties that are preserved as natural areas are subject to more stringent landscaping standards than other lands within the Greenway. There is an emphasis on the use of native plants when revegetating the Greenway and preserving existing vegetation. The percentage of native plants to be used varies with the existing quality and quantity of wildlife habitat. A list of native plants and their wildlife values appears in the Background Document and will be distributed to future land use applicants.

Setbacks

The recommendation for a 25-foot (7.6 m) minimum setback with average setback of 35 feet (10.7 m) in which no nonriver-dependent or nonriver-related uses may locate without a Goal 15 exception is an improvement over the current Greenway Plan that calls for a 25-foot setback only.

Potential

One of the shortcomings of the inventory process is the lack of attention to a site's POTENTIAL for restoration. That deficiency was the one most criticized by everyone involved in developing the rating sheet. The City of Portland planning staff did include a "POTENTIAL" section in their document, "Lower Willamette River Wildlife Habitat Inventory." They stated that "The relative low score that more than 100 sites received was attributable to the lack of the three factors that appear on the inventory rating sheet: Food, Water and Cover . . . these areas could be rehabilitated to provide significant wildlife habitat values."

OTHER PLANNING EFFORTS

Portland Audubon Society has been involved in a number of other planning efforts in cooperation with the Bureaus of Planning, and Parks and Recreation that have influenced wildlife and recreation along the Willamette River. When specific land use issues arise, many of our publications, programs, and field trips are scheduled in order to inform Portlanders about the issues.

City of Portland Goal 5 Update

As with the Willamette Greenway, the statewide land use planning process calls for a periodic review of the other 18 goals, one of which (Goal 5) relates to natural resources. Goal 5 also directs that an inventory be conducted on a citywide basis to determine the location, quantity, and quality of natural resources including wetlands, wildlife habitat, and ecologically significant areas. If there are no conflicting uses (rare in an urban setting), the goal demands that the resource be protected. If there are conflicting uses, the jurisdiction must conduct an Environmental, Social, Economic and Energy Consequences Analysis to determine whether the site(s) will be conserved, fully developed, or partially conserved. This process also will be applied to the Willamette Greenway. The Willamette Greenway wildlife habitat inventory will substitute for a Goal 5 inventory because the procedures are nearly identical.

Oaks Bottom Management Plan

Audubon Society of Portland has prepared a management plan for Oaks Bottom Wildlife Refuge, the most significant site inventoried on both the original Lower Willamette River study and the Willamette Greenway Update wildlife inventory. This 160-acre (64.8 ha) City of Portland park is managed cooperatively by Portland Audubon and the Park Bureau. Audubon Society consults with the City Park Bureau on all parcels of land with wildlife habitat value and makes recommendations regarding habitat enhancement, protection, and maintenance.

Portland Audubon cooperates in public education programs (hikes utilizing city parks; bicycle rides such as our "Ride On The Wild Side" natural history series and classes) with the Park Bureau.

PUBLICATIONS

Portland Audubon Society publishes a monthly newsletter, *The Warbler*, and a quarterly journal, *The Urban Naturalist*. The latter is a publication begun in the summer of 1982 to encourage the appreciation of Portland area urban wildlife. The latest issue (Summer 1986) focused on the Willamette River to coincide with our planning involvement. *The Urban Naturalist* contains articles on both native and nonnative wildlife and plant species and "theme issues" such as the Columbia Slough and Willamette River.

SUMMARY

Cooperation between public agencies and private interest groups has resulted in the most comprehensive wildlife habitat inventory completed to date for a City of Portland planning document. The ongoing Goal 5 inventory promises to be an improvement over the Greenway work. A methodology acceptable to a broad range of interests was developed from a format used in other Portland area jurisdictions and applied as directed by Oregon's statewide land use laws. The City of Portland has, for the Willamette River, and soon will have citywide, site-specific wildlife habitat data on which to base decisions concerning the conservation, preservation, and enhancement of significant natural resources.

Other actions such as neighborhood and regional park planning, public education programs, publication of urban natural history journals, and continued private citizen involvement in the planning process will ensure that Izaak Walton would have been pleased with our efforts to protect one of Portland's most scenic natural features.

Acknowledgments.—I began this project with Linda Dobson, Planner II with the Portland Planning Bureau. Bob Goldie, Planner II started a bit later. They are the most conscientious, cooperative planning team I have worked with. Bob's tenacity in working on the documents and tireless research into wildlife-attracting plants is proof positive that a planner *can* be a biologist!

Martha Gannett, Laurie Causgrove, Virginia Church and the rest of *The Urban Naturalist* "crew," as always, have produced a visually attractive and interesting issue on the Willamette River that was an outgrowth of the Greenway wildlife inventory. Their incredible volunteerism over the past 4 years has done much to educate Portlanders about wildlife in their own backyards.

Special thanks also are due Ralph Thomas Rogers, U.S. Environmental Protection Agency; Joe Pesek and Gene Herb, Oregon Department of Fish and Wildlife; Paul Ketcham, 1000 Friends of Oregon; and Jack Broome, The Wetlands Conservancy.

Funding for the inventory came from Oregon Department of Fish and Wildlife's nongame wildlife fund, the YARG Foundation, Sellwood-Moreland Improvement League, and Portland Audubon.

REFERENCES CITED

Audubon Society of Portland. 1986. *The Urban Naturalist*, Summer issue.

Houck, M.C. and R.T. Rogers. 1984. Wetlands: dirt cheap and disappearing. Landmark 1:12–19. (A publication of 1000 Friends of Oregon.)

Analysis of Small Mammal Community Data and Applications to Management of Urban Greenspaces

CHARLES H. NILON[1] AND LARRY W. VANDRUFF, *Faculty of Environmental and Forest Biology, SUNY College of Environmental Science and Forestry, Syracuse, NY 13210*

Sanders and Rowntree (1984) have described the challenges associated with planning and managing urban greenspaces—areas with soil surface covered by at least some visible vegetative cover (Powell 1982). A variety of user groups, often with conflicting interests, compete for a limited resource. Local governments and conservation groups are taking an increased interest in the management of greenspaces, with wildlife conservation and management a high priority (Syracuse Commission for the Conservation of the Environment 1973, R. Pouyat, New York City Parks Dept. pers. comm. May 1985). Wildlife management is a particular challenge. Although a large body of theoretical and technical information on wildlife management techniques exists (Giles 1978, Schemnitz 1980) there is a lack of information on assessing the value of forested greenspaces for wildlife (D. Urich, Missouri Dept. of Conservation, pers. comm. October 1985). The wide variety of greenspace habitats, and the diversity of former and current land uses and people that surround them, are all factors responsible for this observation.

Biogeographers and planners have focused on classifying the range of habitats that occur within urban areas. These classifications have viewed the urbanization process as a relatively static process determined largely by land use. Brady et al. (1979) developed a 12-level ecological typology for urban areas that placed sites in urban and urbanizing areas along a continuum from completely natural to completely cultural units based on the physical nature of land use zones and the biota associated with them. Spirn (1984) ranked urban habitats along a zonation of man-dominated to uncultivated habitats. Forman and Godron (1986) identified discrete suburban, urban, and megalopolitan landscapes based on a number or landscape features. VanDruff and Rowse (1986) considered landscape features in their analysis of the habitat characteristics associated with the abundance of urban mammals.

In contrast to this static view of urbanization based on an objective method of classifying urban habitats, urban geographers have treated urbanization as a dynamic process. These include the concentric zone model of Park and Burgess (1925), Hoyt's (1939) sector theory of urban land use, and Harris and Ullman's (1945) multiple nuclei theory. Borchert's (1967) four technological epochs have been useful in describing the form of cities based on developments in technology and transportation. Sanders' (1978) study of the dynamics of urban decline used these technological developments to understand periods of growth and decline in several U.S. cities.

As wildlife biologists concerned with the management of greenspaces for a number of wildlife species, we wondered if it were possible to use species abundance data to develop a simple system for grouping greenspaces into categories with similar management needs. To be useful as a management tool, the system should make sense both from an ecological standpoint and correspond to views of the urbanization process held by planners. We used ordination and classification techniques to differentiate 24 greenspaces in the Syracuse, New York metropolitan area based on the small mammal populations found on each greenspace. This small mammal data set is similar to the type of information planners and managers have available when planning the management of greenspaces. Our objectives in this paper are to identify the environmental factors that explain differences between the greenspaces, develop a simple classification system for greenspaces, and relate the environmental factors and classification to measures of landscape quality and pattern.

[1]Dep. of Biology, Morehouse College, Atlanta, GA 30314.

Integrating Man and Nature in the Metropolitan Environment. Proc. Natl. Symp. on Urban Wildl., Chevy Chase, Md., 4–7 November 1986, L.W. Adams and D.L. Leedy, eds. Published by Natl. Inst. for Urban Wildl., 10921 Trotting Ridge Way, Columbia, MD 21044, 1987.

METHODS

We used data from studies of 24 greenspaces in the Syracuse area. Rowse (1980) and Powell (1982) studied the small mammal populations of 21 greenspaces in Syracuse. Mathews (1982) studied the small mammal communities of three wooded areas in suburban and rural Onondaga County, surrounding Syracuse (Fig. 1). We pooled these data and selected for further study the 11 species most likely to be captured in Museum Special traps (Nilon 1986). Relative abundance (total captures of a species ÷ total small mammal captures) was used as an index of species abundance (Table 1).

Ordination and Classification of Small Mammal Data

Ordination is an analytical procedure designed to separate observations in a space defined by ecological variables (Pielou 1984). Both principal components analysis and Bray-Curtis ordination (Pielou 1984) were used to study the arrangement of greenspaces. Because of the similarity in results from the two techniques, we report only the results of principal components analysis ordination. This was a useful technique for our study because it allowed us to analyze the spatial pattern of the greenspaces in a space defined by the small mammal species abundance values. We used life history information for the species to identify differences in habitat requirements and environmental gradients that define the ecological space that separate the greenspaces.

Classification techniques mimic the mental classification procedures used to assign objects to categories (Pielou 1984). We used Ward's Minimum Variance method to

Table 1. Small mammals captured on 24 greenspaces in and around Syracuse, New York.[a]

Species	Number of sites	Average relative abundance (%)
White-footed or deer mouse (*Peromyscus* spp.)	24	52.3
Short-tailed shrew (*Blarina brevicauda*)	22	14.7
Meadow vole (*Microtus pennsylvanicus*)	16	11.0
Norway rat (*Rattus norvegicus*)	10	9.3
Eastern chipmunk (*Tamias striatus*)	8	9.1
House mouse (*Mus musculus*)	5	1.1
Meadow jumping mouse (*Zapus hudsonicus*)	2	0.6
Masked shrew (*Sorex cinereus*)	2	1.4
Woodland jumping mouse (*Napeozapus insignis*)	1	0.3
Southern flying squirrel (*Glaucomys volans*)	1	0.3
Ermine (*Mustela erminea*)	1	0.1
Total		100.2

[a]Captured by Rowse (1980), Mathews (1982), and Powell (1982).

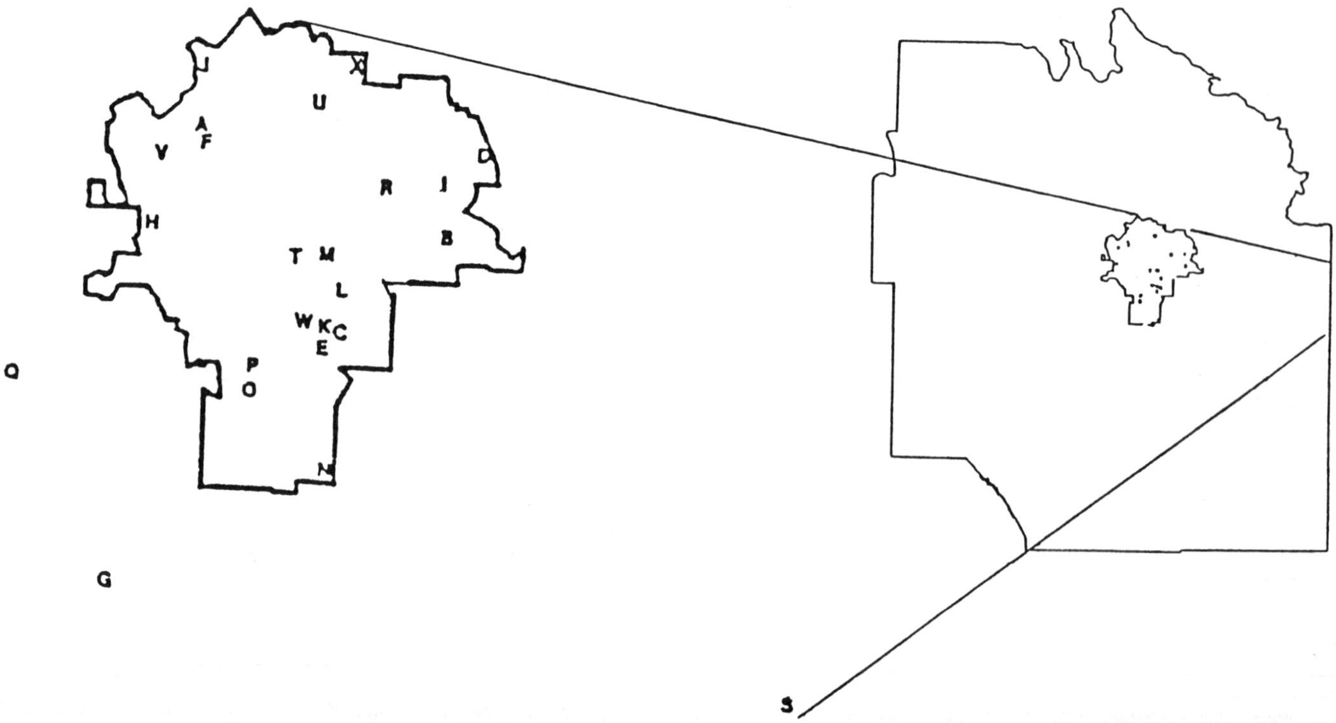

Fig. 1. Location of 24 greenspaces in Syracuse and adjacent portions of Onondaga County, New York.

develop an hierarchical clustering of the greenspaces based on species' relative abundance values.

Landscape Quality and Pattern for Areas Surrounding Greenspaces

Land cover, land use, and landscape pattern variables were measured within the 1-km radius area surrounding the center of each greenspace (Table 2). Land cover and land use data were used to describe landscape quality. The percentage of each cover type and land use within the 1-km radius area was determined by interpreting aerial photographs and land use maps for Syracuse and Onondaga County (Syracuse-Onondaga County Planning Agency 1977), using the homogeneous land use polygon technique (Sanders and Stevens 1984). Landscape pattern variables were measured on the same aerial photographs using procedures described by Bowen and Burgess (1981). We used principal components analysis to identify the landscape quality and pattern variables that best explained differences among the landscapes within 1 km of the center of each greenspace.

Table 2. Landscape quality (land cover and land use) and pattern variables measured within a 1-km radius surrounding greenspace centers.

Landscape Quality
Land cover:
Percent covered by tree canopy
Percent covered by herbaceous cover
Percent covered by bare soil
Percent growing space
Land use:
Percent residential land
Percent institutional land
Percent parks
Percent vacant land
Percent agricultural land
Landscape Pattern
Greenspace area
Greenspace perimeter/area ratio
Average distance from greenspace to other forested areas
Total number of connections between greenspace and other forested areas

RESULTS

Ordination and Classification of Small Mammal Data

Four principal components account for 71% of the variation in the small mammal relative abundance data set (Table 3.) Twenty-eight percent of the ecological distance between sites was explained by the abundance of the masked shrew, woodland jumping mouse, and southern flying squirrel—species associated with mature woodlands (Hamilton and Whitaker 1979, DeGraaf et al. 1981). The second principal component has strong positive loadings for the Norway rat and house mouse—species associated with human disturbance—and a negative loading for *Peromyscus* spp., the most abundant small mammal in eastern woodlands (Hamilton and Whitaker 1979). The third principal component has positive loadings for species associated with old field and meadow habitats, and the fourth component has strong loadings for species associated with old fields and young forests.

Table 3. Principal components (PC) analysis of small mammal abundance data for 24 greenspaces (loadings ≥ +/− 0.30).

Principal component / Species	Loading	Variance explained (%)
PC 1 (Eigenvalue = 3.09)		28.1
Masked shrew	0.56	
Woodland jumping mouse	0.56	
Southern flying squirrel	0.56	
PC 2 (Eigenvalue = 1.90)		17.3
Norway rat	0.60	
Peromyscus spp.	−0.57	
House mouse	0.44	
PC 3 (Eigenvalue = 1.53)		13.9
Eastern chipmunk	−0.63	
Meadow vole	0.54	
Meadow jumping mouse	0.44	
PC 4 (Eigenvalue = 1.28)		11.7
Short-tailed shrew	0.59	
Peromyscus spp.	−0.50	
Meadow jumping mouse	0.35	
Total variance explained		71.0

Slightly over 45% of the variation in species' relative abundance values are explained by the first two principal components (Fig. 2.). The two axes of Fig. 2 separate sites based on the relative abundance of species that inhabit mature forests (X-axis) and the relative abundance of species associated with woodland disturbance and human influence (Y-axis). The location of greenspaces along the axes indicate the presence of environmental gradients of forest cover and disturbance.

Results of the hierarchical classification of greenspaces based on species' relative abundance values are shown in Fig. 3. We found that the dendrogram could be generalized to three groups characterized by the abundance of *Peromyscus* spp. and other frequently captured species—the meadow vole, short-tailed shrew, eastern chipmunk, and Norway rat (Table 4). Group one, dominated by *Peromyscus* spp., includes sites where some degree of site management occurs. Group two includes greenspaces with small mammal populations typical of old fields and different-aged forests in Central

Table 4. Average relative abundance values (%) for species that describe the three greenspace groups based on cluster analysis. (See Fig. 3).

Species	Group 1	Group 2	Group 3
Peromyscus spp.	72.9	39.6	11.3
Meadow vole	5.3	16.4	0
Short-tailed shrew	14.7	16.1	1.4
Eastern chipmunk	0.9	13.7	42.3
Norway rat	1.2	10.5	45.1
Total	95.0	96.3	100.1

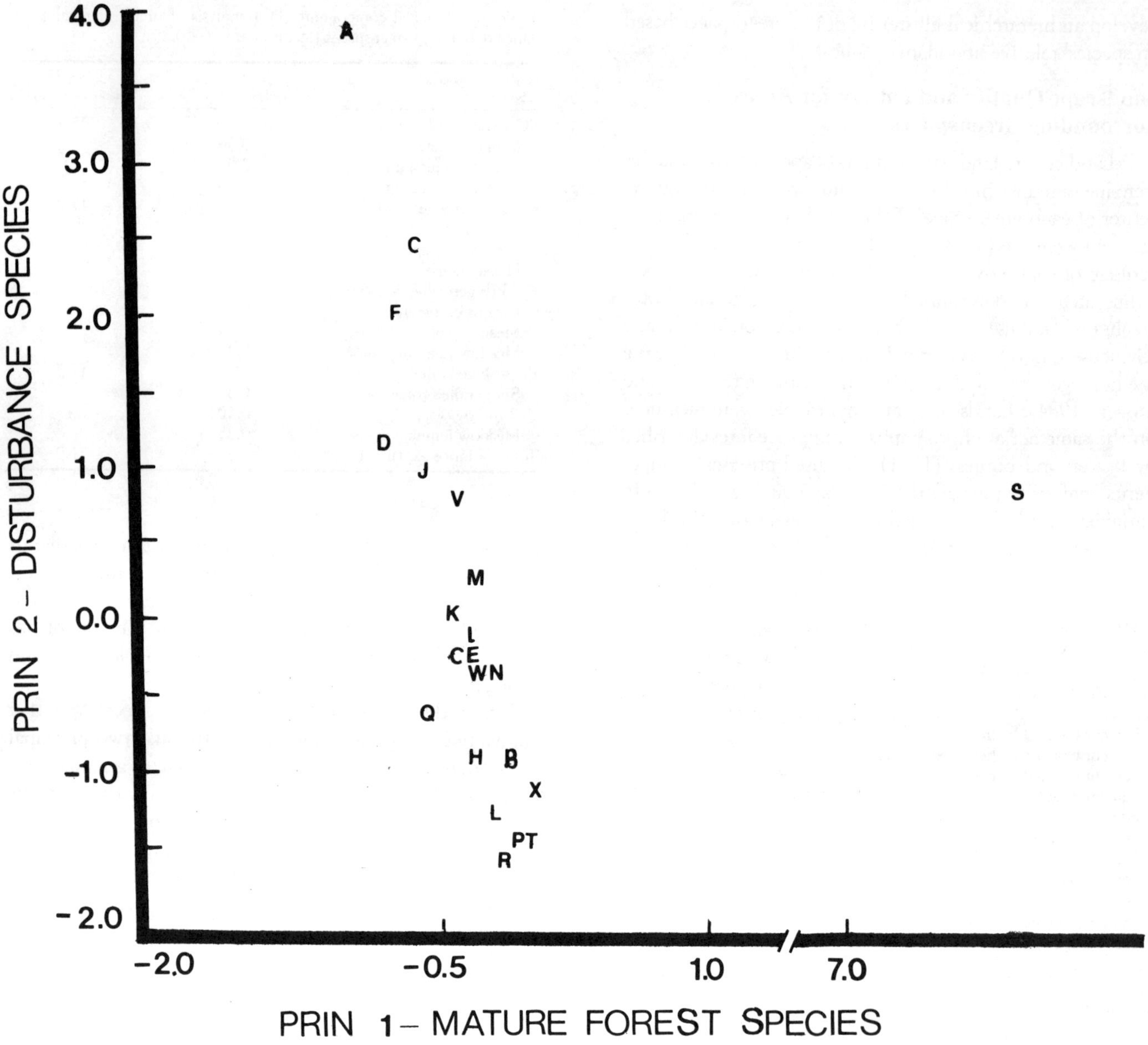

Fig. 2. Ordination of the first two principal components using small mammal relative abundance data for 24 greenspaces.

New York (Townsend 1935). Group three, dominated by the Norway rat and eastern chipmunk, includes greenspaces with a high level of disturbance and human activity.

Landscape Quality and Pattern

Four principal components explain 74% of the variance in the 1-km radius area surrounding the center of each greenspace; slightly over 51% of the variation is explained by the first two principal components (Table 5, Fig. 4). High scores on the PRIN 1 axis (Fig. 4) indicate a high percentage of growing space, canopy, vacant and agricultural land use, and a low degree of greenspace isolation from other forested areas. High scores along the PRIN 2 axis describe areas with a low percentage of canopy cover and residential land use, a high percentage of bare soil, and greenspaces with a high perimeter to total area ratio. The 24 greenspaces fall into three groups when plotted along these axes. Group 1 includes areas on the edge of the city and in suburban and rural areas. These "urban fringe" greenspaces are characterized by predominately vacant and agricultural lands dominated by large amounts of growing space. The second group represents disturbed landscapes. The areas surrounding these greenspaces have low amounts of growing space, with these spaces dominated by bare soil with little canopy or herbaceous cover. The greenspaces are linear with a high perimeter to total area ratio, and a high degree of isolation from other forested areas. The remaining greenspaces (Group 3) form a group defined by the character of

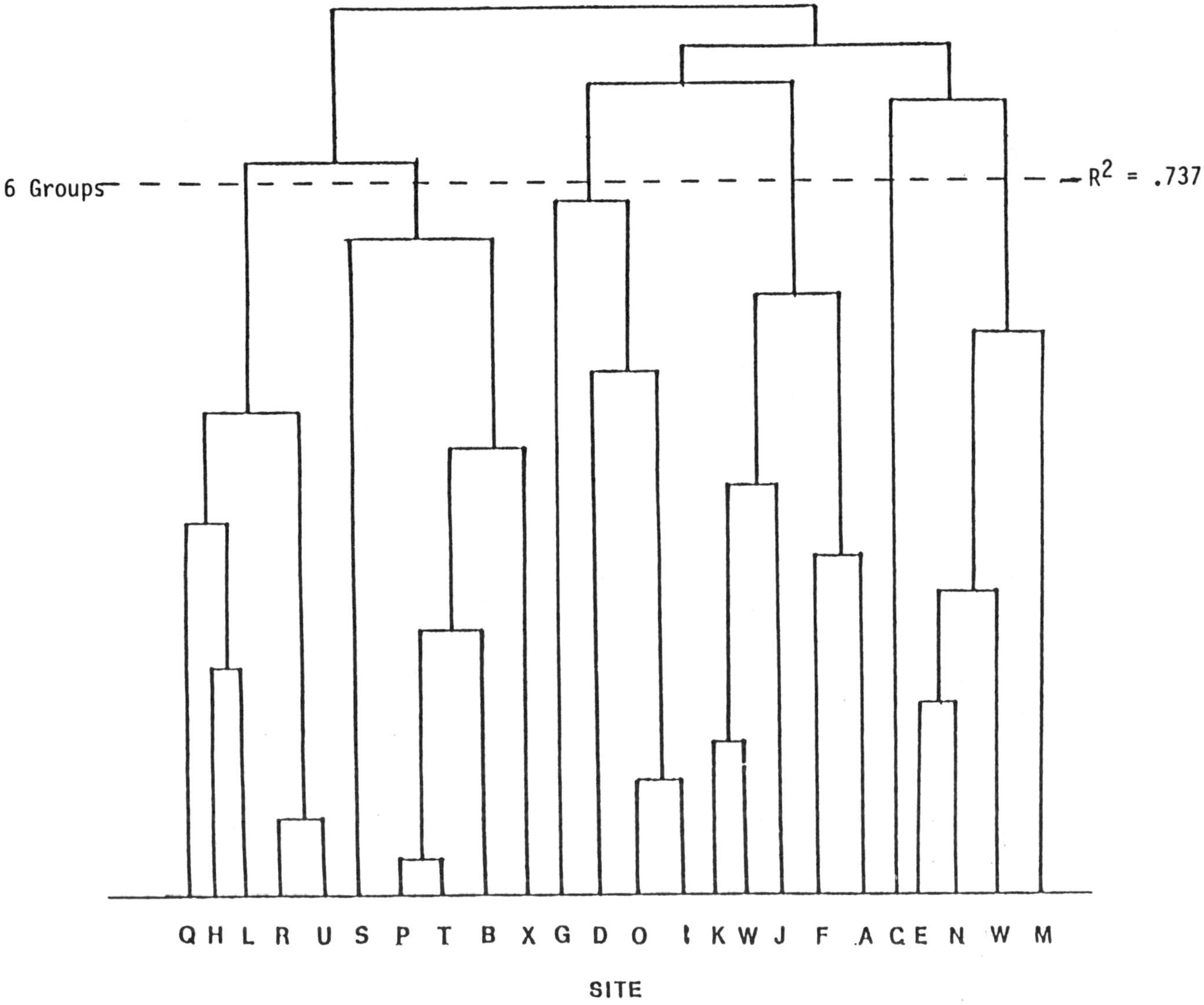

Fig. 3. Cluster analysis of 24 greenspaces based on small mammal relative abundance values.

residential landscapes. Growing space is relatively low compared to the urban fringe group. Landscape features should be expected to vary with the structure of vegetation in residential neighborhoods (Rowntree 1984).

The greenspaces surrounded by urban fringe landscapes have small mammal communities typical of mature forest or old fields. Greenspaces surrounded by disturbed landscapes tend to have small mammal communities typical of disturbed sites. The group of greenspaces surrounded by residential landscapes includes a diversity of small mammal communities reflecting the variability of residential landscapes.

DISCUSSION

Our results indicate that small mammal population data can be used to identify environmental differences between greenspaces. These differences can be attributed to environmental gradients of forest cover and disturbance, and are expressed as three groups of greenspaces with very different small mammal populations. Our results fit the pattern of environmental gradients associated with urbanization that influences the structure and species composition of greenspace vegetation described by Airola and Buchholz (1984), Whitney (1985), and Nilon (1986).

Both the environmental gradients and grouping of greenspaces can be defined in terms of the urbanization process. Landscape quality and pattern data reveal that greenspaces on the edge of the city, and in disturbed and residential landscapes are distinct. These differences can be explained in part by the spatial and technological models of urbanization described at the beginning of this paper. For example, specialized land use zones, such as industrial areas and construction sites along filled wetlands, define unique landscapes. Greenspaces surrounded by these landscapes

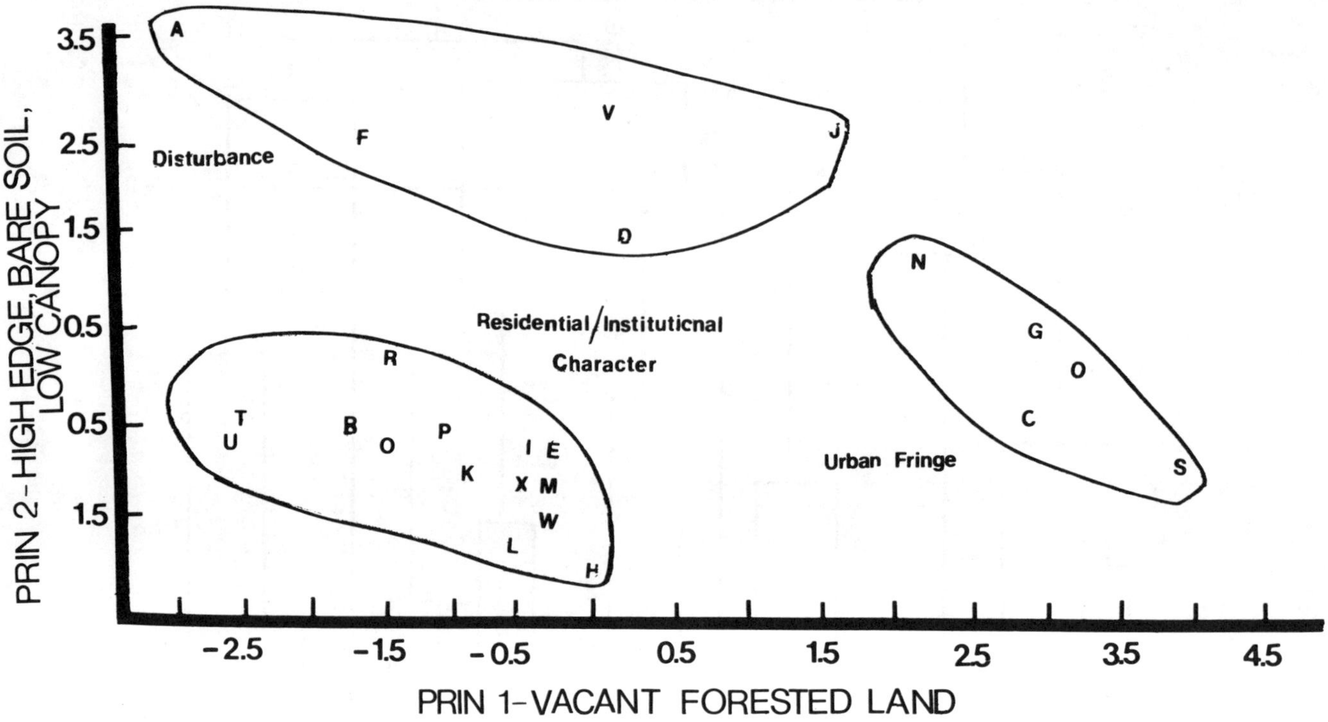

Fig. 4. Greenspaces plotted along axes defined by landscape quality and pattern variables for the 1-km area surrounding the center of each greenspace.

have small mammal populations characteristic of disturbed sites.

Our results suggest that wildlife population data can be used to classify greenspaces into groups with similar management needs. A classification system based on population data provides results that are easy to interpret and meaningful to ecologists, managers, and planners.

Table 5. Principal components (PC) analysis of landscape quality and pattern data for areas within 1 km of the center of each greenspace (loadings ≥ +/− 0.30).

Principal component Variable	Loading	Variance explained (%)
PC1 (Eigenvalue = 4.3)		33.3
Percent vacant land	0.43	
Total growing space	0.41	
Average distance to other forested areas	−0.36	
Percent canopy cover	0.32	
PC2 (Eigenvalue = 2.3)		17.9
Percent bare soil	−0.57	
Percent residential land use	0.40	
Perimeter/total area ratio	−0.38	
Percent canopy cover	0.34	
PC3 (Eigenvalue = 1.7)		13.0
Greenspace area	0.54	
Number of connections to forested areas	0.48	
Percent institutional land use	−0.41	
Average distance to other forested areas	0.39	
PC4 (Eigenvalue = 1.3)		9.8
Percent herbaceous cover	0.68	
Percent bare soil	−0.34	
Percent parks	−0.32	
Total variance explained		74.0

REFERENCES CITED

Airola, T.M. and K. Buchholz. 1984. Species structure and soil characteristics of five urban forest sites along the New Jersey Palisades. Urban Ecol. 8:149–164.

Borchert, J.R. 1967. American metropolitan evolution. Geogr. Rev. 57:301–323.

Bowen, G.W. and R.L. Burgess. 1981. A quantitative analysis of forest island pattern in selected Ohio landscapes. Oak Ridge Natl. Lab. Environ. Sci. Div. Publ. No. 1719. 111 pp.

Brady, R.F., T. Tobias, P.F.J. Eagles, R. Ohrner, J. Micak, B. Veale, and R.S. Dorney. 1979. A typology for the urban ecosystem and its relationship to larger biogeographical landscape units. Urban Ecol. 4:11–28.

DeGraaf, R.M., G.M. Witman, and D.D. Rudis. 1981. Forest habitat for mammals of the Northeast. USDA Forest Serv., Northeastern For. Exp. Sta. and Eastern Region, Amherst, MA. 182 pp.

Foreman, R.T. and M. Godron. 1986. Landscape ecology. John Wiley and Sons, New York. 619 pp.

Giles, R.H., Jr. 1978. Wildlife management. W.H. Freeman and Co., San Francisco. 416 pp.

Hamilton, W.J., Jr. and J.O. Whitaker, Jr. 1979. Mammals of the eastern United States. Cornell Univ. Press, Ithaca, N.Y. 346 pp.

Harris, C.D. and E.L. Ullman. 1945. The nature of cities. Ann. Am. Soc. Pol. Sci. 242:7–17.

Hoyt, H. 1939. The structure and growth of residential neighborhoods in American cities. Fed. Housing Adm., Washington, DC.

Mathews, N.E. 1982. The capability of U.S. Forest Service resources evaluation in assessing small mammal habitat. M.Sc. thesis, SUNY Coll. Environ. Sci. and For., Syracuse, N.Y. 138 pp.

Nilon, C.H., Jr. 1986. Quantifying small mammal habitats along a gradient of urbanization. Ph.D. Thesis. SUNY Coll. Environ. Sci. and For., Syracuse, N.Y. 148 pp.

Park, R.E. and E.W. Burgess. 1925. The city. Univ. Chicago Press, Ill. 239 pp.

Pielou, E.C. 1984. The interpretation of ecological data: a primer on classification and ordination. John Wiley and Sons, N.Y. 263 pp.

Powell, L.J.H., Jr. 1982. The occurrence and distribution of selected mammalian species and their interaction with residents in an urban area. M.Sc. thesis, SUNY Coll. Environ. Sci. and For., Syracuse, N.Y. 113 pp.

Rowntree, R.A. 1984. Forest canopy and land use in four eastern United States cities. Urban Ecol. 8:55–67.

Rowse, R.N. 1980. An abundance survey and habitat affinity analysis of mammals in Syracuse, New York. M.Sc. thesis, SUNY Coll. Environ. Sci. and For., Syracuse, N.Y. 133 pp.

Sanders, R.A. 1978. American urban decline: updating evolutionary trends. Disc. Pap. Ser., Dep. of Geogr., Syracuse Univ., N.Y. 18 pp.

Sanders, R.A. and R.A. Rowntree. 1984. Environmental management through urban forestry on the hillsides of Cincinnati, Ohio. J. Environ. Manage. 19:161–174.

Sanders, R.A. and J.C. Stevens. 1984. Urban forest of Dayton, Ohio: a preliminary assessment. Urban Ecol. 8:91–98.

Schemnitz, S.D. 1980. Wildlife techniques manual. The Wildlife Society, Washington, D.C. 685 pp.

Spirn, A.M. 1984. The granite garden: urban nature and human design. Basic Books, N.Y. 334 pp.

Syracuse Commission for the Conservation of the Environment. 1973. City of Syracuse open space index. Unpub. Rep. 66 pp.

Syracuse-Onondaga County Planning Agency. 1977. Land use plan, Syracuse, New York. Unpub. Rep.

Townsend, M.T. 1935. Studies of some of the small mammals of Central New York. Roosevelt Wild Life Annals 8(2), New York State Coll. For., Syracuse Univ., Syracuse, N.Y. 120 pp.

VanDruff, L.W. and R.N. Rowse. 1986. Habitat associations of small mammals in Syracuse, New York. Urban Ecol. 9:413–434.

Whitney, G.G. 1985. A quantitative analysis of the flora and plant communities of a representative midwestern U.S. town. Urban Ecol. 9:143–160.

Use of Kulcyznski's Similarity Index in Analysis of Urban Avifaunas

ALEXANDER T. CRINGAN, *Department of Fishery and Wildlife Biology, Colorado State University, Fort Collins, CO 80523*

INTRODUCTION

This paper has been written to examine the general question of whether avifaunas of different cities tend to become more similar to each other over time as a result of urbanization. Clearly, certain species of birds are highly successful in urban environments, among them Canada goose *(Branta canadensis)*, rock dove *(Columba livia)*, American crow *(Corvus brachyrhynchos)*, European starling *(Sturnus vulgaris)*, house finch *(Carpodacus mexicanus)* and house sparrow *(Passer domesticus)*, and eventually come to dominate in cities over wide areas as urban biotic communities approach their climax stages. Intuitively, one would answer the above question affirmatively. In this paper, I will suggest how an objective method of expressing similarity, Kulcyznski's index, can be used to examine the question, then analyze trends in Christmas Bird Counts for four selected cities.

If it is true that urbanization leads to increasing similarity in urban avifaunas, then either or both of the faunas being compared has to be changing. Also, if two faunas are converging in similarity, then one, if not both has to be diverging, either from what it used to be, or else from a third fauna not experiencing the same changes. If there is convergence, there must also be divergence, although it is possible that divergence could occur without accompanying convergence.

The specific alternative hypotheses to be examined (rather than tested) are:

(1) that for a given urban area, Christmas Bird Counts tend to be more similar over short than long intervals of time; and

(2) that for different urban areas, Christmas Bird Counts become more similar over time.

METHODS

Criteria for selecting cities for analysis were:

(1) being within a Standard Metropolitan Statistical Area in the Mountain Region of the United States in the 1980 Census (U.S. Department of Commerce 1983);

(2) being east of the Continental Divide; and

(3) having Christmas Bird Counts for 1950, 1960, 1970 and 1980 (American Birds 1971, 1981; Audubon Field Notes 1951, 1961).

Christmas Bird Counts for four places meeting these criteria, Colorado Springs and Fort Collins, Colorado; Casper, Wyoming; and Billings, Montana, for the years 1950, 1960, 1970, and 1980 were analyzed.

Similarity indices may be calculated by comparing either the presence or absence of species in lists, or their relative abundances expressed as percentages of all items on those lists. Sorenson's similarity index (Greig-Smith 1964, Dirschl 1969, Gauch 1973) and Duellman's faunal resemblance factor (Duellman 1965, Armstrong 1972) work with occurrence only, and take the form SI (or FRF) = $(2*c)/(a+b)$, where c is the number of items on both lists, and a and b are the total numbers of items in each of the lists. Kulcyznski's similarity index (Oosting 1956, Hansen et al. no date), like Gauch's (1973) Percentage Similarity, takes into account relative numbers. After expressing each item as a percentage of all items in both lists, it is calculated by summing the lower of the two percentages for all items occurring in both or either list. It may range from 0% to 100%.

A personal computer employing spreadsheet software was used to calculate the similarity indices. Christmas Bird Counts were entered on identically-formatted spread sheets, and the two lists to be compared were merged. Editing

Integrating Man and Nature in the Metropolitan Environment. Proc. Natl. Symp. on Urban Wildl., Chevy Chase, Md., 4–7 November 1986, L.W. Adams and D.L. Leedy, eds. Published by Natl. Inst. for Urban Wildl., 10921 Trotting Ridge Way, Columbia, MD 21044, 1987.

included deletion of rock dove counts and of unidentified birds. Indices were calculated for all species together, then for aquatic birds (loons, grebes, waterfowl, gruiforms, charadriiforms, and kingfishers), raptors and scavengers (falconiforms, strigiforms, crows, ravens, magpies, and shrikes), galliforms, and other terrestrial birds. These categories were non-overlapping and all-inclusive. Species contributing most to dissimilarities were listed in the outputs. I did not attempt to test the significance of differences in similarity indices.

RESULTS

Cross-temporal Similarity Within Areas

All Species.—For all four areas, the similarity indices for all species of birds were greater for 1980cf1970 than for 1980cf1950, and for 1950cf1960 than for 1950cf1980 (Table 1). Viewed retrospectively, mean of indices for 1980cf1970 was 68.5%, indicating similarity, and mean of indices for 1980cf1950 was 38.5%, indicating dissimilarity. Viewed prospectively, mean of indices for 1950cf1960 was 53.5%, and that for 1950cf1980, 38.5%, a pattern of similarity being replaced by dissimilarity. The first alternative hypothesis is supported—Christmas Bird Counts over short intervals of time tend to be more similar than counts at longer intervals of time.

The only species that accounted for >5% dissimilarity in one or more of the cross-temporal comparisons of all species were Canada goose, mallard *(Anas platyrhynchos)*, ring-necked pheasant *(Phasianus colchicus)*, black-billed magpie *(Pica pica)*, Bohemian waxwing *(Bombycilla garrulus)*, European starling, American tree sparrow *(Spizella arborea)*, dark-eyed junco *(Junco hyemalis)*, red-winged blackbird *(Agelaius phoeniceus)*, western meadowlark *(Sturnella neglecta)*, rosy finch *(Leucosticte arctoa)*, and house sparrow. A better idea of processes at work can be gained by examining similarity indices for the designated groups of birds.

Aquatic species.—All counts of aquatic birds for Colorado Springs and Billings were internally similar to very similar to each other. Likewise, excluding the 1950 count of only eight aquatic birds, counts for Casper were similar to very similar to each other. Aquatic bird counts for Fort Collins were very similar in 1950 and 1960, and again in 1970 and 1980, but the 1950 and 1960 counts were from somewhat to very dissimilar from the 1970 and 1980 counts. Changes in relative numbers of Canada geese and mallards accounted for 96.2% of this dissimilarity.

Raptors and Scavengers.—All counts of raptors and scavengers for Colorado Springs, Casper and Billings were internally similar to very similar. For Fort Collins, the 1950 and 1960 counts were very similar to each other, as were the 1970 and 1980 counts, but the 1970 and 1980 counts were dissimilar from the 1950 and 1960 counts. Changes in relative numbers of American crow and black-billed magpie accounted for 79% of the dissimilarity at Fort Collins between 1960 and 1970.

Table 1. Cross-temporal similarity indices (%), Christmas bird counts, 1950–1980.

City Bird group	Retrospective comparison				Prospective comparison			
	1980 cf 1980	1980 cf 1970	1980 cf 1960	1980 cf 1950	1950 cf 1950	1950 cf 1960	1950 cf 1970	1950 cf 1980
Colorado Springs								
All species	100	70	55	50	100	55	55	50
Aquatic species	100	65	55	55	100	95	80	55
Raptors-scavengers	100	65	85	85	100	95	75	85
Galliforms	100	60	60	40	100	0	10	40
Other terrestrial birds	100	70	50	50	100	45	55	50
Fort Collins								
All species	100	65	40	30	100	70	20	30
Aquatic species	100	95	30	15	100	80	10	15
Raptors-scavengers	100	85	40	40	100	80	30	40
Galliforms	100	100	100	100	100	100	100	100
Other terrestrial birds	100	45	45	45	100	55	40	45
Casper								
All species	100	70	80	35	100	45	50	35
Aquatic species	100	80	70	0	100	10	5	0
Raptors-scavengers	100	80	70	70	100	80	70	70
Galliforms	100	60	0	60	100	100	60	60
Other terrestrial birds	100	60	55	50	100	45	75	50
Billings								
All species	100	70	65	40	100	45	35	40
Aquatic species	100	85	85	70	100	70	75	70
Raptors-scavengers	100	60	50	55	100	95	90	55
Galliforms	100	90	90	90	100	100	100	90
Other terrestrial birds	100	75	70	45	100	55	35	45

Galliforms.—Cross-temporal similarity indices for galliforms for Fort Collins and Billings were internally very similar. Those for Colorado Springs and Casper varied greatly.

Other Terrestrial Birds.—Cross-temporal similarity indices for counts of other terrestrial birds ranged from 41–77%. Their patterns varied considerably among places. Few species had any great effect on dissimilarities in these indices. For example, for Colorado Springs, 1950cf1960, eleven species together accounted for 90% of the dissimilarity. There is yet no strong indication of a move in the direction of sustained high similarity in any of these four places, as there is for the other groups of birds.

Cross-regional Similarity Within Years

All Species.—All cross-regional similarity indices comparing Colorado Springs and Fort Collins, all species, were dissimilar, and there was no evident trend in this statistic between 1950 and 1980 (Table 2). Many species contributed slightly to the observed dissimilarities. Counts comparing Fort Collins and Casper displayed convergence, moving from a very dissimilar 16% in 1950 to a somewhat dissimilar 43% in 1980. Counts for Casper and Billings exhibited convergence, moving from a dissimilar 32% in 1950 to a similar 71% in 1980. Species that contributed >5% to dissimilarity in one or more of the cross-regional, all species comparisons were the Canada goose, mallard, ring-necked pheasant, European starling, dark-eyed junco, red-winged blackbird, rosy finch, and house sparrow.

Aquatic Species.—Colorado Springs and Fort Collins counts of aquatic birds were very similar in 1950 and 1960, but very dissimilar in 1970 and 1980 (Table 2). Canada goose, mallard, and American wigeon *(Anas americana)* accounted for most of the dissimilarity in 1970 and 1980. Fort Collins and Casper had very similar aquatic birds counts in 1960, but very dissimilar counts in 1970, when Canada goose, mallard, common goldeneye *(Bucephala clangula)*, and common merganser *(Mergus merganser)* accounted for most of the difference. The index increased in 1980, principally because of an increase in numbers of Canada geese at Casper. Casper's and Billings's counts of aquatic birds were similar to very similar from 1960 through 1980.

Raptors and Scavengers.—Of the four groups of birds examined separately, raptors and scavengers had the highest average cross-regional similarity indices. Counts of raptors and scavengers in Colorado Springs and Fort Collins were similar in 1950 and 1960, dissimilar in 1970, and very similar in 1980. Differences are largely due to differences in numbers of American crows. The crow was well established as a wintering bird in Colorado Springs in 1950, but did not begin wintering in Fort Collins in appreciable numbers until sometime between 1960 and 1970. Counts of raptors and scavengers in Fort Collins and Casper were very similar to similar in 1950 and 1960, but diverged to become dissimilar in 1970, mainly because of the crow. An increase in the magpie:crow ratio in Fort Collins in 1980 allowed the Fort Collins-compared-with-Casper index to rise in 1980, but it was still in the dissimilar range. Raptor and scavenger counts for Casper and Billings were very similar in 1950, and have since diverged slightly, but are still similar.

Galliforms.—Of the four groups of birds examined separately, galliforms showed the lowest average similarity indices. Cross-regional counts of galliforms (Table 2) ranged from completely dissimilar to dissimilar. Such counts for Fort Collins and Billings, not shown, are more similar to each other than for any other pair of areas, owing to the dominance of ring-necked pheasants in both places.

Other Terrestrial Birds.—Cross-regional similarity indices for other terrestrial birds ranged from 44–71%, with one exception, 25% for Fort Collins-compared-with-Casper in 1950 (Table 2). There may be slight convergence between such counts for Fort Collins and Casper, and Casper and Billings, but the trends are inconclusive.

Table 2. Cross-regional similarity indices (%), Christmas bird counts, Colorado Springs (COSP), Fort Collins (FOCO), Casper (CASP), and Billings (BILL), 1950–1980.

Bird group compared / Cities compared	1950	1960	1970	1980
All species				
COSP cf FOCO	48	33	33	43
FOCO cf CASP	16	31	24	43
CASP cf BILL	32	58	58	71
Aquatic species				
COSP cf FOCO	91	79	14	17
FOCO cf CASP	1	78	11	40
CASP cf BILL	1	63	92	72
Raptors-scavengers				
COSP cf FOCO	66	63	40	84
FOCO cf CASP	81	71	23	42
CASP cf BILL	92	82	74	65
Galliforms				
COSP cf FOCO	40	0	0	42
FOCO cf CASP	25	0	0	0
CASP cf BILL	42	0	0	0
Other terrestrial birds				
COSP cf FOCO	62	49	44	53
FOCO cf CASP	25	45	51	46
CASP cf BILL	44	56	52	71

DISCUSSION

Evaluation of Christmas Bird Counts

It is beyond the scope of this paper to evaluate the quality of data incorporated into Christmas Bird Counts. Various aspects of this problem have been reported, starting at least as early as Preston's (1958) work. Horak (1986) recently reviewed a number of papers on this subject. Still, there are some aspects of Christmas Bird Count results as a data-base that are highly relevant to this evaluation of Kulczynski's similarity index.

Representativeness of low-intensity Christmas Bird Counts producing small samples, e.g., Billings, 1950 (N = 337) is certain to be much more variable than that of well-coordinated, high-intensity counts. Usually early counts were of lower intensity than recent counts, and hence early counts are likely to be less representative of the communities sampled than later counts. Similarity indices involving early or other low-intensity counts are as a result going to be more imprecise than indices for high-intensity counts. Small group samples, e.g., Casper, waterfowl, 1950 (N = 8), further increase the likelihood of this kind of error.

Counts of rock doves for these places and years were incompletely reported, and have not been included in the analysis. It seems likely therefore that all similarity indices herein are stated conservatively.

Assumptions in Calculation of Kulcyznski's Similarity Index

Kulcyznski's similarity indices are weighted heavily by species that are abundant in at least one of the lists being compared. Dissimilarity (100%—KSI) is influenced most by the species having the greatest differences between percentages on the two lists. A species comprising 50% of one list, 25% of the other, has the same contribution to dissimilarity as does a species comprising 26% of one list and 1% of the other. Consequently, changes in numbers of abundant species such as the Canada goose and mallard among aquatic birds, crow and magpie among raptors and scavengers, and starling and house sparrow among other terrestrial birds, will usually have the greatest effects on similarity. Species contributing importantly to perceived similarity, such as common goldeneye, American kestrel *(Falco sparverius)*, house finch, dark-eyed junco, and evening grosbeak *(Coccothraustes vespertinus)* generally affect the indices little, because their percentages of birds within their groups are small by comparison.

There are a number of ways the index could be improved. Analysis of a complete year-to-year series of counts would permit regression analysis of the resultant indices. Use of moving averages would eliminate some of the "noise," especially that from erratic species like waxwings. Logarithmic and/or exponential transformations might appropriately reduce the weight accorded abundant species. Also, the groups that I have used might be further subdivided. Exclusion of Canada geese and mallards from aquatic birds would give us a more meaningful index to the similarity of the two lists as to all other aquatic species. Yet another approach would be to convert numbers to species biomass, or even metabolic biomass. One eagle is much more significant than one kestrel bioenergetically.

Non-urban Landscape Features Affecting Similarity

A Christmas Bird Count is conducted within a circle of 7.5-mile (12.1 km) radius, and has an area of 171.5 sq mi (444 sq km). None of these areas considered is entirely urban. Thus the counts reflect the summation of birds occupying urban, suburban, and rural habitats, and the implied effects of urbanization are diluted.

These four cities, all within Standard Metropolitan Statistical Areas (entire counties in these cases) vary in their relation to other cities. Colorado Springs and Fort Collins are within a contiguous block of counties that also includes Pueblo, Denver, Boulder and Greeley, an area that is becoming a metropolis. Casper and Billings are isolated by contrast. Urbanization is proceeding at a different rate within each of these four cities.

Latitude, altitude, and climate importantly affect avifaunas. For example, dark-eyed juncos comprised 19% of other terrestrial birds at Colorado Springs and 2% of those at Billings in 1980. It may be a long time, if ever, before Billings changes enough through urbanization to winter nearly as many juncos as Colorado Springs.

Water conditions profoundly affect aquatic species. Billings and Casper count areas include large rivers, and should always have relatively more goldeneyes and mergansers than Fort Collins and Colorado Springs. Numbers of reservoirs and their relation to cropland account for much of the difference in status of Canada geese between Fort Collins and Colorado Springs.

Another variable affecting Kulcyznski's similarity indices is the juxtaposition of habitats within the count circle. Colorado Springs is more within the foothills and mountains than is Fort Collins, which is much more within the plains. Casper and Billings are insular cities, surrounded by lightly populated grasslands, farmlands and shrublands, and Casper has more foothills and mountains within its count circle than Billings. I have not attempted to relate variance in avifaunal similarity to independent variables such as these.

Species Affecting Similarity Indices

Kulcyznski's similarity index is a very coarse index of avifaunal similarity. In this analysis, only seven species accounted for >10% of the similarity in any of the 36 comparisons made, and only 12 species accounted for >5% of the dissimilarity in any of the cross-temporal or cross-regional comparisons. The most frequent contributor of >10% to similarity was the house sparrow, which made this level of contribution in 17 of 36 comparisons made. The mallard contributed >10% to similarity in 10 comparisons, the European starling in six. Canada goose, dark-eyed junco, red-winged blackbird, and black-billed magpie contributed >10% to the similarity indices in one to three cases each. These seven species, along with rosy finch, ring-necked pheasant, Bohemian waxwing, American tree sparrow, and western meadowlark, contributed >5% to dissimilarity in one or more cases each.

SUMMARY

Christmas Bird Counts for Colorado Springs and Fort Collins, Colorado; Casper, Wyoming; and Billings, Montana, for 1950, 1960, 1970, and 1980 were compared using Kulcyznski's similarity index. The structure of winter bird communities in each of these cities changed between 1950 and 1980. Wintering bird communities of Fort Collins and Casper are becoming increasingly similar, as are those of Casper and Billings. Similarity of winter birds between Colorado Springs and Fort Collins has changed little since 1950. Raptors and scavengers exhibit the greatest cross-regional similarities, galliforms the lowest. In addition to urbanization, several other factors probably influence similarity of winter avifaunas of the cities examined. Improved methods of expressing similarity are suggested, but not tested.

REFERENCES CITED

American Birds. 1971, 1981. Audubon Christmas Bird Counts. Am. Birds 25:445–452, and 35:655–663.

Armstrong, D.M. 1972. Distribution of mammals in Colorado. Univ. Kans., Mus. Nat. Hist. Monogr. 3. 415pp.

Audubon Field Notes. 1951, 1961. Audubon Christmas Bird Counts. Audubon Field Notes 5:163–166, and 15:260–264.

Dirschl, H.J. 1969. Foods of lesser scaup and blue-winged teal in the Saskatchewan River Delta. J. Wildl. Manage. 33:77–87.

Duellman, W.E. 1965. A biogeographic account of the herpetofauna of Michoacan, Mexico. Univ. Kans. Publ., Mus. Nat. Hist. 15:629–709.

Gauch, H.G. Jr. 1973. The relationship between sample similarity and ecological distance. Ecology 54:618–622.

Greig-Smith, P. 1964. Quantitative plant ecology. (2nd ed.) Butterworth's & Co. Ltd., London. 256pp.

Hansen, R.M., T.M. Foppe, M.B. Gilbert, R.C. Clark, and H.W. Reynolds. No date. The microhistological analyses of feces as an estimator of herbivore dietary. Composition Anal. Lab., Range Sci. Dep., Colo. State Univ. 6pp. (mimeo.)

Horak, G.C. 1986. Cumulative impacts of rapid urbanization on avian diversity in northeastern Colorado. Ph.D. dissertation, Colo. State Univ. 135pp.

Oosting, H.J. 1956. The study of plant communities. (2nd. ed.) W.H. Freeman, San Francisco.

Preston, F.W. 1958. Analysis of the Audubon Christmas Counts in terms of the lognormal curve. Ecology 39:620–624.

U.S. Department of Commerce. 1983. 1980 census of population. Vol. 1. Characteristics of the population. Chapter A. Number of inhabitants. Part 1. United States summary.

The Extension Dimension: Public Support and Education

Chairman: Gary J. San Julian, *Extension Wildlife Specialist, North Carolina State University, Raleigh*
Cochairman: Joseph M. Schaefer, *Urban Biologist, Kansas Fish and Game Commission, Wichita*

Role of Extension Specialists as Educators in Urban Areas

Wayne R. Marion, *Department of Wildlife and Range Sciences, 118 Newins-Ziegler Hall, University of Florida, Gainesville, FL 32611*

DeeCee Freiling, *School of Forestry, Fisheries and Wildlife, University of Missouri, Columbia, MO 65211*

Traditionally, Extension Specialists have dealt with agriculture and related problems at the county level through the vast Cooperative Extension Service network. This network has prided itself on responding in a timely and practical manner to special needs identified by one-to-one interaction with local landowners. Times are changing and the Cooperative Extension Service is assuming a greater role in urban areas. The linkage is still there with rural landowners and problems, but the network and scope has expanded to include urban areas and needs as well. Planning, working with larger groups, and evaluation of impacts are focal points for Extension Service activities.

Extension Specialists are involved with expanded roles in both rural and urban settings; they, too, are being encouraged to work with larger groups in a proactive (rather than just reactive) manner. The needs and challenges have never been greater for Extension Specialists to assume a greater leadership role in public education. Extension Specialists are linked to one of the largest communications networks in this country (the Cooperative Extension Service) and this should be used to advantage in reaching groups of educators, planners, and developers. This paper suggests some positive ways in which Extension Specialists can begin to meet the challenges of their continuing and expanding role as public educators. These include working in the urban setting, attempting to upgrade the image of extension by responding to non-traditional programming needs, improving communications, cooperation between agencies, planning, and accountability.

The role of Extension Specialist has greatly expanded in variety and extent. Extension's role once seemed to be a source of information mainly for rural communities. Cooperative Extension's traditional "image" of providing technical assistance in just Agriculture, Home Economics, and 4-H programs also needs to change in many parts of the country. With about 75% of the U.S. population living in urban areas or suburbs, and with a growing trend toward urbanization, Extension must expand its role as an educational and informational system.

Transition into programming for urban situations is a slow process for several reasons. First, large governmental systems are generally slow to respond to needs simply due to their size. The size of the Cooperative Extension network, which literally connects every county in the United States, has both positive and negative aspects. Reluctance to change could be considered to be either positive or negative depending upon your perspective. One perspective is that the Cooperative Extension Service is caught in the middle of a struggle between older, traditional lifestyles and values vs. newer, "modern" lifestyles and values. Certainly, *this* topic is large enough to keep sociologists and others busy for several decades attempting explanations; it also is well beyond the scope of this paper. Suffice it to say that the "wholesome" image of a family farm in America as a dominant lifestyle has changed substantially in the last 3 decades.

Another major reason for Extension's slow response to changing times is that Extension agents and staff were frequently reared in a rural setting and they either lack the expertise or feel uncomfortable in dealing with urban situations and programs. The evolution of the Cooperative

Integrating Man and Nature in the Metropolitan Environment. Proc. Natl. Symp. on Urban Wildl., Chevy Chase, Md., 4–7 November 1986, L. W. Adams and D. L. Leedy, eds. Published by Natl. Inst. for Urban Wildl., 10921 Trotting Ridge Way, Columbia, MD 21044, 1987.

Extension Service's presence and effectiveness in urban situations seems to be a tedious process that is occurring as a "forced" change in many counties. Despite all of these potential changes, the Cooperative Extension Service still "enjoys" grassroots support from agriculture and rural interests for programs of relevance to these people.

Finally, we believe that the "image" of Cooperative Extension referred to above remains as a major stigma in many areas to urbanites approaching Extension for answers to their non-agricultural problems or for assistance with non-agricultural programs. The Cooperative Extension Service must respond to urban needs in the future in order to survive politically. At the same time that Extension may be slow to evolve and modernize its image, it has a vast capability for quickly transmitting *current* information to various user groups. Many states are becoming highly computerized and technology continues to improve in this area. Also, just as computer software must be "user friendly" in order to be effective, Extension personnel are required to present information in layman's terms to be readily understandable to user groups and the general public.

A number of new challenges exist in Cooperative Extension Service programming including working in a "proactive" (rather than just a "reactive") manner and with larger groups (rather than one-to-one interaction). Perhaps the best example of non-productive "reactive" activity over the years has been the Extension Wildlife Specialists' attempts to respond to numerous daily requests for assistance in controlling damage from wildlife. These requests, often from sincere people incurring serious damage to crops and private property, have traditionally been difficult to predict and nearly impossible to include in planning processes. Development of rather extensive literature for distribution addressing animal damage control has been the most typical way for Extension Wildlife Specialists to respond state by state and this has helped with some of the most common problems. The U.S. Department of Agriculture's new program in the Animal, Plant and Health Inspection Service (APHIS) promises to provide some future relief for Extension's involvement in this area. But, as urbanization increases, so do the wildlife-people interactions and it is very likely that a number of agencies or organizations will remain involved in trying to minimize animal damage problems.

As needs increase and funding levels decrease, it becomes imperative for Extension Specialists to strive for improved communications and linkages with other agencies and organizations. A continuing, long-term challenge for Extension Specialists seems to be in improving communications and cooperation with these groups.

Another new major challenge is for the Cooperative Extension Service to change with the times to better respond to user needs in non-traditional areas of Agriculture, Home Economics, 4-H, and Natural Resources. Examples include worksite programming (for working, single parents), educational programs for youth in wildlife (wildlife contests, cooperation with Project Wild), forestry (contests, cooperation with Project Learning Tree), nutrinomics (learning about foods with good nutrition at reasonable prices) and shooting sports (for both adults and youth).

Recognition and appreciation of non-commodity values and aesthetics have not normally been a part of extension programming in the past, but should be in the future. Along with this, natural resources programming should become a more vital part of Extension Specialists' activities. In general, natural resources programs seem to be an exciting part of youth programming in Extension. Also, many larger metropolitan areas are trying different ways to revitalize their downtown sections, and other areas all over town that have fallen into disrepair. The state Extension specialist has an opportunity in these cases to work with community development specialists at the county level, as well as local businessmen and community leaders, city councils, and Chambers of Commerce to understand and implement plantings that not only aesthetically benefit the urban areas, but also provide food and cover for wildlife. There are many plants that are very beautiful, form good screens, provide winter interest, and also fulfill requirements for wildlife.

As with most governmental programs today, Extension has had to become accountable for monies spent and to document impacts on various publics and user groups. The pendulum seems to have swung dramatically toward Extension program planning and evaluation in recent years; Extension Specialists need to be actively involved in both of these processes.

Youth programming is extremely important in both the rural and urban setting. These are the people in our society who are malleable, and most influenced by new ideas or different thinking. The reason is that they are not so set in their ways as are most adults.

Unfortunately, the 4-H clubs are probably much less active and are less visible in many urban areas than they are in rural communities. This means that it becomes very important to contact youth groups of all kinds in urban areas in order to get the message across. Here again, there is a tremendous need and opportunity for Extension to teach the teachers, scout leaders, etc. in order to reach the youth with whom Extension does not traditionally work.

Today's young people are accustomed (as are adults) to a very slick, glossy, "high-tech" world. Extension educators must be ready to perform in today's settings in order to gain interest and/or appreciation from urban youth and adults alike. In urban settings where there is such ready access to cable television and public television, Extension has a perfect outlet for some creative teaching opportunities. People spend many hours each week tuned to this medium.

Wildlife and people are alike in many of their basic needs such as food, shelter, homes, etc. The animals that will survive best in urban surroundings are those that can tolerate the close proximity of humans, and are most flexible and able to adapt to the changing habitat in the urban environment. Extension educators, as well as other "teachers," also must be able to adapt to ever-changing needs and interests in order to survive and be successful in their roles as educators. The greatest diversity of wildlife is found where the habitat provides many different sources and kinds of food and cover in one area. Likewise, Extension Specialists will have the most success reaching the public by branching out with many varied and new methods for disseminating their information.

Training Volunteer Fish and Wildlife Educators for Suburban Programming

ROBERT J. KENT, *Cooperative Extension, Suffolk County, 246 Griffing Avenue, Riverhead, NY 11901*

ROBERT BUERGER, *New York Sea Grant Extension Program, Marine Sciences Research Center, SUNY at Stony Brook, NY 11790*

THOMAS LITWIN, *Seatuck Research Program, Cornell Laboratory of Ornithology, P.O. Box 31, Islip, NY 11751*

Natural resources programs for 4-H youth in New York State have the following goals: (1) to help youth acquire personal values reflecting a commitment to the quality of environment that they desire, (2) to make them acquainted with the principles and practices of conservation, (3) to allow them to explore the resource bases for living systems and to become actively involved in their management and conservation, (4) to enhance their quality of life through natural resource based recreational experiences and skills development, and (5) to help them explore career opportunities in natural resources fields. Cooperative Extension traditionally has relied on trained volunteers to help educate others. In suburban Long Island, where the population exceeds three million people, the need for trained volunteers to assist with program delivery is especially great. A lack of knowledgeable and trained volunteers in natural resources fields has prevented us from reaching many of the program goals locally. Although many 4-H clubs complete natural resources projects, few get beyond the introductory level, often because of the leaders' lack of confidence in the natural resources area.

In recent years, recruiting adults to be traditional 4-H club leaders has proved difficult. In large part, this has been attributed to the dual career family structure, where both parents work outside the home. Parents explain that they do not have the time to help with 4-H clubs on a regular basis. The pool of female homemakers, a traditional source of volunteers in the past, has declined considerably. The rise of the single parent family has compounded the problem.

To combat the problem of few trained volunteers knowledgeable in natural resources, we developed a new program. So that busy people could become involved, we designed the program with a flexible volunteer commitment. Traditional 4-H leaders are generalized and teach a wide variety of subjects. They generally meet with youth groups on a regular, long-term schedule. The new program trains specialized leaders in various fields of natural resources. These leaders might work with existing 4-H clubs, or do their volunteer work in a variety of community settings. The key elements of our new system are to (1) find people already knowledgeable in a natural resource area and to train them to be volunteer educators, (2) provide these trainees with a flexible commitment that will enable them to fit volunteer time into their schedule, and (3) establish a series of short-term special interest programs for youth led by these specialized volunteers as an alternative to traditional 4-H club involvement.

The first pilot subject was sport fishing. Sport fishing is a leading recreational activity on Long Island, resulting in a group of individuals who are knowledgeable about fishing and Long Island waters. Approximately sixty adult sport fishing clubs exist on Long Island.

To attract adults from this pool of experienced anglers, a volunteer training program entitled Master Anglers was developed by staff of the Department of Natural Resources at Cornell University, New York State Sea Grant, and Suffolk County 4-H. Master Anglers would be volunteer sport fishing educators, teaching basic angling skills and wildlife conservation principles. The potential success of this approach was indicated by two existing programs. Many sportsmen volunteer to serve as hunter safety instructors for the New York State Department of Environmental Conservation, and many amateur horticulturalists volunteer to be Master Gardeners for Cooperative Extension nationally.

The planning committee developed a 13-week Master Angler training program. Topics covered in the training

Integrating Man and Nature in the Metropolitan Environment. Proc. Natl. Symp. on Urban Wildl., Chevy Chase, Md., 4–7 November 1986, L.W. Adams and D.L. Leedy, eds. Published by Natl. Inst. for Urban Wildl., 10921 Trotting Ridge Way, Columbia, MD 21044, 1987.

session included ecology of fishes, fisheries management, sportsmanship and ethics, safety, handling of fish and seafood preparation, angling techniques, and teaching techniques. The purpose of the training program was to give participants a broad background in sport fishing-related topics, so they could knowledgeably interact with the public and 4-H clubs. However, it was assumed that volunteers would choose to teach topics in which they already had a strong interest.

It is our hope that through an involvement with sport fishing, young people will reach some of the natural resources goals mentioned earlier. Our strategy is to first get young people interested in fishing, to teach them how to be successful anglers, and then get them concerned and involved with fisheries conservation issues.

The Master Angler program was advertised through the local media. Persons expressing an interest in the program were sent a program schedule, a fact sheet explaining the goals and purpose of the program, and an application form. On the application form, applicants were asked to describe their level of fishing experience, their present involvement in sport fishing activities, and why they wanted to be a Master Angler. Approximately 90 people submitted applications. From that group a class of 31 was selected, including those with the strongest background and desire to do volunteer work. The program was conducted in the fall of 1985. Instructors for the program included staff of the New York State Department of Environmental Conservation, the Coast Guard Auxiliary, locally recognized angling "experts," and Cooperative Extension Sea Grant and 4-H staff.

Twenty-nine people completed the course. In order to graduate from the Master Angler program, each candidate had to attend all the training sessions and prepare a teaching-related project. Each candidate was required to present his project before the group. The purpose of the presentation was to give each volunteer at least one experience speaking in front of a group before course completion. During the final session, participants were given Master Angler diplomas and identifying patches.

Following the training course, all program participants were sent evaluation forms. They rated the program very highly, and expressed a real enthusiasm for the program and its mission. One point mentioned by several participants was their feeling that they needed more instruction on how to become effective teachers.

The volunteers have been active for 8 months. A part-time staff member was hired to coordinate their activities. His responsibility is to help locate volunteer opportunities, and to recruit Master Anglers for specific programs. This is done through a Master Angler newsletter and by telephoning. Some Master Anglers have been very active, but others have yet to fulfill their volunteer commitment.

Master Anglers have been involved in a variety of programs. The availability of Master Anglers was advertised to community groups through Cooperative Extension publications. Libraries have had Master Anglers teach basic angling courses. Two Master Anglers conducted a rod building course, and another organized the clean-up of a freshwater lake. Several Master Anglers helped handicapped adults learn how to fish. Master Anglers also taught classes to 4-H youth at a sport fishing camp.

The successful experience with the pilot program on Long Island led to the development of a Master Angler training program by Cooperative Extension staff working along Lake Ontario. The experience with the program in upstate New York was very similar to the Long Island experience.

The future for the Master Angler program in New York is promising. A second training program is scheduled for the fall of 1986 on Long Island. With experience gained from two pilot programs, staff will be working on program refinement and standardization. The program coordinators will be working to develop (1) a basic course outline for statewide application, (2) a guide for Cooperative Extension agents on how to organize a Master Angler program, (3) a uniform identification system of hats, patches, and diplomas for Master Anglers, and (4) a resource book of angling publications for use by Master Anglers.

Because of the success of the Master Angler program, other natural resource topics were examined for their potential to provide volunteers to instruct youth. The field of ornithology was selected because of its wide appeal and relevance to many natural resource issues. Several local chapters of the National Audubon Society exist on Long Island, and we hoped these clubs could serve as a source of adult volunteers. Cornell University and The National 4-H Council have developed a wide variety of project guides and audio-visual aids that could be used with an ornithology training program.

Staff from the Seatuck Research Program of the Cornell Laboratory of Ornithology, and Cooperative Extension, jointly planned and carried out a Master Birder Training program. Like Master Anglers, these people were to be trained volunteers, willing to help both organizations carry out their educational missions. We were particularly interested in having Master Birders work in two areas. On suburban Long Island, fragmentation and loss of wildlife habitat are critical concerns. We hoped that Master Birders might serve to encourage people to become active in wildlife habitat improvement projects in suburban areas. We also wished to broaden participants' perspective of wildlife management techniques as they might relate to suburban natural resources. Lastly, a birding program would help address the 4-H natural resources goals already mentioned. By introducing more young people to the fascination of observing and studying birds, we hoped to cultivate their interest in the environmental factors affecting bird populations.

A 10-week training program was planned and piloted. Instructors included staff of the Cornell Laboratory of Ornithology, Cornell Cooperative Extension, the New York State Department of Environmental Conservation, and the U.S. Fish and Wildlife Service. As with the Master Anglers, there was an enthusiastic response to the public announcement of the Master Birder program. Eighty applications were received and other names were placed on a waiting list for future programs. From the 80 applications, 30 participants were selected.

The training program was conducted during the spring of 1986. As with Master Anglers, training sessions were scheduled during the evening hours so that working people could attend. Classes were provided in a variety of topics including waterfowl, shorebirds, upland birds, songbirds, and basic ecology and management. Trained Master Birders have taught classes in basic bird identification to community groups, and have worked with handicapped individuals and other special populations to introduce them to birding.

Whereas Master Anglers rated their training session as "excellent," Master Birders rated theirs as "good." Both groups were given a rating scale that included poor, fair, good, and excellent. The birders seemed to be a less uniform group than the anglers, with a wider range of knowledge and greater involvement with the issues surrounding the subject. In contrast to the Master Angler program, finding an appropriate level of instruction for this second group was more difficult.

Two observations were made of the birders that did not seem to apply to the anglers. Generally, the birders appeared to have a desire to improve their own technical skills first, with volunteerism being secondary. In addition, this group seemed more issue oriented, particularly in regard to wildlife management, and had a tendency to be more opinionated. Although this led to very interesting discussions during the classes, it also raised concern regarding the ability of these individuals to present the issues to students and groups objectively.

From the experience with these two programs, a number of conclusions can be drawn. First, it is clear that there is an interest on the part of many people to become involved in special interest natural resources volunteer training programs. It is important that such programs be properly marketed to a target audience to reach potential candidates. It is also necessary to have a clear statement of program objectives and expectations that can be shared with potential candidates. Identifying a candidate's knowledge of the subject and commitment to volunteerism is necessary before accepting the individual into the program. A personal interview would provide additional insight to the person's potential for volunteer educational work.

Refining a program's length and content will be an ongoing process. A program should be at least long enough to build a sense of group identity and purpose, and for the coordinators to get to know all the participants. The longest training period for Master Gardeners in New York State is 100 hours, although most county programs are considerably shorter. Obviously a person will not become an expert in any field as a result of one training program. The term "Master" has caused some confusion. A Master Birder or Angler is not necessarily, in our definition, an expert in bird identification or fishing techniques, but rather someone trained and motivated to teach basic information to others. In addition, these programs were designed to provide programmatic continuity and identity with the long established Cooperative Extension Master Gardener program.

We are encouraged by our experience with both programs. Special interest volunteers, given the opportunity to volunteer when their time permits, can supplement the traditional 4-H volunteer who works in a broad array of subjects and meets with clubs on a regular basis. Trained special interest volunteers can help raise the level of instruction to higher standards because they start with a higher level of specialized knowledge than do many traditional 4-H volunteers.

People get natural resources information from a range of sources, including the media, clubs, and friends. Cooperative Extension is in the fortunate position of being able to teach resource management from a university perspective, with knowledge soundly based in research. We believe it is important that this type of information reach the public to help people understand environmental issues more thoroughly. The use of special interest, trained volunteers can help us reach that goal.

Wildlife and Natural Resources Information and Education Programs for New York City

MICHAEL J. MATTHEWS, *Division of Fish and Wildlife, New York State Department of Environmental Conservation, Delmar, NY 12054*

DOROTHY LEWANDOWSKI, *Department of Parks and Recreation, New York City, The Arsenal, 830 5th Avenue, New York, NY 10021*

INTRODUCTION

During the past 10 years, New York State's Division of Fish and Wildlife has developed an active Urban Wildlife Program. The program has completed an attitude and interest survey of urban residents with regard to wildlife (Brown and Dawson 1978), and an inventory of urban wildlife habitat within New York State (Matthews and Miller 1980, Matthews et al. in press). Other projects implemented by the program include establishing the first urban wildlife park—Tivoli Lakes, Albany, New York (Miller and Matthews 1978); establishing a wildlife shrub planting program for urban and suburban backyards; and assorted information and education programs for the urban public.

Many of these extension and information programs have been directed towards the New York City area. The focus on New York City was indeed necessary and timely. New York City contains almost eight million residents, over 25% of the city land area is still in open space, and most of this open space is the responsibility of the New York City Department of Parks and Recreation (NYCDPR). In 1979, the NYCDPR established an Urban Park Ranger Program in conjunction with an active revitalization of its massive park system (Huber and Matthews 1985). Over 100 NYC urban park rangers combine both patrolling to protect park patrons and educating the public through interpretive walks and programs. This fact was responsible for the start of a sound working relationship between the state and the city. Through the ranger interpretive program, the Department of Environmental Conservation (DEC) could provide factual information on natural resources management. The interpretive program is perhaps the most innovative and expansive in the country. All the rangers have ample opportunity to design and lead programs, and take great pride in doing so. City parks are ideal classrooms where natural and man-made environments converge.

DISCUSSION

One new and important development in the ranger training process is a workshop on urban natural resources management. This program was instituted and developed by the DEC Division of Fish and Wildlife's Urban Wildlife Program. Starting as a pilot project in 1983, a workshop was conducted for 16 rangers. Because of its success, the program was expanded to include all ranger staff. Funding of the 1984 program was provided through the State's wildlife tax contribution program, Return a Gift to Wildlife (RAGTW). The American Museum of Natural History and the New York Botanical Garden in New York City provided conference facilities for the workshops, and New York City's Pelham Bay Park, Central Park, and Van Cortlandt Park served as outdoor laboratories. Lectures at the Museum and Botanical Garden were followed by afternoon field trips in the parks. Workshop participants were treated to lectures by representatives from DEC, National Audubon Society, American Museum of Natural History, State University of New York's College of Environmental Science and Forestry, Cornell University, New York Botanical Garden, New York State Wildlife Rehabilitator Council, NYC Department of Parks and Recreation, and the U.S. Department of the Interior's Gateway National Recreation Area. A workbook also was presented to each ranger that included subjects like urban forestry, backyard wildlife, urban soils, freshwater wetlands, animal damage control, and natural history interpretation. Through this cooperative venture, the state and the city are better able to provide urban residents with a more complete picture of natural resource management via

Integrating Man and Nature in the Metropolitan Environment. Proc. Natl. Symp. on Urban Wildl., Chevy Chase, Md., 4–7 November 1986, L.W. Adams and D.L. Leedy, eds. Published by Natl. Inst. for Urban Wildl., 10921 Trotting Ridge Way, Columbia, MD 21044, 1987.

a trained and professional ranger staff. These workshops are now an important part of the yearly overall ranger training program.

Formal programs are offered by the rangers during the school year to school children in grades three to seven. Created in coordination with the New York City Board of Education, the programs provide environmental education for city youngsters and instill in them a positive attitude toward parks. All topics covered include an activity packet that the teacher utilizes with the students. Word building exercises, food chain games, and street tree care activities are examples. These activities are designed to prepare students for the ranger class and park visits. Topics covered include geology, plants and trees, urban animals, pond life, salt marshes, park history, appreciation, and design. Last year over 50,000 students participated in these programs. With a more streamlined procedure, and the introduction of the activity packets, the rangers hope to increase the number of school children they reach.

In 1986, RAGTW provided funds to produce a set of educational posters and an activity packet. Each poster will depict an animal in a particular park setting. Crotona Park, Bronx—black and gray squirrels (*Sciurus carolinensis*); Van Cortlandt Park, Bronx—raccoon (*Procyon lotor*); Central Park, Manhattan—woodchuck (*Marmota monax*); Prospect Park, Brooklyn—black-crowned night heron (*Nycticorax nycticorax*); Kissena Park, Queens—ring-necked pheasant (*Phasianus colchicus*); and Clove Lake Park, Staten Island—chipmunk (*Tamis striatus*). The posters will be distributed to teachers and school children attending either the Urban Animals or the Ponds and Lakes program conducted by the rangers. Each poster will be accompanied by an educational activity packet prepared by the Urban Park Rangers in cooperation with the Division of Fish and Wildlife's Urban Wildlife Program. This packet will contain activities that the students and teachers can do on their own to familiarize themselves with wildlife and its habitat in New York City.

REFERENCES CITED

Brown, T.L. and C.P. Dawson. 1978. Interests, needs and attitudes of New York's metropolitan public in relation to wildlife. Cornell Univ. Dep. of Nat. Resour. Res. and Ext. Serv. No. 13, Ithaca, New York. 53pp. Multilith.

Huber, R.M. and M.J. Matthews. 1985. Genial hosts in a renovated home. NYS Conservationist 40:12–15.

Matthews, M.J. and R.L. Miller. 1980. New York State's urban wildlife habitat inventory. Trans. Northeast Sect. The Wildl. Soc. 37:11–18.

Matthews, M.J., S. O'Connor and R.S. Cole (in press). Data base for the urban wildlife habitat inventory. Landscape and Urban Planning.

Miller, R.L. and M.J. Matthews. 1978. Tivoli Lakes management plan. NYS Dep. Environ. Conserv. Wildl. Resour. Cent., Delmar, 67pp. Multilith.

Attitudes of Urban Residents Toward Avian Species and Species' Attributes

STEPHEN PENLAND, *Washington Department of Game, 16018 Mill Creek Blvd., Mill Creek, WA 98012*

Traditionally, the Washington State Department of Game, like most other state wildlife management agencies, has dealt primarily with game species and a clientele of hunters and anglers. This long-term involvement with a specific user group and a limited number of animal species has enabled the Department to accurately gauge opinion and sentiment regarding management policies and activities.

Today, nearly three-fourths of Washington residents live in urban areas. Urbanization probably has led to changes in perceptions and attitudes among the general public in the state regarding wildlife, as has been demonstrated in national surveys by Kellert (1976, 1980).

In response to changing needs and demands of Washington residents, the Department initiated a Nongame Program in 1974 and an Urban Wildlife Program in 1981. However, relatively little objective information has been available regarding the non-hunting public's knowledge and attitudes concerning nongame wildlife, especially in urban areas. Such information should be a primary component in the planning of nongame and urban wildlife management activities. This is especially true in light of a proposed statewide initiative that would change the primary source of Department funding from hunting and fishing license revenues paid by a specific user group to include an increase in the state sales tax paid by all Washington residents.

The present study was conducted as part of a larger project of avian habitat relationships in Seattle (Penland 1984). It was intended to provide preliminary information regarding knowledge and attitudes of urban residents toward bird species present in their neighborhoods by comparing known relative abundances of avian species with residents' responses to a questionnaire survey.

METHODS

Birds were censused in 54 residential plots among six Seattle neighborhoods representing a gradient of urbanization. The four census periods included two winter seasons (1979–80 and 1980–81) and two spring seasons (1980, 1981). A questionnaire was distributed at every third house in each of the plots, with a total of 330 questionnaires delivered. The census methods and neighborhood descriptions are given in Penland (1984). The questionnaire elicited information regarding species that had been observed in the neighborhood, as well as attributes of desirable and undesirable birds.

RESULTS

Bird species that I observed more frequently than 0.5 times per census during at least one of the four seasons in any neighborhood are shown in Table 1. Six species—bushtit (*Psaltriparus minimus*), American robin (*Turdus migratorius*), European starling (*Sturnus vulgaris*), house sparrow (*Passer domesticus*), house finch (*Carpodacus mexicanus*), and dark-eyed junco (*Junco hyemalis*)—were observed at this minimum frequency in all six neighborhoods. Of these, the most numerous species in some neighborhoods included the European starling in Madrona and Ballard (16.8 and 10.4 per census, respectively), the house sparrow in Ballard and Queen Anne (7.9 and 6.0 per census, respectively), and the American robin in Queen Anne (5.9 per census). European starlings and house sparrows accounted for 40% or more of all of the birds seen in four of the neighborhoods during at least one of the census periods.

A total of 298 (90%) questionnaires were completed and returned. Of these, 274 (92%) responded to the section that elicited information regarding species present and attributes of desirable and undesirable species.

Identified Species

Respondents were asked to name all the bird species that they had observed at some time in their neighborhood (Table 2). The average number of species named by all

Integrating Man and Nature in the Metropolitan Environment. Proc. Natl. Symp. on Urban Wildl., Chevy Chase, Md., 4–7 November 1986, L.W. Adams and D.L. Leedy, eds. Published by Natl. Inst. for Urban Wildl., 10921 Trotting Ridge Way, Columbia, MD 21044, 1987.

Table 1. Highest average number of birds observed per census (percent[a]) during one of four census periods, Seattle, Washington, 1979–1981.[b]

	More urbanized neighborhoods			Less urbanized neighborhoods		
Species	Ballard	Queen Anne	Madrona	Ravenna	North End	Central
Band-tailed Pigeon					1.5 (8)	.8 (5)
Rock Dove	1.0 (7)	.7 (5)	2.7 (14)		1.0 (6)	3.6 (27)
Violet-green Swallow (*Tachycineta thalassina*)		.9 (7)				
American Crow			1.1 (4)	.6 (6)	1.0 (6)	.7 (5)
Black-capped Chickadee (*Parus atricapillus*)					1.1 (7)	.9 (7)
Bushtit	.5 (4)	.6 (5)	1.1 (5)	3.7 (28)	1.8 (10)	2.7 (18)
American Robin	4.1 (18)	5.9 (26)	3.8 (13)	2.2 (17)	2.4 (13)	4.1 (31)
European Starling	10.4 (45)	9.1 (40)	16.8 (57)	2.1 (16)	2.8 (16)	2.0 (15)
Yellow-rumped Warbler (*Dendroica coronata*)						1.1 (7)
House Sparrow	7.9 (55)	6.0 (44)	3.8 (20)	4.5 (43)	4.8 (27)	2.0 (16)
Evening Grosbeak (*Coccothraustes vespertinus*)					.8 (4)	.6 (4)
House Finch	.7 (5)	1.3 (9)	1.8 (10)	.5 (5)	1.4 (8)	.5 (4)
Pine Siskin (*Carduelis pinus*)					.9 (8)	1.4 (9)
Dark-eyed Junco	1.4 (6)	1.3 (10)	.7 (4)	.9 (12)	2.7 (16)	1.2 (9)
Song Sparrow (*Melospiza melodia*)			.9 (6)			
Total[c]	28	28	33	32	46	36

[a]Percent of total birds (all species) observed during the census period.
[b]Birds observed less frequently than 0.5/census are omitted.
[c]Total number of species observed during the study period.

respondents was 4.6. Only six (2%) respondents named more than 10 species. The average number of species observed, including unidentified species, was 6.4 among all respondents. Seven percent of the respondents could list no birds observed in their neighborhood. American robins were most frequently identified, with 84% of the respondents listing this species. The American crow (*Corvus brachyrhynchos*) ranked second, with 74% of all respondents naming this species. The third and fourth most frequently cited species were the house sparrow (59%) and European starling (43%). Other species that were frequently named included the Steller's jay (*Cyanocitta cristata*) (25%), rock dove (24%), swallow (15%), hummingbird (15%), chickadee (11%), and finch (10%).

Two species were unevenly distributed among the neighborhoods—band-tailed pigeons (*Columba fasciata*), limited to North End and Central neighborhoods, and rock doves, most common in Madrona and Central neighborhoods—and were proportionally cited by residents in those neighborhoods.

Several species were named more frequently than would have been predicted by their known relative abundances. I infrequently censused hummingbirds, yet they were named in all neighborhoods, and by 15% of all respondents. Similarly, I found American goldfinches (*Carduelis tristis*) on just a few occasions during 2 years of censusing, yet this species was named in all but one neighborhood, and by 6% of all respondents. Woodpeckers and Steller's jays were infrequently encountered during my censuses, especially in the more highly urbanized neighborhoods. Yet these birds were named in nearly all neighborhoods and by a relatively large percentage of the respondents, including those in Queen Anne and Madrona where no Steller's jays were found during my censuses. Finally, American crows were named more frequently than might have been predicted by their known relative abundance, especially in the highly urbanized neighborhoods of Ballard and Queen Anne, where they were rarely observed.

Some species were named less frequently than would have been predicted by their known relative abundances. European starlings were most abundant in Madrona, yet far fewer residents named starlings there compared to residents in other neighborhoods. Dark-eyed juncos and bushtits were named less frequently than expected, especially by residents in the North End neighborhood. These two species were either the fourth or fifth most common species I censused among all neighborhoods during the two winter census periods, yet they were named by only 6%–7% of all respondents.

Desirable Species and Species Attributes

Residents were asked which species they considered desirable to have in their neighborhood and the attributes of these desirable birds (Table 3). Eighty percent of the respondents said that there were desirable bird species in their neighborhood. However, most respondents listed fewer than two specific desirable species. The American robin was cited far more frequently than any other species, with 52% of all respondents stating this was a desirable species. The only other species considered desirable by more than 10% of the respondents was the house sparrow. This was due to the large percentage (29%) of the residents in Ballard who favored the species. Some 37% of the respondents said that they liked having all or most species of birds found in their neighborhood.

With regard to desirable characteristics, approximately half of the respondents said they liked the antics of birds while feeding, the grace of flying birds, or other behavioral characteristics (Table 3). Some 41% of the respondents indicated that the color of birds was an important attribute. Birds with pleasant songs or calls were desired by 35% of the residents. Other attributes cited by respondents were consumption of insects and weed seeds (19%), small size (16%), and the absence of offensive characteristics (7%).

Undesirable Species and Species' Attributes

Residents were asked which species and species' attributes they considered to be undesirable (Table 4). More than three-fourths of the respondents in Madrona and Central neighborhoods indicated the presence of undesirable

Table 2. Birds identified at some time during the year by at least 10% of neighborhood respondents in one or more neighborhoods, expressed as the percent of total respondents in each neighborhood, Seattle, Washington, 1979–1981.

	More urbanized neighborhoods			Less urbanized neighborhoods			
Species	Ballard	Queen Anne	Madrona	Ravenna	North End	Central	Total
Hawk, sp.			12		1		1
Gull, sp.	7	11	6	3	1	17	6
Band-tailed Pigeon				2	10	6	4
Rock Dove	31	22	59	10	14	61	24
Hummingbird, sp.	14	6	12	13	23	6	15
Northern Flicker *(Colaptes auratus)*		3		8	11		6
Woodpecker, sp.	3	6	12	3	11	33	8
Swallow, sp.	20	11	12	13	14	11	15
Steller's Jay		17	24	22	41	61	25
American Crow	71	69	88	72	75	78	74
Chickadee, sp.	12	11		5	14	22	11
Bushtit	7	3		13	6	11	7
American Robin	85	92	94	78	81	89	84
Cedar Waxwing *(Bombycilla cedrorum)*		3		3	2	11	3
European Starling	54	64	12	43	33	44	43
House Sparrow	64	75	47	55	52	67	59
Grosbeak, sp.				2	1	11	2
Finch, sp.	7	11	12	13	8	17	10
American Goldfinch	2		12	3	12	6	6
Rufous-sided Towhee *(Pipilo erythrophthalmus)*				5	11	6	5
Dark-eyed Junco	3	3		12	7	6	6
"Blackbird"	3	6	12	8	2		5
None identified	3	3		12	8	6	7
Mean number identified (±S.D.)	3.9 ±2.0	4.2 ±2.2	4.1 ±2.2	4.7 ±4.8	4.8 ±3.8	5.8 ±4.8	4.6 ±3.3
Mean number observed, including unidentified (±S.D.)	5.1 ±2.7	5.8 ±3.1	5.7 ±3.0	6.7 ±5.3	6.4 ±4.7	8.4 ±5.6	6.4 ±4.1
Number of respondents	59	36	17	60	84	18	274

Table 3. Species and attributes identified as desirable by respondents, expressed as the percent of respondents who stated that there were desirable bird species in their neighborhood, Seattle, Washington, 1979–1981.[a]

	More urbanized neighborhoods			Less urbanized neighborhoods			
Species	Ballard	Queen Anne	Madrona	Ravenna	North End	Central	Total
Hummingbird, sp.	2	3		4	3	6	4
Woodpecker, sp.			7		3	6	2
Swallow, sp.	5	7			2	6	3
Steller's Jay			14		11		5
American Crow	2		7	2	3		3
Chickadee, sp.	2			4	5	11	4
American Robin	54	66	43	35	41	44	52
House Sparrow	29	7	14	4	5	11	12
Finch, sp.	2	3		2		6	2
Dark-eyed Junco	2	3	7	4			3
Unidentified species	2	7	29	4	3	17	7
All or most species	29	21	7	44	36	22	37
Desirable characteristics							
Behavior	56	62	86	42	23	50	52
Color	32	35	64	48	24	33	41
Song, call	39	24	14	31	35	39	35
Consume insects	22	14	21	15	28		19
Small size	5	7		8			16
Not offensive	2				18	6	7
Indefinite, or other response	29	10	29	23	29	22	28
No response	20	17		10	21	22	19
Query regarding presence of desirable bird species in respondent's neighborhood:							
Answering "Yes" (%)	70	81	82	87	79	100	80
Answering "No" (%)	22	6	12	3	8		10
No response (%)	9	14	6	10	13		10
Number of respondents	59	36	17	60	84	18	274

[a]Species mentioned by fewer than 5% of the respondents in all neighborhoods are omitted.

species, and 57% of all respondents said there were undesirable birds in their area.

The American crow was disapproved by a majority of those who indicated the presence of undesirable species. This included 84% of the respondents in the North End neighborhood. The European starling was considered undesirable by 34% and the rock dove by 24% of the respondents. Disapproval of the rock dove was highest in the Madrona (54%) and Central (71%) neighborhoods, where this species is most common.

Noise was the most disliked avian attribute, being cited by 63% of the respondents. Residents in the North End neighborhood cited this characteristic most frequently, with an 86% disapproval. The mess associated with nests and roosts on or near houses was cited by 57% of the respondents, with the highest percentages coming from residents in more highly urbanized neighborhoods. The negative effect some species have on other birds, including predation on eggs and young, interference at birdfeeders, and general harassment, also was cited by a majority of the respondents. Other undesirable attributes included consumption of fruit and garden produce (12%), overwhelming numbers (11%), and damage to the house (4%).

DISCUSSION

The number of bird species named or observed by respondents was quite low, especially considering that I censused up to 46 species in one neighborhood and a minimum of 28 species among all neighborhoods. This parallels the limited knowledge of animals found by Kellert (1980) on a national scale. The American robin appears to be of special interest to urban residents in western Washington, because it was the most frequently identified and was con-

Table 4. Species and attributes identified as undesirable by respondents, expressed as the percent of respondents who stated that there were undesirable bird species in their neighborhood, Seattle, Washington, 1979–1981.[a]

	More urbanized neighborhoods			Less urbanized neighborhoods			
Species	Ballard	Queen Anne	Madrona	Ravenna	North End	Central	Total
Rock Dove	29	30	54	8	4	71	24
Steller's Jay				4	4	14	3
American Crow	54	30	39	58	84	50	59
American Robin	3			8			2
European Starling	51	40	8	39	27	21	34
House Sparrow		10		4	4		3
"Blackbird"		5		8	2		3
Unidentified			8		2		1
All or most species			15		4		3
Undesirable characteristics							
Noise	69	20	39	58	86	64	63
Dirty, messy	71	75	77	39	33	71	57
Negative effects on other bird species	77	40	15	50	45	43	52
Consume fruit/garden produce	3	5	15	23	16		12
Great numbers	11	30	15	15	4		11
Damages house		5		8	4	7	4
Other response	3	5	23	4	12	29	10
No response	6	5			2		2
Query regarding presence of undesirable bird species in respondent's neighborhood:							
Answering "Yes" (%)	59	56	77	43	58	78	57
Answering "No" (%)	41	42	23	50	41	17	40
No response (%)		3		7	1	6	3
Number of respondents	59	36	17	60	84	18	274

[a]Species mentioned by fewer than 5% of the respondents in all neighborhoods are omitted.

sidered the most desirable species. Other investigators (Brown et al. 1979, Kellert 1980, Snyder and George 1981) have found similar attractions for robins.

Species that were observed and remembered at frequencies proportionally greater than their relative abundances often were large or noisy birds and were frequently associated with urban wildlife problems. Two other species not fitting this description, but which were frequently observed, may represent special cases of unusual size and behavior (hummingbird) and bright color (American goldfinch). It also is probable that other more common warblers, notably the Wilson's warbler *(Wilsonia pusilla)*, were incorrectly identified as American goldfinches. No definite explanation for the low frequency of starling sightings in the Madrona neighborhood can be offered; they may have been overshadowed by the numbers of larger American crows and rock doves.

Species that were observed less frequently than expected were small, generally nondescript birds. These probably were often the species that were observed but not named by residents, because people frequently asked me about the identification of bushtits and dark-eyed juncos.

The public's inability to name many species and their failure to distinguish many neighborhood species do not appear to be reflected in their interest in urban birds. A substantial majority of respondents reported the presence of desirable species, even among the smaller group of those who had experienced problems with some bird species. Similar attitudes have been found by Brown et al. (1979), Kellert (1980), Snyder and George (1981), Witter et al. (1981), and Shaw and Mangun (1984).

Despite the fact that house sparrows frequently construct their nests in houses, create untidy conditions around the nest site, usurp nest boxes from native bird species, occur in large flocks during most of the year, and have no pleasant song or call (all of which were identified as undesirable attributes), more people considered the species to be desirable than undesirable. An even stronger (73%) favorable attitude regarding house sparrows was found by Dagg (1974) in Waterloo, Canada. The relatively small size of house sparrows was probably their redeeming feature, because the most frequently cited attributes for those approving of house sparrows were their behavioral characteristics and "cuteness."

CONCLUSIONS

Wildlife management agencies are, from the point of view of urban residents, dealing with animals in increasingly remote natural environments and basing their programs on principles of ecology that are not understood by this growing majority of the U.S. population. These changes are likely to result in a decline in the proportion of residents who identify with the programs of their state's wildlife agency and who feel that the agency represents their interests. This can have serious consequences if the wildlife agency must rely on the decisions these urban residents make regarding support for legislative or financial proposals that affect the agency. Urban wildlife programs provide the opportunity to win this support. One of the primary functions of these programs should be to lessen the gap between the public's interest and its knowledge regarding wildlife. Educational programs and activities, such as newspaper columns, classes and workshops, backyard sanctuary programs, species identification posters, winter feeding publications, birdhouse construction manuals, and other means to address the informational needs of the public, should be central to urban wildlife programs.

REFERENCES CITED

Brown, T., C. Dawson, and R. Miller. 1979. Interests and attitudes of metropolitan New York residents about wildlife. Trans. North Am. Wildl. Nat. Resour. Conf. 44:289–297.

Dagg, A.I. 1974. Reactions of people to urban wildlife. Pages 163–165 *in* J.H. Noyes and D.R. Progulske, eds. Wildlife in an urbanizing environment. Planning and Resour. Dev. Ser. 28, Univ. of Mass., Amherst.

Kellert, S. 1976. Perceptions of animals in American society. Trans. North Am. Wildl. Nat. Resour. Conf. 41:533–546.

Kellert, S. 1980. Americans' attitudes and knowledge of animals. Trans. North Am. Wildl. Nat. Resour. Conf. 45:111–124.

Penland, S. 1984. Avian responses to a gradient of urbanization in Seattle, Washington. Ph.D. Dissertation, Univ. of Washington, Seattle, 405 pp.

Shaw, W., and W. Mangun. 1984. Nonconsumptive use of wildlife in the United States. Resour. Publ. 154, U.S. Dep. Inter., Fish & Wildl. Serv., Washington, D.C. 20240. 20 pp.

Snyder, A., and J. George. 1981. Wildlife-related activities and attitudes of Pennsylvanians. Trans. North Am. Wildl. Nat. Resour. Conf. 46: 455–462.

Witter, D., D. Tylka, and J. Werner. 1981. Values of urban wildlife in Missouri. Trans. North Am. Wildl. Nat. Resour. Conf. 46:424–431.

Urban High School Students' Knowledge of Wildlife

CLARK E. ADAMS, *Department of Wildlife and Fisheries Sciences, Texas A&M University, College Station, TX 77843*

JOHN K. THOMAS, *Department of Rural Sociology, Texas A&M University, College Station, TX 77843*

PEI-CHIEN LIN, *Department of Wildlife and Fisheries Sciences, Texas A&M University, College Station, TX 77843*

BRENDA WEISER, *Cypress-Fairbanks High School, Route 12, Box 8B, Houston, TX 77040*

Past assessments have been made of the public's knowledge and understanding of wildlife, selected wildlife management issues, and basic biological, taxonomic, and natural history characteristics of animals in general (Taylor and Samuel 1975, Kellert 1980, LaHart 1981, Byford and Munsey 1984, Kellert 1985, Westervelt and Llewellyn 1985). The particular audiences targeted in those studies respectively were teachers; a national sample of respondents 18 years and older; eighth graders; 4-H conference alumni compared to a cross section of the American public; second, fifth, eighth, and eleventh graders; and fifth and sixth grade students. Each study attempted to develop some association between respondents' wildlife knowledge and attitudes toward wildlife, demonstrated degrees of variation in the wildlife knowledge of groups sampled, and alerted the profession to a critically low level of public knowledge of the biology, taxonomy, and natural history of wildlife or its management.

The present study measured the wildlife knowledge of urban high school students regarding selected mammals. It was a departure from earlier studies in terms of the types of questions used to measure respondents' wildlife knowledge, audience addressed, and purpose of the study. For example, our study focused on urban high school students' ability to identify 16 mammals and to answer the same four natural history questions concerning each mammal rather than cover the broad range of wildlife knowledge questions posed by Kellert and Berry (1980). The current study also provides information concerning the level of public wildlife knowledge and identification of the educational programming required to correct the revealed misinformation on the selected mammals.

STUDY AREA AND METHODS

Harris County is in the east-central section of Texas, within the habitat zones known as the upper and lower coastal plains (U.S. Fish and Wildl. Serv. 1979). The human population of 2,409,547 is greater than that of any of the other 253 counties in Texas. Population density is 1,390 people per square mile. Ninety-six percent of Harris County residents live in urban areas and the urban population grew nearly 40% from 1970 to 1980. Natural areas consisting of municipal parks, refuges, lakes, and reservoirs constitute only 4% of the total county acreage (Clements 1984).

A multiple-choice test was constructed to measure the identification and natural history knowledge of 16 mammals by biology students (N = 213 and 277) enrolled during the 1985 academic year in two urban high schools in Harris County. Biology students were chosen as those who would be the most informed on test components when compared to students in other classes. The test consisted of a series of equally scaled black-line drawings of the cottontail rabbit (*Sylvilagus floridanus*, fox squirrel (*Sciurus niger)*, opossum (*Didelphis virginiana)*, bobcat (*Lynx rufus*), red fox (*Vulpes vulpes*), white-tailed deer (*Odocoileus virginianus*), raccoon (*Procyon lotor*), house mouse (*Mus musculus*), mink (*Mustela vison*), beaver (*Castor canadensis*), plains pocket gopher (*Geomys bursarius*), red bat (*Lasiurus borealis*), striped skunk (*Mephitis mephitis*), buffalo (*Bison bison*), armadillo (*Dasypus novemcinctus*), and cougar (*Felis concolor*). Students identified each animal by choosing its common English name from a multiple-choice list of all sixteen mammals. All animals were present or past endemics of Harris County.

Integrating Man and Nature in the Metropolitan Environment. Proc. Natl. Symp. on Urban Wildl., Chevy Chase, Md., 4–7 November 1986, L.W. Adams and D.L. Leedy, eds. Published by Natl. Inst. for Urban Wildl., 10921 Trotting Ridge Way, Columbia, MD 21044, 1987.

Students then answered a series of four multiple-choice questions on each animal including: (1) what it primarily eats, i.e., meat only (including insects), plants only, both plants and meat, or rotting plants and meat; (2) its level of abundance within Harris County, i.e., extinct, rare, abundant, or never existed in this county; (3) its average weight, i.e., < 1 pound (454 g), > 1 pound (454 g) but ≤ 25 pounds (11.4 kg), >25 pounds (11.4 kg) but ≤ 50 pounds (22.7 kg), or > 50 pounds (22.7 kg); and (4) the impact of urbanization on the animal's abundance, i.e., abundance increased, decreased (but animal still exists), remained about the same, or animal has become extinct. Answers to questions 1 through 4 were verified based on information from Davis (1978), Flyger (1974), Chamberlain et al. (1982), Flyger et al. (1983), Gore and Reagan (1985), and personal communications with C. Winkler and B. Thompson, Wildlife Division, Texas Parks and Wildlife Department and M. Mendoza, Rodent and Predatory Animal Control Service, San Antonio, Texas. Test scoring was based on the values 1 or 0 for correct and incorrect responses, respectively.

RESULTS

T-tests of mean scores between schools (46.99 and 47.21) were not significantly different ($P = 0.722$). Therefore, the combined average score of 47% was used as the cut-off point to designate whether the student population sampled was informed (above the average) or uninformed (at or below the average) concerning the identification, weight, present numbers, eating habits, and effect of the presence of people on each of the 16 mammals used in the study.

Students were most knowledgeable of the cottontail rabbit and least knowledgeable of the opossum, based on total scores for each mammal (Table 1). Even though the majority of students could identify all but one (the opossum) of the 16 mammals illustrated, they demonstrated a progressively greater level of difficulty in answering the four natural history questions on each (Table 1). This may be attributed to a progressive sophistication of knowledge required by each question. These data suggest that urban high school students were most uninformed on the eating habits of eight mammals and the effect of urbanization on the abundance of 12 of the 16 mammals. Students appeared to be especially unaware of the positive influence of alternative food and shelter provided through urbanization on the numbers of mice, raccoons, skunks, bats, squirrels, and opossums, thus identifying needed public educational programming on the ecological relationships of urbanization and species abundance.

Student Misinformation on Wildlife

Name.—The majority of students incorrectly identified the opossum as a rat (60%); a mouse (5%); or a mink, bat, pocket gopher, beaver, or bobcat (<1%). Even though the pocket gopher was correctly identified by 61% of the students it also received an array of incorrect names ranging from opossum (22%); beaver (5%); rat or mink (4%); bat (2%); armadillo or mouse (1%); or cougar, skunk, rabbit or bobcat (<1%). The fox was correctly identified by 76% of the students but others incorrectly called it a wolf (22%); mink or bobcat (1%); or armadillo, cougar, deer, bat, squirrel, or beaver (<1%).

Weight.—The majority of students incorrectly estimated the weight of the pocket gopher as > 1 but < 25 pounds (69%), rather than < 1 pound (10%); bobcat and fox as > 25 but < 50 pounds (47%), rather than > 1 but < 25 pounds (13% and 17% respectively); and the beaver as > 1 but < 25 pounds (72%), rather than > 25 but < 50 pounds (21%).

Table 1. Urban high school students' knowledge of 16 mammals, Harris County, Texas, 1985.[a]

Name	%	Weight	%	Number	%	Eat	%	Effect	%	Sum Score	
Squirrel	99	Buffalo	97	Squirrel	84	Rabbit	89	Deer	73	Rabbit	407
Rabbit	99	Cougar	88	Mouse	83	Bobcat	84	Buffalo	63	Deer	380
Deer	99	Deer	87	Rabbit	81	Cougar	81	Rabbit	50	Buffalo	356
Raccoon	99	Rabbit	87	Armadillo	67	Fox	75	Fox	50	Cougar	346
Bat	97	Skunk	83	Fox	61	Squirrel	70			Squirrel	338
Buffalo	97	Mink	80	Deer	60	Deer	62	Cougar	47	Mouse	319
Armadillo	96	Armadillo	77	Skunk	59	Raccoon	60	Gopher	47		
Bobcat	96	Mouse	76	Opossum	57	Bat	53	Armadillo	46	Armadillo	298
Skunk	96	Raccoon	76	Beaver	56			Beaver	44	Bobcat	286
Cougar	95	Squirrel	74	Gopher	55	Buffalo	46	Bobcat	42	Fox	279
Mouse	90	Bat	55	Buffalo	53	Beaver	43	Mouse	41	Raccoon	274
Mink	88	Opossum	52	Bobcat	51	Gopher	42	Mink	30	Mink	256
Beaver	85					Opossum	40	Opossum	25	Bat	254
Fox	76	Beaver	21	Mink	41	Mouse	29	Squirrel	11	Skunk	252
Gopher	61	Fox	17	Bat	38	Mink	17	Bat	11	Beaver	249
		Bobcat	13	Raccoon	37	Armadillo	12	Skunk	7	Gopher	215
Opossum	34	Gopher	10	Cougar	35	Skunk	7	Raccoon	2	Opossum	208

[a]Knowledge determined by percent correct scores on each mammal's name, weight, present numbers, eating habits, and the effect of the presence of people on its abundance, and by the sum score for each mammal. ($N = 490$ students).

Number Within County.—Many students felt incorrectly that the mink was extinct (28%), abundant (7%), or never existed (25%), rather than rare (40%) in Harris County, Texas. The bat was wrongly considered extinct (10%), rare (48%), or never existed (4%), rather than abundant (38%). The raccoon was incorrectly designated extinct (4%), rare (56%), or never existed (2%), rather than abundant (38%). Cougar numbers were wrongly considered rare (37%), abundant (6%), or never existed (22%), rather than extinct (35%) in Harris County.

Primary Eating Habits.—Urban high school students were uninformed on the eating habits of eight of the 16 mammals used in the study (Table 1). The buffalo, pocket gopher, beaver, and mouse should have been identified as herbivores. Comparatively, between 7% and 23% of the students incorrectly identified the primary eating habits of these mammals as carnivores, 27% to 34% said they were omnivores, and 4% to 28% said these mammals were saprobes. The opossum was identified correctly as an omnivore by less than half (40%) of the students tested and incorrectly as a saprobe (29%), herbivore (18%), or carnivore (13%). The primary eating habits, i.e., meat only (including insects), of the skunk, mink, and armadillo were correctly identified by an extremely small percentage of students. Many students incorrectly identified the skunk as an herbivore (43%), omnivore (34%), or saprobe (16%); the armadillo as an herbivore (42%), omnivore (30%), or saprobe (16%); and the mink as an omnivore (45%), herbivore (26%), or saprobe (11%).

Effect of Urbanization.—Urban students also were uninformed on the effects of people on the relative numbers of 12 of the 16 mammals used in the study (Table 1). Over half (53%) did not know that, as a result of the presence of people, the cougar is presently extinct in Harris County, Texas. Conversely, between 59% and 98% of the students did not know that urbanization promotes an increase of house mice, opossums, squirrels, bats, skunks, and raccoons due to the provision of alternative food and/or shelter resources (Flyger 1974, Chamberlain et al. 1982, Flyger et al. 1983). Between 53% and 69% of the urban students tested were unaware of the relationships among urbanization, loss of habitat, and resultant decreases in the numbers of the pocket gopher, armadillo, beaver, bobcat, and mink. Rather, 4% to 41% of the students felt that these mammals were now extinct in Harris County, Texas.

DISCUSSION AND IMPLICATIONS

Kellert (1985) reported that the general public possesses a limited knowledge of animals. The results of our study agree with Kellert's findings. Further, our results discourage false assumptions of an enlightened public concerning wildlife and we hope they will provide important guidance in wildlife education program development. The majority of urban high school students surveyed in this study seemed to lack an ecological view of wildlife. Over 80% of the students tested lived in a suburb or a major city most of their lives. Their minimal ability to identify the eating habits of eight of the 16 mammals and the effect of the presence of people on the relative abundance of 12 of the 16 mammals may reflect a lack of contact with wildlife given their lifetime residency in an urbanized environment and related life style. It is probably quite difficult for these students to understand the basic ecological principles of food chains and interrelationships without prior knowledge of the eating habits of common representatives of herbivores, carnivores, and omnivores, and knowledge of the effect of urbanization on wildlife habitat. Clearly, future wildlife education program development for the urban resident should emphasize the basic ecological principles of cycles, interrelationships, and diversity exemplified with human-wildlife interactions, and include wildlife-related activities using species common to the urban environment.

REFERENCES CITED

Byford, J. L., and S. Munsey. 1984. Attitudes on wildlife and knowledge retained by 4-H alumni. Trans. North Am. Wildl. and Nat. Resour. Conf. 49:410–420.

Chamberlain, P. A., M. Caroline, and W. A. Wright. 1982. Urban vertebrate pest management: a practical approach. Pages 78–96 *in* R. M. Timm and R. J. Johnson, eds. Proceedings fifth great plains wildlife damage control workshop. Inst. Agric. and Nat. Resour., Univ. Nebraska, Lincoln.

Clements, J. 1984. Flying the colors: Texas. Clements Research Inc., Dallas.

Davis, W. B. 1978. The mammals of Texas. Texas Parks and Wildl. Dep. Bull. 41. 294pp.

Flyger, V. 1974. Tree squirrels in urbanizing environments. Pages 121–130 *in* J. H. Noyes and D. R. Progulske, eds. Wildlife in an urbanizing environment. Coop. Extension Serv. Univ. Massachusetts, Amherst.

———, D. L. Leedy, and T. M. Franklin. 1983. Wildlife damage control in eastern cities and suburbs. Pages 27–32 *in* D. J. Decker, ed. Proceedings of the first eastern wildlife damage control conference. Coop. Extension Serv. Cornell Univ., Ithaca, N.Y.

Gore, H. G., and J. M. Reagan. 1985. White-tailed deer population trends. Texas Parks and Wildl. Dep. Pittman-Robertson Fed. Aid Proj. W-109-R-8, Job Perform. Rpt. 1. 81pp.

Kellert, S. R. 1980. American attitudes and knowledge of animals. Trans. North Am. Wildl. and Nat. Resour. Conf. 45:533–546.

———. 1985. Attitudes toward animals: age-related development among children. J. Environ. Ed. 16:29–39.

———, and J. B. Berry. 1980. Knowledge, affection and basic attitudes toward animals in American society. Publ. No. 024-010 00-625-1, U.S. Government Printing Office, Washington, D.C. 162pp.

LaHart, D. E. 1981. The influence of knowledge on young people's perceptions about wildlife. Proc. Annu. Conf. Southeast. Assoc. Fish and Wildl. Agencies 35:661–668.

Taylor, S. E., and D. E. Samuel. 1975. Wildlife knowledge and attitudes of public school teachers. Proc. Annu. Conf. Southeast. Assoc. Fish and Wildl. Agencies 29:759–765.

U.S. Fish and Wildl. Serv. 1979. Unique wildlife ecosystems of Texas. Region 2. Albuquerque, NM: Dep. of the Interior. 164pp.

Westervelt, M. O., and L. G. Llewellyn. 1985. Youth and wildlife. Publ. No. 498-443-42425, U.S. Government Printing Office, Washington, D.C. 76pp.

Landscape Architecture and Wildlife Habitat Design

Chairman: Jon Rodiek, *Chairman, Department of Park Administration and Landscape Architecture, Texas Tech University, Lubbock*

A General Approach to Landscape Design for Wildlife Habitat

John T. Lyle, *California State Polytechnic University, Pomona, 3801 West Temple Avenue, Pomona, CA 91768*

In recent years, a great deal of effort has gone into establishing a global system of wildlife reserves. The generally accepted goal is to maintain representative samples of the world's major plant and animal communities in a protective status. The work of the biosphere reserves program carried on by Unesco's Man and the Biosphere Project 8 and the Commission on National Parks and Protected Areas of the International Union for Conservation of Nature and Natural Resources (IUCN) are important initiatives in this direction.

Although this is an extremely important effort, indeed one that is essential for maintaining the global gene pool, it is beset by a number of conceptual difficulties. One of these is simply the problem of grouping the world's plant and animal communities. Nature has few sharp dividing lines and any system of grouping is necessarily arbitrary to some degree. There are any number of ways of categorizing biotic communities, but the lines we draw between them are necessarily somewhat fuzzy. The finer the distinctions we make, the larger the number of categories we end up with and the less likely it is that enough reserves can be established to include every community. Conversely, if larger groupings are used, then any number of species that exist on the peripheries of communities are likely to be left out.

And, even if the groupings are large, and the resulting number of communities therefore relatively few, the likelihood of establishing enough permanent reserves in the near future is not great. Even using very coarse categories, such as "tropical humid forests" and "temperate grasslands," IUCN (1980) identified 14 major ecosystem types in the world for which there are either no reserves or inadequate reserves.

Furthermore, even if a full range of reserves can be achieved, they will still include relatively limited areas of land, which will limit the opportunities for speciation to occur. Although the implications of this are little understood, it seems undesirable to limit the diversity of environments in which a community or species occurs and thereby to limit the likelihood of the chance mutation that brings evolutionary change.

For these and other reasons, then, we cannot rely entirely on any system of reserves to maintain the integrity of the global gene pool. Rather, providing suitable conditions for plant and animal communities is a goal for every landscape everywhere, including urban, suburban, and rural landscapes, and a goal that should be seriously pursued at every level of environmental planning and design. Ideally, every regional plan, urban general plan, and design for a city park or a backyard should include specific provisions for wildlife habitat. To date, this has not been commonly done, except in some instances involving rare or endangered species. If planners and designers are to respond to this challenge, we need to establish some approaches and a broad, useful conceptual basis for planning and design for wildlife. The rest of this paper will present a tentative operational system toward that end.

BASIC NEEDS OF WILDLIFE

The two general goals of wildlife management are usually summed up as species richness and featured species enhancement (Leopold 1933). The former involves general management practices, whereas the latter requires specifically focused practices. It is important to keep in mind that these two goals can conflict. By designing for diversity, we might eliminate a particular species, and by designing for

Integrating Man and Nature in the Metropolitan Environment. Proc. Natl. Symp. on Urban Wildl., Chevy Chase, Md., 4–7 November 1986, L.W. Adams and D.L. Leedy, eds. Published by Natl. Inst. for Urban Wildl., 10921 Trotting Ridge Way, Columbia, MD 21044, 1987.

one species, we can limit diversity. Although some situations, especially those involving rare or endangered species, which are protected by federal law, require that we design for featured species, it is much more common and generally more desirable to design for species richness. That is, the most important goal usually is to preserve or enhance, or to establish the integrity of the biotic community. In planning terms, we do this by preserving, enhancing, or establishing suitable habitats, and the first step toward accomplishing that is by providing for basic needs of wildlife. These needs include food, cover, water, and territory, and the requirements of each species are at least slightly different from those of any other. Because the requirements for food and cover are provided primarily by plants, control over wildlife populations is exerted largely through control of vegetation, that is, by what species are planted and in what form. In arid and semiarid cities, wildlife diversity is almost directly proportional to the amount of water available. In other areas, water is less critical but still important. Planning for wildlife, therefore, goes hand in hand with planning the water regime.

Of the major wildlife needs, the requirement for territorial space is the least understood. We know that many animals need territories to call their own, and that the need generally has to do with mating and hunting. As a result of the apparent rigidity of territorial requirements and the variable amounts of space available in cities, the more territorial species, particularly larger species, seem to be at a distinct disadvantage in environments dominated by human beings. When more is known about territorial behavior, it may turn out to be the most limiting of urban wildlife requirements. No matter how many ways we find to increase supplies of food, cover, and water, space will always be at a premium.

HABITAT TYPES

A habitat is a place where the full range of the requirements of a particular species is provided. For landscape planning purposes, we can distinguish six fundamentally different habitat types, all differing in size, form, population potentials, and management practice. These are wild areas, wild patches, wild enclaves, corridors, exotic greens, and wildlife parks. Although the first type probably plays the key role in preserving the global ecosystem structure, the other types play important roles as well. The last four commonly occur in urban areas, and they present particular challenges for wildlife management. In general, the smaller the area, the more intensive the management needed.

Wild Areas

Wild areas are stretches of land not radically altered by human use and large enough to provide a habitat for the full range of species native to that location. In the United States, such areas are usually public lands, including national parks and forests, and lands administered by the Bureau of Land Management. Considering their size and importance, wild areas are usually planned at the subcontinental or global scale.

Management practices in natural areas are primarily directed to keeping human uses under control, usually by restricting the numbers of users, areas of use, and types of use. Areas that are logged and mined are regulated to keep the impacts of those activities on wildlife to a mimimum. In the United States, wilderness areas and wildlife refuges, along with several other categories, are special types of wild areas in which human use is even further restricted in order to maintain the areas' primordial features.

How large should a wild area be? If they are to serve as habitats for the full range of wildlife species, including the top carnivores, quite large areas of land would seem to be implied. Minimum sizes probably vary according to the range needed for the top carnivore in each particular habitat. Sullivan and Shaffer (1975) estimated that the minimum size for the usual full-range wildlife reserve should be between 600 and 700 square kilometers (about 150,000 to 175,000 acres). This is based on providing enough space for at least a few individuals of the top carnivore species. Estimates indicate that each grizzly bear needs about 75 (18,500 acres), each wolf about 60, and each mountain lion about 95 square kilometers. The needs.of other top predators are probably within the same range. Because eight, or even 12, individuals is a very small number, however, and probably not enough to maintain a population indefinitely, this has to be considered a very risky minimum. IUCN (1980) recommended a minimum area of 1,000 square kilometers (about 250,000 acres). In practice, few wild areas, especially in the densely settled European countries, are this large.

Given the state of the world's development, virtually all wildlife habitats, even wild areas in this size range, are surrounded by human activity; they are all islands. Wild areas, however, are more like continents in that they appear to be boundless, at least from within. In the sense that the number of species they can support is not limited by their extent, moreover, they are indeed boundless. The other types of habitat, being seriously limited by their extent, are clearly islands.

This island character is important in considering the wildlife population potential of any landscape. MacArthur and Wilson's (1967) theory of island biogeography provides some guidance. These authors showed that an island develops a community over time that includes a more or less constant number of species. Some species die out, while others migrate in, the number of extinctions equaling the number of immigrations. The rate of extinction correlates with island size; the smaller the island, the larger the number of extinctions per unit area. The immigration rate correlates with the distance to the origins of the migrating species; the closer the island is to other islands, the more new species are likely to arrive. Thus, although there are exceptions, the larger the island, the larger the number of species it is likely to support.

Wild Patches

Wild patches are large enough to be self-maintaining systems with working feedback loops to control their populations as ecologically complete as any area can be without top predators. Usually, they are set aside because of environmental characteristics particularly attractive to wildlife. Usually, they require considerably more intensive management than do wild areas.

Among the best known and most dramatic wild patches in the United States is Jamaica Bay, a 19,200-acre (7,776-ha) marsh less than 10 miles (16.1 km), as the egret flies, from Times Square, New York. Wild patches are usually managed for high levels of species diversity and for large populations. The intensity of management varies, and Jamaica Bay is one of the more intensively managed. Herbert Johnson, who was its superintendent from the time it was named a wildlife refuge in 1953 until the early 1970s, made it a model of the use of urban resources to benefit nonhuman populations. A few examples of his inventive responses to urban change help to illustrate the richness of design possibilities. In the early 1950s, the old railroad trestle over the bay burned, and the Transit Authority proposed to build in its place a new embankment on which to run an extension of the subway. The Parks Department agreed, on the condition that, while dredging, they would build two circular dikes that would be filled with fresh water, thereby creating a new type of environment and considerably expanding the number of species attracted to the area. Once the dikes were in place, they were stabilized with plantings of marshgrasses and other plant species favored by the birds. At the same time, sewage sludge was pumped into the lagoon to cover an island called Canarsie Pol. Marshgrasses quickly invaded this rich new land and made an ideal nesting environment for shorebirds.

Over the years, Johnson planted a variety of trees and shrubs that were particularly favored by certain bird species. Among those planted were the autumn olive, Russian olive, chokeberry, holly, and Japanese black pine. There was no intention to provide a purely native landscape. Rather, it is one designed specifically to accommodate the greatest possible number of bird species. The results are spectacular. Over three hundred bird species are seen in the bay in a typical year, far more than would have appeared there in its natural state.

Wild patches this close to urban areas usually lead precarious lives. In the late 1960s, Kennedy Airport, which lies adjacent to Jamaica Bay, proposed to expand its runways in a manner that would have seriously reduced wildlife populations. After a public furor and an exhaustive impact analysis by an interdisciplinary group, the plan was abandoned. In 1972, Jamaica Bay became part of the newly created Gateway National Recreational Area and thus was gathered under the wing of the National Park Service. Since then, the number of urban wilds under Park Service control has grown considerably, and the results have been promising. Nevertheless, urbanization continues to make encroachments. It now appears that the entire edge of the bay will become a ring of subsidized housing within a few years. The vitality of the refuge will probably depend on the design of this critical edge.

Wild Enclaves

Wild enclaves are smaller than patches, not large enough to be self-sustaining systems but still able to support significant wildlife populations and important for that reason. Sometimes rich habitats manage to survive all the threats and encroachments of surrounding human use and become small spots of wildlife diversity in the midst of cities or farms. Almost invariably, these areas have some exceptional feature that makes them especially attractive to animals, and more often than not, that feature is water. Ponds, streams, marshes, even drainage ditches, usually support rich populations. Among the richest are marsh enclaves, which are invariably alive with waterfowl and other species that thrive around water. Too often, they are continually threatened with obliteration.

In Southern California, the 11-acre (4.5-ha) Madrona Marsh is such an area. This freshwater marsh, which is surrounded by intensive urbanization, supports a rich population of microscopic and macroscopic plants and invertebrates, amphibians and reptiles, and, in particular abundance, migratory waterfowl and resident birds. The small size and the character of the surrounding uses required a complex design process and will require an equally complex management process (Earle 1975).

Systems that identify critical zones provide a strong basis for resolving conflicts and for future control. Considering the precarious existence of most enclaves in the midst of high land prices and urban exigencies, strong conflicting purposes, and volatile emotions, processes of this kind are much needed.

Most enclaves have survived as a result of historical accidents, and we can expect that sooner or later pressures for "higher and better uses" will be brought to bear. The Madrona Marsh continues to exist as an inadvertent byproduct of oil extraction. Some enclaves are the remains of man-shaped environments that have been reclaimed by natural succession.

In regions whose natural vegetation is dense forest, we sometimes find small stands of native woodland surviving in the cities. Though too small to support complete communities of animals, these often feature heavy concentrations of small birds and mammals. A venerable example of this sort of enclave is Wimbledon Common in a suburban area near London, England, which has become a unique kind of urban open space. According to landscape architect Ian Laurie (1979), the cost of maintaining Wimbledon

Common is far less than the cost of maintaining highly developed London parks.

Wild Corridors

In general, the longer the available route of movement in an area, the greater will be the diversity of wildlife. In a large natural area, the number of routes can be almost infinite. But between smaller ones that are not too far apart, and certainly between patches and enclaves, corridors of natural landscape can expand the possibilities of movement in relatively little space. Interconnection by corridors provides an increased array of possibilities for wildlife movement and habitat choice, and is particularly useful for expanding the potentials of the smallest areas and reducing the island effect. Corridor systems are best considered at the regional level.

Urban and rural landscapes are characteristically laced with networks of various kinds, some of which can be fairly easily adapted to attract wildlife. Waterflow networks are perhaps the best, because they provide not only water but the abundant vegetation that usually goes along with it. If the edges of streams, gullies, washes, floodplains, and even flood control channels can be kept open and unimpeded, they can serve as a network of corridors interweaving the wilds with the man-made landscape.

Among the man-made corridors are various types of rights-of-way, including railroads (especially abandoned ones) and powerlines. With some care in design, these can be made to attract animals. Mostly, it is a matter of opening up movement routes that will be beneficial to wildlife and closing those that are likely to bring animals into conflict with human activity. For example, along abandoned railroad rights-of-way, the California Department of Fish and Game recommends using one side for bicycling and hiking and reserving the other side for wild animals.

Wild corridors are especially desirable in areas where it is important to provide habitats for large predators because of human alterations of the natural landscape. In Costa Rica, for example, government policy calls for the creation of new farming settlements in which small tracts of arable land, usually about 20 acres (8 ha), are made available to landless families. As there are few alternatives, these settlements are often carved out of the rain forest. Because of the national concern for their preservation, some undisturbed forest is usually left within the bounds of each settlement. The size of most of these forest remnants ranges from that of enclaves to that of patches—far short of the territory needed by the top predators. The magnificent, elusive jaguar is especially threatened. Little is known about its habits or the extent of its range, except that the latter is immense, probably covering hundreds of square kilometers.

The best solution would probably be to maintain a continuous matrix of rain forest, with the settlements as islands within, rather than the reverse, but this approach would be expensive and would tend to spread settlements far apart, resulting in communication and transportation difficulties. It would also require more land, thus driving settlement deeper into natural areas.

Another possibility would be to group the preserves in larger units spaced closer together. Island theory tells us that these would be far richer habitats, even if they cover no more land than scattered ones.

Finally, if we connect the preserves with corridors, they would be richer still. The corridors might follow streams and rivers and would have to be wide enough to keep animals like the jaguar well away from human settlements. Although they would not effectively replace the larger natural areas of rain forest, they would at lease provide a minimally complete structure in the midst of human activity.

Exotic Greens

Far removed from rain forests and jaguars, exotic greens are man-made landscapes, usually in cities, that are not designed or managed with wildlife as a major concern but nevertheless feature surprisingly large animal populations. It is important to remember that urban landscapes shaped and maintained for specific human uses are far from being in a natural state. Among them are school grounds, urban parks, cemeteries, college campuses, and areas of residential developments, even back and front yards. Usually, they feature exotic species of vegetation that are chosen more for visual effect than for the benefit of wildlife or other ecological reasons. Extensive areas of lawn are common, usually punctuated with a few stands of trees. Often, these places are teeming with wildlife, but diversity is normally limited to a few species of small birds and mammals because the structures of these areas are usually simple and incomplete.

The vegetation of an exotic green is designed to serve the particular functions and image of that place, and these are necessarily different from those of other greens. Thus, each attracts a wildlife population related to its own unique community of plants. One study found, for example, that a reason for the high squirrel population in a cemetery was the area's particular variety of plants, which produced foods at different times throughout the year, assuring a continuous food supply. The closed hours of the cemetery—5 p.m. to 8 a.m.—also seemed to benefit the squirrels, because they had the landscape to themselves during this period. On the other hand, two factors presented greater dangers than the squirrels would find in the wilds. One was automobile traffic, which, although light and slow-moving, killed a large number of squirrels, and the other was disease, which seemed to spread faster than in the wilds. Predation probably took a toll about equal to that in the wilds, because a few red foxes also lived in the cemetery.

In the eastern United States, the red fox is one of the few predators able to adapt to the environment of the exotic green. Foxes have been seen quite frequently in the larger urban parks of most eastern cities where they comprise one of the larger predators.

Exotic greens are the most intensively managed (for human, not wildlife purposes) and heavily used of urban habitats. Consequently, they usually attract the more sociable species, those most tolerant of the human presence.

Wildlife Parks

The examples of this category of wilds are relatively few and highly specialized. They are areas of some size that are specifically designed and managed to accommodate specific exotic wildlife populations. The zoological garden is the most extreme example, although zoos are usually so artificial as to deserve a category of their own. Somewhat less artificial are the several types of wild animal parks where varied species of animals are brought together and allowed to roam freely in a setting that provides them some space and privacy, although it might be quite different in its physiography and vegetation from their native environment. Such parks have been fairly common on royal estates for centuries. A number of estates in England, most notably Woburn Abbey, maintain them. In the United States, wildlife parks usually have a public orientation, functioning essentially as theme parks. Wild Animal Park, near the City of San Diego, is perhaps the best known example.

USEFULNESS OF THE APPROACH

Categorizing habitat areas as outlined in this paper is useful for a number of purposes. It provides a coherent means of dealing with wildlife concerns at each scale of planning. Whereas wild areas are considered components of national or global systems, exotic greens should normally be incorporated into plans at the project or the site level. The types of concerns addressed at each scale, as well as the planning, design, and management practices applied, are quite different.

It should be recognized that this is a tentative operational system, still rough about the edges. Although it has been applied in some planning efforts, it has not yet been polished into a universally applicable planning tool. It will take more applications in practice, as well as more research, to accomplish that. As a working hypothesis, its greatest utility might be as a common frame of reference for research and planning and design, a place where different disciplines can meet.

REFERENCES CITED

Earle, E. 1975. The conservation of natural areas in the context of urban development. M.L.A. Thesis, Calif. State Polytech. Univ., Pomona.

IUCN. 1980. World conservation strategy: living resource conservation for sustainable development. Int. Union for Conserv. of Nat. and Nat. Resour., Avenue du Mont-Blanc, CH-1196 Gland, Switzerland.

Laurie, I. 1979. Urban commons. Pages 231–266 *in* I. Laurie, ed. Nature in cities. John Wiley and Sons, New York.

Leopold, A. 1933. Game management. Charles Scribner's Sons, New York. 481 pp.

MacArthur, R. H. and E. O. Wilson. 1967. The theory of island biogeography. Princeton Univ. Press, Princeton.

Sullivan, A. L. and M. L. Shaffer. 1975. Biogeography of the megazoo. Science 189.

Designing for Urban Wildlife: Results of a 1986 Survey of the Landscape Architecture Profession in Canada

KATHERINE DUNSTER, *Graduate Programme, School of Landscape Architecture, University of Guelph, Guelph, Ontario, Canada N1G 2W1*

INTRODUCTION

This paper summarizes the results of a nationwide survey carried out in 1986. Primary objectives of the survey were to determine: (1) the extent to which the requirements of urban wildlife are considered by Canadian landscape architects in their urban landscape design work, the obstacles they face in undertaking this design work, and the types of information they would use to improve their landscape designs for urban wildlife; (2) how Canadian landscape architects obtained their information about urban wildlife, where they used this information in the design process, and in what types of environments were landscape design projects for urban wildlife being implemented; and (3) the extent to which wildlife management techniques were being used to implement urban wildlife landscape designs. A more comprehensive report is in preparation (Dunster 1986a) that discusses survey results and implications in greater detail.

METHODS

In July 1986, a survey questionnaire was mailed to all 1,105 individual names appearing on the mailing list of the Canadian Society of Landscape Architects (CSLA). The questionnaire mailed was a revised version of an earlier pretest. A covering letter accompanying the questionnaire provided definitions of urban landscape, urban wildlife, herptiles, design, and wildlife requirements to help respondents interpret survey questions.

All respondents were asked to complete Part 1 of the questionnaire regarding personal data, education, and professional qualifications. Confidentiality of this information was assured.

Respondents answering "never" to the question, "Do you consider the requirements of wildlife in your urban landscape design projects?," were directed to several questions that solicited information regarding the obstacles they face in designing for urban wildlife, and the type of information base they would use to begin considering urban wildlife in design. All other respondents were directed to answer all of the questions in the survey.

Several questions were used to elicit information from respondents about urban wildlife design projects. Respondents were asked to describe and list their own projects in one question. Another question asked them to describe and list urban wildlife projects that had been designed by other landscape architects. A final query asked respondents to list any publications they had authored on the subject of urban wildlife landscape design.

Results were tabulated using the SAS Version 5.0 computer statistics package (SAS Institute Inc. 1985).

RESULTS

Of the 1,105 questionnaires mailed, 262 (23.7%) were returned completed and 40 (3.6%) were undeliverable. Returned questionnaires were determined to be usable if the respondent was a member of a provincial landscape architecture association, and, thus, automatically a member of the CSLA (Fig. 1).

Eleven (1%) respondents indicated that they were not involved in urban landscape design, most being employed by national or provincial parks, and 14 (1.3%) of the completed returns could not be used because the respondents were not members of a provincial landscape architecture association.

The 237 usable returns were classified into two categories. Forty (16.9%) individuals reported that they never considered the requirements of wildlife in their urban landscape design projects, and, thus, completed the short form of the questionnaire. The remaining 197 (83.1%) respondents completed the entire form.

Integrating Man and Nature in the Metropolitan Environment. Proc. Natl. Symp. on Urban Wildl., Chevy Chase, Md., 4–7 November 1986, L.W. Adams and D.L. Leedy, eds. Published by Natl. Inst. for Urban Wildl., 10921 Trotting Ridge Way, Columbia, MD 21044, 1987.

Fig. 1. Location of Provincial Landscape Architecture Associations.

Male respondents (75.1%) outnumbered females (24.1%) and several respondents (0.8%) did not state their sex. Nearly all (96.2%) of the respondents were actively practicing landscape architecture (1.7% were students, 1.7% were retired, and 0.4% did not respond), and 75.1% were under the age of 40. Length of practice ranged from 0 to 50 years. Most of the respondents (69.2%) indicated they had been practicing landscape architecture less than 10 years.

Respondents indicated they had taken a wide variety of education programs, the most popular (43.9%) being a Bachelor of Landscape Architecture. Only 1.3% indicated that they had not received formal landscape architecture training.

Most respondents (58.3%) indicated they considered the requirements of wildlife in less than 25% of their urban design projects. Included in this group were the 40 landscape architects who said they never considered the requirements of wildlife in urban design. At the other end of the scale was a group of 32 (13.5%) individuals who said they considered the requirements of wildlife in 76–100% of their urban design projects.

More respondents (94.4%) indicated they had designed urban landscapes to encourage birds than to encourage mammals (49.7%), fish (46.2%), invertebrates (41.1%), or herptiles (18.3%). Fewer respondents indicated they had designed landscapes to discourage wildlife, with mammals receiving the greatest response (16.2%), followed by herptiles (12.2%), birds (6.1%), invertebrates (5.1%), and fish (3.0%).

Information about urban wildlife requirements was obtained from a wide variey of sources. Approximately one third of the respondents could not rank their sources in order of importance and gave them equal ranking. Three (1.5%) did not respond to the question. The remaining 125 (63.5%) landscape architects indicated that books, literature, and library sources were their most important sources of information (42.4%), but data collected from previous work/projects (16%), and experts on staff (16%) also were considered important.

Experts on staff included biologists, limnologists, foresters, and ecologists. Thirty-four respondents specified that they used "other" sources of information, of which only 4 (3.2%) indicated they would rely on their "other" source as their first source of information. Seventeen (50%) of these "other" sources were personal observation and the remainder were friends, local field naturalists, and Ducks Unlimited.

Urban wildlife information was readily available to 42.6% of the respondents whereas 46.7% indicated that the information was only readily available sometimes. Only 10.2% of the respondents indicated they had difficulty interpreting available urban wildlife information, although 45.2% said they sometimes had difficulty. A similar number (41.6%) indicated that they never had difficulty in interpreting the information and 3.0% did not respond to the question.

Urban wildlife information is being used by the respondents in several stages of the design process (Table 1), particularly planting design (84.3%), inventory and analysis (71.7%), and design concept (66.5%). Less than half of the respondents (44.2%) indicated they used the information at the beginning of the design process (terms of reference/client interview) and only 32.5% indicated they used the information as they implemented their designs. Even fewer (24.4%) indicated they used the information in the monitoring and review of projects. Most respondents (78.9%) felt that a sourcebook of information including lists of experts, consultants, literature, or nurseries would be most useful to either improve or consider urban wildlife in their designs (Dunster 1986b).

Slightly more than half (56.3%) of the respondents said suitable food and cover material was available for their planting design specifications. Several (5.1%) did not respond to the question, and 38.6% felt suitable material was not available.

Table 1. Use of wildlife information in the design process for landscape architecture projects.[a]

Stage of design	Percent of respondents
Terms of reference/client interview	44.2
Program	52.3
Inventory & analysis	71.7
Concept	66.5
Master plan	44.7
Planting design	84.3
Implementation	32.5
Monitoring & review of project	24.4
Other	1.5

[a]N = 197.

Designs for wildlife have been undertaken in a wide variety of urban environments (Table 2). Most respondents reported they had designed for wildlife in urban parks or other open spaces (74.6%) and single housing-residential backyards (60.9%). All other categories received less than 30% responses. Other institutional areas specified were cemeteries, nature education centers, arboreta, historical areas, and urban interpretive trails. Other urban design work specified included municipal policy and official plan reports, gravel pit reclamation, stream-river-ravine rehabilitation projects, waterfronts, landfill sites, and landscape management plans.

Table 2. Urban areas where design for wildlife has been undertaken.[a]

Area	Percent of respondents
Single housing/residential backyard	60.9
Multiple housing/apartment open space	29.9
Neighborhood plan	23.4
Urban parks, open spaces	74.6
Institutional: schools	17.3
Institutional: hospitals	12.2
Institutional: universities	11.7
Institutional: zoos	6.1
Institutional: botanical gardens	13.2
Institutional: other	9.6
Industrial	15.7
Central business district	7.1
Streetscapes	16.2
Rights-of-way	16.8
Transportation corridor planning	19.8
Other	12.7

[a]N = 197.

Less than 30% of the respondents used wildlife management techniques to carry out their designs. Most popular techniques used were winter feeding regimes or programs (26.4%), and "pest" species managment control (25.9%). Nesting houses had been erected by 21.3% of the respondents. Brush piles for cover had been constructed by more respondents (16.2%) than rock piles (12.2%). Other artificial methods specified were planting regimes and earthworks to improve aquatic habitat. New species introductions such as fish stocking had been used by 19.3% of the respondents and only 15.3% indicated they had attempted species removal or relocation. Other management techniques employed included the creation, enhancement, protection, and conservation of habitat; control of humans, dogs, and bears; and removal of food sources for airport-dwelling birds. Most respondents (68.0%) felt that project time and budget constraints did not give them enough time to research and consider urban wildlife needs.

All respondents were asked to indicate how often they used native (or indigenous) plant material in their urban planting designs. Thirty percent said they used native plant materials 76–100% of the time, and many individuals specified they were inhibited in doing so by the lack of readily available native plant materials.

Respondents were asked to identify the obstacles that inhibited their urban wildlife design. Fifty-four respondents could not rank their obstacles in order of importance and gave them equal ranking. Thirteen did not answer the question, and of the remaining 170 respondents, 41.8% felt their greatest obstacle was no client demand or interest (Table 3). A wide variety of other obstacles were specified including lack of public awareness, lack of suitable plant stock, lack of support from senior landscape architects or employers, and public resistance to the existence of wildlife in cities.

Table 3. Obstacles to designing for urban wildlife in order of importance.[a]

Obstacle	Relative importance %
No client demand or interest	41.8
No client support (financial)	12.9
No obstacles	12.3
Other	11.8
Personal lack of knowledge	11.2
Bureaucratic obstacles	4.1
Difficulty understanding/using information	3.5
Difficulty finding data/information on wildlife	2.4
Total	100.0

[a]N = 170.

Less than a quarter of the respondents (20.3%) indicated that there were government policies, regulations, by-laws, or other bureaucratic requirements that constrained their ability to consider wildlife in urban designs. Slightly more (22.4%) felt there were none, 5.5% did not respond, and 51.9% did not know. The most frequently listed government constraints were weed control acts or by-laws (22 respondents), property design-maintenance standards (15 respondents), and government apathy or lack of vision (8 respondents). Other government constraints mentioned were public health standards (3 respondents), public liability (3 respondents), pesticide-herbicide regulations (4 respondents), and municipal engineers cause many problems (3 respondents).

CONCLUSIONS

A primary hypothesis of the survey was that very few landscape architects in Canada are aware of a design paradigm shift occurring in the profession in other countries (Baines 1985, Flugel 1986, Rodiek 1986). This new trend in thinking places greater moral responsibility on landscape architects to approach every design project with a much deeper ecological understanding. Not only are the needs of all living beings equally important to consider in this new paradigm, it may be critical to the maintenance of planetary equilibrium and health to understand the relationships and interconnectedness of all species, when modifying environments through design (Lovelock 1979, Myers 1984).

Responses to the questionnaire generally supported the hypothesis. Whether or not it was a part of the client's terms of reference, only 13.5% of the respondents reported that they considered the requirements of urban wildlife in 76–100% of their projects. Over 40% of the respondents felt that a lack of client demand or interest was their greatest obstacle to designing for urban wildlife; more than any of the other obstacles listed. This opinion is not substantiated by a recent survey of the Canadian population (Filion et al. 1983), which reported that 66.8% of Canadians participated in nonconsumptive residential wildlife-related activities. As reported by Filion, some 20.4% of Canadians purchase feed for urban wildlife and 13.4% maintain plants for wildlife in their gardens.

One explanation for this discrepancy may be that landscape architects are just not discussing the importance of considering the needs of urban wildlife with their clients. Only 44.2% reported that they used wildlife information at the first stage in the design process (terms of reference/client interview), perhaps missing the best opportunity to provide the client with information that will promote the positive ecological, social, and economic benefits of urban wildlife, thus gaining client support. An awareness and acceptance of the paradigm shift would allow these landscape architects to consider wildlife, whether or not their client expressed an interest. I should also point out that only 24% of the landscape architects I surveyed responded to the questionnaire. The opinions of the remaining 76% were not known and this fact may have contributed to the discrepancy.

Responses to several of the questions in the survey suggest that although urban wildlife information is available, it may not be in a format that all landscape architects can usefully interpret, use in design, and successfully promote when meeting with clients. Most respondents relied on secondary sources of information (books, literature, library sources) as their first source of information, and 78.9% indicated a sourcebook of urban wildlife information specific to the needs of landscape architects would be very helpful to them. The scientific community has published a considerable volume of information about wildlife requirements, yet few attempts have been made to translate the information into a form that can be assimilated by the landscape architect into the design process. Few respondents reported that they used wildlife management techniques to carry out their designs, which may be a further indication of the need for better information and more inter-disciplinary collaboration between landscape architects, scientists, and wildlife managers.

Design projects for urban wildlife appear to be limited to what landscape architects consider appropriate urban environments for wildlife. Although it is important to continue to design for wildlife in backyards, parks, and open spaces, there are many opportunities to expand these efforts into the design of other urban environments for wildlife. The fact that wildlife exists everywhere in cities in spite of, and because of the actions of man, has important implications for landscape architects entrusted with the privilege of designing our urban landscapes. The recreational role of wildlife in cities outlined by Filion et al. (1983) should provide considerable impetus for landscape architects to consider wildlife in the design and management of all urban landscapes.

Respondents indicated a general lack of awareness about government policies, regulations, by-laws, or requirements that could constrain their ability to consider wildlife in urban designs. This is surprising because 96.2% indicated they were practicing landscape architects, and should therefore, be aware of all the legalities that might affect their design work. Not surprising was the number of respondents who indicated that the "Weed Control Act" was their greatest bureaucratic constraint to designing landscapes for urban wildlife. Whereas many "weeds" are beneficial to wildlife, few can be considered a threat to agriculture in the urban environment.

Many individuals commented that there is a need for more information to be published in periodicals read by landscape architects, especially information about designs that have been implemented. Although a sourcebook is in preparation (Dunster 1986b), all those involved in urban wildlife design should feel a moral and professional obligation to share their information and experiences so that the entire profession will shift more quickly to accepting the new design paradigm.

The positive comments of respondents indicate that the survey has been a useful means of increasing the awareness of Canadian landscape architects about urban wildlife.

Acknowledgments.—I would like to thank my advisor, Denis Stevens for his help in clarifying my ideas and reviewing various drafts of the questionnaire. Thanks are also owed to Bob Dorney and Bob Brown for the encouragement and moral support they have offered. The assistance of the Canadian Society of Landscape Architects in providing their membership list on mailing labels is gratefully acknowledged. I am particularly indebted to Julian Dunster for providing ideas, discussion, and critical reviews of this manuscript.

REFERENCES CITED

Baines, C. 1985. How to make a wildlife garden. Elm Tree Books/ Hamish Hamilton, London.

Dunster, K. 1986a. Designing for urban wildlife: a survey of Canadian landscape architects. In preparation.

Dunster, K. 1986b. A sourcebook of urban wildlife information for Canadian landscape architects. In preparation.

Filion, F.L., et al. 1983. The importance of wildlife to Canadians: highlights of the 1981 national survey. Catalog No. CW66-62/1983E, Canadian Wildl. Serv., Ottawa, Ontario K1A 0H3. 40pp.

Flugel, H-J. 1986. "Fur die Tierwelt Planen." Garten + Landschaft. 5:25–30.

Lovelock, J.E. 1979. GAIA. Oxford Univ. Press, Oxford, England.

Myers, N. ed. 1984. GAIA, an atlas of planet management. Anchor Press/Doubleday, Garden City, New York.

Rodiek, J. 1986. "Wildlife Habitats." Landscape Architecture magazine 76:148.

SAS Institute Inc. 1985. SAS user's guide: statistics. Version 5 edition, SAS Institute Inc, Carey, North Carolina.

Design Criteria for Children and Wildlife in Residential Developments

LISA SCHICKER, *Department of Landscape Architecture, North Carolina State University, Raleigh, NC 27695*[1]

INTRODUCTION

Considerable research on urban ecology and urban wildlife has been carried out during the past 10–15 years. Several books and articles concerning this topic have been published (Schmid 1975, Wilson and Willis 1975, Galli et al. 1976, Leedy et al. 1978, Laurie 1979, Andrews and Cranmer-Bying 1981, Goldstein et al. 1981, Adams and Dove 1984, Hough 1984, Leedy and Adams 1984, Spirn 1984), and several conferences have been held that address wildlife in an urban context (e.g., Noyes and Progulske 1974, Kirkpatrick 1978, Shaw 1986).

Very little, however, has been completed on how *people* relate to wildlife, especially children of urban and suburban areas. By the year 2000, over 90% of all Americans will live in urban areas. Considering that 173 million Americans currently live in urban areas, and that 52 million of these are under 18 years of age (U.S. Department of Commerce 1985), the subject is one that must attract attention. However, relatively little is even known about children's attitudes and behaviors in early stages of life in general, to say nothing of their relation to wildlife.

Perhaps the most thorough and important work concerning children's relationships to wildlife that has been completed was a study sponsored by the U.S. Fish and Wildlife Service (Kellert and Westervelt 1983). In this study, one can find an exhaustive literature review, but as the authors stated, "The focus of most research in this field has not been wildlife, but attitudes toward other environmental issues, such as air and water pollution, overpopulation, recycling and land use." The researchers found that "culture, status, parental occupation and influence, ethnic background, area of residence, scholastic ability, participation in nature activities, books, T.V., family, and friends all can possibly affect children's perceptions of the natural world."

There also is a small amount of literature on the child's use of outdoor environments that was consulted for the present study. Hart (1979, 1983), Lynch (1979), Moore (1978, 1980), Wood (1978) and others (Cohen et al. 1979, Francis 1984, Van Andel 1984) have all reached similar conclusions, which are summarized below.

1. Children play anywhere, and a very small percentage of their time is spent in designed-for-children areas (such as playgrounds). Favorite areas include wildlands, vacant lots, street pavements, and parking areas.
2. Children, especially 5 to 10 year-olds, are the most frequent users of neighborhood space.
3. Most valued feature includes water, sand or dirt, vegetation, loose parts to build with, things to collect, and animal life.
4. Children place great value in being able to find and make places for themselves.
5. Young children play close to home in visible contact with known adults.
6. Active play, like walking, running, and bicycling, is frequently observed.
7. Safety is an important condition of optimal use of an environment.

I have been working with children in an assortment of contexts for the past 8 years as a natural history instructor, exhibit designer at museums and nature centers, and most recently as a National Wildlife Federation Conservation Fellowship recipient. I conducted my research through a series of personal interviews, neighborhood walks, and questionnaires administered to urban and suburban children in Raleigh, North Carolina. Because of my experiences with children, and their parents and teachers, I do not hesitate in saying that access to the richness and diversity of the natural world (including a full range of wildlife) is valuable. It is preferable that exposure to the natural world be at an early age, and, because young children are not very mobile, it is essential that it be within their home range.

[1]Present address: Landscape Architecture Department, California Polytechnic State University, San Luis Obispo, CA 93407.

Integrating Man and Nature in the Metropolitan Environment. Proc. Natl. Symp. on Urban Wildl., Chevy Chase, Md., 4–7 November 1986, L.W. Adams and D.L. Leedy, eds. Published by Natl. Inst. for Urban Wildl., 10921 Trotting Ridge Way, Columbia, MD 21044, 1987.

If it is true that children respond to early exposure to wildlife and wildlands, and if they do not travel far from their homes, then it follows that provisions for wildlife must be made within residential developments. Frequently, landscape architects, architects, planners, and developers involved with the creation of residential subdivisions do not consider needs of children to be important in their designs. A development with only groomed and manicured lawns, culverted streams, few trees, and no wild places to explore may not be as enjoyable an environment as it could be. In what follows, I provide preliminary evidence and support for the concept of including wildlands in residential developments, and I present a few recommendations on how such provisions can be made most effectively.

WHAT I LEARNED FROM 39,000 KIDS

If we are to introduce wildlands into the habitats of children, we must certainly understand the behaviors of children no less well than those of plants and animals. I have, in my teaching lifetime, worked with over 39,000 children. These experiences have created much understanding and awareness of children's behaviors and attitudes toward the natural environment. They are the basis for the recommendations I will be making about the design of residential environments, sharpened and formed, of course, by the more deliberate studies that were conducted for the National Wildlife Federation.

These studies fall into two classes with three groups of children. I administered questionnaires to two groups—196 school children at a Durham elementary school and 51 in a natural history museum course. I also interviewed and took neighborhood walks with 13 children that enabled me to see a little more deeply into the system of behaviors glossed in the questionnaire results. What follows are the results of these studies that pertain to design criteria in residential areas for children and wildlife.

In general, children placed high value on outdoor places for play that allowed for personal investigation and manipulation of materials. There was a high importance placed on secrecy, make-believe, and privacy in outdoor activities. Most favored places for play were located near water (stream, pond, or puddle), bicycle paths (streets, sidewalks, etc), or in sports fields. One of the least preferred outdoor places was the school playground. The home range for children in the study (ages 6–10) was a 5-minute walk from the front door of the house. This distance increased for children who were permitted to ride bicycles freely.

When compared with all outdoor activities, investigation of wildlife was a very significant pursuit. Fifty percent of all recorded outdoor activities directly involved wildlife: collecting, observing, experimenting, or shooting. Wildlife also was used as props in games and construction activities. Generally, children exhibited an "anthropomorphic-paternalistic-experimental" attitude toward animals. Animal investigations, which included acts of "mutilation" were observed and described with frequency. Knowledge was quite limited and the youngsters did not distinguish easily among native, exotic, and domestic animals, nor were they able to identify proper animal and plant habitat associations. Fears about animals were usually unfounded or blown out of proportion, and fears were much greater on paper than in the field. Natural history courses appeared to be influential in improving knowledge, attitudes, and interest in wildlife, as well as in reducing children's fears of certain animals, mainly snakes and other reptiles (Schicker 1986).

Other highly favored outdoor activities included bicycle riding, sports participation, activities in and around water, building and constructing forts and treehouses, and hiding from adults.

Favorite wild animals were the creepy-crawly variety: amphibians, reptiles, insects, and crustaceans. They were mentioned, looked for, and collected more than all others. The high mention rate of animals found on the ground or in the water seems significant. An important comparison of child and adult wildlife knowledge and interest finds that interest for lower forms of animals changes over the years, being extremely interesting and important to children and almost never mentioned by adults (who define and recognize wildlife primarily as birds and mammals).

Children also were very interested in the conditions of their surrounding outdoor environments; they expressed strong opinions and ideas for how their neighborhoods and school grounds should look, preferring a certain amount of untidiness and "undesigned" and "ungroomed" areas for play. They exhibited strong tendencies toward taking active roles in environmental form and change.

DESIGN CRITERIA

How can access to wildlands and wildlife by children be achieved through design? What does a wild habitat located in a residential area look like? What components will provide a place suitable for children's experience as well as provide habitat for wildlife? A compromise must be reached. An area that allows for child access and play will probably provide less than optimal habitat for wildlife, but having perfect habitats is not the point. Areas will be useful only if children can get to them. For example, though a bramble thicket makes an excellent wildlife habitat, children cannot get through dense, sharply thorned, 4-foot-high shrubs.

In general, though, places satisfactory for children's activities also tend to be good wildlife habitats. By utilizing my findings on children's behavior and preference for outdoor activities as well as wildlife habitat management principles, a set of design criteria and a list of appropriate open spaces have been reached (Tables 1–3). Because of the less than optimal conditions for wildlife in residential developments, addressing any of the issues described in Tables 1–3 will inevitably improve the chances of wildlife being seen

Table 1. Landscape design criteria for children (ages 6–10) and wildlife.

Criteria	Most preferred	Acceptable (rank order)
Habitat types	Aquatic; preferably stream with vegetated corridor.	Other aquatic areas; wetlands, ponds, lakes. Forest, vacant lot, grassy field.
Location	Five-minute walk from home; central to neighborhood, linked to other wildlands.	Five-minute bicycle ride from home; along bike paths, sportsfields.
Size	Not important to kids, preferably 2 acres for wildlife.	
Shape	Greenbelt with activity nodes.	Large, circular shape.
Safety	Social safety.	Physical safety.

Table 2. Plant and animal considerations in landscape design for children.

Consideration	Most important	Less important
Animals to encourage	Salamanders, toads, frogs, turtles, insects, crayfish, squirrels, lizards, butterflies.	Songbirds, chipmunks, raccoons, non-poisonous snakes, opossums, birds of prey.
Animals to discourage	Poisonous snakes, stinging insects.	
Plants to encourage	Berry and fruit trees and shrubs edible to both children and wildlife. Good climbing trees.	Combination of native plants: evergreen and deciduous, all different height layers.
Plants to discourage	Poisonous or irritants: poison ivy and nettles.	Thick and impenetrable thorny brambles.

by children. If one were forced to choose a single neighborhood open space that best suits wildlife and kids simultaneously, it should be a greenbelt park along a stream corridor with small patches or clumps of vegetation and pathways that accommodate bicycle travel. The closer to home, the better.

Habitat Types

For children, providing a variety of representative habitats (aquatic, forest, field, and edge), when available, is of paramount importance. Areas good for wildlife and for children's play are not always the areas where intensive residential development is easiest or even recommended. Floodplains and wetlands, for example, are poor for development, but strongly recommended for child's play, wildlife habitat, and foraging territory.

The treatment of water is very important. Leaving unchanneled and unculverted streams and ponds enhances wildlife habitat and provides cherished opportunities for play. Although culverting or channelling of streams is sometimes necessary, it is not the recommended treatment on a large scale. However, culverts are usually a necessity and they happen to be a favorite child's playplace and raccoon adopted habitat! A balance between undisturbed and culverted waters should be considered while siting residential areas. To make aquatic sites accessible, built elements such as small bridges, docks, and observation decks are desirable. If these elements are too expensive to construct, naturally occurring debris should be left in place and will suffice. These are simple suggestions, but they work. There are several pamphlets available from the National Wildlife Federation and county agricultural extension offices that describe methods of creating small ponds. Small retention basins used for runoff during construction could—if retained—provide good aquatic habitat. (As a safety measure, sides on open retention basins should be gently sloped—preferably less than a 3:1 ratio.) Seeding these areas with regional, edible wild seed mixes (such as millet, oats, rye, rice, crabgrass, *Andropogon,* partridge pea and beggar's lice) is recommended. Boardwalks over aquatic habitats are relatively inexpensive and are great for play and watching wildlife.

Location

Considering the needs of both wildlife and children, wild areas should be both ecologically linked to other wild areas (to provide pathways for plant and animal migration) and be as accessible and safe for children as possible. Wildlife areas should be centrally located in residential developments and perhaps buffered by residences instead of roads, with

Table 3. Open spaces that will meet design criteria.

Greenbelt parkways (along stream corridors if present)
Easements and utility lines
Dedicated land
School and church grounds
Wooded privacy clumps and buffers between houses
Areas adjacent to sports fields
Nature trails, backyards, cemeteries

common foot paths allowing access. A central location of this type would provide neighborhood visibility and be within parental shouting distance. Judging from information from the children about preferred playplaces, wildlife habitat also should be interspersed along biking paths (which include the slower, residential streets) and sports fields, where kids spend much of their free time. This would allow them more opportunities to encounter other animals. Also recommended is the provision of vegetative connections to existing greenspaces, which might include parklands, playgrounds, church and schoolgrounds, and cemeteries. Were these spaces left a little less "tidy" and groomed, they would be enjoyed as a playplace for children and be better homes for animals.

Size and Shape

Large acreage is not necessary for play from the child's perspective. Children are resourceful and need very little space to enjoy the natural world. Because of their behavior patterns, children mainly use areas that provide for extensive movement, and this is why I have recommended a greenbelt approach.

Likewise, many wildlife species are resourceful, and readily populate the smallest pocket of derelict land. However, to maintain self-perpetuating populations of any one species, acreage requirements do exist. Because of the limited research on wildlife requirements in urban areas, it is difficult to specify exact sizes. In general, bigger is better, and the suggestion of 2 acres (0.8 ha) based on woodland bird species research is a good place to start (Goldstein et al. 1981).

Wildlife moves most easily through closed tree canopies, extensive shrub masses, and continuous ground covers. Some areas available for play, and which provide wildlife habitat, exist already in planned developments, commonly in the form of undevelopable stream corridors, ravines, wooded privacy buffers between lots, and utility easement land. In the case of easement land, only the vegetative character of the area need be changed to improve its use as wildlife cover and forage. This can be accomplished through less frequent mowing schedules or seeding with edible grains.

Safety

Safety is an important issue that cannot be taken lightly. There are two types of safety to consider: social safety and physical safety. The location and size of habitat within the development are the most important factors in determining social safety of an area. Sometimes, the less "designated" an area is, the less chance it has for attracting social problems. (Public parks are more apt to attract vagrants or molesters than are undesignated wildlands.) Wildlife areas should be centrally located in residential developments if at all possible. Social safety also varies from city to city and issues should be addressed by each individual residential planner according to local conditions.

Physical safety issues mainly concern poisonous plants, insects and snakes, or extreme site conditions that may be harmful to children. The most dangerous site conditions in residential areas include extremely steep or unstable slopes. Although retention ponds used during construction can make great wildlife habitat, they should not be designed as such unless they have shallow area and gentle, sloping sides. The most common potentially harmful plant and wildlife species in North Carolina include poison ivy (and related genera), copperheads, bees, bald-faced hornets, yellow jackets, and fire ants. Although it is impossible to plan against all, certain precautions can be made.

Eradicate poison ivy. If burning is the method used, this should be done before residents move in because poison ivy smoke can be seriously damaging to highly allergic people. The bases of surrounding trees could be soaked with water before burning in order to protect them from also going up in smoke. On the large scale, eliminating all the poison ivy is impractical (and it is great wildlife food); it might be easier to educate residents about the proper identification of these plants.

Remove rock piles. If poisonous snakes are abundant in your geographic area (as they are in North Carolina), this will eliminate a potential hiding site (but this is also a favorite habitat for other, more desirable animal species). It may be comforting to note that a mere one thousand snake bites are reported annually in the United States, with only 3% of these resulting in fatalities. Snake bite fear is worse than snake bites. Proper identification knowledge of poisonous snakes achieved through posters, brochures, and visual signage for residents might also aid in avoiding contact with these passive creatures.

Hornets, yellow jackets, and fire ants nest in the ground and are easily disturbed by children. When disturbed, they sting en masse! If nests are discovered, they should be eradicated.

Most childhood accidents occur in the home, and safety in wildlands need not be overemphasized. Wildlands normally provide safe testing grounds and challenges for growing children. Providing educational materials to residents concerning troublesome plants and animals is the suggested method for avoiding physical safety problems.

SUGGESTIONS FOR ENHANCING CHILDREN'S EXPOSURE TO WILDLIFE

"The city and suburban landscape is a production of conflicting values. It expresses a deep seated affinity with natural things; but these expressions take place only on human terms, subject to the standards of order and tidiness imposed by public values. Design often sets its limits to diversity by establishing landscapes by brute force; adapting a site to a predetermined set of plants which could only survive with the use of machines, fertilizers, herbicides, pruning, mulching and spraying, and many a splendid and rich environment could be kept in a residential setting by simply leaving it alone" (Hough 1984).

This is the best advice for designing an area for kids and wildlife; the best solution is to do nothing at all. But if the site has been cleared or otherwise disturbed, then the case for landscaping with native plants must be strongly made. Successional planting techniques and urban reforestation practices are available (Hough 1984). Planting with edible native species (for kids and animals) is preferred, and the National Wildlife Federation has provided an excellent list of suggested species (for field, forest, and wetland areas) that can be used by any landscape architect, planner, or resident. Involving kids in the planting of native plants is even better!

The following additional small scale suggestions are made to enhance children's exposure to wildlife in their neighborhoods.

- Allow for the preservation and selection of trees conducive to climbing and for the construction of treehouses.
- Provide wildlife observation stations.
- Create vernal pools and manipulate water levels to encourage amphibian and other wildlife habitation.
- Plant and design butterfly meadows.
- Introduce the concept of natural adventure playgrounds.

A detailed description and discussion of these subjects can be found in Schicker (1986).

In addition, at the smallest scale, individual homeowners could be introduced to the National Wildlife Federation's Backyard Wildlife Program. Considering that children prefer to play in close vicinity to their own homes (Wood 1977), this would be the ideal place for introducing wildlife to children. In this program, children and parents participate together in creating mini-havens for wildlife in their own yards. Yards are certified through the Federation if they meet the requirements of providing food, cover, and water to wildlife. Some of the many species of wildlife that have been reported from certified yard owners include the more common squirrels, rabbits, opossums and raccoons, but chipmunks, turtles, salamanders, field mice, toads, frogs,- lizards, muskrats, otters, coyotes, and skunks (depending on geographic location) also have been reported. Backyard Wildlife materials are available to the public for a minimal cost, and landscape architects and planners could benefit from this information as well as recommend its use to developers and homeowners.

Places for Kids and Wildlife in Neighborhoods

Delft, The Netherlands.—In high density complexes in Delft, urban forestry practices have been established, and are providing excellent landscaping as well as important spaces for children's play. These "forested" areas do not resemble the "neat and tidy" school of landscaping, but they have an informal yet functional character of a heavily used landscape. The Dutch believe it is unrealistic to attempt to confine children to specific play areas and the natural wooded areas can handle the wear and tear. Minor pathways are left to be made by residents and children's play; once the paths are established, they are paved.

Village Homes Neighborhood.—Village Homes, a residential development in California, is one of a few examples where kids and wildlife are happily coexisting in a residential setting. New forms of community open space were incorporated into the design such as vineyards, orchards, community bike paths, and natural drainage areas. In Village Homes, over 85% of all water is kept on site, flowing through a series of swales, ponds and channels, supporting natural vegetation, wildlife, and child exploration. Through mapping and favorite place analysis, the use of these open spaces by children has been evaluated by Frances (1984). He found that the pedestrian and bike paths received the most heavy use (24% of total observations), followed by street space (20%), common areas or greenbelts (14%), open drainage areas (8%), and turf areas (13%). The least used areas were the vineyards (0%), orchards (1%), community gardens (1%), private gardens and patios (3%), and playgrounds (4%). Of all community open green spaces, greenbelt commons, turf areas, and natural drainage swales were the most commonly used, pointing to the value of these areas to children. Frances also found that the most "sacred" places for children were the wild or unfinished places such as construction sites and places like "willow pond" or "clover patch." These findings argue for neighborhood design that retains open space in its natural state, which children can manipulate to suit their own needs.

Environmental Yards.—Using natural features to shade play areas, environmental yards offer fantastic experiences for children. Plants and animals, flowers and trees, water and dirt give children the chance to explore their environment, observe life cycles, interact with other living things, and cooperate with nature.

The Washington Environmental Yard (WEY) was founded in 1971 and developed as a cooperative project among neighborhood residents, teachers, administrators, and the children who attended Washington Elementary School located in downtown Berkeley, California (Moore 1980). Landscape architect Robin Moore and school principal Herb Wong coordinated community involvement and efforts on the project through a series of surveys and workshops. The "Yard" was an effort to diversify 1.5 acres (0.6 ha) of asphalt play yard into a variety of play and learning environments, including a haven for wildlife. WEY is open 24 hours a day and is freely accessible to any neighborhood users. A 0.5-acre (0.2 ha) zone, called the Natural Resource Area was completely stripped of asphalt, and now contains ponds, wooded areas and meadows, approximating the natural ecosystem of the Bay Area coastal region. WEY is currently undergoing the test of time; native flora and fauna have reestablished residency on the site and have provided teachers and students with an abundance of environmental and science education lessons.

Another example of an environmental yard is the Wildwood School in Aspen, Colorado. The school was built underground to protect the existing natural environment. The school site is used to teach environmental lessons in ecology, biology, and botany.

The concept of environmental yards could easily be applied to any neighborhood setting, through the use of school sites or neighborhood open spaces, if interest and community commitment are available.

CONCLUSIONS

Small parcels of land, withheld from development and ecologically linked to larger habitat "islands," can serve to distribute wildlife habitat throughout residential areas. This network also can provide environmental experiences for children where they live. A very workable land design solution to these scientific findings is ecologically sited, planned unit developments with greenspaces connecting all available open spaces.

Because of current environmental laws and practices, certain lands are excluded from development and can readily be used for these purposes. However, these areas can be used for an assortment of open space uses, and it is the developers and homeowners who need direction and encouragement for using these areas for kids and wildlife. Encouragement and design implementation must come from all professionals involved, including landscape architects, wildlife biologists, planners, developers, and educators.

From my experiences with children, I contend that experiential, day to day contact with the natural world, parental support and encouragement, and participatory hands-on educational experiences are the greatest and most effective methods for ensuring wildlife awareness and appreciation. I also believe that this experience is essential at an early age. Wildlands in residential developments are the ideal place for these activities to occur. Providing places for children to grow up that are both challenging and naturally beautiful can only make them better decision makers about our environmental future.

REFERENCES CITED

Adams, L.W. and L.E. Dove. 1984. Urban wetlands for stormwater control and wildlife enhancement. Natl. Inst. for Urban Wildl., Columbia, Md. 15 pp.

Andrews, W.A. and J.L. Cranmer-Bying, eds. 1981. Urban natural areas; ecology and preservation. Inst. of Environ. Studies, Toronto.

Beebee, T. 1981. Habitats of British amphibians. Biol. Conserv. 15:241–257.

Cohen, U., A.B. Hill, C.G. Lane, T. McGinty, and G.T. Moore. 1979. Recommendations for child play areas. Center for Architecture and Urban Planning, Univ. of Wisconsin, Madison.

Dennis, J.V. 1985. The wildlife gardener. Alfred E. Knopf, New York.

Francis, M. 1984. Children's use of open space in village homes. Children's Environments Quarterly 1:36–38.

Galli, A.E., C.F. Leck, and R.T. Forman. 1976. Avian distribution patterns in forest islands of different sizes in central New Jersey. Auk 93:356–64.

Goldstein, E.L., M. Gross, and R.M. DeGraaf. 1981. Explorations in bird-land geometry. Urban Ecol. 5:113–124.

Hart, R. 1983. Consideration of the value of natural environments in landscape planning. IPA Newsletter 8:3–8.

Hart, R. 1979. Children's experience of place. Irvington, New York.

Hough, M. 1984. City form and natural process. Van Nostrand Rheinhold Company, New York.

Kellert, S.R. and M.O. Westervelt. 1983. Children's attitudes, knowledge, and behaviors towards animals. U.S. Fish and Wildl. Serv., Washington, D.C. 202 pp.

Kirkpatrick, C.M., ed. 1978. Proceedings, wildlife and people—the 1978 John S. Wright Forestry Conf., Purdue Univ., West Lafayette, Ind. 191 pp.

Laurie, I., ed. 1979. Nature in cities: the environment in design and development of urban green space. John Wiley and Sons, New York.

Leedy, D.L., R.M. Maestro, and T.M. Franklin. 1978. Planning for wildlife in cities and suburbs. FWS/OBS-77/66, U.S. Dep. of the Inter., Fish and Wildl. Serv., Washington, D.C. 64 pp.

Leedy, D.L. and L.W. Adams. 1984. A guide to urban wildlife management. Natl. Inst. for Urban Wildl., Columbia, Md. 42 pp.

Lynch, K. 1979. Growing up in cities. MIT Press, Cambridge, Mass.

Moore, R.C. 1980. Collaborating with young people to assess their landscape values. Ekistics 281, March–April.

Moore, R.C. and D. Young. 1978. Childhood outdoors: toward a social ecology of the landscape. Pages 83–127 *in* Altman and Wohlwill, eds. Children and the environment. Plenum Publishing.

Noyes, J.H. and D.R. Progulske, eds. 1974. A symposium on wildlife in an urbanizing environment. Mass. Coop. Ext. Serv., Amherst.

Schicker, L.K. 1986. Children, wildlife and residential developments. M.L.A. Thesis, North Carolina State Univ., Raleigh. 129 pp.

Schmid, J.A. 1975. Urban vegetation. Dep. of Geog., Univ. of Chicago.

Shaw, W., coordinator. 1986. Integrating wildlife conservation and new residential developments. A symp. held 20–22 January, Univ. Arizona, Tucson. (Proc. in prep.)

Spirn, A.W. 1984. The granite garden: urban nature and human design. Basic Books Inc., New York. 334 pp.

U.S. Department of Commerce. 1985. National data book and guide to sources-statistical abstract of the United States. Bureau of the Census.

van Andel, J. 1984/85. Effects on children's behavior of physical changes in a Leiden neighborhood. Children's Environments Quarterly 1:46–54.

Wilson, E.O. and E.O. Willis. 1975. Applied Biogeography. *In* Ecology and evolution of communities, edited by Cody and Diamond. Harvard University Press.

Wood, D. 1977. Free the children! Down with playgrounds! McGill J. of Ed. 12:227–243.

Urban Wildlife Habitat Research—Application to Landscape Design

RICHARD M. DEGRAAF, *Northeastern Forest Experiment Station, Holdsworth Hall, University of Massachusetts, Amherst, MA 01003*

The basic characteristics of urban-suburban avifaunas in these essentially unmanaged habitats have been determined over the last 2 decades of research. In eastern North America, at least, such avifaunas are dominated by exotic species that achieve high densities, have few breeding species compared to rural environments, few cavity or ground nesters, few if any breeding insectivorous migrant species, and high densities of seed eaters-omnivorous species (Walcott 1974, Erz 1966).

The quality of avian habitats varies greatly among urban-suburban environments; many can be greatly enhanced and others less severely degraded by development if avian habitat needs are incorporated in landscape designs. Within broad limits, a wide variety of forest and edge birds can be managed in such environments.

Urbanization of rural landscapes removes, alters, or replaces most of the natural or existing vegetation (Sharpe et al. 1986). Furthermore, urbanization typically changes the local plant species composition by favoring some native species at the expense of others, and by introducing exotic species, intentionally as landscape plantings and unintentionally as "weeds." Eastern North America supports more than 200 species of forest land birds. Much woodland remains, but the woody vegetation of urbanized environments differs from pre-development conditions not only in species composition (especially the inclusion of many sterile forms), but in sparseness and distribution as well. In most suburbs, trees cover a small fraction of the land surface, and, rather than occurring in clumps like naturalistic stands, are thinly, rather evenly distributed over the landscape as "specimen" plantings. These changes have profound effects on urban and suburban avifaunas.

BIRD-HABITAT ASSOCIATIONS

Two basic sets of factors determine whether a given bird species will breed in a given area. Ultimate factors that actually determine reproductive success, e.g., insects to feed nestlings, often are not evident at the time of arrival or habitat selection. Keys to these factors are perceived through "proximate" or psychological factors, and aspects of the physical habitat, especially vegetation structure, that are generally considered important to many species. Ever since Lack (1933) propounded the idea that birds select breeding habitats by recognizing features that the birds did not generally require for survival, namely vegetation structure, many studies have been conducted to identify the features or patterns that bird species were "programmed" to seek.

Breeding bird species occurring together in a given habitat may not necessarily have similar requirements for combinations of vegetation density and distribution. Bond (1957) showed that a continuum of bird species distribution was related to a forest continuum—the distributions of 25 of 27 species were related to the forest continuum, and the abundance of each species peaked at a different point along the forest continuum. Bond may have actually measured indirectly the structural vegetation "requirements" of birds and noted that several species can occur in the same habitat and not respond to the same set of habitat features.

The implied importance of layered vegetation was examined by MacArthur and MacArthur (1961), who demonstrated that the vertical complexity of forest vegetation (the diversity of vegetation heights and density of foliage at those heights) was associated with breeding bird diversity. In the forest habitats studied, plant species composition was not useful in improving the relationships. Subjected to testing in many habitats, the relationship of bird species diversity to foliage height diversity has been supported in many cases (Karr 1968, Karr and Roth 1971) but not others (Tomoff 1974).

The basic importance of vegetational layers to birds of forested regions generally has been established. Bird species can be considered individually to reveal habitat compo-

Integrating Man and Nature in the Metropolitan Environment. Proc. Natl. Symp. on Urban Wildl., Chevy Chase, Md., 4–7 November 1986, L.W. Adams and D.L. Leedy, eds. Published by Natl. Inst. for Urban Wildl., 10921 Trotting Ridge Way, Columbia, MD 21044, 1987.

nents, including foliage layers, that are associated with each (Fig. 1). However, habitat components that are related to bird species richness—those that tend to benefit the greatest number of species in suburban habitats—are more readily incorporated in landscape design and are more useful in management. Horizontal diversity or patchiness also is important to breeding bird composition. Roth (1976) demonstrated that the number of bird species increased faster than the degree of species overlap in a series of habitats from grasslands to forests, and that horizontal habitat heterogeneity was a better predictor of bird species numbers than was vertical habitat heterogeneity.

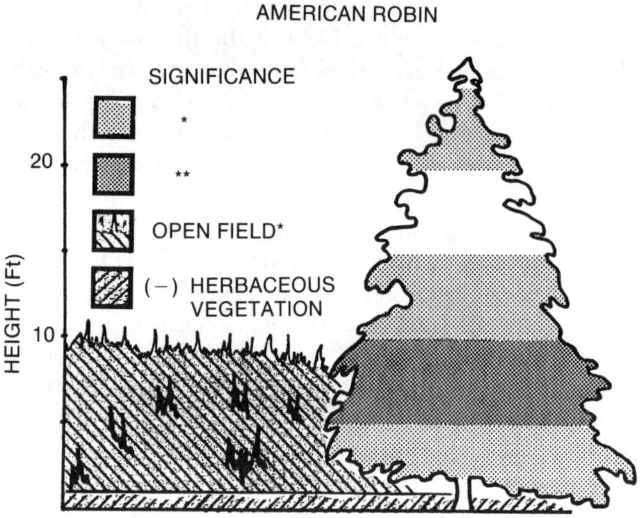

Fig. 1. Suburban habitat associations of breeding American robin (*Turdus migratorius*) in Amherst, Massachusetts; differences are * = $P < 0.05$, ** = $P < 0.01$ (after DeGraaf 1986).

From these studies, it is obvious that both vertical vegetation structure and patchiness are important to breeding bird communities. Suburban habitats, at least in temperate forest regions, have breeding bird communities that are intermediate in species richness. Such areas typically have many more species than urban residential habitats but considerably fewer than rural habitats (DeGraaf and Wentworth 1981). A common result of increased urbanization is a decline in the number of species and a simultaneous increase in total bird density as a relatively few species become very abundant.

Avifaunas of Urban Residential and Suburban Habitats

In New England, differences between urban residential and suburban avifaunas are quite dramatic in the breeding season and during winter. Total urban breeding bird density is more than 2.5 times that in suburban habitats; in winter, total bird density is 1.7 times that of suburbs. Suburbs contained more than 2.5 times as many breeding species and 1.4 times as many species in winter as the urban habitats (DeGraaf and Wentworth 1981). On a functional or guild basis (Root 1967), ground-foraging seed eaters and omnivores are the most abundant groups in both urban and suburban habitats in the breeding season, although members of these guilds are much more abundant in urban habitats (Fig. 2A). These guilds have been found also to dominate the urban and suburban avifaunas of Florida (Woolfenden and Rohwer 1969) and Arizona (Emlen 1974). Insectivorous species are fairly common in suburbs but are nearly absent from urban residential habitats, especially in winter (Fig. 2B).

Differences in urban and suburban avifaunas also are apparent from analyses of nesting substrate guild distributions. Species nesting on tree branches or buildings are more abundant in urban habitats, whereas ground, cavity, shrub, and tree twig nesters are either absent or occur at low densities (DeGraaf and Wentworth 1981).

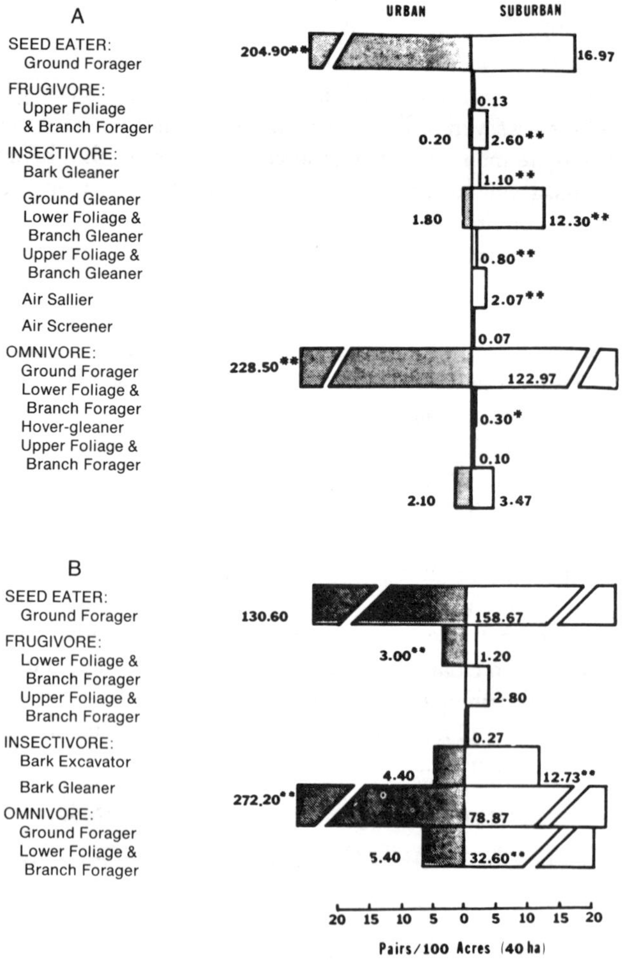

Fig. 2. Breeding season (A) and winter (B) foraging guild distributions in urban residential and suburban habitats; differences are * = $P < 0.05$, ** = $P < 0.01$ (after DeGraaf and Wentworth 1981).

What differences in habitat structure may account for the bird community differences between urban residential and suburban environments? Measures of tree cover and species richness, shrub density, area of weedy growth, and nearness of woodlots all are greater in the suburbs, and likely contribute to the greater avian species richness there. Insectivores are positively associated with the tree features that are characteristic of suburban habitat, and most show an affinity for woodlot nearness. Ground-foraging seed eaters and omnivores, which dominate the urban avifauna, show no affinities for woodlots (DeGraaf and Wentworth 1981).

Suburban Avifaunas and Habitat Associations

Compared to urban habitats, suburbs have more diverse avifaunas. But suburbs vary greatly in habitat structure and thus in their avifaunas. A comparison of the avian foraging guild structures of three types of suburbs revealed several significant differences (DeGraaf and Wentworth 1986). The three types were: MT, an area of large houses, lawns of moderate size, mature trees and shrubs, and large street trees including pin oak *(Quercus palustris)*, American elm *(Ulmus americana)*, and sugar maple *(Acer saccharum)*; YT, a subdivision built on open land with lawns occupying most of the lots, most trees and shrubs small, including small street trees of silver *(A. saccharinum)* and Norway *(A. platanoides)* maples; and OP, a subdivision in which houses were built in a second-growth oak-pine woodland dominated by red oak *(Q. rubra)*, black oak *(Q. velutina)*, red maple *(A. rubrum)*, and white pine *(Pinus strobus)*, in which small clearings were made for houses and small lawns.

Breeding bird censuses conducted over 5 years revealed that species richness and foraging guild numbers were virtually identical in each area, but avifaunas varied greatly. The densities of nine of the 12 guilds differed significantly, reflecting differences in the habitat structure of each suburb type. YT supported the lowest total density, but highest density of insectivorous air screeners, and the fewest ground- and lower foliage-gleaning insectivores; MT supported the highest total avian density, and significantly greater numbers of seed eaters and ground-foraging omnivores; OP supported the greatest number of insectivores, including bark drillers, ground gleaners, foliage gleaners, and air screeners, 5 times the density of insectivores of YT, and 2 times that of MT (DeGraaf and Wentworth 1986).

Among nesting guilds, OP supported the fewest ground-herb nesters, and YT the most. MT supported the most shrub nesters, and OP the fewest. OP supported the most cavity and twig nesters.

When avian foraging and nesting guild distributions are considered in terms of habitat structure, several patterns emerge. Insectivores (except air screeners) are strongly associated with measures of tree cover and show an affinity for woodlots. Seed eaters and ground-foraging omnivores are strongly associated with the area of herbaceous or weedy growth and with large shade trees, but seed eaters avoid woodlots (DeGraaf and Wentworth 1986).

Among nesting guilds, ground nesters are negatively associated with measures of tree cover, and positively associated with openness (area of weedy growth and lawn). Shrub nesters are associated with shrub height, not shrub density. Tree branch, twig, and cavity nesters showed obvious association with measures of tree cover and were negatively associated with lawn area (DeGraaf and Wentworth 1986).

Suburbs are not homogeneous from an avian habitat perspective. A quite wooded habitat is necessary for insectivores—large shade trees will not suffice. Twig and cavity nesters are more abundant in the wooded suburban habitat. Expansive lawns and large shade trees support more seed eaters and ground-foraging omnivores, and more shrub and tree branch nesters.

The Importance of Woody Vegetation

From an analytical point of view, it is difficult to evaluate the effects of vegetation on birds in the developed landscape because the key parameters (layering, species composition, and spatial arrangement) vary almost limitlessly. Individual species' habitat associations can be statistically identified (e.g., Thomas et al. 1977, DeGraaf 1986), but a practical management or design approach necessitates some generalization about the dominant landscape elements and their effects on wildlife. Bird species richness and total woody vegetation volume are fairly closely related—on 60 1-ha (2.5 ac) plots in Amherst, Massachusetts suburbs, 49.6% of the variation in the number of breeding bird species over 5 years could be explained by total woody vegetation volume (Goldstein et al. 1986).

Furthermore, this analysis separated the 65 bird species present into three groups that vary in their sensitivity to vegetation volume and thus their adaptability to built-up areas (Table 1). The first group, 29% of the species, contains those species best adapted to such areas; all are common and are relatively insensitive to the volume of vegetation available, and though some—e.g., wood thrush—were dramatically less common on plots with less woody vegetation, most are able to occupy a broad range of suburban habitats. The second group, 40% of the species, includes those that are able to occur in suburban environments only when vegetation (and other) conditions are unusually suitable (Table 1). These species, on average, occurred where vegetation volume was significantly greater than it was for those in the first group. This second group of species, though not usually the most abundant species even where vegetation volume was high, are still common enough to constitute a regular and extremely valuable component of the suburban avifauna. More importantly, the species in this group are responsive to management, i.e., they can be fairly predictably added to a suburban avifauna where adequate woody vegetation volume is provided (Goldstein et al. 1986).

Table 1. Breeding birds grouped by commonness of occurrence in Amherst, Massachusetts, 1975–1979 (after Goldstein et al. 1986).

Group I: Common and insensitive to vegetation volume
Mourning dove (*Zenaida macroura*)
Blue jay (*Cyanocitta cristata*)
Black-capped chickadee (*Parus atricapillus*)
Tufted titmouse (*Parus bicolor*)
White-breasted nuthatch (*Sitta carolinensis*)
House wren (*Troglodytes aedon*)
Northern mockingbird (*Mimus polyglottos*)
Gray catbird (*Dumetella carolinensis*)
American robin (*Turdus migratorius*)
Wood thrush (*Hylocichla mustelina*)
European starling (*Sturnus vulgaris*)
Red-eyed vireo (*Vireo olivaceus*)
House sparrow (*Passer domesticus*)
Northern oriole (*Icterus galbula*)
Common grackle (*Quiscalus quiscula*)
Northern cardinal (*Cardinalis cardinalis*)
Chipping sparrow (*Spizella passerina*)
Song sparrow (*Melospiza melodia*)
Group II: Suburban environments, manageable
Yellow-billed cuckoo (*Coccyzus americanus*)
Common flicker (*Colaptes auratus*)
Hairy woodpecker (*Picoides villosus*)
Downy woodpecker (*Picoides pubescens*)
Eastern kingbird (*Tyrannus tyrannus*)
Great crested flycatcher (*Myiarchus crinitus*)
Eastern phoebe (*Sayornis phoebe*)
Eastern wood-pewee (*Contopus virens*)
Barn swallow (*Hirundo rustica*)
American crow (*Corvus brachyrhynchos*)
Red-breasted nuthatch (*Sitta canadensis*)
Brown thrasher (*Toxostoma rufum*)
Cedar waxwing (*Bombycilla cedrorum*)
Black-and-white warbler (*Mniotilta varia*)
Yellow warbler (*Dendroica petechia*)
Blackpoll warbler (*Dendroica striata*)
Common yellowthroat (*Geothlypis trichas*)
American redstart (*Setophaga ruticilla*)
Red-winged blackbird (*Agelaius phoeniceus*)
Brown-headed cowbird (*Molothrus ater*)
Scarlet tanager (*Piranga olivacea*)
Rose-breasted grosbeak (*Pheucticus ludovicianus*)
House finch (*Carpodacus mexicanus*)
American goldfinch (*Carduelis tristis*)
Rufous-sided towhee (*Pipilo erythrophthalmus*)
Group III: Uncommon suburban breeding species
Ring-necked pheasant (*Phasianus colchicus*)
Ruby-throated hummingbird (*Archilochus colubris*)
Pileated woodpecker (*Dryocopus pileatus*)
Least flycatcher (*Empidonax minimus*)
Tree swallow (*Tachycineta bicolor*)
Winter wren (*Troglodytes troglodytes*)
Hermit thrush (*Catharus guttatus*)
Swainson's thrush (*Catharus ustulatus*)
Blue-gray gnatcatcher (*Polioptila caerulea*)
Solitary vireo (*Vireo solitarius*)
Warbling vireo (*Vireo gilvus*)
Blue-winged warbler (*Vermivora pinus*)
Yellow-rumped warbler (*Dendroica coronata*)
Ovenbird (*Seiurus aurocapillus*)
Eastern meadowlark (*Sturnella magna*)
Indigo bunting (*Passerina cyanea*)
Purple finch (*Carpodacus purpureus*)
Field sparrow (*Spizella pusilla*)
Swamp sparrow (*Melospiza georgiana*)

The last group constituted 31% of those encountered and consists of uncommon to rare breeding species (Table 1). Some are clearly dependent upon very high volumes of woody vegetation, e.g., pileated woodpecker, but others, such as the meadowlark, clearly are not. Most of this group probably are excluded from built-up areas by psychological factors, predation (especially ground nesters), or the requirements of large unbroken habitat patches of a type not likely to occur in suburbs. Management prospects are likely not promising for this group.

Habitat components to which individual bird species respond, especially foliage layers, have been identified for some common suburban breeding birds (DeGraaf 1986). But landscape design of environments that attract for the most part common or generalist species should be directed toward providing habitat for the greatest number of species.

When suburban bird species richness is analyzed in terms of habitat components, discrete layers of foliage volume do not appear to be important. Such relationships have been demonstrated for forest habitats (MacArthur and MacArthur 1961, Karr and Roth 1971), wherein foliage is arranged more or less in a vertical continuum, and where tree branches interdigitate. But in suburban landscapes, most trees are dispersed as specimens, and other landscape components become important to the breeding bird community. The nearer a woodlot and open field, the smaller the lawn area, the more that "weedy" vegetation is permitted, and the lower the building density, the greater the species richness of the suburban bird community (DeGraaf 1986).

APPLICATION OF HABITAT ASSOCIATIONS TO LANDSCAPE DESIGN

A fairly large literature exists on the values and site requirements of various plants and their arrangement to attract birds to residential grounds (e.g., Terres 1968, Davison 1967, Martin et al. 1951, DeGraaf and Witman 1979). Generally, plants providing persistent fruits, seeds, secure nest sites, and escape cover can indeed attract many bird species from the surrounding landscape to specific sites. To enhance the bird species richness of the landscape as a whole, however, elements of the pre-development landscape must be retained—woodlots and fields (DeGraaf 1986).

Within woodlots there are factors that affect birds, but woodlot size appears to be the characteristic most important to the breeding bird community (Moore and Hooper 1975). Based upon this relationship, designs have been proposed for hypothetical small (Goldstein et al. 1981) and medium scale (Goldstein et al. 1983) residential developments that maximize the patch size of woody vegetation to theoretically maximize the diversity of the bird community.

Not all suburbs or residential cluster developments are built in landscapes that are a mosaic of woodlots and open country. Does suburban development built in woodland, with minimal clearing for houses, have a high number of breeding bird species? Essentially only among insectivores and cavity nesters (DeGraaf and Wentworth 1986). Planted trees, no matter how mature or abundant, apparently do not replace natural forest stands as breeding habitat for insectivorous birds. Edge species will probably continue to thrive in suburbs, but for insectivorous migrant species, which have been used as measures of avifaunal quality (Walcott 1974), natural woodland must be retained where possible.

CONCLUSIONS

The general effects of urbanization on birds—increased abundances of generalist-exotic-omnivorous species and, in forested regions, decreased abundances or elimination of insectivores and ground and tree cavity nesters—can be mitigated by retention of pre-development landscape features and selection of material for the planted environment. Retention of woodlots will provide habitat for some forest birds, especially cavity nesters that depend upon trees containing columns of decayed wood evidenced by dead branches or stems of sufficient size. Such trees are routinely pruned of dead limbs or removed in the planted environment.

Suburbs vary in avian composition depending largely upon the degree to which they alter the pre-existing vegetation. A suburb containing remnants of a closed-canopy, multi-layered forest will support an avifauna quite different from one with mature, but planted, trees and shrubs. The planted environment, no matter how mature, apparently will not suffice as breeding habitat for many insectivorous birds.

In the planted environment, maximizing the crown volumes of trees and shrubs is likely the one management practice or goal that will yield the greatest increases in breeding bird species richness.

The prospects for enhancing urban and suburban avifaunas are good. By retaining pre-development fields and woodlots, increasing vegetation volume, especially in spatially concentrated patches, and by the familiar practice of planting species useful to birds, it is almost certain that the number of breeding bird species can be increased.

REFERENCES CITED

Bond, R.R. 1957. Ecological distribution of breeding birds in the upland forest of southern Wisconsin. Ecol. Monogr. 27:351–384.

Davison, V.E. 1967. Attracting birds: from the prairies to the Atlantic. Thomas Y. Crowell Co., New York. 252pp.

DeGraaf, R.M. 1986. Urban bird habitat relationships: application to landscape design. Trans. North Am. Wildl. and Nat. Resour. Conf. 51:232–248.

DeGraaf, R.M., and J.M. Wentworth. 1981. Urban bird communities and habitats in New England. Trans. North Am. Wildl. and Nat. Resour. Conf. 46:396–413.

DeGraaf, R.M., and J.M. Wentworth. 1986. Avian guild structure and habitat associations in suburban bird communities. Urban Ecol. 9:399–412.

DeGraaf, R.M., and G.M. Witman. 1979. Trees, shrubs and vines for attracting birds: a manual for the Northeast. Univ. of Mass. Press, Amherst. 194pp.

Emlen, J.T. 1974. An urban bird community in Tucson, Arizona: derivation, structure, regulation. Condor 76:184–197.

Erz, W. 1966. Ecological principles in the urbanization of birds. *In* Proc. 2nd Pan-African Ornithological Congress, Pietermaritzburg, Natal, South Africa. Ostrich, Suppl. 6:357–364.

Goldstein, E.L., M. Gross, and R.M. DeGraaf. 1981. Explorations in bird-land geometry. Urban Ecol. 5:113–124.

Goldstein, E.L., M. Gross, and R.M. DeGraaf. 1983. Wildlife and greenspace planning in medium-scale residential developments. Urban Ecol. 7:201–214.

Goldstein, E.L., M. Gross, and R.M. DeGraaf. 1986. Breeding birds and vegetation: a quantitative assessment. Urban Ecol. 9:377–385.

Karr, J.R. 1968. Habitat and avian diversity on strip-mined land in east-central Illinois. Condor 70:348–357.

Karr, J.R., and R.R. Roth. 1971. Vegetation structure and avian diversity in several new world areas. Am. Nat. 105:423–435.

Lack, D. 1933. Habitat selection in birds. J. Animal Ecol. 2:239–262.

MacArthur, R.H., and J.W. MacArthur. 1961. On bird species diversity. Ecology 42:594–598.

Martin, A.C., H.S. Zim, and A.L. Nelson. 1951. American wildlife and plants. McGraw-Hill, New York. 500pp.

Moore, N.W., and M.D. Hooper. 1975. On the number of bird species in British woods. Biol. Conserv. 8:239–250.

Root, R.B. 1967. The niche exploitation pattern of the blue-gray gnatcatcher. Ecol. Monogr. 37:317–350.

Roth, R.R. 1976. Spatial heterogeneity and bird species diversity. Ecology 57:773–782.

Sharpe, D.M., F. Stearns, L.A. Leitner, and J.R. Dorney. 1986. Fate of natural vegetation during urban development of rural landscapes in northeastern Wisconsin. Urban Ecol. 9:267–287.

Terres, J.K. 1968. Songbirds in your garden. Thomas Y. Crowell Co., New York. 256pp.

Thomas, J.W., R.M. DeGraaf, and J.C. Mawson. 1977. Determination of habitat requirements for birds in suburban areas. U.S. For. Serv. Res. Pap. NE-357. 15pp.

Tomoff, C.S. 1974. Avian species diversity in desert scrub. Ecology 55:396–403.

Walcott, C.F. 1974. Changes in bird life in Cambridge, Massachusetts from 1860 to 1964. Auk 91:151–160.

Woolfenden, G.E., and S.A. Rohwer. 1969. Breeding birds in a Florida suburb. Florida State Mus. Bull. No. 13. 83pp.

Public Knowledge of and Preferences for Wildlife Habitats in Urban Open Spaces

SALLY SCHAUMAN, *Department of Landscape Architecture, JO-34, University of Washington, Seattle, WA 98195*

STEPHEN PENLAND, *Washington Department of Game, 16018 Mill Creek Blvd., Mill Creek, WA 98012*

MARILYN FREEMAN, *Department of Landscape Architecture, JO-34, University of Washington, Seattle, WA 98195*

INTRODUCTION

For most cities, one's first impression is of buildings and streets. Yet amid the built environment, the green landscape prevails, sometimes as parks and planned open spaces, but frequently as leftover areas. Although the desirability of urban natural areas is generally agreed upon (Herzog et al. 1982, Ulrich 1986), and their ecological values generally known (McHarg 1969, Spirn 1984), their visual value is only beginning to be explored (Kaplan 1984). Identifying the visual values of urban space is very important because as either remnants or designs, their future often depends on the public's reaction to their appearance. This is especially true for the majority of open spaces, the undesigned remnants. Can't we cut the trees from this hillside to enhance our view? Don't we need parking more than blackberry bushes next to the drainway? Why doesn't the city mow the grass in the old landfill area?

More than likely the public asking these questions would agree that, in general, vegetated urban open space is needed and that all values should be considered in the decision process. Yet this egalitarian understanding does not always surface when a specific site is in question. Agencies managing open spaces must respond to differing, often narrow, public perceptions. One of the open space situations that is least understood is the relationship between the public's knowledge of and preference for wildlife habitats in the city. For example, an agency may fund wildlife educational programs with the belief that a public knowledgeable about urban wildlife species will have more desire to conserve urban habitats. However, it may be that the public's knowledge of wildlife, their recognition of urban habitats, and their preferences for the appearance of these habitats are not working in concert.

This pilot study was directed at the relationships between knowledge, attitudes, and preferences of Seattle, Washington, residents for urban open space with wildlife habitat value. Seattle has a wide variety of open spaces, varying from designed parks to remnant natural areas, including steep hillsides, water edges in industrial or commercial areas, surface drainage ways, sinking landfills, parkways containing transmission lines, water edges at the base of steep slopes, and general "leftover" vegetated landscapes adjacent to various land uses. Many of these areas will never be suitable for development and therefore are presently or potentially valuable for wildlife habitat.

Seattle is a city in a region that takes open space seriously. For example, voters passed an initiative in 1979 to tax themselves in order to preserve farmland in King County. The region prides itself on being environmentally knowledgeable and sensitive. Many people moved originally to the region because of its natural beauty. Although we have no supporting data, we believe that Seattle residents are especially knowledgeable of urban nature and habitats. On the premise that Seattleites have knowledge about urban wildlife and their habitats, we hypothesized that they also have positive attitudes toward urban wildlife habitats, are able to recognize good habitat, and prefer landscapes that are good habitats. The study included a photo preference test, a habitat recognition test, and a questionnaire to determine knowledge and attitudes, and to gather demographic data.

LITERATURE REVIEW

This study follows a first pilot study conducted in a Seattle suburb (Black et al. 1985), and attempts to build on previous results from studies on visual preferences for land-

Integrating Man and Nature in the Metropolitan Environment. Proc. Natl. Symp. on Urban Wildl., Chevy Chase, Md., 4–7 November 1986, L.W. Adams and D.L. Leedy, eds. Published by Natl. Inst. for Urban Wildl., 10921 Trotting Ridge Way, Columbia, MD 21044, 1987.

scapes, on attitudes toward wildlife and wildlife habitat in the city, and on knowledge of wildlife and wildlife habitat.

Landscape Preferences

A recent review of 88 studies indicated research on human responses to vegetation and landscapes is plentiful (Ulrich 1986). For more than 15 years, researchers have studied preference for specific landscape elements (Zube 1976, Brown and Daniel 1984), categorized landscape types and compared viewer preferences among types (Balling and Falk 1982, Herzog et al. 1982, Kaplan and Kaplan 1982, Lyons 1983, Hayward and Weitzer 1984, Schauman 1986), and looked for differences in preference due to demography (Herzog et al. 1982, Lyons 1983, Nasar 1983, Hayward and Weitzer 1984). It is generally agreed that people's preferences are broadly predictable: positive toward natural landscapes in general, and toward trees and green, park-like or pastoral landscapes in particular. Less agreement exists as to the variations in preference due to gender, race, or geographical residency.

Although many landscape preference studies have been conducted, little work relates natural area preference to wildlife habitat value. Pudelkewicz (1981) examined residents' preferences for the planned open spaces of Columbia, Maryland. She used characteristics proposed by Kaplan and Kaplan (1982) and hypothesized three predictors as influencing preference—(1) promised information (mystery, complexity), (2) legibility (coherence, space, texture, edge), and (3) primary landscape qualities (trees, wildlife, water). The same photos used for the preference testing also were rated for wildlife habitat characteristics. She found that trees, complexity, and mystery were the strongest predictors of preference. Her suggestion for designers was to combine less preferred areas with more acceptable areas, or to locate less acceptable areas away from residents' homes. However, designers are not usually involved in the day to day management decisions concerning the appearance of remnant open spaces. These decisions usually result from public attitudes about the appearance of a specific site, one most often covered with volunteer plants arranged by natural selection, not design.

Attitudes Toward Wildlife or Wildlife Habitat

There has been a range of studies to identify variables influencing attitudes toward wildlife, such as interest and knowledge of wild animals (Dagg 1974), the local environment (Gilbert 1982), and wildlife as an amenity (Dick 1982). Most of these studies dealt with attitudes toward wildlife rather than habitat. There is little to suggest that a given attitude toward animals will necessarily indicate a predictable attitude toward the animal's habitat. Only two articles (Pudelkewicz 1981 and Black et al. 1985) attempted directly to determine residents' attitudes toward habitat, and of those, only Black et al. (1985) looked at habitat outside the residents' immediate setting.

Knowledge of Wildlife and Wildlife Habitat

Few studies have examined knowledge of wildlife in relation to attitudes toward wildlife. Leedy et al. (1978) reported that despite their acceptance of many wildlife species in urban areas, a large number of people were unable to identify many of the animals that were sometimes present. Respondents' knowledge in relation to preference has been mentioned only by Kellert (1984), and he placed no emphasis on knowledge of habitat. Gilbert (1982) found that many urban residents appeared not to understand that diversity of vegetation was important in producing a diversity of wildlife species. Black et al. (1985) found that residents had surprisingly high knowledge of certain wildlife species habitat needs, and residents correctly identified water as an important element in habitats. Habitat knowledge was related to preferences by Pudelkewicz (1981), but she related the experts' knowledge to residents' preference.

It seems apparent that little has been done to determine the public's attitudes or knowledge regarding urban wildlife habitats. It is conceivable that the public may have a positive attitude toward urban wildlife as long as it is at no cost to them in terms of accepting undesirable nearby habitat landscapes. Alternatively, it may be that the public really does know what constitutes good urban habitat and factors this knowledge into a preference decision.

Many unanswered questions remain for those agencies dealing with the public on the conservation of urban wildlife habitats. Prominent among these are:

1. What, if any, is the relationship between knowledge of wildlife habitat and landscape preferences?
2. Is there any difference in preferences for habitat based on proximity to respondents' homes?
3. What demographic factors are associated with knowledge of wildlife habitat?
4. What demographic factors are associated with preferences and attitudes toward landscapes?

METHODS

This study was conducted during the period June through September, 1986. Data were gathered by means of a photo preference test and a questionnaire.

Photo Preference Test

Fifteen black and white photographs were chosen to represent typical remnant and designed open space habitats in Seattle. Landscapes were photographed within a 3-week period during sunny, midsummer weather. All photographs were taken with a 35mm camera from the same height above ground level. No details (leaf shape, flowers, or identifiable plants) were visible in the foreground. All scenes excluded built structures (buildings, roads, utility poles), animals, trash, people, and water. The photographs were differentiated mainly by amount of ground cover, numbers and distribution of trees and shrubs, and distribution of vegetative heights. The scenes ranged from treeless, mowed grass areas to a mixed, uneven-aged forest to a dense coniferous stand.

Seven wildlife biologists rated the expected wildlife diversity of each picture on a five-point scale from 5 = Most Diversity to 1 = Least Diversity. The biologists' mean ratings for each picture were used to group the photographs into five categories from "most diverse habitat" to "least diverse habitat." The 3- by 5-inch (7.6 by 12.7 cm) pictures were then randomly arranged, assigned a letter from A to O and mounted on a gray board containing the words "WE NEED YOUR OPINION."

Questionnaire

Preference.—A written questionnaire was used to record preference responses and elicit attitudes toward and knowledge of wildlife habitat in the city. Preference scores for each of the 15 scenes were solicited on a scale of Like Very Much(1), Like Somewhat(2), Neither Like nor Dislike(3), Dislike Somewhat(4), and Dislike Very Much(5). Respondents were asked first for their preference on all 15 photos as if the scene were "somewhere in the city," and then the preference question was repeated as if the scene were "across the street from your house." Finally, respondents were asked to identify and give a one-word description of their most preferred and least preferred scenes.

Attitudes, Knowledge, and Demographic Data.—The second section of the questionnaire contained 11 opinion statements, such as "Nearby greenery and open spaces are important attractions to me when choosing a neighborhood in which to live." Respondents were asked to indicate if they Strongly Agree(1), Agree(2), Neutral(3), Disagree(4), or Strongly Disagree(5).

Sections three and four were designed to discover the levels of verbal and visual knowledge of respondents regarding wildlife-habitat relationships. Section three was a series of eight questions based on wildlife-habitat interactions, such as: "One way that homeowners can attract robins is to put out a birdhouse for them in the spring." We asked respondents to "Agree" or "Disagree," and a score was determined by the total number of correct responses of each respondent.

In the fourth section, we solicited visual knowledge of habitats by having the respondents rate the original 15 photographs for wildlife diversity, using the same scale as the wildlife biologists. To obtain a score for the habitat recognition section, we subtracted each respondent's ratings of habitat from the experts' mean ratings. This yielded a "difference" score that was used in subsequent analyses.

The fifth section of the questionnaire asked for the following demographic information: gender, ethnicity, age, number in household under 15 years, home ownership, dwelling type, schooling, family income, childhood environment, and outdoor activities.

Data Collection

Data collection sites consisted of a card table and chairs set up at six Seattle supermarkets during the month of August, 1986. Locations were selected if they were not on major commute routes so that they would draw from local residents. We administered the questionnaire in four predominantly white neighborhoods and two predominantly black or mixed-race neighborhoods. Only those passers-by who showed an interest in the display board were asked if they wanted to help us with a survey of open space in the City of Seattle. Eighty-five people volunteered to complete the survey (Table 1).

Table 1. Demographic characteristics for questionnaire respondents compared to the city-wide population, Seattle, Washington, 1986.

Variable	Seattle[a]	Study respondents
Population	493,846	85
Median age	32.4	40
Median family income	$22,096	$27,500
Completed 4 yrs. college	28.1%	35.8%
Owner occupied housing	51%	53.2%
Ethnicity		
White	80%	79.3%
Black	9.5%	15.9%
Other	10%	4.8%

[a]Source: Neighborhood Profiles. 1980. Seattle Post-Intelligencer

RESULTS

We used one verbal and one visual measure for both preference and knowledge. One method of determining knowledge was the number of correct responses to the questions regarding wildlife-habitat interactions. The visual measure of knowledge was the difference between the respondents' and the experts' rating given to each scene based on its expected relative habitat diversity. The two measures of preference consisted of the rating given to each photograph and the rated response to each attitude statement.

Knowledge of Wildlife Habitat and Landscape Preference

We found some correlation between the respondents' ability to recognize habitat diversity and their preference for a landscape. However, only four "somewhere in the city" and six "across the street" scenes had significant positive correlations (Table 2). Additionally, two scenes (E, I) "somewhere in the city" and one scene (E) "across the street" had significant negative correlations between recognition and preference. Scene I is a highly preferred golf course with a mowed lawn and tall deciduous trees. Respondents who chose this scene as their first preference described

Table 2. Kendall Rank-order Correlation between habitat diversity recognition and two types of preference, Seattle, Washington, 1986.

Scene	R-value	Probability
For scene "somewhere in the city other than your neighborhood"		
L mixed species woodland with shrubs	0.2770	0.003
O tall grass, shrubs & trees	0.2700	0.004
E tall grass, shrubs	−0.2365	0.008
G tall grass, shrubs & trees	0.2322	0.010
I mowed golf course	−0.2115	0.025
H tall grass, cattails & trees	0.2002	0.024
For scene "across the street from your house"		
E tall grass, shrubs	−0.3756	0.001
O tall grass, shrubs & trees	0.2795	0.003
H tall grass, cattails & trees	0.2749	0.003
B mixed height deciduous woodland	0.2648	0.005
D dense, mixed woodland	0.2432	0.008
G tall grass, shrubs & trees	0.2162	0.014
L mixed species woodland with shrubs	0.1984	0.024

it as "neat," "pastoral," "clean," "friendly," "safe," "pleasing to the eye," and "open." The other scene (E) "somewhere in the city," correlating negatively, was a tall grass—low shrub landscape that was rated low in preference but high in habitat value. Respondents who ranked this as their lowest preferred scene described it as "flat," "weedy," "boring," "unkempt," "dry," "the pits," and "scrubby."

The second measure of knowledge, a score based on the number of correct responses to the wildlife-habitat interaction questions, was not significantly correlated with the respondents' visual ability to recognize habitat diversity. Therefore, these verbal and visual measures seemed to be dealing with different aspects of wildlife knowledge. Nevertheless, the second measure of knowledge showed little correlation with landscape preference (Table 3). Six "somewhere in the city" scenes demonstrated significant positive correlations, and one such scene had significant negative correlation. Only two scenes had significant positive correlations between the respondent's score on the wildlife habitat questions and preference for landscapes "across the street." Respondents who chose these scenes as their first preference gave reasons for their choice such as "depth," "trees," "balance," "beauty," "open and sunny," "peaceful," "diverse," and "natural."

Table 3. Kendall Rank-order Correlation between the number correct on knowledge test and two types of preference, Seattle, Washington, 1986.

Scene	R-value	Probability
For scene "somewhere in the city other than your neighborhood"		
O tall grass, shrubs & trees	0.2140	0.01
C mixed species woodland	0.2127	0.01
H tall grass, cattails & trees	0.1999	0.017
K mature trees, high mowed grass	−0.1962	0.021
G tall grass, shrubs & trees	0.1933	0.02
L mixed species woodland with shrubs	0.1611	0.038
B mixed height deciduous woodland	0.1502	0.05
For scene "across the street from your house"		
B mixed height deciduous woodland	0.1641	0.035
G tall grass, shrubs & trees	0.1634	0.036

The results of relating both the visual recognition of habitats and the verbal score of knowledge seem to indicate that knowledge is related to preference, but not strongly so. This may differ from Dagg's (1974) conclusion that preference and knowledge were related because they each correlated with other factors. Ulrich's (1986) literature review did not cite any articles relating knowledge to landscape preferences.

Preferences regarding open spaces were measured through responses to a set of attitude statements. These verbal responses, when individually correlated with verbal knowledge measured by the score on the wildlife habitat questions, revealed no significant correlations. However, we believe that a better approach in this type of study would be to derive a single score of verbal preference for each respondent based on his or her combined responses to the attitude questions.

Although there appear to be relatively few correlations between the measures of wildlife habitat knowledge and landscape preference in this study, people do appear to be able to recognize relative values of habitat. The respondents' ranking of the scenes based on habitat diversity differed significantly from the biologists' ranking in only three photos. We inferred that the general public can recognize, perhaps intuitively, landscapes for their habitat value, whether or not they have knowledge of wildlife-habitat associations.

Habitat Preferences in Relation to Proximity to Respondent's Residence

Respondents were asked to rate their preference for each scene based on whether the landscape was located "somewhere in the city" or "across the street." When comparisons were made between the ratings for the two locations (T-test of the means of preference and Repeated Measures Analysis of Variance), significant differences were found between the two groups, with "somewhere in the city" locations being preferred. We inferred from this that preference for a natural landscape decreases as its location moves close to one's home. This conclusion is consistent with Balling and Falk (1982) and Lyons (1983) who found significant differences between preferences for natural scenes based on whether one would visit a place or have it as a part of one's daily experience.

In a simple inspection of the ranking of scenes, some further differences were revealed. Scene C, a mixed height and species woodland, was both preferred by the respondents and rated excellent habitat by respondents and the biologists. Scene A, deciduous new growth woodland, though rated good habitat by the respondents, was one of the least preferred "across the street," but ranked higher if located "somewhere in the city." Reasons given for not liking this scene by respondents who rated it as their lowest preference were "dense," "unkempt," and "too much timber." Scene E, a tall grass, low shrub area with no trees, was the least preferred landscape in either location; it was rated medium (respondents) and low (biologists) for habitat value.

Demographic Factors and Knowledge of Wildlife Habitat

We found few demographic factors showing significant relationships with either the verbal or visual measures of knowledge. For the number correct on the wildlife-habitat interaction questions, only *age* ($\chi^2 = 9.11$, $p = 0.0105$) and *households with children under 15* ($\chi^2 = 4.27$, $p = 0.0387$) showed a significant relationship with verbal knowledge. When we examined visual recognition of habitats with demographic data, we found that only *households with children under 15* (χ^2 range = 10.7–12.3, p range = 0.01–0.03) and *number of activities this year* (χ^2 range = 10.0–13.7, p range = 0.006–0.04) demonstrated significant relationships. We concluded that little relationship seemed to exist between knowledge of wildlife habitat and demographic factors. This conclusion differs from Dagg (1974) who found age, education, and work status to be significant and Kellert (1984) who found relationships with wildlife knowledge and education, race, and income.

Demographic Factors and Preferences-Attitudes Toward Landscape

We also attempted to find relationships between demographic factors and either attitude or preference. Many of the demographic characteristics showed some relationship with a few individual attitude statements, but the data are inconclusive.

The variable *ethnicity* was related to preference more frequently than any other demographic variable. It was a significant factor in eight scenes if they were located "somewhere in the city" (χ^2 range = 11.6–18.0, p range = 0.001–0.03) and in 10 scenes if they were located "across the street" (χ^2 range = 13.3–26.6), p range = 0.001–0.09). Another demographic factor, *activity level,* was second in importance but had only five significant relationships with preferences for scenes. We concluded that race may relate to preference in yet to be determined ways and that other factors seemed to be unimportant.

Hayward and Weitzer (1984) stated the importance of collecting demographic information when surveying residents' preferences. Researchers have found correlations of preferences or attitudes with age, home ownership, sex, location, urban vs. rural, and history of residence (Dagg 1974, Balling and Falk 1982, Gilbert 1982, Lyons 1983, Schroeder 1983). However, some researchers have found contradictory results regarding some of these same variables (Faulkenberry 1974, Lyons 1983). We tend to agree with Pudelkewicz (1981) who believed there was little to support the conclusion that a relationship between demography and preference exists.

CONCLUSIONS

This study was based on the premise that knowing preference will provide some understanding of how people may react in certain landscape decision situations. Our results indicated that preference does change as the landscape comes in closer proximity to one's home territory. The presence of open space received greater approval if located "somewhere in the city" than it did if located "across the street."

From the correlations of both verbal and visual knowledge with landscape preference, we concluded that knowledge regarding the interaction between wildlife and habitat does relate somewhat to preference. However, this is not a strong association and other, yet unidentified, factors appear to affect landscape preference. The public's visual ability to recognize habitat diversity was surprisingly good, for it did not differ significantly from the opinion of the experts. Because the verbal knowledge did not correlate with the respondents' recognition of habitat diversity, we inferred that, for these subjects, visual ability may be an intuitive and unconscious judgement. People are able to read the landscape and identify good habitat. Furthermore, this visual reading ability seemed to correlate with preference. Perhaps if this ability were raised to a conscious understanding through education, it could be an effective means of ensuring a more informed public who will have clearer conservation goals for remnant urban habitats. More research is needed to determine to what degree education might change people's conservation decisions, especially for those landscapes close to home and easy to see, smell, and touch.

REFERENCES CITED

Balling, J. D. and J. H. Falk. 1982. Development of visual preference for natural environments. Environ. and Behav. 14:5 28.

Black, S., P. Broadhurst, J. Hightower, and S. Schauman. 1985. The value of riparian habitat and wildlife to the residents of a rapidly urbanizing community. Pages 413–416 *in* First North Am. Riparian Conf. Tucson.

Brown, T. C. and T. C. Daniel. 1984. Modeling forest scenic beauty: concepts and application to Ponderosa Pine. Res. Pap. RM-256, USDA For. Serv., Fort Collins.

Dagg, A.I. 1974. Reactions of people to urban wildlife. Pages 163–165 *in* J. H. Noyes and D. R. Progulske, eds. A symposium on wildlife in an urbanizing environment. Planning and Resour. Dev. Ser. 28, USDA For. Serv., Amherst, Mass.

Dick, R. E. 1982. An analysis of human responses to contacts with wildlife in urban parks. Ph.D. Thesis, Univ. of Wash., Seattle. 162pp.

Faulkenberry, G. D. and C. D. Cowan. 1974. Oregon wildlife preferences and activities survey. Oregon State Univ., Corvallis.

Gilbert, F. F. 1982. Public attitudes toward urban wildlife: a pilot study in Guelph, Ontario. Wildl. Soc. Bull. 10:245–253.

Hayward, D. G. and W. H. Weitzer. 1984. The public's image of urban parks: past amenity, present ambivalance, uncertain future. Urban Ecol. 8:243–268.

Herzog, T., S. Kaplan, and R. Kaplan. 1982. The prediction of preference for unfamiliar urban places. Population and Environ. 5:43–59.

Kaplan, R. 1984. Impact of urban nature: a theoretical analysis. Urban Ecol. 8:189–197.

Kaplan, S. and R. Kaplan. 1982. Cognition and environment: functioning in an uncertain world. Praeger, New York. 287pp.

Kellert, S. R. 1984. Urban American perceptions of animals and the natural environment. Urban Ecol. 8:209–228.

Leedy, D. L., R. M. Maestro, and T. M. Franklin. 1978. Planning for wildlife in cities and suburbs. FWS/OBS-77/66, USDI Fish and Wildl. Serv., Washington, D.C. 64pp.

Lyons, E. 1983. Demographic correlates of landscape preference. Environ. and Behav. 15:487–511.

McHarg, I. L. 1969. Design with nature. Doubleday, Garden City. 197pp.

Nasar, J. L. 1983. Adult viewers' preferences in residential scenes: a study of the relationship of environmental attributes to preference. Environ. and Behav. 15:589–614.

Pudelkewicz, P. J. 1981. Visual response to urban wildlife habitat. Trans. North Am. Wildl. and Nat. Resour. Conf. 46:381–389.

Schauman, S. 1986. Scenic value of countryside landscapes to local residents. Natl. Symp. on Social Sci. in Resour. Manage. Oregon State Univ., Corvallis. 230pp.

Schroeder, H.W. 1983. Variations in the perception of urban forest recreation sites. Leis. Sci. 5:221–230.

Spirn, A. W. 1984. The granite garden: urban nature and human design. Basic Books, New York. 334pp.

Ulrich, R. S. 1986. Human responses to vegetation and landscapes. Landscape and Urban Planning 13:29–44.

Zube, E. H., ed. 1976. Studies in landscape perception. Univ. of Mass., Amherst. 169pp.

Greenways for Americans[1]

HAL SALWASSER, *President's Commission on Americans Outdoors, Washington, D.C.*[2]

"they should form a framework of . . . parks and forests connected by a series of paths and trails . . . for . . . general outdoor living."

Benton MacKaye (1929)

RECOMMENDATION

Establish a network of private, local, and state GREENWAYS to provide people with access to open spaces close to where they live and to link together the rural and urban spaces in the American landscape.

BACKGROUND

Imagine getting on a bicycle, a horse, a trail bike, or simply donning a back pack at Pine Cliff, North Carolina, and crossing the country along a continuous network of greenways. Perhaps your trip only goes as far as a city park in Roanoke, Virginia, or maybe it concludes in Wicasset Bay, Maine. It could have taken you all the way to Montana de Oro State Park in California or to the Willamette River Greenway in Oregon. And it could include stops along the way for trout and bass fishing, quail hunting, a leisurely canoe trip, or a reunion with old school chums on the Appalachian National Trail.

The byways for this trip of the future are Greenways that reach out from communities all across America to link cities, towns, farms, ranches, parks, refuges, deserts, alpine, wetlands, and forests into a vast and varied network of open spaces for recreation and conservation. Many of the pieces of the network are already there: greenways along rivers, old rail lines, floodways, Heritage Corridors, wetlands, and big game migration routes. It is time to hook them up.

Farfetched? Bold? Audacious? You Bet! Just like the Interstate Highway System was several decades ago and pioneering the West was several centuries ago. Even more far out, we are going to build this network of Greenways for Americans with private capital, local initiative, lots of sweat equity, and only a helping hand from the general public at large.

So, what are these greenways? They are natural areas where recreation and conservation are the primary uses and values. Fingers of green that come in many shapes and sizes, serve many purposes, and derive from many different beginnings: biking and hiking trails along abandoned rail lines, boating and fishing sites on ribbons of bright water restored from neglect in an earlier time, zones of wildland on vacant lots for "just messing around" after school or work, and belts of grasslands, shrubs, and forest surrounding and threading their way through cities and countrysides like the capillaries of a giant circulatory system. They can be like spokes on a big wheel, the rim of the wheel, the patches and connections in a weblike network, or just individual strips and bands of natural lands and waters.

This country has committed vast tracts of lands and waters and invested enormous sums of money in its heritage of federal and state parks, forests, and reserves (500 to 700 million acres [202 to 283 million ha] open to recreation). They are world class resources, and remain bulwarks in our recreation estate. But they tend to be far from where people live and limited in their ability to meet the growing diversity of America's recreation and conservation needs. Seventy-five to 80 percent of Americans live in urbanizing areas. They need open spaces close to home. And they need the pride that comes from accomplishments that result from individual ideas and actions. Greenways can meet those needs.

Greenways for Americans will be based on getting the most from existing resources and programs, and tapping the

[1]A preliminary draft of the President's Commission on Americans Outdoors.

[2]Present address: USDA Forest Service, Box 2417, Washington, D.C. 20013.

Integrating Man and Nature in the Metropolitan Environment. Proc. Natl. Symp. on Urban Wildl., Chevy Chase, Md., 4–7 November 1986, L.W. Adams and D.L. Leedy, eds. Published by Natl. Inst. for Urban Wildl., 10921 Trotting Ridge Way, Columbia, MD 21044, 1987.

power of market forces and individual initiative. A variety of mechanisms will be used to build the system including:

- recognition/registration of sites that already meet the goals,
- incentives to private interests to make lands and waters available for recreation; including law enforcement, protection of property rights, limitation to liability, and encouragement to provide services that are better delivered by the private sector,
- Conservation Reserves and Conservation Easements under the 1985 Farm Bill,
- elimination of federal subsidies for new development in 100-year floodplains and elimination of disaster aid for property losses in floodways,
- challenge grants from the Trust for Americans Outdoors and private corporations and foundations to stimulate local matching funds when acquisition by local, state, or non-profit groups is deemed appropriate,
- broader application of existing authorities to use abandoned rail lines and utility corridors for the public good, and
- local, county, or state recreation fees to fund operations and maintenance on public areas.

Greenways for Americans is a bold idea with the magic to stir people to action. But Greenways themselves are not new. We wish to spread the concept, like a prairie fire, across the American landscape by focusing on the potential values of Greenways to local communities and of a Greenways network to regions and the entire country, encouraging more consistent application, stimulating grass roots initiative, and emphasizing the roles of private and local interests in recreation and conservation.

GOALS

- Provide Americans with access to open spaces and wildlands for the widest possible variety of outdoor activities close to home.
- Conserve the great American landscape, in all its diversity, and the full potential for human interactions with that heritage.
- Increase the roles of private enterprise and local governments and groups in recreation and conservation.
- Encourage local pride and celebration in the quality and availability of outdoor assets.
- Diversify and strengthen local economies and lifestyles through enhanced recreation opportunities.
- Leverage federal investments in recreation and conservation with local dollars (including private investments) and "sweat equity."
- Link urban and rural areas into a diverse network for the dual purposes of recreation and conservation of natural resources.

ELEMENTS OF A GREENWAYS NETWORK

The Greenways network is envisioned to include any site, public or private, that is managed in a predominantly natural state for conservation of resources and recreation opportunities. For example:

- Greenways along river and stream courses [about 3 million miles (4.8 million km) potential; Corps of Engineers and local floodplains managers could be major partners],
- Greenways along old rail lines [about 120,000 miles (193,000 km) potential; railway corporations and trails coalitions could be major partners],
- Greenways along wildlife migration routes (State wildlife agencies and landowners major partners),
- Greenways along utility corridors (unknown extent; utility company and ORV groups partners),
- Greenways along scenic roads and highways (Blue Highways; AAA, Federal Highway Users partners), and
- Greenways along landforms, trails, paths, flood protection zones, and linear parks.

The network will result from using Greenways to connect existing recreation and conservation areas, thereby enhancing the values of both those areas and the Greenways. For example, units of the:

- National Forest System,
- National Park System,
- National System of Public Lands,
- State Parks and State Wildlife Areas,
- City and County Parks,
- Greenline Parks of mixed ownership, and
- Private lands managed at least partly for recreation uses, such as California's Ranches for Wildlife.

Greenways Examples (there are hundreds more)

New York Staten Island Greenbelt
Regional Parks, Oakland, California
Maryland Open Space Program
Illinois-Michigan Canal Natural Heritage Corridor
Yakima Greenway, Washington
Bicycle trail along Interstate 70 in Colorado

Potential Partners in Coalitions for Greenways (just a few examples of national groups with strong grass roots programs and chapters)

TransAmerica Trails Network
Trout Unlimited's Living Brightwater Trust
Izaak Walton League of America's Save our Streams
Trust for Public Land
Rails to Trails Conservancy
Garden Clubs of America
National Trails Council

Heritage Trails Fund
American Hiking Society
Walkways Center
Bicycle USA
Rail and utility companies
State fish and wildlife, forestry, and recreation agencies
State and local chambers of commerce and tourism boards
National Institute for Urban Wildlife
American Rivers Conservation Council
American Farmland Trust
Association of State Flood Plain Managers
The Nature Conservancy
American Forestry Association
ORV groups
State and local highway agencies
Private landowners

Some Examples of Local Action and Coordination

Grass Roots Ikes Program
Coordinated Resource Management Planning

Suggested Local Roles

Goal setting, inventories, and priorities
Planning and management coordination
Major funding and sweat equity
Operations and maintenance

Suggested Federal Roles

Champion the concept—Exec. Order, new law, marketing with assistance from an advertising agency working through the national offices of grass roots groups
LWCF challenge grants
Enforce existing statutes on environmental quality and property rights
Logistics and brokering technical assistance

POTENTIAL BENEFITS

- reduced flood damage
- wildlife habitat; plant and animal conservation
- water table recharge in wetlands and healthy riparians
- aesthetics of the landscape
- enhanced community pride and identity
- lower cost than major federal acquisition program
- more effective use of limited land area for conservation
- concurrent uses by compatible industries
- enhanced awareness and appreciation for wildlands
- more diverse local economies from tourism

Urban Wildlife Research and Management

Chairman: Eric G. Bolen, *Associate Dean, The Graduate School, Texas Tech University, Lubbock*

Cochairman: Larry W. VanDruff, *Professor, State University of New York, Syracuse*

Summer and Winter Distribution of Introduced Bird Species and Native Bird Species Richness within a Complex Urban Environment

Arthur M. Johnsen[1] and Larry W. VanDruff, *College of Environmental Science and Forestry, State University of New York, Syracuse, NY 13210*

INTRODUCTION

Relative to native ecosystems, the urban ecosystem is severely disturbed and dominated by man and his artifacts (Stearns and Ross 1978). There is an apparent paucity of native wildlife and an abundance of a few exotic (introduced) species, notably the house sparrow (*Passer domesticus*), starling (*Sturnus vulgaris*), rock dove (*Columba livia*), Norway rat (*Rattus norvegicus*), and house mouse (*Mus musculus*). These species, along with uncontrolled and feral domestic dogs and cats, are often the most conspicuous animals in the city. Given their visibility, it is tempting to characterize these introduced species as ecological aberrants that thrive at the expense of more desirable native species. These species appear to be extremely successful in human settlements and, prior to their introduction from Europe (Laycock 1966), were most likely already adapted to the habitat types they occupy in North America. An understanding of the relationships between attributes of the urban environment and wildlife abundance must be gained so that the wildlife manager can make recommendations about the design or redesign of urban areas.

A number of recent investigations (Thomas et al. 1974, Lucid 1974, Paulick 1976, DeGraaf 1978, Gehringer 1980) have used stepwise multiple regression analysis in an attempt to discover which attributes of the urban environment can be used to predict variability in the relative abundance of birds. The stepwise multiple regression technique is used to express the relationship between a criterion variable (in this case bird abundance) and a linear combination of weighted predictor variables. Starting with the predictor variable that accounts for the greatest amount of the variance in the criterion variable, only those predictors meeting some predetermined measure of usefulness are added to the equation. In this way, a large set of habitat variables can be reduced to a smaller set that is relevant to a given species. The square of the multiple correlation coefficient (R^2) is a measure of the extent to which the selected predictor variable set "accounts for" the observed variability in the criterion variable. A review of the studies cited above does not provide a consistent set of habitat attributes accounting for variability in introduced bird abundance. These studies were heavily weighted toward vegetational attributes of the environment. The current study was designed to investigate bird-habitat relationships with greater emphasis on the man-made component of the urban environment.

STUDY AREA

Syracuse is centrally located in upstate New York and is approximately centered at 42°2′30″ North Latitude and 76°7′30″ West Longitude. The corporation limits include 16,425 acres (6650 ha) (SOCPA 1977b) and the metropolitan area is approximately 17,300 acres (7000 ha) in size (Rowse 1979). The city has grown from a population of 200 in 1820 to nearly 200,000 by 1970 (SOCPA 1977b). Syracuse is typical of northeastern cities of its age, having developed from the center outward. The central business district (CBD) and the oldest residential areas are at the

[1]Present address: New York State Dep. of Environ. Conserv., Wildl. Resour. Cent., Delmar, NY 12054.

center. Toward the periphery, smaller commercial areas and newer residential areas were added as the city developed. As this development moved outward, older residential areas in the center of the city became dilapidated. Here many homes became low-income rental property or were razed and replaced by multiple dwelling units or commercial and institutional structures (SOCPA 1977b).

All areas of the city can be placed in the traditional land use categories of commercial, light industrial, residential, institutional, and open space. Only the heavy industrial category is lacking (SOCPA 1977a). The dominant land use type is residential (38%). Open land of various types comprises 29%. A full description of the physiography, climate, soils, and biota of Syracuse is reported elsewhere (Rowse 1979, Syracuse Conservation Advisory Council 1979).

House sparrows and starlings were introduced in New York City, approximately 175 air miles (280 km) from Syracuse in 1850 and 1890, respectively (Bull 1974, pp. 539–541). Rock doves were established in the Great Lakes region and the northeastern American Colonies at the beginning of the 18th Century (Schorger 1952), and feral populations probably existed in Syracuse prior to the arrival of the other two introduced bird species.

METHODS

Study Sites

For the 1970 U.S. Census, Syracuse was divided into 63 census tracts. The tracts, of variable area, were calculated to include roughly equal numbers of people. For the purposes of this study, 20 of these census tracts were selected so that tracts that were predominantly commercial, light industrial, high density residential, and low density residential were all represented. The sample included areas of both old and new development.

Within each of the 20 census tracts, five street segments, evenly dispersed throughout the tract, were selected from a city street map. This scheme yielded a total sample of 100 city streets. The sample was later reduced to 99 when data collection on one street had to be terminated because all of the buildings and vegetation were razed to make room for a bus garage.

Bird Counts

Eight summer and eight winter bird counts were made on each of 99 streets over a period of 2 years. Transects were walked over a pre-established segment of 328 feet (100m). All birds seen within 82 feet (25 m) of either side of the street were tallied by species by a single observer advancing over the transect at a constant rate of approximately 0.62 miles/hour (1 km/h). Only birds to the side and ahead of the observer were counted. Flying birds were counted only if they were, in the judgment of the observer, flying into or out of the count area or if they appeared to be "hunting" (e.g., raptors and gulls) within the area.

Summer counts were made between 1–4 hours after sunrise from mid-July to the first week in September, 1979 and 1980. This summer period has been considered post-breeding for the three introduced species (Erskine 1976) but nest behavior was observed in all three species in late July. Summer counts were not made during rain or for 1 hour following rain or when wind velocity exceeded 3 Beaufort (13–19 km/h) or when the temperature exceeded 90°F (33°C).

Winter counts were conducted between 10:00 a.m. and 2:00 p.m. from mid-January to mid-March, 1980 and 1981. All procedures were the same as those for summer except that winter counts were not made during heavy snowfall or when wind velocity exceeded 19 miles/hour (30 km/h) or when the temperature was below 5°F (−15°C).

Habitat Attributes

Twenty-eight habitat variables that were judged to be nonredundant and that emphasized the built environment and human activity were selected and measured for each of the 99 transects. These were as follows: average numbers of dogs, cats, children, adults and moving automobiles encountered while making the bird counts; numbers, within the count area, of bird feeders, windows and doors per unit building volume, linear wires, transverse wires, T.V. antennas, ventilation louvres, separate buildings, and holes in buildings; total building volume and mean age of buildings; proportions of aluminum siding and brick construction within each count area; proportions of commercial, industrial, and vacant land within an area of 125 acres (50 ha) surrounding the transect; proportions of pavement, coniferous cover, deciduous cover, herbaceous cover, and number of separate vegetation patches within an area of 2.5 acres (1 ha) surrounding the transect; distance of the transect from the central business district; and human population density and proportion of dwellings occupied by owners for the city blocks adjacent to the transect.

In order to determine if the set of original variables could be described by a simplified set of compound variables and to provide a set of uncorrelated predictor variables, the 28 habitat variables were subjected to principal components analysis and VARIMAX rotation (Nie et al. 1975). Conceptually, this procedure is simply the rotation of a set of 28 uncorrelated (orthogonal) axes into best alignment with the 28 original variables within the constraints of the VARIMAX criterion.

The results of this procedure yielded little "simplification" of the variable set. The first two principal components in the solution were each highly correlated with more than one of the original variables. The first was positively correlated with number of buildings, number of windows and doors per unit building volume, and transverse wires. This principal component is labeled "structural complexity." The second principal component was positively correlated with area of herbaceous cover and negatively correlated with area of pavement and is termed "herbaceous-pavement tradeoff."

The third through the 26th principal components each had high to moderate correlations with one of the original habitat variables and are named, in each case, for the most highly associated variable. The 27th and 28th principal components were each unrelated to any of the original variables.

All of the variability in the original set of variables is expressed in the set of 28 principal components. Each of the principal components is statistically independent of all others.

Table 1. Simple correlations (r) among exotic bird abundance indices and native bird species richness, Syracuse, New York, summer 1979–1980.

	Rock dove	Starling	Native species richness
House sparrow	.077	.437*	.042
Rock dove		.110	−.380*
Starling			.009
Native species richness			

*$p < 0.05$.

Table 2. Simple correlations (r) among exotic bird abundance indices and native bird species richness, Syracuse, New York, winter 1980–1981.

	Rock dove	Starling	Native species richness
House sparrow	.157	.405*	.182*
Rock dove		.085	−.218*
Starling			−.086*
Native species richness			

*$p < 0.05$.

RESULTS AND DISCUSSION

Bird Counts

Bird counts for the first and second years of the study were combined. In each season, each of the three introduced bird species occurred on more than 90% of the transects and represented the highest number of total encounters. In summer, house sparrows, starlings, and rock doves accounted for 79% of the 9,889 individual birds encountered as follows: house sparrows, 45%; starlings, 14%; rock doves, 20%. In winter, the three introduced species accounted for 94% of 9,902 individual encounters as follows: house sparrows, 31%; starlings, 36%; rock doves, 27%.

In summer, simple correlations among the three introduced species and native bird species richness (number of native bird species recorded) revealed a small, inverse relationship between rock dove abundance and native species richness (Table 1). Also, house sparrow abundance was positively correlated with starling abundance. Though these relationships are statistically significant, they are weak.

In winter, the relationship between house sparrows and starlings was maintained, there was a small positive relationship between house sparrows and native species richness, and small negative relationships between both rock dove and starling abundances and native species richness (Table 2). Again, these relationships tend to be weak.

Table 3. Elements of the final regression equations for native bird species richness, Syracuse, New York, 1979–1981.

Season		Principal Component	β	Cum. R^2
Summer	P_{22}	(building volume)	−.335	.133
	P_7	(number of feeders)	.311	.209
	P_2	(herbaceous-pavement tradeoff)	.300	.299
	P_4	(area coniferous cover)	.295	.386
	P_3	(number of adults)	−.278	.464
	P_{12}	(area deciduous cover)	.278	.541
	P_{19}	(number of automobiles)	−.259	.608
	P_5	(number of children)	−.204	.649
	P_8	(number of linear wires)	.195	.687
	P_{10}	(age of structures)	−.176	.718
	P_{25}	(proportion dwellings owner occupied)	.097	.742
	P_{23}	(distance from CBD)	.094	.765
	P_{18}	(human population density)	−.075	.779
	P_{20}	(area commercial land use)	−.063	.790
Winter	P_4	(area coniferous cover)	.375	.141
	P_2	(herbaceous-pavement tradeoff)	.282	.220
	P_5	(number of children)	−.270	.294
	P_{10}	(age of structures)	−.212	.338
	P_{20}	(area commercial land use)	−.198	.378
	P_{21}	(number vegetation patches)	.194	.415
	P_7	(number of feeders)	.191	.452
	P_{12}	(area deciduous cover)	.184	.486
	P_{16}	(number of louvres)	.183	.519
	P_{23}	(distance from CBD)	.177	.550
	P_6	(number of holes)	−.158	.575
	P_{17}	(area industrial land use)[a]	.156	.600

[a]Area of industrial land use is negatively correlated with P_{17}.

Bird-Habitat Relationships

Stepwise multiple regression was performed using the indices of abundance for the three introduced species and native bird species richness as criterion (dependent) variables and all 28 principal components as predictor (independent) variables. Table 3 shows, for those principal components entering the final equations for native bird species richness, beta-weights and cumulative R^2 values for each season. Because the principal components were used as predictor variables, the values of the beta-weights can be interpreted as measures of the relative importance of the components in predicting the criterion variable (Darlington 1968).

In summer, 14 principal components accounted for 79% of the observed variability in this index. Richness tended to increase with increases in number of feeders; areas of coniferous, deciduous, and herbaceous cover; number of linear wires; proportion of dwellings owner occupied; and distance from the CBD. Richness decreased with increases in building volume; numbers of adults, automobiles, and children; age of structures; human population density; and area of commercial land use. For winter observations, 60% of the variability in native bird species richness was explained by 12 principal components. In winter, building volume, number of automobiles, number of adults, number of linear wires, proportion of dwellings owner occupied, and human population density dropped out of the equation. Positive relationships with number of vegetation patches and number of louvres and negative relationships with area of industrial land use and number of holes were added.

Table 4 shows the results of the stepwise multiple regression solutions for house sparrows, rock doves, and starlings. The distribution of house sparrows was unrelated to that of native bird species richness in summer and weakly related in winter. In both summer and winter, house sparrows responded positively to structural complexity and negatively to building volume. The former component, which accounted for 7% of the variability in summer and 9% in winter, did not emerge as relevant to the distribution of native bird species richness. In summer, house sparrows showed slight affinities for numbers of children, increased distance from the CBD, and human population density. Together, these components seem to relate to the intensity of human residential use which, in turn, may be related to

Table 4. Elements of the final regression equations for house sparrows, rock doves, and starlings, Syracuse, New York, 1979–1981.

Species Season		Principal Component	β	Cum. R^2
House sparrow	P_5	(number of children)	.296	.088
Summer	P_1	(structural complexity)	.266	.158
	P_{23}	(distance from CBD)	.218	.206
	P_{18}	(human population density)	.198	.245
	P_{22}	(building volume)	−.184	.279
Winter	P_1	(structural complexity)	.291	.085
	P_7	(number of feeders)	.268	.157
	P_{16}	(number of louvres)	.249	.219
	P_{13}	(number of T.V. antennas)	.213	.264
	P_{22}	(building volume)	−.191	.301
	P_4	(area of coniferous cover)	−.188	.336
	P_{21}	(number of vegetation patches)	.174	.366
Rock Dove	P_2 }	(herbaceous-pavement tradeoff)[a]	−.246 }	.173
Summer	P_2^2 }		.224 }	
	P_3	(number of adults)	.235	.225
	P_{10}	(age of structures)	.195	.263
	P_6	(number of holes)	.183	.296
	P_{21}	(number vegetation patches)	−.178	.328
Winter	P_2	(herbaceous-pavement tradeoff)	−.299	.089
	P_{10}	(age of structures)	.254	.154
Starling	P_9	(proportion aluminum siding)	.227	.052
Summer	P_{28}		.195	.090
Winter	P_1	(structural complexity)	.334	.111
	P_{18}	(human population density)	.282	.191
	P_5	(number of children)	.252	.254
	P_{22}	(building volume)	−.249	.316
	P_3	(number of adults)	−.179	.348
	P_{10}	(age of structures)	.174	.378
	P_{21}	(number vegetation patches)	.169	.407
	P_4	(area of coniferous cover)	−.160	.433

[a]First order polynomial term meets statistical criteria.

an increased food source from refuse. Waste food has been observed to be an important food source for house sparrows (Guth 1979). Part of the observed shift in house sparrow habitat preference from summer to winter can be explained by noting which habitat attributes were deleted or added to the predictive equations between seasons. In winter, number of children, distance from the CBD, and human population density were replaced by positive responses to number of feeders, number of ventilation louvres, number of T.V. antennas, and number of vegetation patches and a negative response to area of coniferous cover. The biological relevance of bird feeders is obvious. Larger areas of coniferous cover were, in this study, associated with suburban sites and the negative relationship to this component may indicate that house sparrows tended to move toward the central city in winter. Numbers of louvres, T.V. antennas, and vegetation patches may all be associated with increased shelter.

In both seasons, rock dove abundance was inversely related to native bird species richness. This observation was probably due to the great abundance of rock doves in some central city locations that entirely lacked native species. In summer, rock dove abundance was related to the herbaceous-pavement tradeoff by a "U-shaped" function. Rock dove numbers declined as area of pavement decreased, reached a minimum, and then increased. In winter, the relationship between rock dove abundance and this component was linearly decreasing. These observations probably resulted from increased nesting activity in the summer when the birds tended to move toward residential areas to nest. In both seasons, rock doves demonstrated an affinity for older structures. These two components were the only ones that emerged to explain winter rock dove distributions and accounted for only 15% of the total variability. In summer, rock doves responded positively to number of adults and number of holes and negatively to number of vegetation patches.

Starling abundance was unrelated to native bird species richness. In summer, two principal components accounted for only 9% of the total variability in starling abundance. The first of these, proportion of buildings with aluminum siding has no obvious interpretation. The second is virtually independent of the measured habitat variables. In winter, the components that predicted variability in starling abundance were structural complexity, human population density, number of children, building volume, number of adults, age of structures, number of vegetation patches, and area of coniferous cover. The pattern was quite similar to that for house sparrows in summer. In winter, starlings may have used residential areas, vacated by house sparrows, for food and shelter.

Though equations based on stepwise evaluation of the principal components of habitat variation measured in this study accounted for a relatively high proportion of the variability in native bird species richness, variability in the abundances of the three introduced species was poorly described. The introduced species tended to be distributed independently of native bird species richness. For the most part, summer starlings and winter rock doves were distributed randomly relative to the measured habitat variables. House sparrows tended to move out of areas of heavy residential use in winter and were replaced by starlings.

REFERENCES CITED

Bull, J. 1974. Birds of New York State. Doubleday/Nat. Hist. Press, Garden City, N.Y. 655 pp.

Darlington, R.B. 1968. Multiple regression in psychological research and practice. Psychol. Bull. 69:161–182.

DeGraaf, R.M. 1978. Avian communities and habitat associations in cities and suburbs. Pages 7–24 *in* C.M. Kirkpatrick, ed. Wildlife and people. Purdue Univ., W. Lafayette, Indiana.

Erskine, A.J. 1976. Chronology of nesting in urban birds as a guide to timing of censuses. Am. Birds 30:667–672.

Gehringer, S.D. 1980. Songbird-habitat relationships in an urban environment. M. Sc. Thesis, Pa. State Univ., State College. 110 pp.

Guth, R.W. 1979. The junk food guild: birds and mammals on picnic grounds and in residential areas. Ill. Audubon Bull. 189:3–7.

Laycock, G. 1966. The alien animals. Nat. Hist. Press, Garden City, N.Y. 240 pp.

Lucid, V.J. 1974. Bird utilization of habitat in residential areas. Ph.D. Thesis, Va. Polytech. Inst. and State Univ., Blacksburg. 164 pp.

Nie, N.H., C.H. Hull, J.G. Jenkins, K. Steinbrenner, and D.H. Bent. 1975. SPSS: Statistical package for the social sciences. McGraw-Hill, New York, N.Y. 576 pp.

Paulick, R.K. 1976. The determination of habitat components utilized by avian species in a planned suburban community. M. Sc. Thesis, Pa. State Univ., State College. 118 pp.

Rowse, R.N. 1979. An abundance survey and habitat affinity analysis of mammals in Syracuse, New York. M. Sc. Thesis, State Univ. of New York, Syracuse. 130 pp.

Schorger, A.W. 1952. Introduction of the domestic pigeon. Auk 69:462–463.

Stearns, F. and J.E. Ross. 1978. The pressures of urbanization and technology. Pages 199–217 *in* H.P. Brokaw, ed. Wildlife and America. Council on Environmental Quality, Washington, D.C.

Syracuse Conservation Advisory Council. 1979. City of Syracuse urban natural resource inventory. 82 pp.

SOCPA (Syracuse-Onondaga County Planning Agency). 1977a. Syracuse land use plan: proposed land use by neighborhood. (DRAFT). 68 pp.

SOCPA (Syracuse-Onondaga County Planning Agency). 1977b. Land use plan, Syracuse, NY.

Thomas, J.W., R.M. DeGraaf, and J.C. Mawson. 1974. A technique for evaluating bird habitat. Pages 159–162 *in* J.H. Noyes and D.R. Progulske, eds. Wildlife in an urbanizing environment. Planning and Resour. Dev. Ser. No. 28, Holdsworth Nat. Resour. Cent., Amherst, Mass.

Factors Influencing the Distribution and Abundance of Burrowing Owls in Cape Coral, Florida

TED WESEMANN AND MATTHEW ROWE, *Department of Biology, Appalachian State University, Boone, NC 28608*

INTRODUCTION

Birds have often been used to assess the impact of human activity on the environment (e.g., Carson 1962). The dangers of pesticide misuse discussed in Carson's essay were, at least in part, identified by the decline of many songbird populations in the United States. Moreover birds, because of their size and mobility, provide an excellent tool for assessing environmental changes that might occur over relatively short intervals of time or distance (but see Morrison 1986). Perhaps this is why habitat selection has been studied in more detail in birds than in any other group of animals (Krebs 1978, Cody 1985). Most of these studies, however, have focused on birds in "natural" environments (see Cody 1985, and other references therein). Habitat selection by birds in urban or other human-modified habitats has received much less attention (but see Emlen 1974; Gehlbach 1986a, b; and the papers by Roth, and Johnsen and VanDruff in this volume), even though it is in just such habitats where birds might provide a very useful measure of environmental quality or at least environmental change. The burrowing owl (*Athene cunicularia*) provides an excellent opportunity to study habitat selection in an urban bird.

BACKGROUND

Burrowing owls are small owls found only in the western hemisphere. Three aspects of burrowing owl natural history distinguish these owls from most other owl species (for more background on burrowing owl ecology, see Coulombe 1971, Thomsen 1971, and Martin 1973). First, burrowing owls are frequently active during the day. Second, these owls often nest in loose colonies. And third, burrowing owls nest underground. Two subspecies of burrowing owls are present in North America. The western subspecies (*A.c. hypugaea*) has been well studied. Two aspects of the biology of the western burrowing owl appear to influence both its regional and local abundance. First, it prefers areas of short vegetation, being resident throughout much of the arid grasslands and prairies of western North America (Coulombe 1971, Thomsen 1971, Butts 1973, Martin 1973). And second, this subspecies rarely, if ever, digs its own burrow (Butts and Lewis 1982, Green 1983). Instead, it occupies the abandoned dens of colonial, burrowing rodents such as ground squirrels (*Spermophilus beecheyi*) and prairie dogs (*Cynomys ludovicianus*) (Rowe et al. 1986). The local abundance of western burrowing owls thus appears strongly affected by the presence and abundance of burrowing rodents (Butts and Lewis 1982).

The biology of the eastern subspecies (*A.c. floridana*) has received much less attention. This subspecies breeds throughout Florida and southward into the Bahamas and West Indies. In Florida, this owl has traditionally inhabited the open prairies of the south and central parts of the state and, like its western cousin, prefers areas of short vegetation (Hennemann 1980). Unlike the western subspecies, however, the Florida burrowing owl excavates its own burrow (Neill 1954, Courser 1976). The absence of colonial, burrowing rodents in Florida may explain why the Florida burrowing owl both digs its own burrow and is less communal than its western counterpart (Eckert 1974). Burrow availability thus does not appear to be as critical a limiting factor for the eastern subspecies of the burrowing owl. It should be noted that burrows abandoned by gopher tortoises (*Gopherus polyphemus*) may occasionally be used by owls in Florida (Betz 1932, Harrison 1975). Such use is probably rare, however, as owls and tortoises prefer different habitats (Pennock 1922, pers. obs.).

Several authors have reported decreasing burrowing owl populations in the West (Collins 1979, Aufforth 1981). This decline is blamed both on the loss of habitat to development and the loss of nesting sites due to poisoning campaigns against ground squirrels and prairie dogs (Butts and Lewis 1982). Several reports from Florida also suggest that

Integrating Man and Nature in the Metropolitan Environment. Proc. Natl. Symp. on Urban Wildl., Chevy Chase, Md., 4–7 November 1986, L.W. Adams and D.L. Leedy, eds. Published by Natl. Inst. for Urban Wildl., 10921 Trotting Ridge Way, Columbia, MD 21044, 1987.

burrowing owl populations may be declining in that state (Nicholson 1954, Norris 1978). Clearing of land for commercial, residential, and agricultural development is obviously continuing in Florida, as elsewhere, and has caused the decline of many species. Yet Ligon (1963) and Courser (1979) have recorded significant range expansion of the burrowing owl throughout Florida. As mentioned earlier, short prairie-like vegetation appears to be a critical habitat requirement for these owls, and the clearing of land for development often provides this open habitat. Moreover, Martin (1973) stated that the burrowing owl is the raptor least affected by human disturbance; owls are commonly found within city limits in the West (Eckert 1974). It is just such urban and disturbed areas where much of the recent research on burrowing owls has been conducted (Coulombe 1971, Thomsen 1971, Courser 1976). How can such conflicting reports be interpreted? Might development be both the boon and the bane of the burrowing owl in North America? These and other questions prompted our investigation of the factors affecting burrowing owl distribution and abundance in Cape Coral, Florida. The objective was to examine a well-established population of burrowing owls in an urban environment, and specifically, to identify the habitat parameters that make these areas attractive to owls.

METHODS

Study Site Description

Cape Coral is located on the southern Gulf coast of Florida. The city is on a peninsula bounded by Matlacha Pass on the west and the Caloosahatchee River on the east (Fig. 1). Earlier in this century, homesteaders cleared much of this land of palmetto-pine forests for agriculture (Zeiss

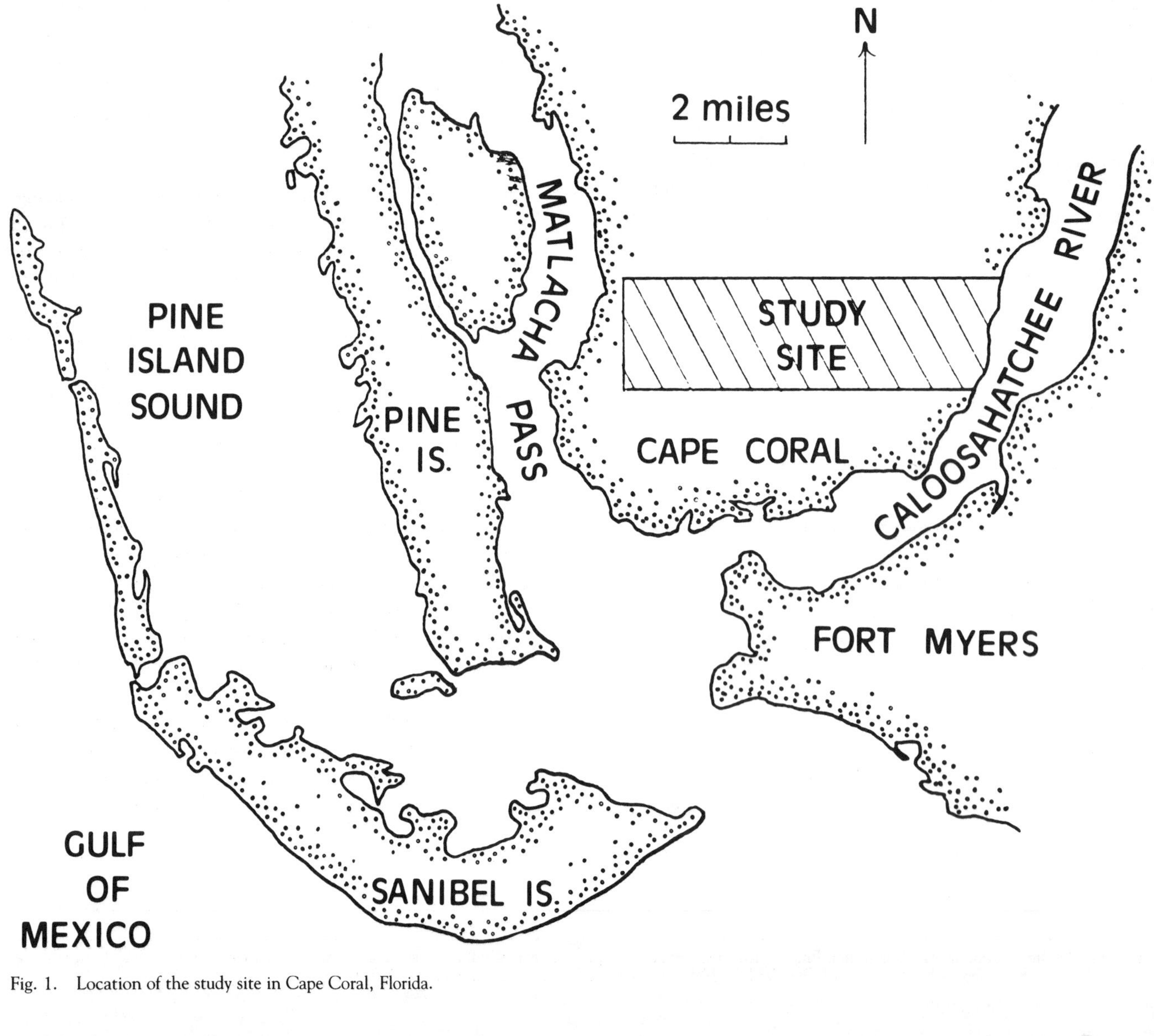

Fig. 1. Location of the study site in Cape Coral, Florida.

1983). Unfortunately, no published reports on the status of burrowing owls in Cape Coral from this period have been found, but densities were probably low. In the 1950's, the Gulf American Land Corporation purchased the land, most of which was being used as cattle range at the time. An extensive system of canals was excavated. The dredged material was used to fill marshes and mangrove swamps, thus elevating the land several meters above sea level in order to build on it. The developers were ambitious—cutting, dredging, and filling cleared an area of approximately 100 mi^2 (161 km^2), and probably opened this area for colonization by burrowing owls. Residential and commercial construction began in 1958 in the southeast corner of the peninsula (Bernard 1983), and has since been gradually continuing northward and westward. Development is most dense in the east, moderate in the center of the peninsula, and negligible in the west. The availability of vacant habitat for burrowing owls, therefore, is graded from east to west. For this reason, a 6-mile-long (9.6 km) east-to-west transect across the entire peninsula was selected for study (Fig. 1). The transect was 2 miles (3.2 km) wide and encompassed approximately 12 mi^2 (19.3 km^2). Vegetation in vacant lots is mowed regularly by city mowing crews, thus maintaining a short-grass habitat throughout the study site.

The study site was subdivided into 14 study areas. With the exception of the areas on the eastern and western boundaries (areas bounded by the river and the pass, respectively), each study area equaled approximately 1 mi^2 (1.61 km^2). The two eastern edge and two western edge areas each encompassed about half this area.

With the exception of a municipal golf course and one scrubland area, all the land in the study site was within 55 yards (50 m) of a road. It was therefore possible to search for owls and burrows by automobile. The study site was searched five times: in December, 1984; in March, May, and September, 1985; and in March, 1986. The location of each burrow was plotted on maps of each study area and designated as a home, satellite, or inactive burrow. Burrowing owls often utilize several, nearby satellite burrows in addition to the home, or nest, burrow (Thomsen 1971, Butts 1973). When a burrow was located, a wooden stake with an identifying number was driven into the ground near the entrance. The number of owls at each home burrow was recorded. Also noted was the collapse or destruction of any burrows and the cause, where determinable.

Factors Influencing Burrowing Owl Distribution and Abundance

During the study, data on four factors that might be affecting burrowing owl distribution and abundance in Cape Coral were compiled. These factors are briefly outlined below (see Wesemann 1986 for further details).

Percent Development.—Development here refers to both residential and commercial structures and landscaping. Percent development might be a critical factor because burrowing owls are ground nesters and require vacant lots for burrows. Owls obviously cannot burrow in parking lots. They also apparently find it difficult to dig through the thick, fibrous grasses, such as *Zoysia sp.* that constitute the lawns of Cape Coral.

It was possible to calculate precisely how much undeveloped, vacant land was available to owls in each study area by using the Land Use Survey Data Sheets compiled monthly by the City of Cape Coral.

Soil Composition.—Because the Florida burrowing owl usually excavates its own den, soil composition may be a critical factor for these owls. The soil of Cape Coral is identified as the Matlacha Series (SCS 1984), which is characterized by poorly drained deposits that have been leveled for urban use. This soil is composed of shell fragments, limestone fragments, and mixed sands. In order to determine soil composition in each of the study areas and correlate this with owl distribution, four sites per mi^2 were systematically sampled. These samples were analyzed to determine percent sand (USDA 1951), as sandy soils should be more easily excavated by owls (Butts and Lewis 1982). The soil samples from each area were used to calculate the average percent sand per study area. Values from each study area were then used to calculate the average "sandiness" of the study site as a whole.

After sampling soil composition systematically, soil samples next to 30 randomly selected burrows were taken to determine what type of soil the owls might actually be selecting. These samples also were analyzed and average percent sand at burrows was calculated.

Prey Abundance.—Prey availability appears to play a significant role in habitat selection by raptors (see Janes 1985, and references cited therein). Most reports of the diets of Florida burrowing owls are described in very general terms (but see Lewis 1973, Hennemann 1980). The consensus from both western and Florida studies is that burrowing owls most frequently eat insects, but that vertebrates may be more important by virtue of their greater biomass (Jaksić and Marti 1981). Two measures of prey abundance, one for vertebrate prey and one for invertebrates, were therefore included in this study.

Because little prey analysis had been done in Florida, pellet analyses were conducted to determine what the owls in Cape Coral were eating. Seventy pellets collected in December, 1984, and 70 pellets in May, 1985, were analyzed. These (see Wesemann 1986) and other diet analyses (Lewis 1973, Marti 1974, Tyler 1983) identified ground-dwelling insects as the prey item most frequently taken by burrowing owls. Pitfall traps were therefore used to estimate the relative abundance of insects in each of the 14 study areas. Trapping was systematically conducted in May and September, 1985, with a minimum of two traps per study area each month. The contents from each trap were oven-dried and weighed. Data from the May and September samples were pooled. Grams of insects/trap/study area were then calculated and used as a relative measure of insect prey abundance for statistical analyses.

The most frequently taken vertebrate prey in the pellet samples was the brown anole *(Anolis sagrei)* (Wesemann 1986). Although these lizards represent only about 3% of the owls' diet on an item basis, it is one of the largest items eaten by the owls and constitutes a large portion of the biomass taken by the owls in Cape Coral (Wesemann 1986). We therefore censused anoles across the study site. One developed lot and an adjacent vacant lot in each study area were randomly selected and searched on foot. The total number of anoles sighted per lot was recorded.

Data on each of the four factors were compiled and correlated with number of adult owls/vacant ha. Using owls/vacant ha is more accurate than total number of owls/study area because the actual available habitat for owls varies between study areas. Also, we used the number of adult owls in May, 1985 (rather than any of the other four census periods), for calculating the dependent variable (number of owls/vacant ha) as this was the height of the breeding season when the greatest number of owls were present. Although birds must also select habitat in both wintering quarters as well as during migration, breeding may place additional pressures on animals to choose optimal habitat (Cody 1985). The May census was therefore deemed the most appropriate for assessing the environmental variables important to burrowing owls. Results were not, however, significantly altered when data from the other censuses were used. A multiple linear regression (SPSS New Regression, Hull and Nie 1981) was calculated using owls/vacant ha (Fig. 2B) as the dependent variable, with percent development, percent sand, insect abundance, and anole abundance (Fig. 2C) as the independent variables. The output from this analysis also provided values for the univariate correlation of number of owls/vacant ha with each of the independent variables. All univariate statistical tests are from Bruning and Kintz (1977).

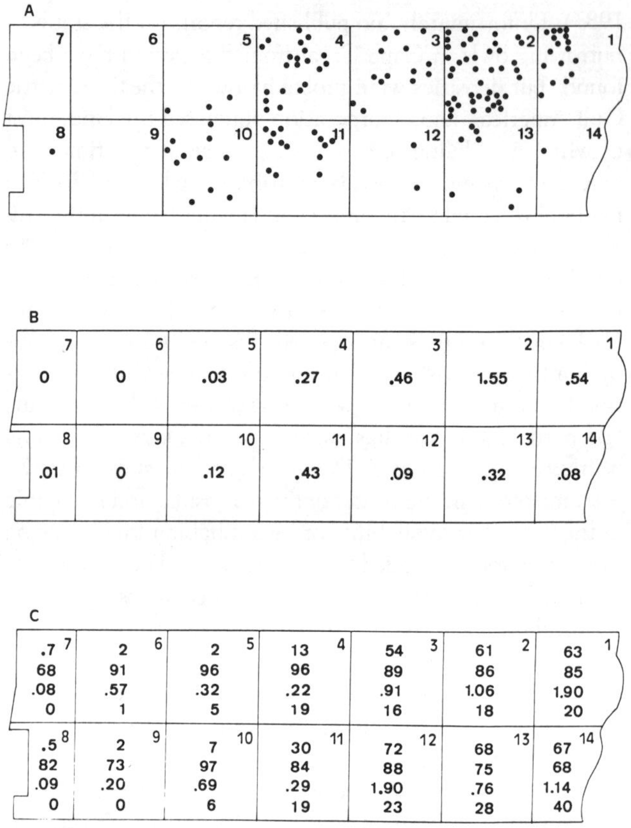

Fig. 2. Distribution of home burrows (A), number of adult owls per vacant hectare (B) in the 14 study areas, May, 1985, and factors influencing owl distribution and abundance (C). Values presented in (C) for each study are, from top to bottom: percent development, average percent sand, and insect (gm/trap) and anole abundance (number/developed lot).

RESULTS

Burrowing Owl Distribution and Density

Study Area 2 had the densest population of owls with 87 adults in 45 home burrows (Fig. 2A, B). This may be the highest breeding density recorded for any raptor species in North America. It certainly surpasses by far any previously recorded densities for burrowing owls. Both Coulombe (1971) and Norris (1978), for example, suggested that burrowing owl densities in optimum habitat may be approximately 20 owls per mi^2. Study Area 2 had over four times this density of adult burrowing owls.

The number and density of owls in Cape Coral are not, however, static. Burrowing owl numbers tend to increase in spring and decrease in autumn (Wesemann 1986). This probably reflects the dispersal of owls after the breeding season, which also has been noted by other investigators in Florida and in the West (Courser 1976, Martin 1973). Readers interested in the population dynamics of burrowing owls in the Cape Coral area are encouraged to see Wesemann (1986).

Factors Influencing Owl Distribution

Percent Development.—There is a well-defined gradient of development across the study site, with the areas of greatest development in the east. In May, 1985, the percent of residential and commercial development ranged from 0.5% in the western Study Area 8 to 72% in the eastern Study Area 12 (Fig. 2C). The correlation between number of owls/vacant ha in May and percent development was positive but not significant ($r=0.498$, $0.05<P<0.10$, $df=12$; Fig. 3A).

Soil Composition.—The mean percent sand per study area ranged from 67.8% in Study Area 7 to 97.3% in Study Area 10 (Fig. 2C). These measures may be less reliable than we had hoped, as there appeared to be extreme variability in "sandiness" even within areas. Therefore it is not surprising that the correlation between number of owls/vacant ha in each study area in May and percent sand in each area

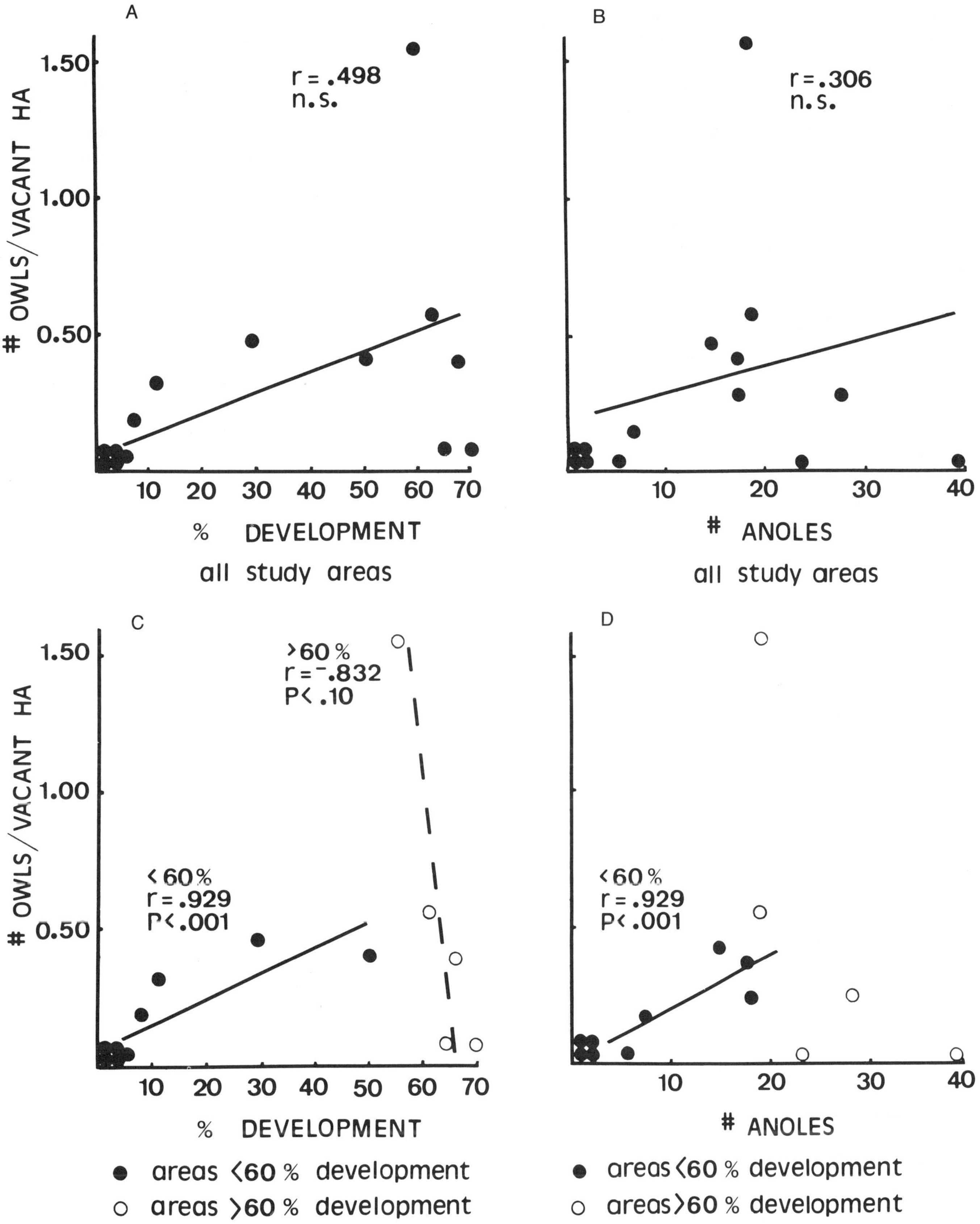

Fig. 3. Owl density in relation to percent development (A,C) and anole abundance (B,D), Cape Coral, Florida, May, 1985.

was not significant ($r=0.113$, $P>0.20$, $df=12$). This lack of correlation between percent sand and number of owls/vacant ha may thus correctly reflect the high variability of sandiness within areas. The soil next to 30 burrows also was analyzed to determine what type of soil the owls might actually be selecting within a given area. The mean percent sand at these 30 burrow sites was 94.6%. The average sandiness of the entire study site, however, was only 84.1% (calculated by averaging across all 14 study areas, Fig. 2C). The difference between average percent sand of the study site and percent sand at the 30 randomly selected burrows was highly significant ($t=7.82$, $P<0.001$, $df=42$). This suggests that the owls indeed prefer very sandy soils, probably because these soils are easier to excavate (Butts and Lewis 1982). Burrowing owls may thus be excluded from certain sites within a given study area because the soil is too hard, even though soil composition, per se, may be too variable to explain differences in burrowing owl densities between study areas.

Incidentally, 14% of the 301 burrows (home, satellite, and inactive) counted during the entire study were destroyed by automobiles, mowers, home construction, or directly by people. Although this figure may seem high, nearly 37% of the censused burrows collapsed from apparent natural causes, such as flooding from rainstorms or because the burrows were too shallow. A univariate correlation between percent collapsed burrows per area and percent sand per area was significant ($r=0.787$, $P<0.01$, $df=10$). This suggests a trade-off for the owls in their choice of a burrow site. Owls prefer sandy soils in which to burrow, but these soils collapse more easily. Collapsed burrows were redug and reused in 15 instances. Two burrows were even redug twice after collapses. Such persistence demonstrates a remarkable site tenacity by these owls, suggesting that the benefit of digging in sandy soils outweighs the potential cost of burrow collapse.

Prey Abundance.—Insect abundance ranged from a low of 0.08 gm/trap in Study Area 7 to a high of 1.90 gm/trap in Study Areas 1 and 12 (Fig. 2C). The correlation between number of owls/vacant ha in May and grams of insects/trap was positive but not significant ($r=0.326$, $P>0.20$, $df=12$).

The mean number of anoles across all 14 study areas on developed lots was 13.93 per lot, significantly greater than the mean number of anoles on vacant lots, which was only 0.5 per lot ($t=4.08$, $P<0.001$, $df=26$). The low number of anoles on vacant lots was expected because the lack of vegetation on vacant lots in Cape Coral results in poor habitat for anoles, which frequent trees and shrubs (Behler and King 1979). Because of the low number of anoles on vacant lots, this measure was not included in subsequent calculations. The correlation between number of owls/vacant ha in May and anole abundance on developed lots was positive but not significant ($r=0.306$, $P>0.20$, $df=12$; Fig. 3B).

To summarize, none of the univariate correlations between number of owls/vacant ha and any of the four factors examined (percent development, percent sand, insect abundance, and anole abundance) were significant. None of these variables, by itself, appears to explain differences in burrowing owl densities across the study areas. A multiple linear regression (Hull and Nie 1981) was thus computed to determine if the four factors combined could reliably predict the number of adult owls/vacant ha.

This multiple regression also was not significant ($R=0.698$, $P>0.15$, $df=4,9$). Only 48.7% of the variability in the dependent variable (number of adult owls/vacant ha) was explained by all four factors combined. There were, however, significant univariate correlations among several of the independent variables themselves, namely: percent development with insect abundance ($r=0.818$, $P<0.001$, $df=12$); percent development with anole abundance ($r=0.857$, $P<0.001$, $df=12$); and anole abundance with insect abundance ($r=0.588$, $P<0.05$, $df=12$).

When the number of owls/vacant ha was plotted with percent development in all 14 areas (Fig. 3A), a pattern emerged. The number of owls/vacant ha appeared to peak at around 60% development. In fact, it looked as though urbanization might even have a negative effect on the number of owls/vacant ha above this 60% development level (variability certainly increases). The 14 study areas were therefore divided into those less than and those greater than 60% development. The univariate and multivariate analyses outlined above were then repeated. Several significant relationships were revealed when analyses were split in this manner. On the univariate level, the number of owls/vacant ha was now significantly correlated with development below the 60% level ($r=0.929$, $P<0.001$, $df=7$; Fig. 3C, solid regression line). Owl density actually appeared to be negatively affected by levels of development greater than 60% ($r=-0.832$, $0.05<P<0.10$, $df=3$; Fig. 3C, dashed regression line). The lack of a relationship between owl density and anole abundance previously reported (Fig. 3B) also changed; below 60% development the number of owls/vacant ha and anole abundance were now significantly correlated ($r=0.929$, $P<0.001$, $df=7$; Fig. 3D).

When the multivariate analysis was repeated using only those areas with less than 60% development, the regression was highly significant ($R=0.993$, $P<0.001$, $df=4,4$). Moreover, 98.6% of the variability in the dependent variable (number of owls/vacant ha) could be explained by the four independent variables acting simultaneously. Although only one of the four independent variables, anole abundance, contributed significantly, *by itself,* to the prediction equation (reg. coef. $=0.014$, $t=3.45$, $P<0.03$), percent development was close to being significant (reg. coef. $=0.005$, $t=2.36$, $P<0.08$). The fact that anole abundance and percent development are the most important variables in the multiple regression is not surprising given their highly significant univariate correlations with owl densities (below 60% development), mentioned above. It also is no surprise that little of the variance in the dependent variable was uniquely explained by any given independent variable. Anole abundance, for example, explained only an additional 4.27% of the variability in the number of owls/vacant ha after entry of the other independent variables into the regression. Most of the variance in owl density is shared among all four factors, a result consistent with the high correlations among several of the independent variables themselves.

Multivariate analysis of those study areas greater than 60% development was not possible due to the small sample size ($N=5$).

DISCUSSION

The distribution of adult burrowing owls at the study site in May, 1985 (Fig. 2A), suggests that owls are selecting areas of high residential development over adjacent, less urbanized tracts. Indeed, owl densities in Cape Coral are actually highest in areas with 54% to 64% urbanization. Why? The answer appears to be food. The significant univariate correlations of percent development with the abundance of both anoles and insects suggest that where there are more houses there is more food for burrowing owls (see Emlen 1974, and Gehlbach 1986a,b for additional examples of urban effects on avian food supplies). But why should this be so? Insects may be more common in developed areas because the diversity and abundance of vegetation is greater in the landscaped, urban areas. Perhaps more importantly, these areas are artificially watered all year long, unlike the undeveloped tracts. The greater abundance of anoles in the urban areas may simply be related to this positive correlation between percent development and insect abundance. The ground-dwelling insect species sampled in this study included many species eaten by both anoles and burrowing owls. Anoles, therefore, may be selecting urban areas both because of the enhanced vegetative cover as well as the greater availability of their insect prey. But not only do the developed areas have more anoles per house, they also have more houses, meaning that the total number of anoles available to owls in highly developed zones is much greater than in less developed areas. The owls appear to be tracking this increased insect and anole availability in urbanized areas, at least up a point. Owl density was significantly correlated with percent development, but only when the most urbanized areas ($>60\%$ development) were excluded from analysis (Fig. 3C). When development surpasses 60%, owl densities drop, even though anole and insect abundance continue to rise. In areas with greater than 60% development, then, other environmental or behavioral factors must interfere with the benefits owls derive from the greater prey availability in urban areas. One such adverse factor expected to increase with percent development is the level of disturbance to owls by humans, such as burrow vandalism, harassment by pets, and increased owl mortality from collisions with automobiles. Another factor that may explain the decrease in owl densities in areas with greater than 60% development is simply insufficient open space. Burrowing owls may require a critical minimal area of vacant land (e.g., for hunting); once this minimum is surpassed by development, the area may become less suitable for burrowing owls.

Which of the two prey groups, insects or anoles, best explains the positive relationship between owl density and urbanization at levels below 60% development? Though insects are taken more frequently, anoles are larger and may constitute a significant portion of the biomass taken by burrowing owls in Cape Coral (Wesemann 1986). Moreover, there is limited evidence that owls in Cape Coral increase their take of anoles during the breeding season, when energy stress might be highest (Wesemann 1986). A similar pattern is exhibited by spotted owls (*Strix occidentalis*), which select larger prey while feeding young than during courtship and incubation (Barrows, pers. comm.). The availability of prey with greater biomass (anoles) when young are being fed may be a critical factor in habitat selection by burrowing owls in Cape Coral. This is supported by the singly significant contribution of anole abundance to the multiple linear regression. Remember, however, that many of the independent variables were correlated among themselves; identifying any single factor as the best predictor of owl density in Cape Coral would therefore be misleading.

One other aspect of habitat selection that may be influencing the present distribution of burrowing owls in Cape Coral needs mentioning; i.e., site fidelity or philopatry. Many bird species will consistently return to old nesting sites, even if the habitat there is deteriorating (Krebs 1978). Such site fidelity may mean that some species of birds exhibit little "choice" when selecting habitats (see Cody 1985). Burrowing owls are known to be at least mildly site tenacious (Martin 1973, Aufforth 1981). In addition to optimum habitat selection, then, the present distribution of owls in Cape Coral may reflect an original colonization by this species of the southeast corner of the peninsula. Burrowing owls appear to be moving into the less developed western areas of the peninsula as the eastern areas reach intolerable levels of residential development (Wesemann 1986). Even then, the owls may only move a short distance because they are site specific. Nonetheless, the results of our analyses strongly suggest that owls are actually attracted to areas of moderate housing density.

EPILOGUE

Urbanization appears to have both positive and negative effects on burrowing owl densities in southwestern Florida. By cutting forests and draining swamps, development has opened new habitat for burrowing owls to colonize, and urban areas are rich in the prey species eaten by owls. Yet, too much development drives owls away. What, then, will be the fate of the burrowing owl in Florida? The owls' breeding range may still be expanding in the state due to continued clearing of land for development. A naive conclusion might suggest these owls will benefit from urbanization, but this is a shortsighted view. Urban property is usually too valuable to humans not to develop residential communities far beyond the tolerance level of burrowing owls. Any benefit the owls will realize in terms of newly-available habitat and enhanced prey abundance will be short-lived. Courser (1976) has already documented decreasing owl numbers in urban areas. The period between initially opening the habitat for owl colonization and the point where development exceeds the tolerance limits of the owls will undoubtedly decrease as the demands on the land by an expanding human population increases.

This owl is currently classified as a species of special concern by the state of Florida (Heller, pers. comm.). Ironically, this affords the owls protection from harassment by individuals but little legal protection from development. A building permit can be postponed until young owls are fledged, but because no one monitors active burrows, construction crews are on their honor to report nesting sites. Naturally, this is rare, and destruction of both nests and nesting habitat continues.

On a positive note, Cape Coral residents in Study Area 1 reported an increase in the number of owls after a temporary decline several years ago. Although this area presently has a 63% level of development, there is little further home construction, possibly due to the inflated cost of these preferred riverside lots. Because the rate of new home construction will probably continue to be greatest in the areas where lots are less expensive, the high cost of real estate in highly developed areas may leave enough vacant lots for the burrowing owls to survive in these areas.

Equally encouraging, the Florida Department of Game and Freshwater Fish is now exploring the possibility of using this research as a foundation for maintaining healthy populations of burrowing owls in developed areas such as Cape Coral (Millsap, pers. comm.). With sound management criteria and a public desire, continued urban expansion need not spell the doom of this unique owl in Florida.

Acknowledgments.—We wish to thank Jane and Doris Davidowski for their encouragement and for their participation in this project. We also appreciate the friendly assistance provided by the City of Cape Coral. Drs. Jeffrey Butts, Mary Connell, and Edgar Greene offered constructive comments on an earlier draft of the manuscript. This research was supported by grants from the Graduate School and the University Research Council of Appalachian State University.

REFERENCES CITED

Aufforth, A.K. 1981. The burrowing owl in North Dakota. North Dakota Outdoors. April.

Behler, J.L. and F.W. King. 1979. The Audubon Society field guide to North American reptiles and amphibians. Alfred A. Knopf, New York, N.Y.

Bernard, E. 1983. Lies that came true. Anna Publishing, Inc., Ocoee, Fl.

Betz, H. 1932. Burrowing owls in Pinellas County, Florida. Auk 49:478.

Bruning, J.L. and B.L. Kintz. 1977. Computational handbook of statistics. Scott, Foresman and Co., Glenview, IL.

Butts, K.O. 1973. Life history and habitat requirements of burrowing owls in western Oklahoma. M.Sc. Thesis, Oklahoma State Univ., Stillwater.

Butts, K.O. and J.C. Lewis. 1982. The importance of prairie dog towns to burrowing owls in Oklahoma. Proc. Okla. Acad. Sci. 62:46–52.

Carson, R. 1962. Silent Spring. Houghton Mifflin Co., Boston, Ma.

Cody, M.L. 1985. An introduction to habitat selection in birds. Pages 4–56 *in* M.L. Cody, ed. Habitat selection in birds. Academic Press, Inc., Orlando, Fl.

Collins, C.T. 1979. The ecology and conservation of burrowing owls. Pages 6–17 *in* P.P. Schaeffer and S.M. Ehlers, eds. Owls of the west: their ecology and conservation. Natl. Aud. Soc., Western Education Center, Tiburon, Ca.

Coulombe, H.N. 1971. Behavior and population ecology of the burrowing owl in the Imperial Valley of California. Condor 73:162–176.

Courser, W.D. 1976. A population study of the burrowing owl near Tampa, Florida. M.Sc. Thesis, Univ. of South Florida, Tampa.

———. 1979. Continued breeding range expansion of the burrowing owl in Florida. Am. Birds 33:143–144.

Eckert, A.W. 1974. The owls of North America. Doubleday and Co., Inc., Garden City, N.Y. Pp. 163–176.

Emlen, J.T. 1974. An urban bird community in Tucson, Arizona: derivation, structure, regulation. Condor 76:184–197.

Gehlbach, F.R. 1986a. Population and environmental features that promote adaptation to urban ecosystems: the case of eastern screech owls *(Otus asio)* in Texas. Paper presented at 19th Int. Ornithol. Congress. Ottawa, Canada.

———. 1986b. Odd couples of suburbia. Nat. Hist. 95:56–66.

Green, G.A. 1983. Ecology of breeding burrowing owls in the Columbia Basin, Oregon. M.Sc. Thesis, Oregon State Univ., Corvallis.

Harrison, H.H. 1975. A field guide to birds nests. Houghton Miflin Co., Boston, Ma.

Hennemann, W.W. III. 1980. Notes on the food habits of the burrowing owl in Duval County, Florida. Fl. Nat. 8:24–25.

Hull, C.H. and N.H. Nie. 1981. SPSS update 7–9: New procedures and facilities for releases 7–9. McGraw-Hill Book Co., N.Y.

Jaksić, F.M. and C.D. Marti. 1981. Trophic ecology of *Athene* owls in mediterranean-type ecosystems: a comparative analysis. Can. J. Zool. 59:2331–2340.

Janes, S.W. 1985. Habitat selection in raptorial birds. Pages 159–188 *in* M.L. Cody, ed. Habitat selection in birds. Academic Press, Inc., Orlando, FL.

Krebs, C. 1978. Ecology: the experimental analysis of distribution and abundance. Harper and Row, New York, N.Y.

Lewis, J.C. 1973. Food habits of Florida burrowing owls. Fl. Nat. 1:27–29.

Ligon, J.D. 1963. Breeding range expansion of the burrowing owl in Florida. Auk 80:367–368.

Marti, C.D. 1974. Feeding ecology of four sympatric owls. Condor 76:45–61.
Martin, D.J. 1973. Selected aspects of burrowing owl ecology and behavior. Condor 75:446–456.
Morrison, M.L. 1986. Bird populations as indicators of environmental change. Pages 429–451 *in* R.F. Johnston, ed. Current Ornithology, Vol. 3. Plenum Press, New York, N.Y.
Neill, W.T. 1954. Notes on the Florida burrowing owl. Fl. Nat. 27:67–70.
Nicholson, D.J. 1954. The Florida burrowing owl: a vanishing species. Fl. Nat. 27:3–4.
Norris, D. 1978. Florida's burrowing owl. Fl. Nat. 51:4–6.
Pennock, C.J. 1922. Florida burrowing owls. Wilson Bull. 34:21.
Rowe, M.P., R.G. Coss, and D.H. Owings. 1986. Rattlesnake rattles and burrowing owl hisses: a case of acoustic Batesian mimicry. Ethology 72:53–71.
SCS. 1984. Soil Survey of Lee County, Florida. U.S. Dep. of Agric., Soil Conservation Service.
Thomsen, L. 1971. Behavior and ecology of burrowing owls in the Oakland municipal airport. Condor 73:177–192.
Tyler, J.D. 1983. Notes on burrowing owl *(Athene cunicularia)* food habits in Oklahoma. Southwestern Nat. 28:100–102.
USDA. 1951. Soil survey manual. 18:207.
Wesemann, T. 1986. Factors influencing the distribution and abundance of burrowing owls *(Athene cunicularia)* in Cape Coral, Florida. M.Sc. Thesis, Appalachian State Univ., Boone, North Carolina.
Zeiss, B. 1983. The other side of the river: historical Cape Coral. B. Zeiss, Publisher, Cape Coral, Fl.

Assessment of Habitat Quality for Wood Thrush in a Residential Area

ROLAND R. ROTH, *Department of Entomology and Applied Ecology, University of Delaware, Newark, DE 19717-1303*

INTRODUCTION

Songbirds on a residential lot may be considered an asset, especially if the birds are visually or auditorially pleasing and create no nuisance or pest situations. Certain habitat features can attract individual birds to a site and contribute to their success, i.e., act as proximate and ultimate factors of habitat selection (Hildén 1965). Finally, habitat can be preserved and enhanced (i.e., managed) so as to maintain or improve its attractiveness and usefulness to songbirds without serious loss of aesthetic qualities. Translating these three assertions into reality is not easy in an urban environment. One not only must identify a set of variables associated with presence and success of a species or set of species; one also must determine which have functional significance and how to produce and maintain those features in a way that is feasible and acceptable for the site, the homeowner, and the neighbors. This paper concentrates on the first task, identification of variables, for a migrant passerine, the wood thrush *(Hylocichla mustelina)*.

Its song, appearance, and lack of nuisance qualities (unless one dislikes bird songs at dawn) make the wood thrush an asset to a residential area and thus a species worth attracting and holding. Wood thrushes are more tolerant of forest fragments and edges than most tropical forest migrants (Whitcomb et al. 1981) and occur in residential areas with a semblance of forest-like habitat. With some attention to habitat protection and maintenance during and after construction, a builder and resident can make an area attractive and useful to the species.

In this paper, I use multiple regression and comparisons of extreme groups to identify factors associated with seven measures of presence and success of wood thrushes living on individual residential lots. The measures represent management goals ranging from the simple, aesthetic one of presence of birds to population-oriented ones about breeding success, site fidelity, and general quality. The double-screening yields a preliminary list of 16 variables representing general habitat features also reported by other workers. I estimate limits of quality for the variables and the probabilities of achieving management goals with the caveat that the models are preliminary and untested.

STUDY AREA

The 32-acre (1a = 0.405 ha) study area of 70 lots and two intervening streets was in the center of Arbour Park, a residential area built from 1966–'68 in Newark, Delaware, on a wooded slope and terrace above a forested floodplain. Non-street and -sidewalk area equaled 29 acres. A street and one row of homes separated the study area from adjacent, undeveloped woodland or parkland of various areas and depths (Fig. 1).

The extent to which forest vegetation and conditions remained varied considerably among lots (Fig. 1). All still had trees in the rear yard, but the extent varied from a few trees at the extreme rear border to solid tree canopy extending to the house. Some had retained original trees (especially American beech, *Fagus grandifolia*) as specimens or groups in the side and front yards, often of sufficient size and number to produce a solid tree canopy there as well. The collective effect of these trees was a continuous, semi-forested strip 38–350 ft (1ft = 0.305m) wide through the center of each block. Some owners had retained the natural forest understory (leaf litter, herbs, shrubs) in the rear areas. Others had cleared the understory and often substituted bare ground, moss, or ornamental ground cover for herbs and leaf litter.

American beech had a frequency of 33% in the canopy (above 15 ft) along transects that sampled entire lots (see Methods, Profile Transects). The next four highest frequencies belonged to maples, *Acer* spp., mostly *rubrum* (17%); tulip poplar, *Liriodendron tulipifera* (13%); sweetgum, *Liquidambar styraciflua* (9%); and white oak, *Quercus alba* (8%). Beeches comprised 20% of all stems ≥ 1 inch (1 in = 2.5 cm) dbh in the rear strips (see Methods, Belt Transect).

Integrating Man and Nature in the Metropolitan Environment. Proc. Natl. Symp. on Urban Wildl., Chevy Chase, Md., 4–7 November 1986, L.W. Adams and D.L. Leedy, eds. Published by Natl. Inst. for Urban Wildl., 10921 Trotting Ridge Way, Columbia, MD 21044, 1987.

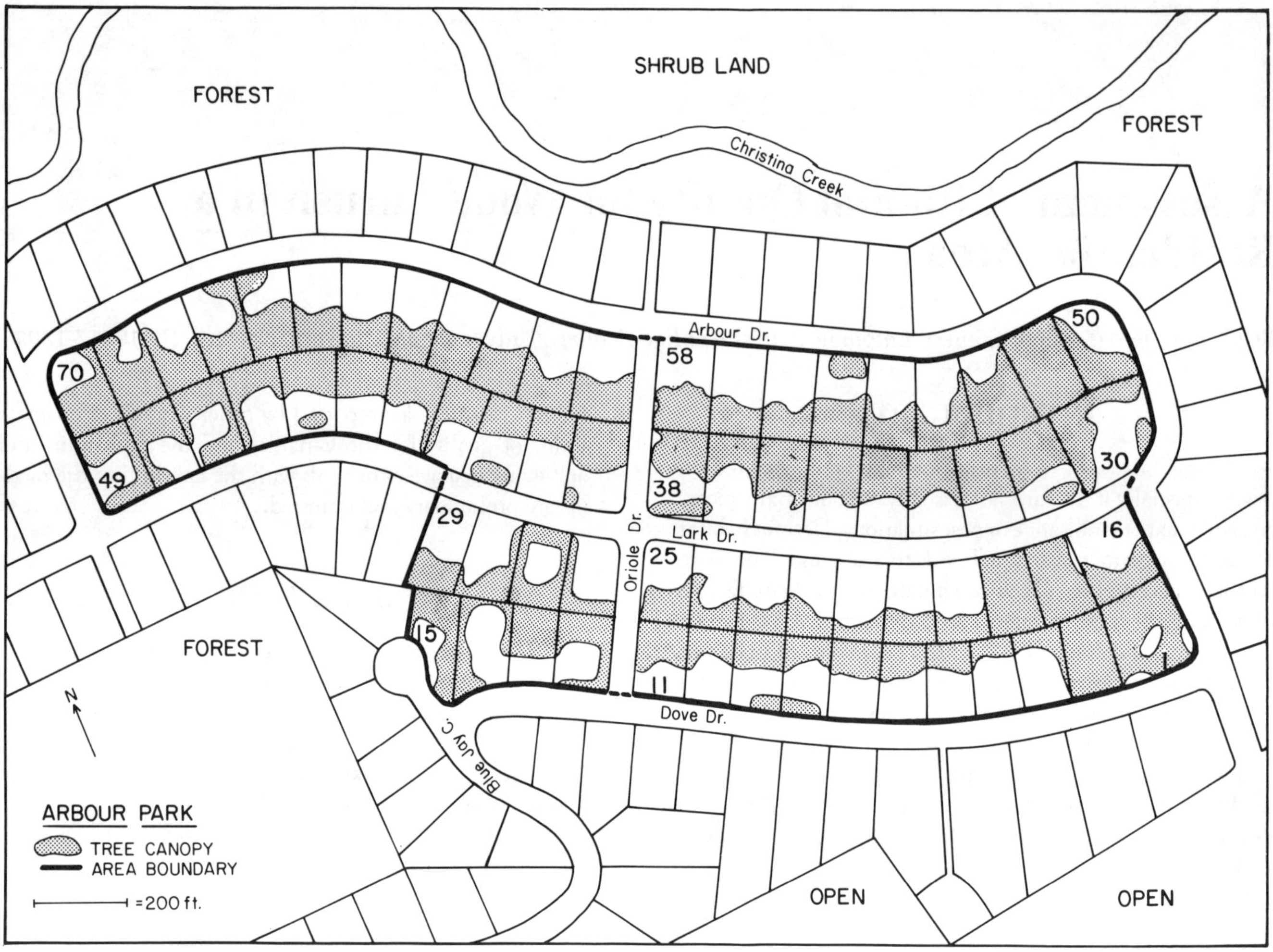

Fig. 1. Map of Arbour Park study area and surroundings. Lots are numbered sequentially from lower right to left.

Yellow poplar (12%), maples (10%), sweetgum (8%), American hornbeam, *Carpinus carolinianum* (8%), and black gum, *Nyssa sylvatica* (6%) had the next higher relative densities there. *Viburnum* spp., mainly *dentatum* and *prunifolium* (4%), and flowering dogwood, *Cornus florida* (3%), also were in the understory. Shrubs (1–2 in dbh) were 49%, and trees (≥ 5 in) 38%, of the stems in the strips.

METHODS

Habitat Characteristics

Profile Transect.—Three transects perpendicular to the long axis of the house, through the center of the lot and at a prescribed distance from each edge, sampled various vegetational components between the front walk and rear line. Sample points were 15 ft apart, yielding 26–43 points/lot.

A 1-inch rod 10 ft long was set vertically at each sample point. The type of ground cover on which the pole rested was recorded. In this analysis, I used only four of those recorded: moss, litter (leaves, dead stems, compost), bare ground, and grass. I also recorded whether bark or foliage touched the pole at least once in each 1-foot interval between 1 and 15 ft. This technique allowed calculation of cover for various height intervals.

At each point, I also estimated the portion of sky blocked by plant cover above 15 ft in each of four 0.5- by 0.5-in squares secured to the end of a tube 4.5 in long held vertically. Thus, the total number of estimates was 4X the number of sample points. I recorded all species that comprised the canopy above 15 ft at each point. This permitted calculations of frequency of occurrence of canopy trees.

Belt Transect.—I sampled density and diameter of woody stems (≥ 1 in) in the rear-yard strips using a belt transect 11 ft wide centered 30 ft from the back line. The transect ran parallel to the rear property line and from edge to edge of each lot.

Water Conditions.—In July, 1982, an assistant sketched a detailed map of springs, seeps, depressions, and drains and characterized them as moist, soggy, or with standing, seeping, or trickling water. I later gave each lot a score ranging from 0 (no wet spots) to 4 (surface water) based on that map.

Tree Cover.—Areas of significant, solid tree canopy (Fig. 1) were mapped by pacing. Isolated groups were included if they consisted of several large trees. The area of tree cover was determined from the maps by polar planimetry.

Birds

Wood thrush data were collected from 2 May–10 August 1980–'83 between 8:00 am and 5:30 pm EDT. Agreements with the residents precluded work outside these hours and on weekends. Frequent searches for nests and regular monitoring of them determined number of nests built and fledgling production.

General mist-netting and captures of females flushed from nests and males attracted by song-playbacks yielded information on spatial use. Color-banding the adults and nestlings allowed me to determine ownership of nests and fledglings, to recognize returning birds, and to determine spatial use of the area.

Detections of birds made during daily work as well as during intentional censuses were plotted on field maps. These records plus nest and capture locations comprised composite maps from which I determined usage areas ("territories") for individual pairs. I drew the borders conservatively, ignoring extreme movements of individuals from the general cluster of observations. Some territories overlapped in space but not in time. I compromised on boundaries where records for adjacent pairs overlapped spatially and temporally.

Variables

Dependent Variables.—Six dependent variables were quantifications of six points along a continuum of management goals (Table 1). The goals with respect to each lot were: (1) annual inclusion in a territory; (2) annual use for significant life activities, e.g., nesting, feeding, or singing; (3) annual use for nesting; (4) production of young; (5) production of young by birds significantly using the lot; and (6) return of adults in subsequent years.

YRSOVLP measures the simplest goal: birds present in yard. The data for it and No. 2 came from the composite maps. YRSACT evaluates a property in terms of its contribution to a pair's life based on the occurrence of significant activity on the lot. A territory might include a property, but because of habitat limitations, the birds might use it very little. Significant activities were nesting, unless on the extreme edge of the property, or repeated observations of feeding or singing.

Variables 3–5 focus on the critical aspect of reproduction. I chose YRSWNST instead of number of nests because a high number of nests may indicate a high degree of failure as well as an attractive site. Two better measures are the number of young produced—on the lot itself (TOTYG) and by all territory owners significantly using the lot (YGOVTER). The latter gives value to a lot for contributing to success even if no nest is on the lot itself.

Variable 6 measures the property's capacity to hold birds. Numerous studies have shown greater site fidelity or return rates for birds that have been successful (Gauthreaux 1982, Greenwood and Harvey 1982). In a sense, RETURNS may measure the bird's assessment of quality. A return within one territory width has been used to quantify site fidelity (Harvey et al. 1979). I used a more stringent criterion for counting a return; the bird's subsequent territory had to include the lot used previously.

A seventh dependent variable is a composite measure of quality, QUASCOR, calculated as follows. I determined the number of times a lot fell into the upper two or lower two performance classes for each of the other six dependent variables. (See Fig. 2 for those classes.) When I subtracted the number of lows from the number of highs, a value within the range of +6 (all upper classes) to −6 (all lower classes) resulted. To eliminate problems of sign, I sequentially numbered each value in the range starting with zero for −6. Thus, QUASCOR ranged from 0 to 12.

Independent Variables.—The list of variables that were tested (Table 2) is greatly reduced from the many possibilities in the data collected. I eliminated species and ground cover types that were of low abundance, were little used by wood thrush for nesting, or which previous experience indicated would be irrelevant to the goals of this analysis. I ignored all but one combinational variable for the sake of simplicity.

Variables 1–9 come from the belt transect data and only describe the forested strip in the rear yards. They reflect the effects of owners' thinning activities as well as natural spatial variation in species composition.

Variables 10–14 reflect two methods of indexing density of cover in space, variations on themes tried before (e.g., Karr 1968, Karr and Roth 1971, Roth 1979). They use data from the profile transects. VLCO (Nos. 10–12) calculates cover as a percent of the number of intersections of height intervals and sample points in space. That is, it equals [total contacts over all heights and sample points/(number of sample points × number of heights being considered)] × 100. In contrast, PTCO (Nos. 13–14) equals

Table 1. Dependent variables determined for each house lot.

1. YRSOVLP—Number of years in which ≥ 25% of lot used.
2. YRSACT—Number of years with significant activity on the lot. See text.
3. YRSWNST—Number of years with ≥ 1 nest regardless of outcome.
4. TOTYG—Total number of fledglings in 4 years.
5. YGOVTER—Total number fledged by parents significantly using (See Variable 2) a lot.
6. RETURNS—Number of cases in which a lot was reused by a previous user, even if a year intervened without return.
7. QUASCOR—A composite of Variables 1–6. See text for calculation.

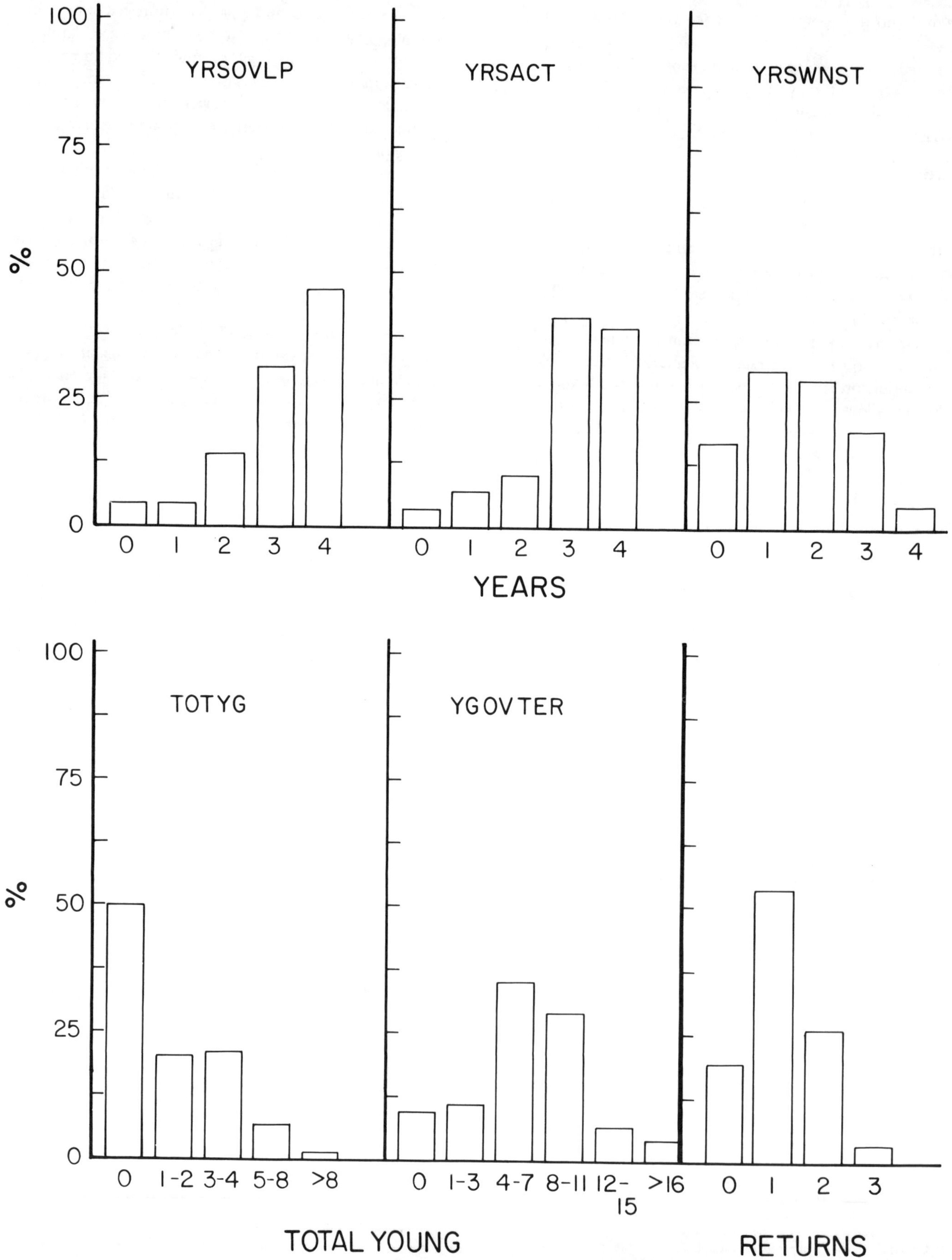

Fig. 2. Frequency distributions of 70 lots in Arbour Park on the six simple measures (Table 1) of habitat quality.

Table 2. Independent variables determined for each house lot and used in the analysis.

1. SHRD—Shrub density (1–2 in dbh)
2. TRED—Tree density (≥ 5 in dbh)
3. STMD—Stem density (≥ 1 in dbh)
4. ABD—Density of American beech[a]
5. VIBD—*Viburnum* density[a]
6. HD—American hornbeam density[a]
7. MD—Maple (*Acer* spp.) density[a]
8. SGD—Sweetgum density[a]
9. TPD—Tulip poplar density[a]
10. VLCOTOT—Volume cover at 1–15 ft. See text for calculation.
11. VLCOLO—Volume cover at 1–7 ft. See 10.
12. VLCOHI—Volume cover at 8–15 ft. See 10.
13. PTCOLO—Percent cover 1–7 ft. See text for calculation.
14. PTCOHI—Percent cover 8–15 ft. See 13.
15. CANCOV—Mean percent of sky covered by vegetation ≥ 15 ft above ground.
16. ABF—American beech frequency. Percent of points over which American beech occurred in canopy ≥ 15 ft.
17. HF—American hornbeam frequency. See 16.
18. MF—Maple frequency. See 16.
19. SGF—Sweetgum frequency. See 16.
20. TPF—Tulip poplar frequency. See 16.
21. LA—Area of the lot.
22. TA—Area covered by significant tree canopy.
23. TLRAT—Proportion of lot covered by significant tree canopy.
24. BGF—Bare ground frequency. Percent of sample points at which bare ground occurred.
25. GF—Grass frequency. See 24.
26. LF—Litter frequency. See 24.
27. MSF—Moss frequency. See 24.
28. BGMF—Frequency of bare ground or moss. See 24.
29. WAI—Water index. See text.
30. NE—Neighbor effect. See text.

[a]All stems ≥ 1 in.

[the number of sample points with ≥ 1 contact in the height interval desired/the number of sample points]. The two methods gave values significantly correlated with one another ($r = 0.91$, $p < .0001$ for VLCOLO vs. PTCOLO and 0.82, $p < .0001$ for VLCOHI vs. PTCOHI).

CANCOV and frequencies of certain canopy species (Nos. 16–20) describe tree features over the entire lot because they come from the profile transect data. TA and TLRAT come from the tree cover maps. Lot area (No. 21) was included because *ceteris paribus* the probability of a lot being used increases as its area increases.

Of the several types of ground cover tested (Nos. 24–28), leaf litter should attract and grass discourage this ground-foraging forest species. Moss and bare ground were used because of their considerable variation in frequency among lots and because of their occasional use as foraging substrates.

The Water Index (No. 29) was included because of the apparent importance of moisture conditions to habitat selection in wood thrush (Bertin 1977). Neighbor Effect (No. 30) was the only non-habitat variable. I calculated this index by awarding a point to a lot for each lot contiguous with it (including corners) that held at least one nest during a year. The sum of the points over 4 years was the index. NE should be positively related to YRSOVLP, YRSACT, and RETURNS. If birds are nesting in a yard adjacent to yard Y, they are likely to use Yard Y also. NE should be negatively related to YRSWNST and TOTYG. If birds have a nest in a yard adjacent to Yard Y, the chances are low that any other bird will have a nest in Yard Y because of territoriality. If the birds' nest survives long enough to produce young, there is even less chance that those birds or any others will move into Yard Y. I had no basis for predicting how NE should relate to YGOVTER or QUASCOR.

Analysis.—I used two techniques to identify characteristics associated with success and failure with respect to the seven measures of quality (dependent variables). The first screening used the MAXR method of multiple regression (SAS 1982). MAXR yields a series of "best" equations (though not necessarily with the highest R^2), one for each number of variables specified, rather than one final model as some procedures do. "Best" means largest increase in R^2 over the previous model that had one less variable. An independent variable can be strongly related to the dependent variable but be eliminated because it explains some of the same variation, but less, than another does.

From the pool of 30 independent variables (Table 2), I obtained the 1- to 20-variable models for each dependent variable. From each of the seven sets of 20 models, I selected one as "best." The subjective selection was a compromise among several criteria: (1) where R^2 ceased to increase by ≥ 1.5% per step; (2) maximum R^2; (3) where Mallow's C_p was low and less than p (the number of dependent variables plus one, Draper and Smith 1981: 299–301); (4) minimal number of regression coefficients with significance levels of $p > 0.1$; and (5) a biologically sensible combination of variables.

The second screen isolated variables that distinguished poor lots from good ones. (I will describe lots ranking high on any dependent variable variously as good, better, or high and will use appropriate contrasting terms for low-ranking ones.) Groups of good and poor lots were constituted separately for each of the seven dependent variables. I tried to combine performance classes so as to meet the criteria of equal and adequate N's, maximum number of significant differences, and biological reason. The variety of frequency distributions of performance classes (Fig. 2) precluded any uniformity of N's or of the number or symmetry of classes combined. I identified significant differences between means of high and low groups with t-tests deemed appropriate by F-tests for equality of variances. Arcsin transformations of variables that were percentages (e.g., Nos. 10–20, 23–28, Table 2) had negligible effect on the probabilities and no effect on outcomes of the tests. Significance was set at $p \leq 0.05$ although values up to 0.1 were considered notable for a screening study such as this one.

Variables in each regression model that also appeared as notable in the t-tests became "final variables" (FV's), for which I determined "quality limits" (QL's) as follows. I combined the poor and good groups used for each FV separately, ranked the lots by scores, and located the lot representing the 15th percentile of the good lots. That is, 85% of the good lots had scores equal to or higher than that lot's score, which became the QL. I could then calculate the probability that a lot above or below that limit was a good performer for that particular quality measure using as a base the number of all lots, good plus poor, above and below the limit.

RESULTS

General Data

The number of wood thrush pairs using the area for at least part of the season include territories that extended off the study area and are not population densities (Table 3). The activity spaces or "territories" usually touched 3–5 lots, but some were largely in 1 or 2 or touched 8–12 during a summer of repeated nesting. Although most activity occurred in the wooded strip and backyards, birds sometimes used other parts of a lot. Several nests were built in front yards, over street-side walks, and over driveways. The number of nests in every year was about twice the number of pairs, but we did not have two nests for every pair. Some pairs nested once and left the area whereas others had more than two attempts. The number of fledglings ranged from 17–39 per year (Table 3).

Patterns in the Dependent Variables

The frequency distributions of performance varied considerably among the six simple measures except for YRSOVLP and YRSACT (Fig. 2). Most lots had activity in ≥ 3 years. Even lots with zeros received occasional or peripheral use.

The high proportion of lots used by birds for 3 or 4 years (YRSOVLP, YRSACT) was not reflected in similar proportions holding nests in 3 or 4 years. Twelve lots never had a nest built within them to my knowledge (Fig. 2, YRSWNST). Three held nests in every year.

Only six lots produced ≥ 4 young (Fig. 2, TOTYG), but 80% contributed to the production of ≥ 4 birds during the 4 years (Fig. 2, YGOVTER). Ten of the 12 lots that had no nests contributed, by being used significantly by birds nesting in neighboring lots, to the production of 2–15 young.

Most lots had at least one adult return (Fig. 2). The reasonable maximum for this variable would be six, one pair with exclusive use of a lot in 1980 and returning for the next 3 years. Only two adjoining lots achieved half of that. In that case a male returned twice, and one of his mates returned once.

Table 3. Number of pairs of wood thrush on the study area, number of nests, and number of young fledged during each year at Arbour Park.

Year	Pairs	Nests	Fledglings
1980	20	39	22
1981	22	40	17
1982	13	26	39
1983	14	29	34

Spatial Patterns in Quality

Similar Quality.—Instances of both isolated and clustered lots of similar quality occurred. For example, lots with nests in 4 years (Nos. 2, 25, and 66, Fig. 1) were widely scattered, but some clusters with 3 years' nesting use existed, e.g., Nos. 36–39 and 52–54. Lots producing (≥ 5 young) were not clumped, but a large cluster (Nos. 31–33, 50–54) that produced ≥ 3 young appeared. All lots that recorded ≥ 2 returns were in groups of 2–6, e.g., Nos. 1, 2, and 16 and Nos. 42–44, 62–64.

The few lots with zeros or ones for YRSOVLP and YRSACT were scattered. A large block that had nests in ≤ 1 year consisted of Nos. 3–7 and 19–21. Six lots (12–15, 26–27) scoring ≤ 3 for YGOVTER were neighbors. Lots that never had birds return to them were isolated except for Nos. 66, 67, 69, and 70.

Juxtaposed Extremes.—Some high-performing lots bordered lots of the lowest category. In the most extreme example, Lot 2 with nests in all years (8 nests) produced 12 young while Nos. 1 and 3 never had nests. Lot 3 received a zero for every variable.

Regression

General.—I report only the sign, relative importance, and significance of each independent variable (Table 2) that contributed to the models chosen because this paper deals with the screening stage of identifying important habitat variables. Presentation of complete regression equations that imply prediction and generalization is inappropriate. All of the models selected were significant regressions ($p < 0.0001$). The sign of the regression coefficient of some variables is illogical, an artifact of intercorrelation of independent variables in multiple regression. One way of detecting this is through comparison of the sign with that for the correlation coefficient, r, for that variable in the correlation matrix.

Four variables (TRED, VLCOTOT, PTCOHI and BGF) did not appear in any of the models. Six appeared only once and none appeared more than four times. At the beginning of the following segments dealing with the model for each dependent variable, I present: the significant ($p \leq 0.10$) and notable ($0.1 < p \leq 0.15$) variables (SV, NV) in descending order of their importance to the regression, the percent of variation explained by the model (R^2), the C_p, and, for comparative purposes, R^2 for a 20-variable model. Variables with a negative slope are in parentheses.

YRSOVLP.—[SV: ABF, MF, HD, (BGMF), (GF), TPF, and (TA); NV: (MD) and PTCOLO; R^2 = 51%; C_P = 1.17; R^2_{20} = 59%]. The model includes a positive association with vegetation in the subcanopy (hornbeam density and cover at 1–15 ft) and frequency of three common canopy species (beech, maples, and tulip poplar). Beech and maple contributed most to the regression ($F = 24.4$, $p < 0.0001$ and $F = 8.3$, $p = 0.006$). Tree area was negatively related. The illogical sign is confirmed as an artifact by the positive correlation coefficient ($r = 0.364$, $p < 0.002$). Two other negative associations are logical—frequency of grass and of bare ground plus moss.

YRSACT.—[SV: ABF, MF, HD, (MD), (LA), PTCOLO, and (TPD); NV: (NE); R^2 = 44%; $C_p = -3.37$; R^2_{20} = 52%]. This model and the previous one had 5 variables in common. Frequency of beech and maples were again the most important ($F = 17.9$, 16.4, respectively; $p < 0.0001$). The negative slope for TPD conflicts with a positive, but insignificant, correlation coefficient. The negative sign for lot area is unexpected but agrees with the correlation matrix. The expected positive association with NE did not occur.

YRSWNST.—[SV: (NE), (SGF), TPD, ABF, (STMD), SHRD, (MSF), SGD, and ABD; NV: (LA) and VIBD; R^2 = 54%; $C_p = 0.26$; R^2_{20} = 59%]. NE was by far the most significant contributor ($F = 28.3$, $p < 0.0001$) and was logically negative. The six density variables reflect the importance of dense cover, especially in the understory (e.g., shrubs, *Viburnum*). Beech was represented by both frequency in the canopy and density. The incongruously negative slope for stem density conflicts with a positive, but insignificant, correlation. Sweetgum frequency was also negative in the correlation matrix ($p = 0.07$).

TOTYG.—[SV: (NE); NV: ABD; R^2 = 25%; $C_P = -12.9$; R^2_{20} = 39%]. Although additional variables would have raised R^2, the numerous, very large probabilities of the slopes rendered the model of doubtful value. The strongly negative ($F = 12.8$, $p = 0.0006$) Neighbor Effect is as expected. American beech again appears, this time as density.

YGOVTER.—[SV: HD, (SHRD), ABD, (HF), TA, (NE), VLCOLO, and MSF; NV: (VLCOHI); R^2 = 44%; $C_P = -0.33$; R^2_{20} = 53%]. This model is enigmatic. There is a hint that greater vegetation cover in the rear strips was associated with greater production (SHRD, despite its negative sign, ABD, HD, VLCOLO, and TA). Three of the negative variables (SHRD, VLCOHI, and HF) had positive, though insignificant, r's ($p = 0.42$, 0.61, 0.30, respectively). Argument could be made for the association of NE with YGOVTER to be positive or negative. Both its slope and the correlation coefficient ($r = -0.25$, $p = 0.03$) were negative.

RETURNS.—[SV: (TLRAT), TA, WAI, VIBD, HD, CANCOV, SGF, and (HF); NV: (MF); R^2 = 39%; $C_P = -0.81$; R^2_{20} = 49%]. Six variables in the model represent trees (canopy cover; frequency of hornbeam, maples, and sweetgum; area of trees; and tree:lot area). The negative slope for maple contrasts with an insignificant, positive r. Hornbeam frequency had both a negative slope and correlation. Hornbeam is a minor canopy species (above 15 ft) with thin leaf cover. That its density, in contrast, is positively related to RETURNS indicates its contribution to understory density, along with *Viburnum*. A very large slope ($b = -3.9$) and negative sign for TLRAT probably were artifacts; TLRAT had $r = 0.11$ ($p = 0.36$). The water index appears for its only time in this model.

QUASCOR.—[SV: LF, TPF, and CANCOV; NV: SGD; R^2 = 30%; $C_P = -8.2$; R^2_{20} = 44%]. QUASCOR showed little commonality with the other models. Litter frequency made its only appearance and was the main contributor to the regression ($F = 4.63$, $p = 0.04$). Two of the variables were related only to conditions in the wooded, rear yards (density of sweetgum and litter frequency). The other two variables (canopy cover and frequency of tulip poplar) strongly relate to those areas also.

Group Comparisons

General.—The second screening tested means of variables from groups of lots with high and low performances on each quality measure. The groups were constituted from Fig. 2 as follows: YRSOVLP and YRSACT—4 vs. ≤ 2 yrs.; YRSWNST—≥ 3 vs. ≤ 1 yrs.; TOTYG—≥ 5 vs. ≤ 2 young; YGOVTER—≥ 8 vs. ≤ 7 young; RETURNS—≥ 2 vs. ≤ 1 returns. The high group for QUASCOR scored ≥ 3 (i.e., lots were in the upper two ranks for at least 3 of the 6 measures and no more than once in one of the two lower ranks. The low group (≤ 3) scored in the lower two ranks at least 3 times and not in the upper two more than once.

The t-tests yielded at least one significant difference between groups for 22 variables and a notable difference for one more (Table 4). The more successful group of lots had the higher mean in most cases. Exceptions were all cases for grass frequency (GF), two cases for neighbor effect (NE), and one case for SGF. This pattern also was generally the case for most comparisons that were not significantly or notably different. Significant differences ($p \leq 0.05$) were most numerous for litter frequency (LF), GF, frequency of tulip poplar (TPF), and the proportion of lot covered by trees (TLRAT). Sixteen of the 23 notable variables (Table 4) also appeared in at least one regression model, thereby becoming "final variables" to be examined further.

Final Variables and Quality Limits

Only slight overlap of final variables (FV's) occurred among the seven dependent variables (Table 5). Some of those had similar quality limits (QL) for different success measures, e.g., HD, CANCOV, ABF, TPF, and NE (Table 5). QL's in 3 cases involving SGF and NE are upper rather

Table 4. Means ± (SE) of independent variables for groups of lots representing low (L) and high (H) success for each dependent variable. (N) at top of each column. Densities in stems/a; cover values, TLRAT, and frequencies in percents; tree area in acres. WAI and NE are unitless. See Tables 1 and 2 for explanation of variables. Values rounded after tests.

	Dependent variable													
	YRSOVLP		YRSACT		YRSWNST		TOTYG		YGOVTER		RETURNS		QUASCOR	
Independent variable	L (16)	H (32)	L (14)	H (27)	L (34)	H (16)	L (49)	H (6)	L (42)	H (28)	L (20)	H (50)	L (10)	H (9)
SHRD											218 (39)	360[a] (78)	62 (28)	360 (106)
TRED									171 (16)	244 (33)				
STMD									448 (56)	647 (89)	463 (50)	691[a] (118)	293 (41)	749 (197)
ABD	52 (16)	128 (21)					82 (14)	170[a] (65)	77 (12)	142 (27)			79 (22)	165[a] (41)
VIBD											10 (6)	40[a] (15)		
HD			9 (7)	58 (19)					20 (6)	69 (20)				
TPD							59 (14)	137[a] (65)	41 (9)	92[a] (25)	43 (10)	109 (30)	19 (7)	132[a] (61)
VLCOTOT	6 (0.4)	7[a] (0.5)	5 (0.6)	7 (0.6)					6 (0.3)	8 (0.6)			5 (0.5)	7 (0.9)
VLCOLO			2 (0.4)	3[a] (0.3)					2 (0.2)	3 (0.4)			1 (0.3)	3 (0.5)
VLCOHI	3 (0.2)	4 (0.3)	4 (0.4)	5 (0.3)					4 (0.2)	5 (0.3)				
PTCOLO			15 (3)	22[a] (3)					19 (2)	25 (3)			10 (2)	23 (4)
PTCOHI	29 (2)	36 (2)	30 (2)	37 (2)	33 (1)	37[a] (2)			32 (1)	37[a] (2)			31 (2)	36[a] (1)
CANCOV	47 (3)	61 (2)			51 (2)	62 (2)					54 (2)	60[a] (3)	47 (4)	65 (2)
ABF	22 (4)	40 (3)			28 (3)	39 (4)								
MF			13 (4)	20[a] (2)									9 (3)	22 (8)
SGF					10 (1)	6 (1)					8 (1)	11[a] (2)		
TPF	10 (2)	15 (1)	9 (2)	14 (1)					10 (1)	17 (2)			6 (2)	15 (2)
TA	0.18 (0.02)	0.26 (0.02)			0.20 (0.02)	0.26 (0.02)							0.19 (0.02)	0.28 (0.02)
TLRAT	38 (3)	57 (3)			44 (.03)	56 (.04)			47 (2)	56[a] (4)			39 (1)	59 (1)
GF	38 (3)	24 (2)	35 (3)	26[a] (3)	33 (2)	25 (3)	31 (2)	21 (5)	33 (2)	25 (3)			41 (4)	26 (4)
LF	17 (3)	31 (2)	19 (4)	30 (3)	21 (2)	31 (3)			21 (2)	30 (3)	23 (2)	29[a] (3)	13 (5)	37 (4)
WAI			0.4 (0.2)	1.2 (0.3)							0.7 (0.1)	1.3 (0.3)		
NE					7.4 (0.4)	6.2[a] (0.6)	7.1 (0.3)	5.0 (1.2)			6.4 (0.4)	7.5[a] (0.4)		

[a]Differences at 0.05 < p ≤ 0.1. All other differences at p ≤ 0.05.

Table 5. Quality limits of final variables for each measure of success as determined by multiple regression and t-tests of extreme groups. See Table 4 for units of values.

Independent variable	Dependent variable						
	YRSOVLP	YRSACT	YRSWNST	TOTYG	YGOVTER	RETURNS	QUASCOR
ABD				168[b]	38[b]		
VIBD						34[b]	
HD		29[b]			34[b]		
VLCOLO					1		
VLCOHI					3		
PTCOLO		10					
CANCOV						52	60
ABF	24		23				
MF		8					
SGF			10[a]			5	
TPF	7						8
TA	0.2						
GF	37[a]						
LF							24
WAI						1[b]	
NE			8[a]	8[a]			

[a]85th percentile because relationship negative.
[b]Minimum non-zero value of high lot used due to large number of ties among zeros or unusual distribution. See text.

than lower limits because the variables were inversely related to success.

The chance that a lot performed well if the value of its FV was ≥ QL exceeded 50% for most of the FV's (Table 6). E.g., a lot that had a beech frequency of ≥ 24% (Table 5) had an 82% chance (Table 6) of having birds present for 4 years. Probability of high performance when FV < QL was generally below 30%, but in some cases was over 40%, e.g., HD-YRSACT.

The highest probabilities of success when the QL was surpassed occurred under YRSOVLP, YRSACT, and QUASCOR. Not all of those carried stiff penalties to success for being below the threshold. Chances of high success if below QL ranged from 5% (GF-YRSOVLP) to 48% (HD-YRSACT) (Table 6).

A few FV's had many zeros and ties between high and low performance lots when the lots were ranked (ranked data not shown). This made determining the 15th percentile

Table 6. Percent chance and (N) of high performance by a lot with a final variable (FV) equal to or above (A) and below (B) the quality limit for that FV. See Table 5 for quality limits.

Independent variable	Dependent variable													
	YRSOVLP		YRSACT		YRSWNST		TOTYG		YGOVTER		RETURNS		QUASCOR	
	A	B	A	B	A	B	A	B	A	B	A	B	A	B
ABD							44 (9)	4 (46)	45 (49)	29 (21)				
VIBD											50 (12)	24 (58)		
HD			89 (18)	48 (23)					59 (27)	26 (43)				
VLCOLO									45 (53)	29 (17)				
VLCOHI									41 (58)	42 (12)				
PTCOLO			74 (31)	40 (10)										
CANCOV											50 (44)	15 (26)	73 (11)	13 (8)
ABF	82 (33)	33 (15)			70 (33)	12 (17)								
MF			77 (30)	36 (11)										
SGF					42 (33)	18 (17)					51 (49)	19 (21)		
TPF	77 (35)	38 (13)											73 (11)	13 (8)
TA	82 (33)	33 (15)												
GF	79 (34)	5 (14)												
LF													89 (9)	10 (10)
WAI											35 (34)	22 (36)		
NE					40 (35)	13 (15)	14 (36)	5 (19)						

of the high group for the purpose of calculating probabilities of success tedious and hid biological meanings. Those and other special cases are noted now.

The chances of success above and below QL for HD and VIBD (Table 6) are based on lots having some or none, respectively, of the species. Some high performance lots lacked the two species, especially hornbeam, thus reducing the penalty for its absence. Those lots almost invariably were rich in beech.

The QL's for beech density (Table 5) equal the lowest, non-zero values for a high lot in the list. They represent the 33rd and 21st percentiles for high scores for TOTYG and YGOVTER, respectively. I used those values because a few high-scoring lots lacked beech. When one of those was the 15th percentile and was far below the rest of the good lots, a distorted probability of success resulted. Those few lots invariably were well stocked with hornbeam and *Viburnum.* Members of the high group for TOTYG had beech densities $\geq$ QL or had none at all. In between were 36 low scorers that had beech densities $<$ QL. The situation for YGOVTER was more diffuse; only 10 poor lots were below QL.

The QL for WAI was 1, which represented presence of moist gullies but no sogginess. Lots with an index ≥ 1 had a low probability of having ≥ 2 birds return in 4 years (35%, Table 6). Raising the QL to ≥ 2 (minimum of some sogginess) raised the probability to 53%.

DISCUSSION

The final variables that survived the double screening were surely important to the variation in achievement of the management goals among the lots of Arbour Park (Table 5). Although I have considered different measures of success throughout the analysis, most of them are related. E.g., a lot cannot produce young if it has no birds or nests. Consequently, I will treat all FV's as collectively important in differentiating successful from unsuccessful lots rather than restricting them to the specific measures under which they appear (Tables 5 and 6). That some variables appeared in more than one column supports that approach. I restrict discussion to the FV's although some of the variables surviving only one screening also may be correlated with or contribute to the habitat conditions represented by the FV's.

What do the FV's generally indicate about habitat of desirable lots? Dense, shade-casting canopy is reflected by greater density and frequency of beech, greater area under trees, and greater canopy cover. Beech was the only species significantly correlated with CANCOV and TA ($p < 0.0001$). A second feature is a shrubbiness and understory component represented by greater density of hornbeam, *Viburnum* spp., maples, PTCOLO, VLCOLO, and VLCOHI. All were correlated with shrub density ($p \leq 0.007$). Frequency of tulip poplar in the canopy may manifest the shrubbier, more-recently disturbed spots in the woods prior to development of Arbour Park. It was most strongly correlated with hornbeam ($p = 0.02$) and shrub density ($p = 0.07$). Most of the high scoring lots had less than 37% of the ground in grass (Table 5). This reflects a trade-off generally with tree cover and litter. The higher water index reflects the presence of wet soil. The negative association of sweetgum frequency above 15 ft with density of shrubs, hornbeam, *Viburnum,* and even sweetgum itself, and its only positive one being with beech density, suggests that SGF was associated with success because it represents large sweetgums in older, less recently disturbed sections.

My results agree with two other studies of wood thrush habitat despite differences in sampling and analytical techniques. Soil moisture, shrub cover, and trees $\geq$ 40 ft were three of the variables Bertin (1977) found to be important in Vermont woodlands. His shrub layer overlapped parts of my "LO" and "HI" layers. I did not measure tree height, but the tree frequencies among the FV's certainly include trees $\geq$ 40 ft tall. A *Viburnum* species and "early successional stage" were notable aspects of his wood thrush territories also visible in some of the good lots at Arbour Park.

James et al. (1984) reported "high densities" of wood thrush in forests of this region dominated by tulip poplar and sweetgum. Forests farther west with "peak densities" included beech and sugar maple *(Acer saccharum).* A set of habitat measurements from Maryland forests, including residential areas with beech and tulip poplar, characterized nesting habitats as having tall trees, dense canopy cover, and many understory trees. Shrubs were of minor import.

Speculation on the functional value of some of the variables is warranted. The role of litter in harboring invertebrate food for this largely ground-foraging (Bertin 1977, pers. obs.) bird is certain. I frequently saw them feeding in compost piles or in leaf litter, occasionally on bare ground or moss, or in sparse grass under ornamentals, and rarely, if ever, in grass. Moisture is important for producing mud or wet leaf mold (Forbush and May 1955:379) for nest-building, and probably for keeping soil invertebrates accessible.

Beech was a FV four times including YRSWNST, TOTYG, and YGOVTER. It was the site for 67% of the nests, the next closest being *Viburnum* spp. at 11%. However, nests in beech were no more successful than those in other sites (Roth, unpublished data). Its stiff limbs and tight leaf layers may make beech attractive for nesting, but its high use also probably was a function of its high relative frequency in the canopy (86%). The dense shade cast by beeches also may help maintain a cooler, moister soil.

Although the R^2's for the regression models are not high, the models significantly describe part of the variation of each measure of habitat quality. Some improvement in R^2 may be possible by use of additional variables (as shown by the 20-variable models), transformations or interactions of the current ones, or of ridge regression to compensate for intercorrelation of dependent variables. Some of the "noise" may be in the dependent variables, e.g., as a result of a missed nest or a miscount of fledglings that put a house lot in the wrong class, or of stochastic events such as nest failure that had nothing to do with habitat. Finally, the single lot may be of the wrong scale to demonstrate distinct patterns (Wiens et al. 1986). The clusters of lots of similar quality and the notable neighbor effects imply merit in a similar analysis using groups of contiguous lots.

From a strictly statistical viewpoint, my results describe conditions in Arbour Park and only should be used for recommendations for enhancing wood thrush habitat there or nearby. Even then, caution should be used because the conclusions are from preliminary, associational stages of multiple regression and are untested. The results may be generalizable with caution for mesic deciduous areas of the mid-Atlantic area east of the Blue Ridge Mountains. James et al. (1984) clearly showed the fallacy of going beyond that distance because preferred habitat features change over the species' range.

Given those caveats and with no consideration of relative merits of plant species for landscaping, I offer the following guidelines for having a better than 50% chance of providing nesting habitat for wood thrush: a minimum of 0.2a (8,700 ft^2) of tree cover, preferably contiguous, with a canopy that blocks at least 70% of the sky and under which one maintains natural leaf litter, native shrubs, and moist soil. American beech is the most desirable tree, but others such as sweetgum and maples forming good canopies over shrubs may be acceptable. Success of such landscaping as wood thrush habitat will improve considerably if adjoining lots provide similar juxtaposed patches to produce a larger area.

SUMMARY

The study uses data from a 4-yr study of a banded, breeding population of wood thrush in a residential area. Thirty habitat features were screened for association with seven measures of habitat quality based on the birds' use, reproductive effort, and site fidelity on individual lots.

A double-screening approach using multiple regression and comparisons of extreme groups produced 16 variables strongly associated with at least one of the measures. As a group, these "final variables" (FV's) represented a dense tree canopy, shrubby understory, soil moisture, and leaf litter. The results reflect features identified by others as important aspects of wood thrush habitats elsewhere. Occurrence of nests and production of young on a lot were negatively affected by presence of nests on neighboring lots.

A quality limit (QL) for each FV equaled the 15th percentile value of the variable among high-performance lots. Estimated chance of high performance for a lot if it had an FV value $\geq$ QL was 35–89% and 5–48% if the value of the FV $<$ QL. Tentative guidelines using these first-stage, untested results are suggested for attracting and enhancing success of the birds.

Acknowledgments.—This paper would not have been completed without Brad Sample's yeoman work on the computer, Vicki Taylor's and Cindy Cairo's dedication and skill on the word processor, and the residents of Arbour Park, who graciously allowed ready access to their yards. Paul Kendra was a valuable field assistant for 3 years. John Pesek provided valuable statistical advice, any misuse of which is my responsibility. Rich Leibfried recorded vegetation data for me *gratis*. Sherry and Chad Roth helped greatly with preliminary data compilation. I thank them all. The research was supported by the McIntire-Stennis Cooperative Forestry Research Program. This report is published as Miscellaneous Paper No. 1150 of the Delaware Agricultural Experiment Station, and Contribution No. 576 of the Department of Entomology and Applied Ecology, University of Delaware, Newark, Delaware.

REFERENCES CITED

Bertin, R. I. 1977. Breeding habits of the wood thrush and veery. Condor 79:303–311.

Draper, N. R. and H. Smith. 1981. Applied regression analysis. 2nd Ed. John Wiley and Sons, New York. 407 pp.

Forbush, E. H. and J. B. May. 1955. A natural history of American birds of eastern and central North America. Bramhall House, New York. 554 pp.

Gauthreaux, S. A., Jr. 1982. The ecology and evolution of avian migration systems. Pages 93–168 *in* D. S. Farner, J. R. King, and K. C. Parkes, eds. Avian biology, Vol. VI. Academic Press, New York.

Greenwood, P. J. and P. H. Harvey. 1982. The natal and breeding dispersal of birds. Ann. Rev. Ecol. Syst. 13:1–21.

Harvey, P. H., P. J. Greenwood, and C. M. Perrins. 1979. Breeding area fidelity of the great tit (*Parus major*). J. Anim. Ecol. 48:305–313.

Hildén, O. 1965. Habitat selection in birds. Ann. Zool. Fenn. 2:53–75.

James, F. C., R. F. Johnston, N. O. Wamer, G. J. Niemi, and W. J. Boecklen. 1984. The Grinellian niche of the wood thrush. Am. Nat. 124:17–30.

Karr, J. R. 1968. Habitat and avian diversity on strip mined land in east-central Illinois. Condor 70:348–357.

Karr, J. R. and R. R. Roth. 1971. Vegetation structure and avian diversity in several New World areas. Am. Nat. 105:423–435.

Roth, R. R. 1979. Vegetation as a determinant in avian ecology. Pages 162–174 *in* L. Drawe, ed. Proc. First Welder Wildlife Foundation Symposium.

SAS. 1982. SAS user's guide: statistics. SAS Institute, Cary, North Carolina. 584 pp.

Whitcomb, R. F., C. S. Robbins, J. F. Lynch, B. L. Whitcomb, M. K. Klimkiewicz, and D. Bystrak. 1981. Effects of forest fragmentation on avifauna of the eastern deciduous forest. Pages 125–205 *in* R. L. Burgess and D. M. Sharpe, eds. Forest island dynamics in man-dominated landscapes. Ecol. Studies No. 41., Springer-Verlag, New York.

Weins, J. A., J. T. Rotenberry, and B. Van Horne. 1986. A lesson in the limitations of field experiments: shrub-steppe birds and habitat alteration. Ecology 67:365–376.

Recreating a Herpetofaunal Community at Gateway National Recreation Area, New York

ROBERT P. COOK AND CLIVE A. PINNOCK, *National Park Service, Gateway NRA, Floyd Bennett Field, Brooklyn, NY 11234*

INTRODUCTION

Gateway National Recreation Area's Jamaica Bay Wildlife Refuge consists of 9,155 acres (3,705 ha) of salt-water bay, marsh, and uplands scattered among 25 islands in south Brooklyn and Queens, New York. Established in 1948 by the New York City Department of Parks and Recreation, the National Park Service took over its management in 1972. In recognition of Jamaica Bay's long history of human impacts, and with a vision for its future potential, management is based on "policies directed towards the preservation and restoration of natural processes and landscapes to perpetuate significant wildlife species and their habitats" (USNPS 1979).

LAND USE CHANGE AND HERPETOFAUNAL IMPACTS

To appreciate the rationale for restoration requires an understanding of land use changes and their impacts in this area. Jamaica Bay was originally 26,000 acres (10,522 ha) of shallow bay and salt marsh located at the western end of Long Island (Hassler 1845, Jamaica Bay Environmental Study Group 1971). It was surrounded by the dunes, shrublands, and deciduous forests of present day Brooklyn, Queens, and Nassau counties. Though our knowledge of the original herpetofauna is incomplete (Schlauch and Burnley 1968), historic records for Long Island in general give some indication of the past. Noble (1927) listed 39 species as indigenous to Long Island, and Schlauch (1978a) considered 37 species definitely indigenous plus 12 others as possibly. Most, but certainly not all, of these species likely occurred in the three counties bordering Jamaica Bay.

Urbanization of Long Island followed a general pattern of agricultural development, and a later period of concurrent agricultural decline and increased urbanization. Once at this stage a cycle of decay and renewal ensued (Schlauch 1978a). The early communities surrounding Jamaica Bay engaged in agriculture, fishing, shipping, and resort development (Black 1981), but the most dramatic changes have occurred in this century, a period of rapid urbanization on western Long Island (Schlauch 1976).

As part of this process, draining and landfilling reduced the marshes of Jamaica Bay. Along the bay's periphery, fill created areas for residential and highway development, "sanitary landfills," and Kennedy Airport (Black 1981). Today Jamaica Bay has been reduced to 13,000 acres (5,261 ha), due mostly to this loss of peripheral marshes (Jamaica Bay Environmental Study Group 1971). On the islands, dredge spoil deposition created upland habitats where only salt marsh had existed. Because these islands had, since 1948, become the Jamaica Bay Wildlife Refuge, a program of habitat improvements was undertaken which, in conjunction with successional changes, has led to the present habitat diversity of Jamaica Bay.

As these insular habitats were being created, the mainland herpetofauna was undergoing the general decline, extirpation, and reduction to remnant populations that typically accompanies urbanization (Campbell 1974, Dove 1985). Most of Brooklyn's original herpetofauna is now extinct, and in Nassau county 24 of 35 indigenous species are considered extinct or endangered (Schlauch 1978b). One problem with assessing impacts is that the historic literature gives few specific locations for widespread species. We do know, however, that the eastern hognose snake *(Heterodon p. platyrhinos)* formerly occurred in the Rockaways (Engelhardt et al. 1915), and species such as the smooth green snake *(Opheodrys v. vernalis)* and the eastern mud turtle *(Kinosternum s. subrubrum)*, were common throughout this area (Ditmars 1896, Engelhardt 1913, Murphy 1916).

Integrating Man and Nature in the Metropolitan Environment. Proc. Natl. Symp. on Urban Wildl., Chevy Chase, Md., 4–7 November 1986, L.W. Adams and D.L. Leedy, eds. Published by Natl. Inst. for Urban Wildl., 10921 Trotting Ridge Way, Columbia, MD 21044, 1987.

HERPETOFAUNAL INVENTORY

Ruler's Bar Hassock, the Bay's main island, is the most accessible and has the greatest diversity of habitats. It contains 372 acres (151 ha) of uplands and 140 acres (57 ha) of impoundments (Bridges 1976). A herpetofaunal inventory conducted in 1979–80 was based on observation at freshwater ponds, searches under debris, use of aquatic funnel traps, and interviews of local naturalists.

As a result, Fowler's toad *(Bufo woodhousei fowleri)*, northern diamondback terrapin *(Malaclemys t. terrapin)*, and eastern garter snake *(Thamnophis s. sirtalis)* were found to occur as breeding populations, and individuals of eastern box turtle *(Terrapene c. carolina)*, eastern painted turtle *(Chrysemys p. picta)*, red-eared slider *(Chrysemys scripta elegans)*, and snapping turtle *(Chelydra serpentina)* also were recorded. The diamondback terrapin is a salt marsh species, thus indigenous, and the snapping turtles may have been remnant individuals of a nearly-extirpated native population. The remainder of these species, however, are known either for their urban tolerance or for being popular as pets (Schlauch 1976, Klemens 1985). Their presence on the island is most likely recent, and the result of deliberate or inadvertent release by humans.

The conclusion from the 1979–80 inventory was that the herpetofauna then present was only a portion of the native species potentially capable of being supported by the diverse habitats present. Considering the dispersal barriers posed by urbanization (Campbell 1974) and the salt waters of Jamaica Bay, such a faunal impovishment was not surprising.

HABITAT IMPROVEMENTS AND COMMUNITY RE-CREATION

Considering the paucity of herpetofauna on Ruler's Bar Hassock, and the continuing urbanization pressures on remnant mainland populations, a program of habitat improvements and animal transplants was formulated. The object was to take advantage of the recently created uplands and recreate a herpetofaunal community resembling, as close as possible, that which had formerly occurred on the now urbanized mainland. This would be consistent with the Refuge's mandate (USNPS 1979) and could help preserve local gene pools threatened by further urbanization. Similar programs had been proposed in theory by Campbell (1974) and used in Great Britain to protect endangered populations of *Bufo calamita* (Beebe 1973). Our program would differ only in its attempt to transplant several species, rather than just one.

Before transplanting animals, a number of habitat improvements were made. Terrestrial microhabitats were enhanced by placing piles of boards, driftwood, leaves, and woodchips in various habitats. Four small freshwater ponds, ranging in size from 0.4 acres (0.16 ha) to 700 square feet (65.1 square meters) were created by bulldozer or hand and planted with submergent and emergent vegetation.

Candidate species for transplanting were those native to Long Island and, based on literature, personal observation, and discussions with local herpetologists, adapted to the habitats present on Ruler's Bar Hassock. Because animal transplants can be controversial, the following guidelines were adopted to ensure that the program accomplished its goals without adverse complications:

1. Long Island has been isolated from continental New York for at least 3,500 years (Strahler 1966) and its fauna is somewhat different (Connors 1971). In order to preserve local gene pools, and utilize animals best adapted to local conditions, only individuals collected on Long Island would be released.
2. Animals released would come from populations currently facing extirpation or large enough to sustain collection.
3. Lower trophic level species would be released first.

Adhering to these criteria, transplants began in 1980 and are ongoing. Different species were collected at different life stages, and some species (e.g., spring peeper, *Hyla crucifer*) were collected at more than one life stage. All snakes and turtles released were marked using scale clipping and carapace notching, respectively (Woodbury 1956), but amphibians were released unmarked.

The numbers of animals of a given species that were released varied, as did the number released in a given year, because the program has been possible only by opportunistically integrating it into other aspects of daily refuge operations. Generally, as experience, knowledge of a species' occurrence, and networking with others knowledgeable of local herpetofauna increased, the number of individuals released also increased. The role of networking cannot be overemphasized. As the program gained momentum, the network grew until, by 1984, much of the collecting was done by volunteers who lived in proximity to habitats undergoing development. A typical pattern of release is that of the smooth green snake; 11, 8, 27, and 33 individuals were released in 1981, '82, '83, and '84, respectively. After 1984, intensive collecting of green snakes was discontinued and activities primarily have consisted of population monitoring.

Monitoring efforts vary by species and consist of observations at breeding ponds, use of aquatic funnel traps, searches under boards and debris, and miscellaneous encounters (e.g., road kills and animals found by visitors). In monitoring the results of these transplants, a basic pattern of events was anticipated and has, in fact, occurred. The first event is documenting overwinter survival. Second is confirmation of breeding or production of offspring, determined by records of neonates, metamorphs, and unmarked individuals of species marked before release. Offspring records, however, do not necessarily prove establishment because some impregnated females were released. Determining species establishment is difficult, and we have been conservative in such pronouncements. When a pattern of continuing records of progeny over the course of 2–3 years emerges, combined with evidence of a spread from the focal point of introduction, it is fairly safe to conclude establishment.

A full assessment of results will require another 10–20 years, but data so far have been encouraging. Individuals of 11 species have been released and two of these are established (Table 1). Spring peeper and northern brown snake were deemed established within 3 and 4 years, respectively, and releases have been discontinued. In the case of the brown snake, releases began in 1980 and young were being produced by 1982. Because of limited staff time, intensive monitoring (i.e., capture and marking) of brown snake neonates was discontinued in 1984 to allow a shift in effort towards species not yet established.

Successful overwintering has been documented in all species except the eastern milk snake (*Lampropeltis t. triangulum*), and offspring also have been recorded for the box turtle, painted turtle, green snake, and black racer (*Coluber c. constrictor*) (Table 1).

The lag time in determining the outcome of many of the releases is due to a combination of factors. Much of the habitat these inherently hard to find animals (Dove 1985) were released into is impenetrable, and at the low densities they occur at following release, and without any tracking devices, they are simply hard to recover. For example, a box turtle released in 1980 was first recaptured in 1985. Differences in fecundity allow some species, such as anurans and ovoviviparous snakes, to more quickly exploit empty niches, and thereby build their densities up to readily detectable levels. A final factor is the number of individuals of a species released in a given year. Although it is preferable to collect and release large numbers of a species at once, so their density will be as high as possible, this was not always practical.

DISCUSSION

Rather than attempt to discuss in detail the incomplete returns of our releases, we will focus on our perceptions of the implications of this program.

At the site specific level, it seems reasonable to conclude that many, but not all, of the species released will become established. The failure of some species to become established points to possible errors in judgment on the suitability of species for the habitat available, or to poor technique. As previously mentioned, this project is being carried out at something of a grass roots level. Considering the continued urbanization occurring in this area, it was felt that to defer action until major funding was available is unrealistic, and would result in lost opportunities to salvage local populations. Thus, being only partially successful is preferable to doing nothing.

Table 1. Population status of amphibians and reptiles released on Ruler's Bar Hassock Island, Jamaica Bay Wildlife Refuge, New York, New York, 1980–1986.

Species released	Year	No. of individuals	Overwinter survival	Breeding records	Established
Spring peeper	80–83	58 adult 3600 larvae	Yes	Innumerable	Yes
Green frog	85–86	15 adult	Yes	a	a
Red-backed salamander	83–86	361 juvenile 1443 adult	Yes	6 offspring recorded	a
Northern brown snake	80–81	23 juvenile 49 adult	Yes	42 offspring recorded from 83 to 9/1/84	Yes
Smooth green snake	81–86	17 juvenile 64 adult	Yes	9 offspring recorded	a
Eastern hognose snake	84–85	21 hatchling 4 adult	Yes	a	a
Eastern milk snake	84–85	13 juvenile 9 adult	a	a	a
Black racer	85–86	4 juvenile 17 adult	Yes	13 offspring recorded	a
Snapping turtle	83–85	320 hatchling 11 juvenile 35 adult	Yes	a	a
Eastern painted turtle	82–85	28 juvenile 295 adult	Yes	6 offspring recorded	a
Eastern box turtle	80–86	12 juvenile 183 adult	Yes	3 offspring recorded	a

[a]Insufficient elapsed time or data to determine.

Future efforts here, or carried out by others, should consider maximizing the number of individuals released simultaneously by using husbandry techniques, and by establishing a network of trained volunteer collectors from the start.

The grass roots nature of this program, though it does have its drawbacks, has conferred one great advantage that others can use. This is the fact that significant efforts at salvaging and managing urban herpetofauna can be carried out by agencies and institutions with limited funds. Now that urbanization impacts on herpetofauna are better understood, there is a growing effort to manage amphibians and reptiles in urban environments. This, we assume, is based on the realization that without such actions, many more populations will disappear around urban areas. Habitats and extirpated species are being restored, and threatened populations transplanted to protected habitats (Beebe 1973; NJDEP 1984, 1985; Gates et al. 1985).

Protected urban bioenclaves may offer opportunities for further salvaging of endangered populations. In Gateway National Recreation Area, for example, many areas are former landfill and present opportunities similar to those found on Ruler's Bar Hassock. Throughout the New York City area, and we would suspect in many other places, decommissioned landfills are in the process of being revegetated. Because many are unsuited for human habitation or wholesale public use, they have become *de facto* wildlife refuges. Their suitability as sites for managing and salvaging herpetofauna should be considered.

Jamaica Bay has a history of initial abuse for which more recent efforts at restoration are attempting to compensate. It is unreasonable to expect that the entire preurbanization fauna can be preserved, but as a result of this program the continued existence of many of these species within New York City is ensured. By adapting the principles of this program, and learning from both its successes and mistakes, the herpetofauna of other urban areas also might be managed to preserve local gene pools and "enliven the city with sounds and sights" (Campbell 1974).

REFERENCES CITED

Beebe, T. J. C. 1973. Observations concerning the decline of the British amphibia. Biol. Conserv. 5:20–24.

Black, F. R. 1981. Jamaica Bay: A history. Cult. Resour. Manage. Study No. 3, USDI Natl. Park Serv., Washington, DC. 116 pp.

Bridges, J. T. 1976. Vegetation survey, soils map, and estimate of plant health conditions at Jamaica Bay Wildlife Refuge. Natl. Park Serv.—New York Bot. Garden Coop. Res. Unit, Bronx. 73 pp.

Campbell, C. A. 1974. Survival of reptiles and amphibians in urban environments. Pages 61–66 *in* J. H. Noyes and D. R. Progulske, eds. Wildlife in an urbanizing environment. Univ. of Mass. Coop. Ext. Serv., Amherst. 183 pp.

Connors, P. F. 1971. The mammals of Long Island, New York. Bull. 416, New York State Mus. and Sci. Serv., Albany. 78 pp.

Ditmars, R. L. 1896. The snakes found within fifty miles of New York City. Abst. Proc. Linnean Society, New York, 8:9–24.

Dove, L. E. 1985. Reptiles and amphibians. *Urban Wildl. Managers Notebook*—6. Supplement to *Urban Wildl. News* Vol. 8. 8 pp.

Engelhardt, G. P. 1913. The reptiles of Long Island. Mus. News 8:128–129.

Engelhardt, G. P., J. T. Nichols, R. Latham, and R. C. Murphy. 1915. Long Island snakes. Copeia 17:1–4.

Gates, J. E., R. H. Stouffer, Jr., J. R. Stauffer, Jr., and C. H. Hocutt. 1985. Dispersal patterns of translocated *Cryptobranchus alleghaniensis* in a Maryland stream. J. Herpetol. 19:436–438.

Hassler, F. R. 1845. Map of New York Bay and harbor and the environs. Survey of the coast of the United States. United States Coast Survey Depot. Washington, DC.

Jamaica Bay Environmental Study Group. 1971. Jamaica Bay and Kennedy Airport: a multidisciplinary environmental study. Vol. 1: Conclusions, recommendations, summary. Natl. Acad. of Sci./Natl. Acad. of Eng., Washington, DC. 56 pp.

Klemens, M. W. 1985. Survivors in megalopolis: reptiles of the urban Northeast. Discovery 18:22–25.

Murphy, R. C. 1916. Long Island turtles. Copeia 33:56–60.

NJDEP. 1984. Research results: Eastern Tiger Salamander. NONGAME NEWS, Spring 1984. New Jersey Dep. of Environ. Protection, Div. of Fish, Game, and Wildl. p. 6.

NJDEP. 1985. Amphibian habitat restored, amphibians introduced. NONGAME NEWS, Summer 1985. New Jersey Dep. of Environ. Protection, Div. of Fish, Game, and Wildl. p. 3.

Noble, G. K. 1927. Distributional list of the reptiles and amphibians of the New York City region. Guide Leafl. Ser. No. 69, Am. Mus. Nat. Hist., New York. 9 pp.

Schlauch, F. C. 1976. City snakes, suburban salamanders. Nat. Hist. 85:46–53.

Schlauch, F. C. 1978a. Urban geographical ecology of the amphibians and reptiles of Long Island. Pages 25–41 *in* C. M. Kirkpatrick, ed. *Wildlife and people.* John S. Wright Forestry Conf. Proc., Dep. of For. and Nat. Resour., Purdue Univ. and the Indiana Coop. Ext. Serv., West Lafayette.

Schlauch, F. C. 1978b. New methodologies for measuring species status and their application to the herpetofauna of a suburban region. Engelhardtia 6:30–41.

Schlauch, F. C. and J. M. Burnley. 1968. Distributional survey of the indigenous herpetozoans of Long Island. Engelhardtia 1:34–37.

Strahler, A. N. 1966. A geologist's view of Cape Cod. Nat. Hist. Press, Garden City, New York. 117 pp.

USNPS. 1979. General management plan, Gateway National Recreational Area. USDI Natl. Park Serv., Washington DC. 180 pp.

Woodbury, A. M. 1956. Uses of marking animals in ecological studies: marking amphibians and reptiles. Ecology 37:670–674.

Deer-human Interactions and Research in the Chicago Metropolitan Area

JAMES H. WITHAM AND JON M. JONES, *Illinois Natural History Survey, Rt. 4, Box 178, Elgin, IL 60120*

White-tailed deer (*Odocoileus virginianus*) possess adaptive characteristics that enable effective utilization of habitats near human population centers—an increasingly common occurrence in North America (Shoesmith and Koonz 1977, Ashley 1982, Iker 1983, Moen 1984). In such areas, the resultant increased frequency of deer-human interactions produces wildlife management challenges that require a complex blending of ecological, political, and socio-economic considerations.

Deer numbers in the greater Chicago metropolitan area of northeastern Illinois have increased substantially since the 1960's. In Cook County, the second most populous county in the United States with more than five million human residents, a system of county forest preserves sustains sizeable deer herds amidst areas of intensive suburban development. Interacting factors of a high density human population, large numbers of deer, and inviolate, but increasingly insular habitat, currently foster a seemingly ubiquitous array of deer-human encounters. In this paper we: (1) describe typical deer-human interactions in Cook County, and (2) discuss the role of the Chicago Urban Deer Study as a precursor to an urban deer management program.

DEER HABITAT PRESERVATION IN COOK COUNTY

The Cook County Forest Preserve District (CCFPD) is a mosaic of more than 30 discrete refuges that range 16–6,070 ha in size and comprise 11% (27,080 ha) of the Cook County landscape. The CCFPD has acquired land since 1915 for the "purpose of protecting and preserving the flora, fauna, and scenic beauties . . . in their natural state and condition, for . . . the education, pleasure, and recreation of the public" (Wendling et al. 1981). About 20% of CCFPD land has been developed for educational and recreational uses which include five nature centers, the Brookfield Zoo, and the Chicago Botanical Gardens. Non-developed properties are native hardwood forests, reforestations, riparian habitat, old fields, and leased agricultural fields.

OVERVIEW OF DEER-HUMAN INTERACTIONS IN NORTHEASTERN ILLINOIS

The importance of positive interactions between deer and people in an urban setting should not be understated. Langenau et al. (1984) provided a relevant overview of the values of white-tailed deer. Observations of urban wildlife, particularly large mammals such as deer, are high quality non-consumptive experiences that stimulate environmental awareness and foster a broader appreciation for natural resources among the urban public. Many homeowners that live near forest preserves have attracted deer into their yards, much like avian species, with supplemental feed during winter. Photographers have found that urban deer are good subjects for close-up photography because they are tolerant of human disturbances.

Consumptive use of deer in Cook County is limited. Firearm hunting is prohibited. Archery deer hunting on private and state-owned lands is permitted by the state; however, a conflicting county ordinance prohibits the taking of deer by bow (Dziedzina 1984). The carcasses of deer involved in vehicle collisions in Illinois may be utilized by the public.

The array of negative deer-human interactions in northeastern Illinois is extensive (Table 1). Most forest preserves in Cook County support resident deer herds; private property adjacent to forest preserves has been developed. Deer frequently move from preserves onto private suburban properties to feed on ornamental plantings—a daily pattern typical during winter when the forage within hardwood forests is scarce.

Integrating Man and Nature in the Metropolitan Environment. Proc. Natl. Symp. on Urban Wildl., Chevy Chase, Md., 4–7 November 1986, L.W. Adams and D.L. Leedy, eds. Published by Natl. Inst. for Urban Wildl., 10921 Trotting Ridge Way, Columbia, MD 21044, 1987.

Table 1. Negative deer-human interactions that occur in urbanized northeastern Illinois.

I. Browsing or antler rubbing damage to ornamental, cultivated, or special collections of plants
   A. Ornamental plantings and home gardens
   B. Cultivated (crops)
   C. Collections (arboretums)
II. Browsing damage to naturally occurring or restored plant associations
III. Spacial conflicts with accident potential
   A. Highway vehicle accidents
   B. Airports
   C. Dispersal into commercial or residential sites that contain no suitable deer habitat or escape cover
IV. Transmission of diseases, parasites, and toxicology
   A. California encephalitis
   B. Lyme Disease
   C. Parasites
   D. Heavy metals, pesticides, PCB's
V. Negative agency-public and interagency relationships resulting from deer-related incidents

Example—Northbrook, northern Cook County.

Deer observations were uncommon during the late 1960's in residential areas of Northbrook, a northern Cook County municipality adjacent to the Des Plaines River forest preserves. Deer numbers increased substantially between 1970–1986. Homeowners initially enjoyed seeing more deer near their properties and some promoted increased contact by establishing supplementary feeding stations in their yards. Low-level browsing of ornamental plantings was generally tolerated, although some damage was reported to the Illinois Department of Conservation (IDOC). Deer repellents were tried by some homeowners; damage abatement was moderately successful with herds at low densities. Some deer, named by residents and known by distinctive physical characteristics, used the same residential areas annually and formed traditional use patterns that were learned by offspring. Deer habituated to common residential disturbances. Some residents continued to provide supplemental feed. Over time, browsing damage to ornamental plantings increased with deer numbers. Complaints were registered with the IDOC; deer repellents were not effective at higher deer densities. In 1986, deer density on the northern Des Plaines River forest preserves exceeded 39 deer/km^2. Homeowner attitudes toward deer were polarized—some continued to provide supplemental feed—others threatened to shoot deer or involve political representatives. Concerns were expressed regarding potential health hazards associated with children playing in yards littered with deer fecal pellets, and, the transmission of Lyme disease (Warner 1986, Miller 1987). The IDOC, responsible for wildlife species management, and the CCFPD as the refuge landowner, lay precariously straddled on a volatile no-win urban deer issue.

Agricultural land-use has declined with increased urbanization of Cook County. Deer densities have remained low to moderate (<8 deer/km^2) in the more rural areas of northwest and southern Cook County where agricultural land-use remains. In recent years, depredations by deer on corn, soy bean, and orchard crops have been insignificant; issuance of IDOC deer depredation permits to reduce damage to commercial crops has been rare (F. Loomis, IDOC, pers. commun.).

The Chicago Botanical Gardens (121 ha, Cook County) and the Morton Arboretum (607 ha, DuPage County) have reported deer damage to plant collections maintained for scientific, educational, and aesthetic uses. Property boundaries of both arboretums adjoin county forest preserves.

Example—Chicago Botanical Gardens (CBG), Glencoe.

The CBG, owned by the Cook County Forest Preserve District and managed by Chicago Horticultural Society, lies adjacent to preserves on the North Branch of the Chicago River. The common fenceline is not deer proof. Deer herd density on the adjacent preserve is moderate. Deer browse or rub antlers on plants that have high scientific and/or economic values. The CBG receives donations from wealthy urban patrons. Using the terminology of Kellert (1980), the values of these patrons are typically humanistic, moralistic, and ecologistic. Anti-hunting and anti-cruelty attitudes are prevalent. Deer are viewed as a natural component of the CBG. The CBG administration is sensitive to deer issues, in part, because of a publicized arrest of a CBG employee who shot deer on CBG property during 1985. Increasing the height or electrifying the boundary fence may significantly disturb some patrons because of historic association to World War II internment. As landowner, the Cook County Forest Preserve District views deer removal on the CBG as a high-risk political liability.

The protection and maintenance of native plant and faunal associations is mandated in the forest preserve charter. Although most forest preserve land is undeveloped, no control of development is possible on adjacent private properties. These peripheral sites of brush/grassland and agriculture have traditionally provided seasonal habitat for deer. Suburban development on these lands has reduced total deer habitat, and ultimately, has caused greater reliance on the preserve resources. The level of deer impact on preserve vegetation is influenced by the rapidity of the development of adjacent properties, and, the subsequent degree of refuge insularity.

Example—Busse Woods Nature Preserve (BWNP), northern Cook County.

The BWNP is a 177-ha site of high quality dry mesic upland forest, mesic upland forest, mesic hardwood, northern flatwoods, and shrub swamp/marsh vegetative types. The property, a dedicated State Nature Preserve and Registered Federal Natural Landmark, is owned by the Cook County Forest Preserve and lies within the 1,536-ha Ned Brown Preserve. Land-use adjacent to the Ned Brown Preserve includes a large indoor shopping mall, two tollways, two state highways, residential development, and more than 20 high rise corporate buildings. Airspace is within the O'Hare International Airport Terminal Control Area with jets passing over BWNP on final approach at 600 m agl. The Ned Brown Preserve has been developed for recreational use with paved bike trails, picnic groves, a model airplane flying field, and a 241-ha reservoir with recreation facilities. An estimated two million visitors used the Ned Brown Preserve during 1985 (Dwyer, unpubl. data). Two hundred ninety-three deer were counted on the Ned Brown Preserve during an aerial survey in 1984. Deer concentrate in the BWNP during winter. Forest understory plants have been severely impacted, deer-vehicle accidents on adjacent roads are common, and deer suffer from chronic malnutrition.

Spacial conflicts have occurred when deer move from protected habitats into areas of high human use. Deer-vehicle accidents are the most common type of conflict. Cook County has the highest number of reported deer-vehicle accidents among 102 counties in Illinois (IL. Dep. Trans., unpubl. data). Economic losses sustained from deer-vehicle accidents in Cook County averaged $1,306 in 1985 (Witham and Jones, unpubl. data). During spring 1986, a minimum of 11 incidents of deer in "unusual" urban locations, such as a grocery store, travel agency, high school, and race track were reported. Most incidents were handled by police or local animal control personnel with varying success. A periodic concern results from deer on or near airport runways.

Example—O'Hare International Airport, Chicago.

> The O'Hare International Airport is located less than 1 km from forest preserves on the Des Plaines River. Deer habitat, consisting of woodlots/shrub-grasslands and a tree nursery, are located near major airport runways. A small (< 30 deer) resident herd exists on airport property; numbers may be supplemented by immigration from nearby forest preserves. Concern over deer near runways became acute in 1982 when an American Airlines commercial jet struck and killed a buck during takeoff (Iker 1983). Subsequently, the IDOC, U.S. Fish and Wildlife Service, and O'Hare Airport Authority reduced deer numbers. Professional shooters collected 16 deer in 1982 and five deer in 1983. The removals produced negative responses from the media. During the last 4 years, O'Hare Airport safety personnel have maintained three box traps during winter. Less than 10 deer have been live captured; traps have been vandalized by airport personnel.

The role of deer as a health hazard to humans has received recent attention in northeast Illinois. Regionally, most adult deer are hosts for California encephalitis-var Jamestown Canyon virus (P. Grimstad, unpubl. data; Issel et al. 1972; Grimstad et al. 1982). However, the IDOC does not view the transmission of J.C. virus as a serious hazard to the public (A. Woolf, S. Il. Univ., typescr. memo to IDOC, 1985). Lyme disease, a zoonoses with arthritic and flu-like symptoms, is caused by a spirochete transmitted by the deer tick (*Ixodes dammini*). The public most likely to contract Lyme disease are individuals who live near high density deer herds, or those using deer habitat for recreation or by occupation during spring or summer (Moen 1984, Woolf 1986, Miller 1987).

The actions of agencies responding to deer incidents have received intense examination from the public and media. Agencies view any action involving deer as a political liability. Media attention often focuses on individual traumatic incidents such as an attempted capture of a deer in an unusual location or euthanizing an injured animal. If the actions are criticized, then the involved agency will avoid similar responses in the future. Such avoidance is the basis for interagency reluctance to become involved in urban deer management.

Example—Arlington Heights incident.

> A displaced yearling buck ran through a window of a travel agency and was eventually captured by village police. The deer was restrained by ropes and transported to a local forest preserve without contacting county officials. The injured deer was released but remained at the site and was found simultaneously by public recreationists and county police. The recreationists wanted the deer to be sent to a veterinarian, whereas, the police chose to shoot the animal because it appeared to have broken legs. The officers discharged six shots to kill the deer. Questions of public safety, police competence, and animal rights involved in the incident became focal points of newspaper articles; radio and television news teams interviewed participants. Following this incident, a county forest preserve policy was invoked stating that no deer incidents would be handled by forest preserve employees. Months later, the incident was raised as an issue during elections for county board commissioner.

THE CHICAGO DEER STUDY: A TRANSITIONAL STEP TOWARD MANAGEMENT

The Chicago Urban Deer Study was developed as a vehicle to facilitate transition into a permanent urban deer management program. Several advantages have been derived by using research as lead-in to management. Wildlife research, relative to direct management, is fairly well received by agencies and the urban public. The leverage gained during successful research forms precedence that extends to management programs. And, research is experimental, affording the flexibility necessary to identify and explore a range of alternatives for management issues.

In 1983, the IDOC contracted the Illinois Natural History Survey (INHS) to study white-tailed deer ecology, deer-human interactions, and experimental management options in northeastern Illinois. Selection of research emphasis was guided by anticipated future management needs that included: (1) collection of baseline data to establish herd and habitat profiles, (2) assessment of deer-human interactions, (3) development of interagency cooperation, (4) public awareness and participation, and (5) pilot studies to explore issues and to establish management precedents.

The first 3 years of research have been successful. Preliminary baseline data were collected, deer-related damage was assessed, cooperative contacts among agencies and the public were developed, and the experimental manipulation of a high density herd was initiated.

Postmortem examinations were performed on more than 1,000 deer carcasses collected over a 23-month period. Indices of physical condition were used to develop comparative herd profiles. Postmortem examinations provided baseline data on longevity, productivity, parasitology, and toxicology. Minimum herd densities were determined from annual aerial counts during winter. Preliminary integration of these data suggest that deer herds on urban refuges exhibit a wide range of physical conditions (chronic malnutrition to robust) and densities (ca 1–39 deer/km^2).

Typical deer-human interactions were discussed previously in this paper. However, INHS research has focused on the three principal types of negative deer-human interactions. Recorded incidences of deer damage to ornamental and scientific plantings have been mapped. Trends in deer-vehicle accidents were determined; average economic loss per accident was estimated from questionnaire responses. Impact of high density deer herds on the composition, density, and structure of forest understory vegetation has been documented and is monitored annually on selected sites.

Although principal funding was provided by the IDOC, we have continued to develop interagency support opportunistically. The INHS (Department of Energy & Natural Resources) has donated administrative assistance and support facilities based at the University of Illinois, Champaign. The CCFPD contributed office facilities and logistical help. Additional contracts for special studies were solicited from the CCFPD and the Illinois Nature Preserves Commission.

We discovered that most organizations, when approached with forethought, were cooperative. Perhaps the best example involved a network of 89 organizations (police, highway maintenance, forest preserves etc.) that reported the locations of deer carcasses that were collected and used for postmortem examinations. Also, cooperative research was developed with the Brookfield Zoo and Michigan State University that added supportive data for interherd profile evaluations.

Communication with organizations and the public has been an integral part of INHS duties. Research personnel have met annually with a Community Liaison Committee—high level administrators who represent 17 agencies and organizations with an expressed interest in urban deer (Table 2). The Liaison Committee has provided an opportunity for dissemination of project information and functioned as a forum for community input. Information provided by INHS personnel has been the basis of numerous newspaper articles, radio interviews, and television news stories. Technical and popular articles have been published; slide presentations have been regularly given to public and professional audiences. The study has used over 200 volunteers (solicited from local colleges, conservation organizations, sportsmens clubs, and police departments) to restrain deer that were live-captured with rocket nets. Students from nine colleges and universities have been employed as hourly workers or intern research assistants.

Table 2. Agencies and organizations with representatives serving on the Community Liaison Committee for the Chicago Urban Deer Study.

American Humane Association
Brookfield Zoo
Cook County Forest Preserve District
DuPage County Forest Preserve District
Fund for Animals
Great Lakes Outdoor Writers
Illinois Audubon Society
Illinois Department of Conservation
Illinois Natural History Survey
Illinois Nature Preserves Commission
Illinois Wildlife Federation
Lake County Forest Preserve District
McGraw Wildlife Foundation
Morton Arboretum
O'Hare International Airport
Sierra Club
U.S. Department of Agriculture

The most controversial segment of the program has been the experimental manipulation of the Ned Brown Preserve (NBP) deer herd. A formal removal plan was developed at the request of the Illinois Nature Preserve Commission and the CCFPD. The objectives were to: (1) reduce deer browsing pressure to a level that enables the regeneration of forest understory vegetation, (2) decrease the number of deer-vehicle accidents on adjacent highways, and (3) improve average physical condition of the resident deer herd. During 1985–87, the herd was reduced to a specified density, and, will be maintained at or below that level until the end of the study. The removal program has yielded valuable information on the economics of various removal techniques, insight on carcass utilization options, survival and movements of translocated deer, and public attitudes on herd reduction.

DISCUSSION

The preservation of large areas of deer habitat in Cook County, serving as refugia among an increasingly developed suburban landscape, has produced an environment where long-term deer-human conflicts are unavoidable. These conflicts will change spatially and temporally—influenced by dynamic site-specific interactions of deer, humans, vegetation, and abiotic factors. The projected instability of deer herds on Cook County's refuge system dictates the need for developing a permanent urban deer management program.

Traditionally, deer management in the Chicago metropolitan area has been reactive. This has been a strategy of avoidance with action implemented only in response to complaints and crises. Ironically, crises are often emotionally charged situations where actions are most vulnerable to critical examination by media and the public. The pervasive attitude that urban deer management in Chicago is a "no-win" situation was derived from negative experiences that have resulted from ill-prepared crisis responses. We suggest that this can be changed through implementation of a proactive deer management program. On a limited scale, the INHS research program has repeatedly demonstrated that a proactive approach to deer management can be successfully implemented in the Chicago metropolitan area.

The exact structure of a permanent management program has not been formulated at this time. However, the structure and scope of residual management will depend, to a large degree, on the successes and failures of the INHS Urban Deer Research Program. During 1987, formal recommendations will be presented by the INHS to the principal agencies. Recommendations will be regionally specific but will be consistent with criteria listed in The Wildlife Society's position statement on wildlife damage control (TWS 1985).

Acknowledgments.—This report is a contribution of Federal Aid in Wildlife Restoration Project W-87-R, the Illinois Department of Conservation, the U.S. Fish and Wildlife Service, and the Illinois Natural History Survey, cooperating. The Illinois Department of Conservation and the U.S. Fish and Wildlife Service have no responsibility for the form and content of data in this report or for the conclusions reached.

REFERENCES CITED

Ashley, R.F. 1982. Milwaukee's dear deer. Wisc. Nat. Resour. 6:6–11.

Dziedzina, D. 1984. Bowhunting for deer prohibited in Cook County. Outdoor Notebook 4:28.

Grimstad, P.R., C.L. Shabino, C.H. Calisher, and R.J. Waldman. 1982. A case of encephalitis in a human associated with a serologic rise to Jamestown Canyon Virus. Am. J. Trop. Med. Hyg. 31:1238–1244.

Iker, S. 1983. Swamped with deer. Natl. Wildl. Oct–Nov, 5:11.

Issel, C.J., D.O. Trainer, and W.H. Thompson. 1972. Serologic evidence of infections of white-tailed deer in Wisconsin with three California group arboviruses (La Crosse, trivittatus, Jamestown Canyon). Am. J. Trop. Med. Hyg. 21:985–988.

Kellert, S.R. 1980. Public attitudes toward critical wildlife and natural habitat issues. Phase I. Doc. No. 024-010-00-623-4. Washington, D.C., Govt. Printing Office. 138pp.

Langenau, E.E., Jr., S.R. Kellert, and J.E. Applegate. 1984. Values in management. Pages 699–720 *in* L.K. Halls, ed. White-tailed deer, ecology and management. Stackpole Books, Harrisburg, Pa. 870pp.

Miller, J.A. 1987. Ecology of a new disease. BioScience 37:11–15.

Moen, A.M. 1984. Deer management at the Crane Memorial Reservation and Wildlife Refuge. Cornerbook Press, Lansing, N.Y. 90pp.

Shoesmith, M.W. and W.H. Koonz. 1977. The maintenance of an urban deer herd in Winnipeg, Manitoba. Trans. North Am. Wildl. and Nat. Resour. Conf. 42:278–285.

TWS. 1985. Position statement on wildlife damage control. The Wildlifer, No. 210.

Warner, R. 1986. Ticks and deer team up to cause trouble for man. Smithsonian, Apr. pp.131–145.

Wendling, R.C., S.J. Gabriel, J.F. Dwyer, and R.L. Buck. 1981. Forest Preserve District of Cook County, Illinois. J. For. 79:602–605.

Woolf, A. 1986. Lyme disease. Outdoor Highlights. Illinois Dep. of Conserv., Springfield. 14:3–5.

A Strategy for Controlling Rabies in Urban Skunks and Raccoons[1]

RICHARD C. ROSATTE, PAULA M. KELLY-WARD, AND CHARLES D. MACINNES, *Ontario Ministry of Natural Resources Wildlife Branch, Research Section, P.O. Box 50, Maple, Ontario, Canada LOJ 1EO*

INTRODUCTION

Southern Ontario, Canada, is currently the rabies capital of North America. More than 35,000 cases of animal rabies have been reported in the last 25 years. In fact, over 1,700 diagnoses were made during the first 6 months of 1986. As well, 2,000 humans received post-exposure treatment due to contact with potentially rabid animals in Ontario during that period (Ontario Ministry of Health 1986).

The major vectors of rabies in southern Ontario are red foxes *(Vulpes vulpes)* and striped skunks *(Mephitis mephitis)*. Foxes account for approximately 45% of the annual cases and skunks 20%. Domestic animals, especially cattle, are also commonly reported with rabies but the great majority of these infections are due to contact with rabid foxes and skunks. Foxes account for the majority of rabies diagnoses in rural agricultural areas of southern Ontario; however, in city areas, skunks are the more important carriers. In fact, 56% of all diagnosed skunk cases occurring in York County between 1980 and 1985 were reported in metropolitan Toronto (Rosatte 1986). This is most interesting as metro Toronto, which is encompassed by York County, is less than 20% of the total county area.

Methods for controlling rabies have ranged from allowing the disease to run its course, to vaccination of domestic animals, to vaccination and population reduction of wildlife (Baer 1975, Steck et al. 1982, Rosatte et al. 1986). The strategy to control rabies in rural areas of southern Ontario involves dropping baits containing rabies vaccine from aircraft into suitable fox habitat (Johnston and Voigt 1981). However, the current oral rabies vaccine and bait that are effective in foxes do not cause any immunity in skunks. Therefore, there was urgent need to evaluate the cost, effectiveness, and feasibility of alternate means for reducing rabies in urban areas.

We believed that the most acceptable mode of rabies control, in the absence of an effective oral vaccine, was to trap animals, vaccinate by injection, and release them. The studies reported here were designed to test the feasibility of such a strategy. Specific objectives were to:

(1) determine the habitats most frequently used by urban skunks and raccoons *(Procyon lotor)*,
(2) estimate the amount of effort required to live-trap a significant proportion of local populations, and
(3) evaluate the effectiveness of a commercial (inactivated virus) rabies vaccine to produce immunity in skunks and raccoons.

Such results will provide input to an overall urban rabies control strategy. Raccoons were studied as well as skunks due to their great numbers, in case control of rabies is necessary in that species in the future.

STUDY AREA

Metropolitan Toronto, centered at lat. 43°42′N, long. 79°25′W, was selected as the study area. It is an approximate 600-km² urban complex comprised of the cities of Scarborough, North York, Etobicoke, York, Toronto, and the borough of East York. The population is approximately 2.5 million with an average density of 10,750 people/mi² (4,200/km²).

MATERIALS AND METHODS

Radio-tracking

Live-trapping began in May 1984 in an attempt to radio-collar 30 animals (20 skunks, 10 raccoons) in metropolitan Toronto. Live-traps (#106, #108 Tomahawk) baited with sardines were placed in areas frequented by skunks and

[1]Ont. Minist. of Nat. Resour. Wildl. Branch, Contrib. No. 86-02.

Integrating Man and Nature in the Metropolitan Environment. Proc. Natl. Symp. on Urban Wildl., Chevy Chase, Md., 4–7 November 1986, L.W. Adams and D.L. Leedy, eds. Published by Natl. Inst. for Urban Wildl., 10921 Trotting Ridge Way, Columbia, MD 21044, 1987.

raccoons as indicated by residents responding to a news release. Upon capture, animals were immobilized with ketamine hydrochloride (20–30 mg/kg) and fitted with a collar containing a transmitter, antenna, and battery package (150–152 Mhz, Ont. Minist. Nat. Resour. Electronics Lab., Maple). Expandable radio-collars were used on juvenile skunks to accommodate weight gain during the fall.

All collared animals were ear-tagged, vaccinated against rabies (Imrab inactivated rabies vaccine), given an antibiotic, and released at the point of capture following recovery from the anesthetic. Collared animals were monitored during the day, five times/week when possible, May 1984–March 1985. All animals were not radio-tracked for the entire period as recapture of collared animals to obtain blood samples for rabies vaccine efficiency determination began in November. Radio collars were removed at that time.

Trap-Vaccinate-Release

Three areas were chosen for intensive study (Fig. 1). Each area (0.1 mi^2) (0.25 km^2) was divided into trapping grids (328 ft × 328 ft) (100 m × 100 m). Three live-traps were placed in each grid wherever signs such as a den, scats, or a runway were evident. Traps were not placed at grid intersections where trapping was not feasible, e.g., roadways, high-rise apartment complexes, or large parking lots. The number of grids totalled 20, 17, and 20 for study areas 1, 2, and 3, respectively. Different-sized traps [#105 (20″×7″×7″) (51 cm × 18 cm × 18 cm), #106 (26″×9″×9″) (66 cm × 23 cm × 23 cm), #108 Tomahawk (32″×10″×12″) (82 cm × 26 cm × 31 cm)] were placed in each grid to determine if a particular-sized trap was selective for any one species. Traps were baited with sardines.

The three study areas were trapped one at a time in succession for 10-day periods (9 nights) between 3 June and 13 November 1985. A 4-day break was taken between each trapping period. This tactic allowed each area to be trapped four different times.

Captured skunks and raccoons were immobilized with a mixture of ketamine hydrochloride (20–30 mg/kg of body weight) and xylazine hydrochloride (10:1). Animals were ear-tagged for identification, weights and measurements taken, a blood sample taken via jugular vein or cardiac puncture, vaccinated against rabies (Imrab), and allowed to recover. When the animals were fully mobile, they were released at the point of capture.

Collected blood samples were allowed to clot or centrifuged and sera drawn off with a needle and syringe. Sera

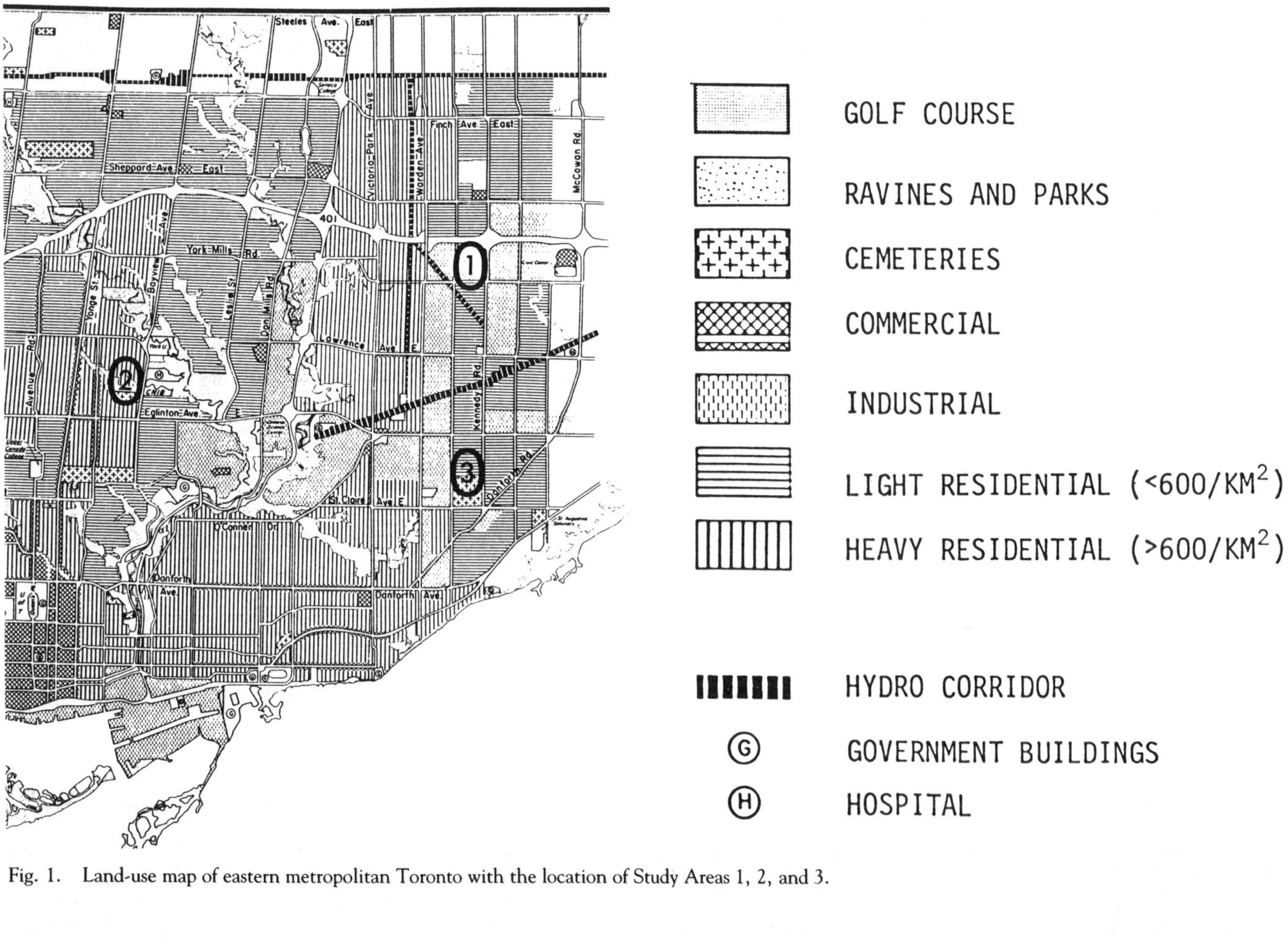

Fig. 1. Land-use map of eastern metropolitan Toronto with the location of Study Areas 1, 2, and 3.

samples were stored in 2-ml provials at −6°F (−21°C) and later sent to Kansas State University for detection of rabies serum neutralizing antibodies.

Data Analysis

Home range was calculated using the minimum area method. A 2-sample t-test was used for comparison of mean home range and movements of skunks and raccoons, and recapture rates of adult and juvenile animals. Trapping effort data were compared using Chi-square 2 × 2 contingency tables (Zar 1974).

RESULTS

Radio-tracking

Skunks.—Twenty-nine skunks (17 juveniles, 12 adults) were fitted with radio-collars. However, due to transmitter malfunction (4), mortality (1), and slipped collars (9), only 15 (6 juveniles, 9 adults) animals had sufficient data for home range and movement determination. No differences between sex and age classes were noted. Mean home range for all cohorts was 0.25 mi^2 (0.02–0.73) [0.64 km^2 (0.05–1.88)] and the average distance moved from the point of capture was 0.63 mi (0.25–1.6) [1.02 km (0.4–2.6)] (Table 1).

Table 1. Movements and home ranges of radio-collared skunks and raccoons, Toronto, Ontario, May 1984–March 1985.[a]

Species	Number (N)	Age/Sex	Home range ($\bar{x}$) mi^2 (km^2)	Movement ($\bar{x}$) mi (km)	Fixes (N)
Raccoon	6	AM	0.23 (0.58)	0.68 (1.1)	414
Raccoon	4	AF	0.07 (0.18)	0.31 (0.5)	728
Skunk	4	AM	0.32 (0.83)	0.58 (0.93)	217
Skunk	5	AF	0.20 (0.51)	0.50 (0.81)	477
Skunk	4	JM	0.35 (0.90)	0.99 (1.6)	193
Skunk	2	JF	0.04 (0.11)	0.40 (0.65)	86

[a]A = Adult, J = Juvenile, M = Male, F = Female.

Raccoons.—Twelve adult raccoons were radio-collared; however, one animal lost its collar and another was killed by a dog. Of the 10 remaining raccoons, no differences were noted between home ranges and movements of adult males and females. Mean home range for both males and females was 0.16 mi^2 (0.03–0.56) [0.42 km^2 (0.07–1.37)] and the average distance moved from the point of capture was 0.5 mi (0.19–1.1) [0.8 km (0.3–1.8)] (Table 1).

Denning Sites.—Both skunks and raccoons used multiple dens as well as different types of dens for summer and fall resting sites, and during the winter denning period (Table 2). Skunks used burrows under houses and associated structures in residential areas. Ground burrows and refuse piles also were utilized by skunks in field-ravine areas. Trees were used almost exclusively by raccoons as den sites in ravine areas, whereas houses and trees were equally important as den sites in residential areas.

Table 2. Number and type of dens used by radio-collared skunks and raccoons, Toronto, Ontario, May 1984–March 1985.

Species number (N)	Number of different dens used $\bar{x}$ (range)	Number of different types of dens used $\bar{x}$ (range)
Skunks (15)	13.9 (6-27)	1.9 (1-5)
Raccoons (12)	18.5 (3-31)	2.3 (1-4)

Trap-Vaccinate-Release

A total of 709 captures (5,273 trap-nights) was made in the three study areas of metro Toronto between 3 June and 13 November 1985. Fifty-two different skunks were captured a total of 189 times and 90 different raccoons were captured on 342 occasions. Other captures (plus recaptures) included 115 cats, 42 groundhogs (*Marmota monax*), and 21 miscellaneous animals.

Skunk Capture Success.—More skunks were captured in the field habitat ($P < 0.001$) than in all other habitat types for combined study areas. There also were greater numbers of skunks taken in the residential habitat than in the cemetery or forest habitat ($P < 0.001$, Table 3).

Table 3. Raccoon and skunk capture success/habitat type/combined study areas, Toronto, Ontario, 3 June–13 November 1985.[a]

Habitat type	Trap nights (TN)	Skunks/TN (N)	Raccoons/TN (N)
Cemetery	1130	0.005 (6)	0.07 (76)
Residential	1295	0.02 (29)	0.08 (105)
Field	1573	0.10 (150)	0.02 (23)
Forest	1125	0.004 (4)	0.12 (138)

[a]Does not include 150 trap-nights in industrial and park habitat where no skunks or raccoons were captured.

Raccoon Capture Success.—Capture success for raccoons was greater in the forest ($P < 0.001$) and residential ($P < 0.025$) areas when each was compared against all areas combined. However, there were greater numbers of raccoons captured in the forest than in residential areas when only those two areas were compared against each other ($P < 0.005$, Table 3).

Capture Success by Area and Trapping Period.—The time of individual trapping periods varied between study areas, but the intervals between periods, and approximate season of each period were similar (Table 4). In Study Area

Table 4. Comparison of trapping results among the three study areas, Toronto, Ontario, 3 June–13 November 1985.

Trapping period / Date	Area 1				Area 2				Area 3			
	1 June 3 -12/85	2 July 16 -24/85	3 Aug. 26- Sept. 3/85	4 Oct.7 -16/85	1 June 17 -26/85	2 July 29- Aug. 7/85	3 Sept. 10 -19/85	4 Oct. 21 -30/85	1 July 1 -10/85	2 Aug. 12 -21/85	3 Sept. 23- Oct. 2/85	4 Nov. 4 -13/85
SKUNKS CAPTURED												
total	7	92	34	31	2	2	1	2	4	7	4	3
different[a]	4	15	13	14	2	2	1	1	3	6	4	3
new[b]	4	14	7	7	2	2	1	1	3	5	3	3
RACCOONS CAPTURED												
total	2	4	3	1	37	86	87	33	24	43	20	2
different[a]	2	4	3	1	21	34	32	14	13	19	11	2
new[b]	2	2	2	1	21	23	11	4	13	9	2	0
OTHER CAPTURES												
cats	14	5	5	11	4	3	5	5	27	17	11	8
groundhogs	25	10	5	1	0	0	0	0	1	0	0	0
misc.	2	0	0	1	1	0	1	2	1	3	2	8
Trap Nights	484	368	404	466	359	365	423	427	393	521	527	536
Animals/Trap night												
including tripped traps	0.10	0.30	0.12	0.10	0.12	0.25	0.22	0.10	0.15	0.13	0.07	0.04
minus tripped traps	0.11	0.33	0.13	0.11	0.24	0.42	0.30	0.14	0.16	0.16	0.08	0.04

[a]diff. skunks (raccoons) refers to different individual skunks (raccoons) captured per trapping period.
[b]new skunk (raccoon) captures refers to different individuals captured during all trapping periods.

1, skunks were captured more frequently in Period 2 ($P < 0.001$) than in the other three periods. In Area 2, raccoons were taken more frequently during Periods 2 and 3 than in 1 and 4 ($P < 0.001$, Table 4), and in Area 3, more raccoons were taken during Period 2. Too few raccoons were encountered in Area 1, and too few skunks in Areas 2 and 3 to detect inter-period differences.

Capture Success Between Areas.—More skunks were taken in Area 1 than in 2 or 3 ($P < 0.001$). Area 2 produced more raccoon captures than Area 3 ($P < 0.001$), which in turn had more than Area 1 ($P < 0.001$) (Table 4).

Recapture Success of Adult and Juvenile Skunks and Raccoons.—Greater numbers of juvenile skunks were subsequently recaptured than adults ($P < 0.025$, Table 5), and they were recaptured more often ($P(t) < 0.05$, Table 5). Among raccoons, there was no difference noted in the number of juveniles and adults subsequently recaptured ($P > 0.05$). However, individual juveniles were recaptured more frequently than adults ($P(t) < 0.05$, Table 5).

Time of Trapping.—Eighty-one percent of the total captures were taken during the first 4 nights of trapping for combined study areas and trapping periods. Few new animals (excluding recaptures) were captured after Trapping Day 5.

Capture Effectiveness/Trap Type.—Capture success of skunks was not different for the three trap types. However, there were greater numbers of raccoons caught in #106 and #108 traps than in the #105 trap ($P < 0.001$, Table 6).

Trap Interference/Study Area.—Greater numbers of traps

Table 5. Capture-recapture success of adult and juvenile skunks and raccoons for combined study areas, Toronto, Ontario, 3 June–13 November 1985.

Trapping period	No. of first-time captures subsequently recaptured				Mean number of times recaptured in all subsequent periods (range)				Number of first-time captures not subsequently recaptured			
	Skunks		Raccoons		Skunks		Raccoons		Skunks		Raccoons	
	A	J	A	J	A	J	A	J	A	J	A	J
1	3	0	22	8	2 (1–3)	0	2.6 (1–6)	4.5 (1–7)	6	0	5	0
2	0	14[a]	3	22	0	8 (1–16)	1.3 (1–2)	5.9 (1–19)	4	1	5	4
3	0	4	1	5	0	2.25 (1–4)	2 (1)	4.4 (1–9)	5	2	1	8
4	2	3	1	0	1 (1)	1 (1)	0 (0)	1 (1)	2[b]	2	2[b]	1
TOTAL	5	21	27	35	1.6 (1–3)	5.9 (1–16)	2.4 (1–6)	5.3 (1–19)	17	5	13	13

[a]not including 2 juveniles that died before recapture.
[b]not including 2 adults submitted for rabies diagnosis.

Table 6. Skunk and raccoon captures/trap type, Toronto, Ontario, 3 June–13 November 1985.

	Trap type		
	105	106	108
Skunks captured	55	75	59
% captured	28	40	32
Raccoons captured	34[a]	141	167
% captured	10	41	49

[a]97% juveniles captured between 1 Aug. and 3 Sept./85.

were tripped in Study Area 2 than in Study Areas 1 and 3 ($P < 0.001$). However, there also were more traps tripped in Study Area 3 than 1 ($P < 0.001$, Table 7).

Table 7. Percent traps tripped/study area/trapping period, Toronto, Ontario, 3 June–13 November 1985.

	Trapping period			
Study area	1	2	3	4
1	8.4	8.9	8.4	12.2
2	47.9	41.0	26.1	31.0
3	11.9	16.1	12.1	9.0

Percent of Skunks and Raccoons Captured and Vaccinated.—An estimate of the percent of the populations of skunks and raccoons that were captured and vaccinated was determined by dividing the number of different animals captured in a trapping period by the estimated population size as determined by the weighted mean method (Begon 1979). An estimated 83% of the skunks for combined study areas and trapping periods were captured. Ninety-two percent of the raccoons were captured.

Rabies Vaccine Effectiveness.—Eighty-six percent of the different skunks receiving vaccine had detectable levels of rabies neutralizing antibody. Geometric mean titers were 2.65 and 2.81 International Units (I.U.), for samples taken 30–79 and 80–100 days post-vaccination, respectively. An even higher percentage of the raccoons (98%) vaccinated produced rabies antibody. Mean titers of samples 30–79 and 80–100 days post-vaccination were 4.73 and 2.46 I.U., respectively. Antibody was still detectable up to 3 months post-vaccination.

DISCUSSION

If Trap-Vaccinate-Release (TVR) is to succeed in reducing rabies in urban environments, several considerations must be addressed.

(1) A significant portion of a local vector population must be trappable within reasonable time and cost restrictions.

(2) Dispersal into and out of the target population must be low enough that the vaccinated population is not diluted too rapidly.

(3) The vaccine must be effective in a high proportion of animals.

(4) The best time of year to trap and vaccinate must be determined.

In fact, these components are intimately inter-related. Work with urban feral dogs suggested that if 80% were vaccinated, rabies transmission virtually ceased (Tierkel 1975, Beran 1982). Steck et al. (1982) claimed that rabies died out when over 60% of a fox population was immunized. The difficulty lies in delimiting a "local" population. If vectors are very mobile, vaccination will have to cover a large area. By contrast, if movements are smaller, barriers to rabies may be established by instituting TVR in belts. Animal movements also will affect trappability, as very mobile individuals may be elsewhere when traps are in a specific area.

Biological Considerations

The study plots used in this investigation were small, but produced useful information. An estimated 83% of skunks and 92% of raccoons using the 0.25-km^2 plots were captured during the four trapping periods. In fact, trapping for rabies control should probably start after 1 August as we captured few juveniles in June. As well, young should be at least 12 weeks old before vaccination (Black and Lawson 1980).

Animal Movements.—Radio-tracking showed little dispersal in summer or fall in either species. However, we tracked only a few animals, and overall population density was unknown, so the conclusion of low movement is tentative. In 1986, we are expanding tracking of skunks, and conducting TVR trials on 24 1-km^2 plots, to provide better information on this point.

Movements of both skunks and raccoons in metro Toronto were smaller than comparable studies in rural environments. Home ranges of 1.2–2.0 mi^2 (3–5 km^2) and movements of 12–60 mi (20-100+ km) have been reported for skunks (Storm 1972, Bjorge 1977, Sargeant et al. 1982). Even more extensive home ranges of 4–10 mi^2 (10–25 km^2) and movements of 164 mi (264 km) have been noted for raccoons in rural areas (Lynch 1967, Schnell 1970, Fritzell 1978). However, our observations are more comparable to those in other urban areas (Cincinnati, Washington D.C.) (Schinner 1969, Hoffmann and Gottschang 1977, Manski and Hadidian 1985).

Differential Use of Habitat.—Skunks and raccoons were trapped in different habitats. For skunks, the capture success was greater in open field than residential, cemetery, industrial, or forested park. For raccoons, the order was almost reversed; forested-park greater than residential, industrial, cemetery, or open field. Den locations determined by telemetry supported those rankings.

Knowledge of habitats that support abundant skunks and raccoons in terms of greatest trapping success is clearly useful for planning future trapping studies. We have prepared a land-use map of metropolitan Toronto. The 1986–

87 trapping program should provide estimates of numbers of animals and trapping success related to land-use.

Vaccination Rate.—The vaccine data combined with the proportion of populations trapped indicated that 71% of the skunks (83% trapped × 86% immunized) would be protected against rabies. Similarly, 90% (92% trapped × 98% immunized) of the raccoons would be immunized. Within the limits of the present samples, that suggests that enough animals could be immunized to reduce rabies dramatically.

Logistical Considerations

Anyone faced with the practical problem of optimizing the proportion of target animals immunized given budget constraints will ask the biologist a series of questions:

(1) How large an area must be trapped to contain or exclude rabies?
(2) How many traps are required per unit area?
(3) Where, exactly, should traps be put?
(4) How long should traps be run in one area?
(5) How often should I return to a previously trapped area?
(6) How many traps can one trapper handle?
(7) What kinds of traps are best?
(8) How much will a trapping program cost per unit area?
(9) How much human interference will I encounter when trapping in an urban area?

The size of the area to be trapped will largely depend on the geography of the area, the size of the rabies outbreak area, and the biology of the vector species. For example, if the rabies infected area is surrounded on three sides by geographical barriers such as rivers, lakes, or habitat unsuitable for the vector species, the best tactic to implement would be to create a vaccination belt of immune animals. The size of the belt or buffer zone would depend on the extent of movement of local animal populations. In our study, skunk and raccoon movements were very small. Therefore, a buffer zone 3 km wide should be sufficient to either contain an outbreak of rabies or prevent the progression of an outbreak into the area. However, if a very large area is infected with several localized rabies outbreaks, a better tactic may be to vaccinate areas that are predicted to be rabies "hot spots." Again, the size of the area vaccinated will depend on the movements of the vector species. For example, a 2-km^2 area in the City of Toronto was the site of a major skunk rabies outbreak in 1983, but rabies was not reported there during 1984 or 1985. Therefore, an outbreak might occur in 1986. The tactic employed would be to vaccinate a large portion of the skunk population in the 2-km^2 area as well as within 3 km of the potential outbreak boundaries. This would contain the outbreak or prevent immigrating infected animals from transmitting the disease into the area as an approximate 50-km^2 buffer zone would have been created.

The data indicate that fields and residential areas were important to skunks in terms of capture success, whereas raccoons were trapped more often in forested-park and residential areas. Our study was limited to three areas; however, we are currently trapping 24 different areas to determine if these habitat types support similar populations of skunks and raccoons throughout all of metro Toronto. Preliminary results indicate trappers should focus the majority of their traps in fields and residential areas if targeting for skunks in metro Toronto. Traps should be placed near denning sites such as porches, sheds, garages in residential areas, and ground burrows, runways, or wherever signs such as scats or tracks are present.

The TVR strategy would not be appropriate if it required 2 weeks to capture the majority of animals in an area. During this study, more than 80% of the skunks and raccoons were captured in each study area during the first 4 nights of trapping. The short time-span in which the majority of the skunks and raccoons can be captured also will greatly reduce the amount of labor necessary to implement the control strategy. However, the size of the area being trapped and the number of traps set will determine the duration of the trapping period. We are currently setting between 25 and 100 traps per 1-km^2 area to compare capture success over 4 nights trapping. It appears the maximum number of live-traps one trapper can handle daily is 100.

Skunks were captured equally as well with the three different types of live-traps. However, the smallest-sized trap (#105) caught fewer raccoons than the two larger traps (#106, #108). Also, most of the raccoons caught in the small trap were juveniles trapped in August. Therefore, to be selective in terms of skunk captures, the smaller trap should be used exclusively to exclude raccoons.

The high number of recaptures for both skunks and raccoons suggests live-trapping is a feasible technique to capture and vaccinate as most animals do not become trap-shy. Many "new" animals were captured during each trapping period that had not been captured during a previous trapping period. That reflects the small size of the study areas. Several home ranges of individual animals undoubtedly overlapped the study areas. However, a rabies control program would cover a much larger area than the current study areas, encompassing several animals' home ranges. Therefore, a high proportion of new captures per trapping period would not be as likely.

The cost of controlling rabies in the urban environment is obviously of utmost importance to the success or failure of the program. This program, which involved one full-time technician ($11.00/hr) between June and November 1985, one ½-ton truck, 100 live-traps, gas, oil, and vehicle insurance for 6 months averaging 100 km/day, bait for the traps, and rabies vaccine, cost approximately $18,500.00. During this study, three areas were trapped four times each, alternately for 9-night periods. In a control situation, a study area (1 km^2) need only be trapped for 5 nights and during one period. That would enable a technician to trap and vaccinate a 25-km^2 area between June and November. The cost would be less than $20,000, a small price to pay for rabies control. Considering the larger cities of metro Toronto are approximately 100 km^2, one 25-km^2 quarter could be trapped and vaccinated per year. Alternately, only the potential rabies hot spots could be vaccinated; however, a method of predicting where outbreaks are to occur would have to be implemented. Regardless, the cost of the control strategy is not a major obstacle considering the overall cost of rabies in Ontario.

Perhaps one of the most important considerations for rabies control is whether residents in the area will support the program. That related directly to the amount of human interference with the traps. The majority of traps tripped in Study Areas 1 and 3 were due to animals digging under the traps in attempts to reach the bait. Thirty-seven percent of the traps in Study Area 2 were tripped. Two residents who were against trapping of wildlife for any purpose were responsible for the majority of this interference. Obviously, if many people are opposed to the method of rabies control and are willing to interfere, the TVR strategy will in all likelihood be unsuccessful. A much more thorough publicity campaign is needed to alleviate the problem of human trap interference.

In summary, the data suggest trap-vaccinate-release is a feasible strategy to employ as a method of rabies control for skunks and raccoons in an urban environment such as metropolitan Toronto. However, human attitudes toward the program and public communication will play major roles in determining the success of any such strategy if undertaken. Further research is needed to determine if specific habitat types (i.e., fields, residential areas) throughout all of metro Toronto also support high populations of skunks and raccoons. These studies are currently under way.

Acknowledgments.—The study was supported by the Rabies Advisory Committee, Dr. A.J. Rhodes, Chairman, and the Ontario Ministry of Natural Resources, Wildlife Research Section, Maple. The success of the research program was attributed to the input of many people including D. Voigt, D. Johnston, Dr. S. Smith, F. Matejka, P. Bachmann, L. Virgin, D. Briggs, R. Bramwell, J. Topping, S. Slavec, C. Heydon, F. McKay, J. Lotimer, P. Anson, G. Smith, B. Heron, W. Davenport, and T. Berman. A. Chui drafted the figure. E. Brolly typed the manuscript.

REFERENCES CITED

Baer, G.M. 1975. Wildlife vaccination. Pages 261–266 *in* G.M. Baer, ed. The natural history of rabies. Vol. II. Academic Press, N.Y.

Begon, M. 1979. Investigating animal abundance: capture-recapture for biologists. Univ. Park Press, Baltimore, Md. 97pp.

Beran, G.W. 1982. Ecology of dogs in the central Phillippines in relation to rabies control efforts. Comp. Immun. Microbiol. Infect. Dis. 5:265–270.

Bjorge, R.R. 1977. Population dynamics, denning and movements of striped skunks in central Alberta. M.Sc. Thesis, Univ. of Alberta, Edmonton. 95pp.

Black, J.G., and K.F. Lawson. 1980. The safety and efficacy of immunizing foxes using bait containing attenuated rabies virus vaccine. Can. J. Comp. Med. 44:169–176.

Fritzell, E.K. 1978. Habitat use by prairie raccoons during the waterfowl breeding season. J. Wildl. Manage. 42:118–126.

Hoffmann, C.O., and J.L. Gottschang. 1977. Numbers, distribution and movements of a raccoon population in a suburban residential community. J. Mammal. 58:623–636.

Johnston, D.H., and D.R. Voigt. 1981. A baiting system for the oral rabies vaccination of wild foxes and skunks. Comp. Immun. Microbiol. Infect. Dis. 5:185–186.

Lynch, G.M. 1967. Long-range movement of a raccoon in Manitoba. J. Mammal. 48:659–660.

Manski, D., and J. Hadidian. 1985. Rock Creek raccoons: movements and resource utilization in an urban environment. Natl. Park Serv., Prog. Rep., Washington, D.C. 40pp.

Ontario Ministry of Health. 1986. Monthly Zoonosis Report. Rabies in Ontario for June 1986. Public Health Branch, Toronto. 5pp.

Rosatte, R.C. 1986. Preliminary studies on the feasibility of urban rabies control. Proc. 7th Great Plains Wildl. Damage Control Workshop. San Antonio, Texas. pp. 78–91.

Rosatte, R.C., M.J. Pybus, and J.R. Gunson. 1986. Population reduction as a factor in the control of skunk rabies in Alberta. J. Wildl. Dis. 22:459–467.

Sargeant, A.B., R.J. Greenwood, J.L. Piehl, and W.B. Bicknell. 1982. Recurrence, mortality, and dispersal of prairie striped skunks, *Mephitis mephitis,* and implications to rabies epizootiology. Can. Field Nat. 96:312–316.

Schinner, J.R. 1969. Ecology and life history of the raccoon (*Procyon lotor*) within the Clifton suburb of Cincinnati, Ohio. M.Sc. Thesis, Univ. of Cincinnati, Ohio. 60pp.

Schnell, J.H. 1970. Rest site selection by radio-tagged raccoons. Minn. Acad. of Sci. 36:83–88

Steck, F., A. Wandeler, P. Bichsel, S. Capt, and L. Schneider. 1982. Oral immunization of foxes against rabies. Zbl. Vet. Med. 29:372–396.

Storm, G.L. 1972. Daytime retreats and movements of skunks on farmlands in Illinois. J. Wildl. Manage. 36:31–45.

Tierkel, E.S. 1975. Control of urban rabies. Pages 189–201 *in* G.M. Baer, ed. The natural history of rabies. Academic Press, New York, N.Y.

Zar, J.H. 1974. Biostatistical analysis. Prentice-Hall Inc., Englewood Cliffs, N.Y. 620pp.

The Effectiveness of Translocation Control of Minneapolis-St. Paul Canada Goose Populations

JAMES A. COOPER, *Department of Fisheries and Wildlife, University of Minnesota, St. Paul, MN 55108*

Extirpated by market and subsistence hunting over much of its southern breeding range during settlement, the Canada goose *(Branta canadensis)* has been reestablished in the midwestern and eastern United States and Canada. This successful wildlife restoration resulted from federal, provincial, state, and private programs (Nelson 1963, Dill and Lee 1970, Cooper 1978). Canada goose release in urban-suburban environments began in the 1950s; a decade later, the species was breeding in Denver, Minneapolis-St. Paul, Detroit, Toronto, Wilmington, and the suburbs of Boston, and several New York, New Jersey, and Connecticut communities (Hawkins 1970).

Although noting nuisance goose complaints, Hawkins (1970) concluded that the bird's aesthetic qualities outweighed the nuisance aspect, and, that with enlightened management, difficulties could be minimized. However, metropolitan Canada goose populations and nuisance complaints have grown at phenomenal rates (Laycock 1982, Oetting 1983). For example, Hawkins (1970) estimated the Metropolitan Twin Cities population at 448 birds in 1968; currently I estimate this population at 10,000–12,000 birds. Complaints of goose droppings on golf course greens and fairways, docks and swimming beaches, and lawns are frequent and widespread. In addition, locally breeding geese use the Minneapolis-St. Paul International Airport area and have become a serious aircraft hazard. Five Twin Cities' communities, the Federal Aviation Administration, and Metropolitan Airport Commission are currently funding population reduction research programs and at least six other communities are considering population control.

Capture and transportation of flightless Canada geese to a distant site **(translocation)** has been used to control nuisance urban populations in Massachusetts, New York, Michigan, Ontario, and elsewhere. Published reports on this procedure suggest that it is effective with few birds returning to the capture sites (Martz et al. 1983, Converse 1985). This paper presents the results of research in the Twin Cities of Minnesota that indicate translocation effectiveness may be significantly lower and discusses translocation limitations.

METHODS

Flightless adults and goslings were drive-trapped in June and early July in 1982, 1984, 1985, and 1986 and transported elsewhere by truck. Adult and 1984 immature birds were legbanded and released in Oklahoma; other young geese were transported to Minnesota sites. Oklahoma was selected as a release area because, based on 2,000+ band recoveries from 1974 to 1981, Twin Cities Canada geese did not winter in or migrate through Oklahoma.

Rates of translocated bird return to the capture sites were determined by reading legbands in spring and fall each year with spotting scopes, and from drive-trap recaptures. Breeding females in 1985 and 1986 were identified by the presence of brood patches (Hanson 1959).

In an attempt to reduce adult return to Minnesota, the Oklahoma Department of Wildlife Conservation clipped 1–2 inches (2.5–5.0 cm) from the distal three or four primaries on one wing and pulled the primaries on the other wing in 1985. The 121 geese treated in this manner had been previously translocated. By pulling primaries, flight was delayed by 1 month (mid-August) and by clipping primaries, the birds had an imbalance in wing lift. The latter was presumed to be sufficient to prevent migration.

RESULTS

Flightless adult and young geese were drive-trapped at and translocated from one, two, six and six Twin Cities' communities in 1982, 1984, 1985, and 1986, respectively. The 15 capture sites included six suburban lakes, six park-nature center lakes, two golf courses, and one corporate headquarters pond complex. Two hundred sixty-one adults

Integrating Man and Nature in the Metropolitan Environment. Proc. Natl. Symp. on Urban Wildl., Chevy Chase, Md., 4–7 November 1986, L.W. Adams and D.L. Leedy, eds. Published by Natl. Inst. for Urban Wildl., 10921 Trotting Ridge Way, Columbia, MD 21044, 1987.

and 195 goslings were removed in 1982, 530 and 480 in 1984, 375 and 486 in 1985, and 198 and 309 in 1986 (Table 1). One hundred ninety-five immatures were translocated to Carver Park Reserve (20 miles [32 km] SW of the trap site) in 1982, 424 sent to Oklahoma in 1984, and 798 were released at Minnesota sites 50+ miles (80+ km) from the capture site in 1985 and 1986. Legbands were placed on 256, 200, and 489 young in 1984, 1985, and 1986, respectively.

After the 1982 translocation, the Minneapolis population decreased 55% (505 to 225) in 1983, and gosling production declined 43% (193 to 110). Based on legband readings from females with broods, 18 of 29 (62%) of the breeding females were translocated geese. This population recovered to 1982 levels by 1984 with 373 adults and 192 goslings captured (Table 1). After the 1984 removals, the Minneapolis population declined by 49% (565 to 286) and production was 40% lower (192 to 116). In 1985, 170 adult geese were captured in Minneapolis, 46% fewer than in 1984, and in 1986, 58 were caught, a decline of 66% from 1985. Overall, Minneapolis removals resulted in a 90% drop in adults and a 69% decrease in young produced from 1984 to 1986. At the other sites, adult decline in the first year after translocation was 38%, and reproduction was 37% lower. Second year translocation decreases were 43% for Golden Valley adults and 43% for production. Overall, Golden Valley adults declined 70% and reproduction 69% after 2 years of removal.

Oklahoma translocated adult geese returned to the capture sites at a significantly ($P<0.05$) higher rate than immatures released in Minnesota or in Oklahoma. Eight of 195 (4%) immatures translocated to Carver Park, none of the 1985 Minnesota released young, and four of 256 (2%) of the Oklahoma released immatures returned to the capture sites. In contrast, 33 (13%), 101 (23%), and 72 (28%) of translocated adults returned (Table 2). The clipping of the outer primaries on one wing did not significantly ($P>0.05$) reduce adult return rates. Thirty-three of 121 (27%) of these birds returned in 1986.

Based on brood patch data from 1985 and 1986 recaptures, returning translocated geese made up a high proportion of the breeding populations. In 1985, 43 of 87 (49%) brood patch females captured were translocated geese; the proportion was 47 of 88 (53%) in 1986. Seventy-six percent of the 1986 Minneapolis brood patch females were Oklahoma translocated geese.

DISCUSSION

The results of this study demonstrate that translocation can reduce nuisance populations of Canada geese in urban-suburban communities. Breeding populations were 40–50% and 70–90% lower, and reproduction reduced by 30–40% and 60–70% after 1 and 2 years of removal, respectively. Without the high (12–28%) return of translocated adults, particularly breeding females, the effectiveness of the techniques would have been far greater. Translocated adult females constituted 50% of the breeding females in 1985 and 1986. Moreover, the rate of translocated bird return rose with time (Table 2), suggesting that additional adult translocations to

Table 1. Canada goose translocations from the Twin Cities of Minnesota, and released or uncaptured geese, 1982, 1984–86.

Location year	Translocated			Brood patch females	Not captured
	Adult	Immature	Total		
Edina					
1985	20	6	26	3	3
1986	3	8	11	2	3
Golden Valley					
1984	157	288	445	33	6
1985	81	155	236	36	0
1986	46	89	135	23	0
New Brighton					
1985	38	68	106	13	0
1986	19	36	55	8	0
Minneapolis					
1982	261	195	456	—	50[a]
1984	373	192	565	55	11[a]
1985	170	116	286	51	14[a]
1986	58	60	118	25	20[a]
Plymouth					
1985	22	43	65	10	0
1986	51	100	151	21	6
Richfield					
1985	44	98	142	18	17
1986	21	16	37	9	3
Total	1,364	1,470	2,834	307	133

[a]Released at capture site.

Table 2. Twin Cities recapture and observation of 1,616 banded Canada geese translocated from the Twin Cities to Minnesota and Oklahoma sites, 1982, 1984–85.

	1982		1984		1985		Total return
	Adult	Immature	Adult	Immature	Adult	Immature	
Number banded	261	195	447	256	257	200	
First observed in 1983	18	5					23
First observed in 1984	12	3					15
First observed in 1985	1	0	76	4			81
First observed in 1986	2	0	25	0	72	0	99
Total	33	8	101	4	72	0	218
Percentage	13	4	23	2	28	0	13

the same area will be less effective. In contrast, young birds can be moved very short (20 miles or 32 km) distances from the capture site without significant returns.

My findings differ from Converse's (1985). She reported fewer than 3% of the legbanded Canada geese translocated as far north as Maine and as far south as Georgia returned to her southeastern New York-southwestern Connecticut study area. These birds, unlike the Minnesota populations, were non-migratory and it may be that Canada geese that migrate have a much higher likelihood of returning to the capture sites.

Control of urban-suburban Canada goose populations is expensive (Martz et al. 1983) and in Minnesota costs are paid primarily from local government funds. In addition, goose control is highly visible with frequent media coverage and controversy. The birds are easily counted, thus population reduction projections must be accurate or program creditability is diminished. Thus it is critical that population reduction projections be based on a realistic estimate of translocation bird return.

Ultimately, translocation will be self-limiting as states and provinces willing to accept translocated geese meet their goose restoration goals. Long-term urban goose population reductions will have to be based on other techniques. These include reproduction reduction by physical or chemical means, increased mortality via additional hunting where possible, and perhaps trapping and slaughter for human consumption.

Acknowledgments.—Funding for this research was provided by the University of Minnesota Agricultural Experiment Station, the Cities of Minneapolis, Golden Valley, and New Brighton, General Mills Corporation, the Federal Aviation Administration, and Metropolitan Airports Commission. I thank the Minnesota Department of Natural Resources, the Oklahoma Department of Wildlife Conservation, the U.S. Fish and Wildlife Service, and the U.S. Department of Agriculture for coordinating permits and assistance with capture and translocation. Many people contributed to this project. I thank Tim Anderson and Arlis Olson, Metropolitan Airports Commission, and Oren Burckhardt and Les Case, Federal Aviation Administration for their coordination of funding and access to the airport facilities. Nancy Burgstahler and Mary Mitchell, U.S. Fish and Wildlife Service, Richard Wetzel, U.S. Department of Agriculture, Roger Johnson, Lloyd Knudson, Jon Parker, Tim Wallace, and others with Minnesota Department of Natural Resources, Jontie Aldrich and other Oklahoma Department of Wildlife Conservation personnel provided invaluable assistance. Mari Smaby, Wayne Winkleman, Terry Birkenstock, Lori Hawkins, Tom Roster, Judi Mikolai, Caroline Yineman, and Mike Palanuk, University of Minnesota, assisted with banding, population surveys, translocation, and data processing.

REFERENCES CITED

Converse, K.A. 1985. A study of resident nuisance Canada geese in Connecticut and New York. Ph.D. thesis, Univ. Mass., Amherst, 84pp.

Cooper, J.A. 1978. The history and breeding biology of the Canada geese of Marshy Point, Manitoba. Wildl. Monogr. 61. 87pp.

Dill, H.H. and F.B. Lee, eds. 1970. Home grown honkers. U.S. Dep. Inter., Fish and Wildl. Serv., Washington, D.C. 154pp.

Hanson, H.C. 1959. The incubation patch of wild geese: its recognition and significance. Arctic 12:139 150.

Hawkins, A.S. 1970. Honkers move to the city. Pages 120–130 *in* H.H. Dill and F.B. Lee, eds. Home grown honkers. U.S. Dep. Inter., Fish and Wildl. Serv., Washington, D.C.

Laycock, G. 1982. The urban goose. Audubon 84:44–47.

Martz, J., L. Pospichal, and E. Tucker. 1983. Giant Canada geese in Michigan: experiences with translocations and nuisance management. Pages 57–59 *in* M.A. Johnson, ed. Transactions of the Canada goose symposium. North Dakota Chapter of The Wildlife Society.

Nelson, H.K. 1963. Restoration of breeding Canada goose flocks in the North Central States. Trans. North Am. Wildl. and Nat. Resour. Conf. 28:133–150.

Oetting, R. 1983. Overview of management of Canada geese and their recent urbanization. Page 52 *in* M.A. Johnson, ed. Transactions of the Canada goose symposium. North Dakota Chapter of The Wildlife Society.

Habitat Enhancement Techniques for the El Segundo Blue Butterfly: An Urban Endangered Species

RICHARD A. ARNOLD, *Entomological Consulting Services, 50 Cleveland Road #3, Pleasant Hill, CA 94523*

AUDREY E. GOINS, *Chevron Corporation, P.O. Box 7924, San Francisco, CA 94120*

INTRODUCTION

The El Segundo blue, *Euphilotes battoides allyni* is a lycaenid butterfly (Fig. 1) that is one of only 13 insects recognized as endangered or threatened species in the U.S.A. It is a denizen of the El Segundo sand dunes in the Los Angeles, California, metropolitan area. Urbanization has destroyed or degraded nearly 99% of this sand dune system. Thus, the butterfly was designated as an endangered species by the U.S. Fish and Wildlife Service in 1976. Today the butterfly, whose wingspan is about as large as a dime, survives at only two small dune remnants: a 302-acre (122 ha) parcel at the Los Angeles International Airport, and a 1.6-acre (0.6 ha) sanctuary at the Chevron, U.S.A. Refinery in nearby El Segundo, California.

Despite its diminutive size, the El Segundo blue butterfly (ESB) is an important indicator of the "health" of its habitat. A complex food web, of which the butterfly is but one component, characterizes the ecology of a pre-urban sand dune. Several other insects, spiders, small mammals, and birds feed on the ESB, which in turn feeds on its larval foodplant Seacliff buckwheat *Eriogonum parvifolium* (Polygonaceae), and is a minor pollinator of this plus a few other dune plants. Furthermore, ESB population numbers are greatest where its foodplant thrives. The endemic buckwheat, a perennial shrub, is a poor competitor where weeds, annual grasses, and ground covers have invaded dune remnants. Other endemic organisms that are now rare at the El Segundo Dunes are the parasitic scaly-stemmed sand plant (*Pholisma arenarium*), legless lizard (*Anniella pulchra*), coast-horned lizard (*Phrynosoma coronatum*), coastal little pocket mouse (*Perognathus longimembris*), Belding's savannah sparrow (*Passerculus sandwichensis beldingi*), American peregrine falcon (*Falco peregrinus anatum*), Dorothy's dune weevil (*Trigonoscuta dorothea dorothea*), Lange's dune weevil (*Onychobaris langei*), Lora Aborn's moth (*Lorita abornana*), Henne's Eucosman moth (*Eucosma hennei*), and Ford's dune moth (*Psammobotys fordi*). As the buckwheat and butterfly thrive in dune areas where weeds are minimal, monitoring the endangered butterfly helps to gauge habitat quality of this sand dune ecosystem.

This paper presents preliminary findings of a long-term, dune habitat enhancement project conducted at Chevron's sanctuary for the endangered butterfly. Enhancement activities were initiated in 1982 to arrest declining numbers of the El Segundo blue and its buckwheat foodplant. This observed decline is strongly correlated with deteriorating habitat conditions due to encroachment and increasing abundance of various weeds, coupled with loss and senescence of the buckwheat. Collectively, these factors have resulted in: (1) limited natural seedling establishment by the buckwheat plus other dune endemic plants, (2) a skewed age-distribution of the buckwheat plants, and (3) a reduced biomass of buckwheat flowers. Primary enhancement techniques have included weed abatement, plus propagation and outplanting 1,504 buckwheat seedlings in 1983, 1984, and 1986. Subsequent annual monitoring has focused attention on: (1) survival rates and flower production of resident buckwheat seedlings, (2) survival rates and flower production of the outplanted buckwheat seedlings, and (3) the El Segundo blue population and its response to enhancement efforts. All enhancement activities are consistent with management needs outlined in the El Segundo blue's Recovery Plan (Arnold 1981).

BACKGROUND INFORMATION

Life History of the El Segundo Blue

The ESB has only one generation per year, i.e., it is univoltine. The adult flight season ranges from about 6 to 8 weeks in any given year. It may begin as early as late June

Integrating Man and Nature in the Metropolitan Environment. Proc. Natl. Symp. on Urban Wildl., Chevy Chase, Md., 4–7 November 1986, L.W. Adams and D.L. Leedy, eds. Published by Natl. Inst. for Urban Wildl., 10921 Trotting Ridge Way, Columbia, MD 21044, 1987.

Fig. 1. An adult El Segundo blue butterfly perched on a flowerhead of the Seacliff buckwheat. Photo: R.A. Arnold

and terminate as late as early September. Adult emergence is generally synchronized with the peak flowering period of Seacliff buckwheat.

All phases of the butterfly's life history and behavior are closely associated with the buckwheat flowers. Adults obtain their primary nourishment by drinking the nectar of the flowers; they perch on the buckwheat flowers to locate mates; courtship and mating often occur on the flowers; and females oviposit on the flowerheads. Larvae are cryptically colored to match coloration of the buckwheat blossoms and complete their development in about 4 weeks while feeding on buckwheat flowers. Larvae pupate in flowerheads of the buckwheat or among the leaf litter at the plant's base.

The butterfly's primary predators are spiders, other insects, small mammals, lizards, and birds, and it's main parasites are tachinid flies and braconid wasps. Ants frequently tend older butterfly larvae, a symbiotic relationship known as myrmecophily. The butterfly larvae secrete a sugary liquid known as honeydew, which the ants readily imbibe. Presumably the ants protect the larvae from parasites and predators, as is known to occur in other lycaenid butterflies (Pierce and Mead 1981).

In general, larvae of most butterflies feed on one or a few closely related species, but as adults, they drink nectar from a variety of plants that usually are unrelated to their larval foodplants. In contrast, both the larval and adult stages of ESB are dependent not only upon a single plant species for all of their nutrition, but on the flowers of that plant. This dual dependency of ESB on the Seacliff buckwheat makes it much more vulnerable to loss and deterioration of habitat. However, this dependency also facilitates management efforts, as most enhancement actions can focus on increasing the numbers of flower-producing buckwheats.

Reason for Decline

Today the ESB is found in less than 1% of its original geographic range. The El Segundo Dunes formerly extended about 36 square miles (181 sq km) along the shore of Santa Monica Bay, from Marine Del Rey to San Pedro (Cooper 1967). Due to their proximity to Los Angeles, these coastal dunes have been largely destroyed or altered by urbanization, industrialization, highway construction, sand mining, airport expansion, and planting of ground covers, notably *Carpobrotus* (ice plant) and other landscape species to stabilize the aeolian sands.

Population dynamics of ESB also are closely allied with the Seacliff buckwheat. Although individual plants may live 20 years or more, young plants generally do not flower until their second year of growth. Juveniles and older plants do not produce as many flowers as middle-aged buckwheats, which support the most ESB butterflies. Field observations suggest that most solitary buckwheat plants less than about 5 years of age do not produce enough flowers for ESB larvae to effectively utilize them (Arnold 1983). Thus, survival of the ESB is dependent upon maintenance of middle-aged buckwheat plants, plus recruitment of younger plants to replace older individuals that senesce. Small dune remnants require assistance to maintain this mixture of buckwheat age classes.

For example, Chevron fenced its dune remnant and designated it a sanctuary for the endangered butterfly in 1975. Although this action protected the property from further degradation by off-road vehicles and sporadic sand removal, subsequent monitoring of the butterfly revealed that its population numbers were declining as habitat quality deteriorated (Arnold 1983, 1986). Encroachment by weeds, annual grasses, and ground covers rapidly stabilized the dune remnant. As the abundance of alien plants increased, numbers of perennial dune plants, including the buckwheat, decreased because establishment of their seedlings was limited, or their seedlings were overgrown by the more rapidly growing weeds. Thus, the age-structure of the buckwheat population gradually shifted to consist of more older individuals rather than an even mixture of juvenile, middle-aged, and older plants. As these surviving buckwheats aged, they produced fewer flowers, the essential food supply for the butterfly, which caused the observed decline in butterfly numbers.

Furthermore, the small size of aeolian dune remnants inhibits operation of natural ecological and physical processes that encourage seedling establishment and growth of several perennial, endemic dune plants, including the buckwheat. Under natural dune conditions, the buckwheat grows in patches, with each patch generally consisting of individuals that are similar in age. Windblown, redeposited sand provides new sites for buckwheat seedling establishment. At Chevron's sanctuary, there is no upwind reservoir of sand that can be redeposited onsite to create new areas for seedlings. Thus, primary management actions at the sanctuary have focused on reducing the weed cover and increasing the numbers of younger and middle-aged buckwheats to produce more flowers for the ESB.

Annual monitoring studies of the butterfly and buckwheat since 1977 indicate that habitat quality in the sanctuary deteriorated between 1977 and 1983 (Arnold 1983, 1986). ESB census estimates, based on capture-recapture and stage frequency data, indicate that population numbers declined dramatically during this 8-year period (Fig. 2). For example, in 1977 Arnold (1983) marked 197 ESB adults in 1 day of a capture-recapture study and 647 in a 9-day period. In contrast, only 241 adults were marked during a 28-day period in 1984 (Arnold 1986). Similarly, the number of resident buckwheats declined about 30% during this 7-year period and flower production declined about 70%. The decline in numbers of butterflies and buckwheats is strongly correlated (correlation coefficient = 0.9578, Fig. 2) suggesting that the site was at carrying capacity. Clearly, improved habitat quality was necessary to increase ESB numbers. Refer to Arnold (1983, 1986) for a more detailed description of butterfly census methods and results.

STUDY SITE

All field studies were performed at the El Segundo Blue Sanctuary, a 1.6-acre dune remnant located at the Chevron, U.S.A. Refinery. Arnold (1978) listed the dominant vegetation observed at the site. Fig. 3 illustrates the distribution of resident buckwheats, weeds, annual grasses, and ice plant. A total of 40 quadrats was laid, each measuring 50 feet by 50 feet (15.25m by 15.25m). These same 40 quadrats have

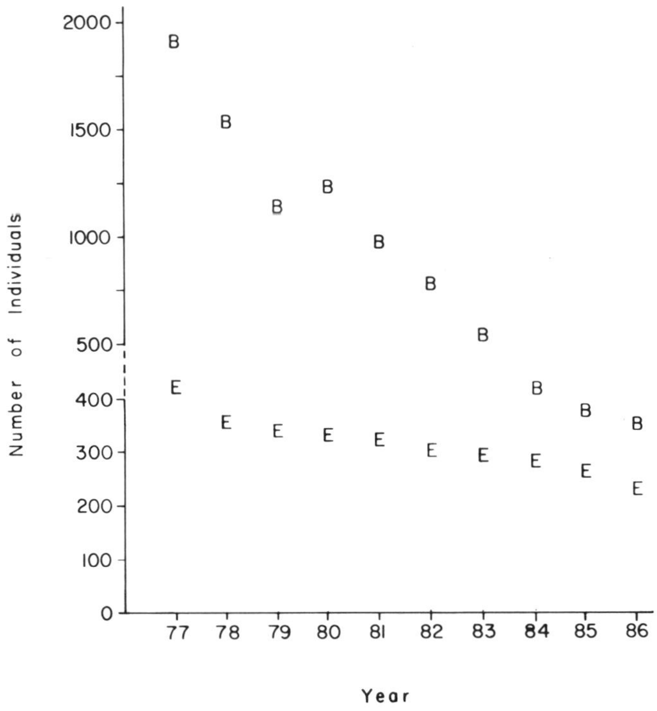

Fig. 2. Relationship between *Eriogonum parvifolium* (E) and *Euphilotes battoides allyni* (B) numbers during the period 1977–86. Plant numbers are based on annual counts. Butterfly numbers are based on actual population sizes calculated from capture-recapture and stage-frequency data. The values for E and B are positively correlated (correlation coefficient = 0.9578).

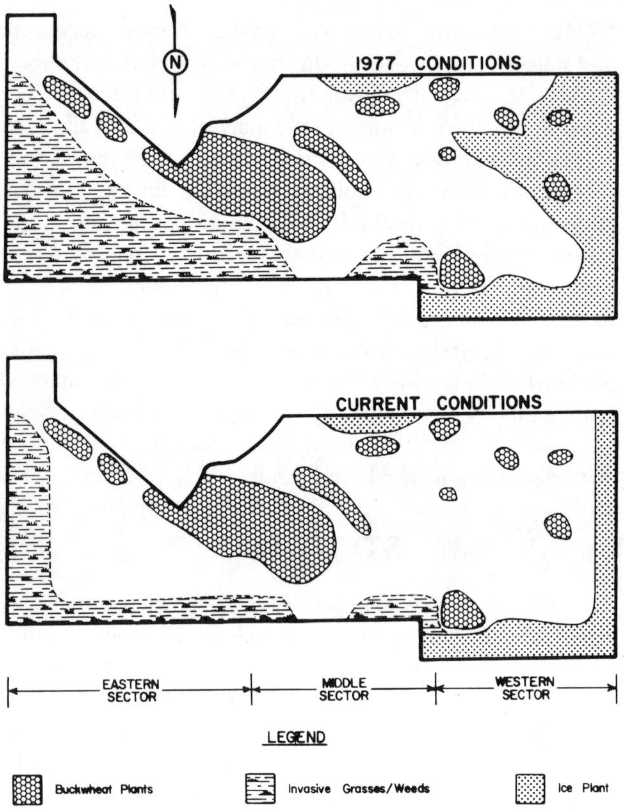

Fig. 3. Dune study site at Chevron USA Refinery in El Segundo, California, illustrating resident and outplanted buckwheat patches; and former and current distribution of ice plant, weeds, and grasses.

Scale: 1 in. = 80 ft.

been used since 1977 as the sampling unit for all butterfly and vegetation studies. Each quadrat was assigned a unique number and the four corners of each quadrat were marked by surveyor's flags. Refer to Arnold (1983) for additional details on the study site.

The sanctuary was divided into three subsites to compare and contrast seedling survival rates. These three areas are characterized by differences in topography, exposure to prevailing winds, and degree of weediness. The western third of the sanctuary includes the highest elevations and originally was the crest of a dune. In 1977, this subsite was dominated by a vegetative cover of *Carpobrotus* and supported less than 20% of all resident buckwheat (Fig. 3). The primary topographic feature of the middle third of the sanctuary is a steep slope. Upper elevations are quite exposed, but lower elevations on the lee side of the crest are more protected. This lower portion of the sanctuary supported the highest species diversity of native plants, but had an extensive cover of annual grasses and *Erodium* (filaree). The eastern third of the sanctuary includes the lowest elevations of the entire site. Approximately one-half of this lowest subsite, adjacent to the middle subsite, shares a similar diversity of native plants and degree of weed cover, but the other half is dominated by annual weeds and *Carpobrotus*. This portion of the sanctuary is more protected from the wind than other subsites.

METHODS

Buckwheat Survey

The distribution of resident buckwheat plants has been mapped each year since 1977 by walking the entire sanctuary and noting the locations of individual plants as well as patches of plants. Numbers of *E. parvifolium* were censused by counting. In addition, the following data were collected for each plant: (1) location within the study area (i.e., quadrat number), (2) date, (3) health (healthy or stressed), (4) number of branches, (5) number of flowers in bloom, (6) numbers of flowers in bud, (7) number of flowers having set seed, (8) total number of flowers (sum of items #5, 6, 7), and (9) estimated age. The age of each plant was subjectively estimated based on the senior author's personal experience growing over 1,000 *E. parvifolium* plants from seed and 10 years of monitoring this plant at the Chevron refinery and other sites. Health also was scored in a subjective manner, but can be verified quantitatively by looking at the ratio of total flower number to the number of branches. Most branches of healthy plants terminate in a flower, thus the ratio of total flowers to branches is approximately 1.0 or sometimes higher. Stressed or senescent buckwheats usually have far fewer flowers than branches, thus the ratio is much less than 1.0.

Buckwheat Propagation and Outplanting

In the late summer or early fall of each year, buckwheat seeds are collected. Care is exercised to prevent collecting seed from flowerheads that support developing larvae or pupae of ESB. Seeds for the 1983 outplanting were sown in 5-inch (13cm) diameter clay pots. Seeds for the 1984 and 1986 outplantings were sown in paper tubes. Seedlings have been grown from both scarified and non-scarified seed and no difference in germination success has been noted. Germinated seedlings were transferred to 3-inch (8cm) diameter clay pots or 1-inch (2.5cm) diameter paper cones (often used for trees and other plants that have long taproots). A soil mix of two-thirds sand and one-third peat moss was used for germination. A thin layer of vermiculite was sprinkled on the surface to help retain moisture.

Seedlings were outplanted during the winter rainy season to minimize the need for supplemental watering. Coastal southern California has a Mediterranean climate, i.e., there is a rainy season in the winter and spring, plus a dry season in the summer and fall. Native dune plants, such as the Seacliff buckwheat, have adapted to these climatic conditions by producing an extremely long taproot for obtaining water during the dry season. Buckwheat seedlings, which are generally about 6 months old at the time of outplanting, may have taproots as long as 2 feet.

To reduce the usual time lag between buckwheat seedling establishment and utilization by ESB, seedlings were outplanted in groups of 10. Eight seedlings were outplanted at equal intervals around the perimeter of a circle with a diameter of 1 yard (ca. 1m). Two seedlings were positioned nearer the center of the circle. By arranging the outplanted seedlings in this manner, the collective growth of surviving buckwheats mimics that of an older and larger solitary buckwheat plant. Because the ESB is attracted to buckwheats with numerous flowers, the butterflies should be attracted to the younger plants growing in clusters, thereby reducing the time lag necessary for butterflies to utilize these buckwheats, compared to solitary plants.

This arrangement also facilitated data collection during subsequent monitoring studies. Samplers could easily monitor the status of individual seedlings within each cluster by always orienting northward when collecting data. This eliminated the need to tag each seedling with an identification number. The same nine data items, as scored for the resident buckwheats, also were recorded for all outplanted seedlings each year after outplanting.

The outplanting procedure is described below:

1. Immediately before outplanting, the location for each group of seedlings within the study site was demarcated by a stake bearing an identification number.
2. At each stake, weedy vegetation growing in a 5-foot (1.5 m) diameter circle was cleared.
3. Eight holes, each measuring about 4 inches (10 cm) in diameter and 6 inches (15 cm) deep, were dug at equal intervals around an imaginary circle measuring 1 yard (ca 1 m) in diameter. Two other holes were placed in the center nearer the stake that identifies each circle.
4. A pinch of Ammonium Sulfate crystals was placed in the bottom of each hole for the 1983 outplantings to promote root growth.

5a. Seedlings grown in clay pots in 1983 were removed from the pots; the roots were loosened, especially if they were matted or in a ball; and the seedlings and the potting mix were placed in the holes. The seedlings rested at or about 0.25 inches (0.6 cm) above ground level.

5b. Seedlings grown in paper tree tubes (1984, 1986 outplantings), were planted as a unit directly into the ground at or about 0.25 inches (0.6 cm) above ground level.

6. Seedlings were watered in with Dexon Benlate solution (1.08 grams of Dexon with 0.76 grams of Benlate per gallon of water) using about 300 ml of solution per buckwheat. This solution was used to prevent "damping off," a condition caused by fungi that attack the seedlings when they become wet.

After outplanting, supplemental watering was applied only if the seedlings started to wilt during the rainy season. No water was applied during the dry season. If seedlings receive too much water during the rainy season, their taproots stay near the surface rather than working their way deep into the sand where they can reach water needed during the dry season. In using this approach, seedling mortality rates due to lack of water might be higher, but the individuals that survive should be hardier, live longer than plants that require regular watering, and be adapted to survive the natural weather conditions. Fertilizer was omitted for similar reasons.

Three batches of buckwheat seedlings have been outplanted at the Chevron sanctuary since the habitat enhancement program was initiated: (1) 574 seedlings, arranged in 61 clusters in November 1983; (2) 560 seedlings, arranged in 56 clusters in December 1984; and (3) 370 seedlings, arranged in 37 clusters in February 1986. The majority of clusters contained 10 seedlings. The remainder of this paper discusses results for seedlings outplanted in 1983 and 1984.

RESULTS

Resident Buckwheat Survey

Naturally-growing individuals of *E. parvifolium* are patchily distributed within the sanctuary. These buckwheats range in age from about 1 to 20 years, but the distribution of age-classes is skewed towards older individuals as there have been very few seedling or young plants established in recent years. For example, in 1984, 285 plants were censused (Fig. 2), but only 27 naturally-germinated seedlings were noted during that census. Most of these (25 of 27) were found in the middle and eastern subsites of the sanctuary, where *Carpobrotus* and grasses were cleared. Mean annual mortality of mature buckwheats has averaged around 10%, and until 1985 had always exceeded seedling recruitment. However, 32 naturally-germinated seedlings were noted during the 1985 census, while only 21 buckwheats were lost.

Outplanted Buckwheat Survey

Of the 574 buckwheat seedlings that were outplanted in November 1983, 29.1% had died by July 1984, 61.1% by the summer of 1985, and 67.8% by the summer of 1986. In the three subsites where buckwheats were outplanted, the survival rate of seedlings during 1984 was greatest (74.7%) in the eastern subsite. Survival rates in the middle and western subsites were nearly identical, 55.0% and 59.0%, respectively. Seedling survival rates were probably lower in these two areas because younger buckwheats were outplanted there. Also, the middle subsite suffered some loss of individuals due to erosion during the winter rainy season, plus some accidental mortality due to inadvertent disturbance. In addition, seedlings in the western subsite were more exposed to the wind, which can dessicate young plants.

This initial group of outplanted buckwheats included 212 juvenile plants that were 1 year old and 362 seedlings that were less than 6 months old at the time of outplanting. In each of the 3 years following outplanting, juveniles had significantly higher survival rates, produced more flowers than the younger seedlings, and had a greater percentage of individuals produce flowers (Table 1).

Flower production by the outplanted seedlings was greatest in the eastern subsite where most of the seedlings were older than 1 year at the time of outplanting and had been pruned one or more times prior to outplanting. Pruning stimulates branching, hence flower production in buckwheat plants. Seedlings outplanted in the middle and western subsites were generally younger, had not been pruned, and produced fewer flowers.

Of the 560 buckwheat seedlings outplanted in December 1984, 45% were still living during the summer of 1985, but only 28% survived until the next summer (Table 1). Their survival rate during the first year after outplanting was noticeably lower than that for the 1983 juveniles or seedlings, and may be due to a combination of factors. First, most were placed in the western and middle subsites where the microclimatic conditions are somewhat harsher. Furthermore, very little rain fell between 1 January and 30 April 1985, a period that usually receives about one-half to two-thirds of the total seasonal precipitation. Although their survival and flowering rates were comparable to the 1983 seedlings at the end of 2 years, flower production was slightly lower, 21.3 flowers per plant vs. 29.2 flowers per plant (Table 1).

ESB Utilization of Outplants

Butterfly utilization was measured two ways: (1) by observed adult ESB visits to flowers for nectar, or to bask, perch, mate, and oviposit; and (2) by incidence of observed larval foraging. In each habitat subsite during the period 1984–1986, the frequency of adult butterfly visits to flowering outplants has increased annually, while visits to resident buckwheats declined (Fig. 4). During this period, the resident buckwheat population grew older and produced fewer and fewer flowers. At the same time, a portion of the outplants survived and produced a greater percentage of the total number of flowers in each subsite. Butterfly visits to flowering outplants during the first year after outplanting are generally low (2%–14%), as most seedlings do not flower until their second season. Butterfly visits during the second season increased, ranging from 8%–38% for all samples. By 1986, some of the surviving outplants in the eastern sector were 4 years old. At this time, 73% of all ESB visits were noted on the outplants versus only 27% on residents.

Table 1. Survival and flowering rates for outplanted buckwheat plants, Chevron's El Segundo Sanctuary, 1983–1986.

	Outplanted		
	1983		1984
	Juveniles	Seedlings	Seedlings
First year:			
% survival	83.0	63.4	45.0
% flowering	82.4	52.8	37.7
x̄ # flowers	30.3	13.9	11.9
Second year:			
% survival	57.1	29.8	28.0
% flowering	94.2	75.9	77.1
x̄ # flowers	86.1	29.2	21.3
Third year:			
% survival	45.3	24.6	—[a]
% flowering	87.5	76.4	—
x̄ # flowers	125.4	72.4	—

[a]data to be analyzed.

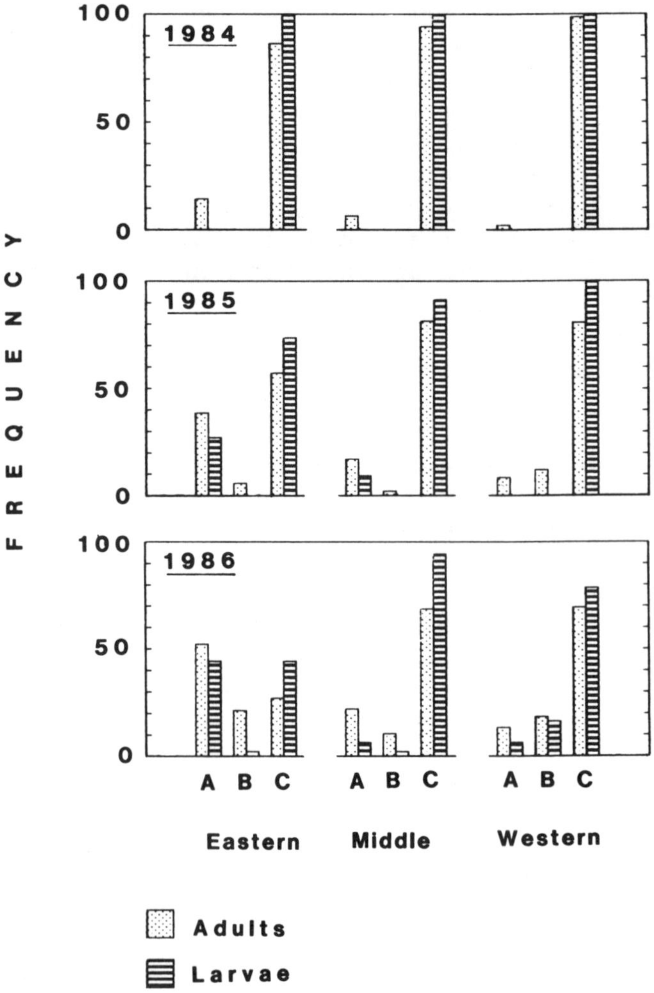

Fig. 4. Percent frequency of ESB adult and larval utilization of outplanted and resident buckwheats in three subsites (Eastern, Middle, and Western) at the Chevron sanctuary during 1984, 1985, and 1986. A = 1983 outplanted juveniles and seedlings, B = 1984 outplanted seedlings, and C = resident buckwheats.

Although adult visitation to outplant flowers is an important first step in rehabilitating the habitat, it is essential that ESB larvae forage on the flowers if the butterfly population is to be maintained. Whereas solitary seedlings generally do not produce enough flowers to sustain larvae until the plants are about 5 years old, larvae have been observed foraging on outplanted seedling clusters at 2 years of age. The incidence of larval foraging activity on outplants also has increased annually, albeit more slowly than adult visits. During 1986, 46% of all observations of larvae in the eastern subsite were noted on the 4-year-old outplants from 1983.

DISCUSSION

Native dune flora are adapted to a number of dynamic processes that create a balance between stability and movement of sand. Many of the perennial plants characteristic of the El Segundo Dunes are dependent upon secondary deposits of aeolian sand for the establishment and growth of their seedlings (Purer 1936). Alien annual plants, such as the grasses and *Erodium,* and other exotics like *Carpobrotus,* form dense ground covers that severely limit, and often prohibit, seedlings of the native perennial plants from getting established. Even if the natives establish some seedlings, the weedy annuals often outcompete them because they can grow and multiply faster. Because the ESB is dependent on foodplants whose distribution is patchy and changes with time, sufficient area must be available to provide for the patch dynamics (i.e., small disturbances and successive stabilization by native vegetation, followed by succession in the vegetation and disruption by the wind) that are an integral part of the natural dunes processes (Pavlik 1979). Truncation of the area occupied by the sand dune community leaves little room for development of the open pioneer and dune scrub communities that would normally characterize these dunes. This natural succession has been disrupted at the Chevron sanctuary by the invasion of dune grasses and ice plant that bind together sand grains and stabilize the dunes (Clark 1977). In addition to their aggressive growth, some ice plants are known to alter substrate conditions in a manner that favors their growth thereby allowing the ice plants to out-compete native plants (Vivrette and Muller 1977).

The collective result of these factors is that the resident buckwheat population now consists primarily of older, often senescent individuals with minimal recruitment of younger buckwheats. As the resident buckwheats age, they produce fewer flowers, resulting in the observed decline of ESB numbers. Management practices are needed to promote the establishment and growth of native dune plants, including buckwheat, and to ensure the perpetuity of the ESB. These practices include gradual replacement of weeds and annual grasses by non-aggressive, non-noxious flora. Because the sanctuary's small size limits natural dune processes important for the establishment of native flora, including buckwheat, it will require continual management.

Preliminary results of Chevron's habitat enhancement efforts are encouraging and suggest that continued rehabilitation may be able to stabilize buckwheat numbers and continue to support the endangered butterfly. Between 1977 and 1984 estimated population numbers of ESB declined 70%. Census estimates for 1985 and 1986 suggest that this rapid decline has been slowed. The 1986 estimate was only 6% less than the 1985 census, which was only 10% less than the 1984 estimate. As more outplanted buckwheat seedlings survive and flower, a gradual increase in ESB numbers is expected.

Although the resident buckwheat population continues to age and produce fewer flowers, natural seedling establishment exceeded mortality for the first time in both 1985 and 1986. These seedlings were generally located in areas where weeds had been removed earlier and we believe that continued weed control will encourage natural seedling establishment by the buckwheat. Although these observations are encouraging, outplanted seedlings probably will provide most of the new buckwheat established at the sanctuary for the next several years.

Several other dune endemic perennials, notably *Abronia umbellata, Croton californicus, Erysimum suffrutescens, Lotus scoparius,* and *Phacelia ramosissima,* have become established in areas manually cleared of weeds. These results are encouraging as continued natural establishment of these endemics may minimize the need for their future propagation and outplanting.

Many of the outplanted buckwheats flowered earlier than expected, especially those seedlings that were pruned during propagation. Numerous ESB adults were attracted to these flowers during their 1984, 1985, and 1986 flight seasons, particularly in the eastern subsite of the sanctuary. Also eggs, larvae, and pupae of the ESB were noted in a few flowers produced by the seedlings. These results are extremely encouraging and suggest that the ESB will begin to utilize clusters of seedlings earlier than solitary buckwheats that would require several more years of growth to produce a similar number of flowers. If this time lag can be continually reduced, then population numbers of the butterfly should increase as buckwheat flower numbers increase at the sanctuary.

Nearly 2 years after outplanting, seedling survival for the 1983 batch of buckwheats was better in the eastern and middle subsites of the sanctuary (48.8% and 43.3%, respectively) than in the western subsite (20.7%). The latter subsite is more exposed to the wind, which could dessicate young seedlings. Only about a 10% mortality rate between the 1984 and 1985 census counts was observed in the eastern and middle subsites, which suggests that the surviving buckwheats may be well established in these areas. Also, flower production by the outplanted seedlings was greatest in the eastern subsite.

Compared to the 1983 seedlings, the 1984 seedlings suffered a greater mortality rate, 55% versus 29%, during their first summer after outplanting. This can be partially attributed to three factors: (1) relative lack of rain after 1 January 1985, (2) the younger age of 1984 seedlings at the time of their outplanting, and (3) most 1984 seedlings were outplanted in the western subsite where weather conditions were harsher.

As many as 60 seedlings may have been accidentally destroyed in the western sector when a weather station was installed in the sanctuary by an outside contractor. Chevron has since erected a sign along the boundaries of the sanctuary to advise refinery personnel about the presence of endangered species habitat there. This action should prevent such potential accidents in the future.

Survival rates and mean flower production by outplanted juvenile seedlings have been noticeably higher than for younger seedlings. Also, ESB adults and larvae have foraged on juvenile plants sooner after outplanting than on younger seedlings. These findings suggest that we should outplant more of the older seedlings in future years. Older seedlings also might suffer less mortality in the exposed areas of the sanctuary where younger seedlings have not fared well.

Overall survival rates of outplanted buckwheat seedlings at the sanctuary compare favorably with results of similar rehabilitation efforts at the Antioch Dunes in Contra Costa County, California (Arnold, unpublished data). There, another species of buckwheat has been outplanted annually since 1979 to benefit the endangered Lange's metalmark butterfly. These results suggest that management efforts at the Chevron sanctuary are progressing about as well as can be expected at this time.

SUGGESTED MANAGEMENT RECOMMENDATIONS

Several positive steps have been taken at the Chevron sanctuary to improve habitat quality and reverse the downward trend in ESB numbers. Because the buckwheat clusters generally require about 3 to 4 years of growth to produce enough flowers to benefit the ESB and a substantial number of seedlings die before reaching this minimum age, management efforts must continue for several years to improve habitat quality. Based on our preliminary findings, we offer the following recommendations for continued management of the sanctuary:

1. Additional buckwheat seedlings should be outplanted in all subsites of the sanctuary to increase buckwheat numbers and flower production to stabilize the ESB population. In light of the observed survival rates, a minimum of 500–600 should be outplanted annually for at least the next 2 to 3 years. The use of juvenile plants versus younger seedlings as outplants should be investigated further.
2. Survival rates of outplanted seedlings have been markedly lower in the western and middle subsites compared to the eastern slope. Soil samples from all three subsites should be analyzed to determine if chemical and nutrient levels are abnormal where seedlings have fared poorly. Also, juveniles should be outplanted in the western subsite to see if they fare any better than young seedlings.
3. Manual clearing of weeds, grasses, ice plant, and filaree should be continued as it promotes natural seedling establishment by not only the buckwheat but also several other native dune plants. Continued weeding efforts may minimize the need to propagate these other dune plants at a later date.
4. Annual monitoring of buckwheat seedling survival, flowering, and utilization by ESB should be continued to evaluate the success of habitat improvement efforts.
5. Annual monitoring of ESB's status at the sanctuary should be continued. Butterfly population numbers should gradually increase as buckwheat seedlings mature and produce more flowers.
6. Other native dune plants growing at the sanctuary should be inventoried and monitored throughout management efforts. If necessary, seedlings may need to be grown and outplanted to prevent formation of a monoculture of buckwheat.
7. The status of native and introduced ant species that tend ESB larvae at the sanctuary should be determined. Because the ants presumably afford the larvae some protection from parasites and predators, their needs should not be neglected.

Acknowledgments.—All work was performed under permit issued to R.A. Arnold by the Wildlife Permit Office of the U.S. Fish & Wildlife Service. We thank the Tree of Life Nursery (San Juan Capistrano, California) and Tom Lemieux (University of California, Berkeley) for growing buckwheat seedlings, plus Dr. Robert Raabe (Plant Pathology Dep., University of California, Berkeley), and Alice Howard for technical assistance with germination and propagation methods. The U.S. Fish & Wildlife Service (Sacramento Office) provided funds for propagation of buckwheat seedlings. We also thank Norm LeRoy, Bob Ray, Kristen Birtwhistle, Brenda Smyth, Al Swanson, and Rod Spackman of the Chevron USA, El Segundo Refinery for logistical and financial support and Bob Foss, Chevron Corporation for preparation of figures.

REFERENCES CITED

Arnold, R.A. 1978. Survey and status of six endangered butterflies in California. Calif. Dep. of Fish & Game, Non-Game Wildlife Investigations E-1-1 Study V, Job 2.20. Final rep. 95 pp.

Arnold, R.A. 1981. El Segundo blue recovery plan. Agency Review Draft. U.S. Fish & Wildl. Serv. 45 pp.

Arnold, R.A. 1983. Ecological studies on six endangered butterflies (Lepidoptera: Lycaenidae); island biogeography, patch dynamics, and the design of habitat preserves. Univ. of Calif. Publ. in Entomol. 99:1–161.

Arnold, R.A. 1986. Studies of the El Segundo blue butterfly—1984. Calif. Dep. of Fish & Game, Inland Fisheries Branch. Adm. Rep. No. 86-4.

Clark, J.C. 1977. Coastal ecosystem management. The Conserv. Found., Wiley Interscience, New York.

Cooper, W.S. 1967. Coastal dunes of California. Geol. Soc. Amer. Mem. 104.

Pavlik, B.M. 1979. Botanical studies near the Monterey, San Francisco, and San Pablo Bays. U.S. Fish & Wildl. Serv. Publ. 10188.

Pierce, N.E. and P.S. Mead. 1981. Parasitoids as selective agents in the symbiosis between lycaenid butterfly larvae and ants. Science 211:1185–1187.

Purer, E.A. 1936. Studies of certain coastal sand dune plants of Southern California. Ecol. Monogr. 6:1–88.

Vivrette, N.J. and C.H. Muller. 1977. Mechanism of invasion and dominance of coastal grassland by *Mesembryanthemum crystallinum* L. Ecol. Monogr. 47:302–318.

Policy and Programs: How We Work Together and Who Pays

Chairman: STEPHEN R. KELLERT, *Associate Professor, Yale University, New Haven, Connecticut*
Cochairman: JAMES R. LYONS, *Staff Director, Committee on Agriculture, U.S. House of Representatives, Washington, D.C.*

European Approaches to Urban Wildlife Programs

GEORGE M A BARKER, *Nature Conservancy Council, England HQ, Northminster House, Peterborough, PE1 1UA, Great Britain*

INTRODUCTION

It is clearly not possible to describe all the European urban wildlife programs here. The range of these programs is great, from large-scale international campaigns to small site-related projects and individual research studies. The subjects of these programs are diverse and include ecological research, town planning, recreation, education, heritage conservation, sociological research, pollution control, and politics, among others. The number of these programs is enormous and is growing. Virtually every country in Europe has some active program and in many practically every major city has a number of schemes in progress.

This paper will categorize some of the main approaches to urban wildlife programs in Europe and will, in some categories, describe in a little more detail examples of schemes illustrating that kind of approach. It will concentrate on programs relating to the built-up areas rather than the complementary and closely inter-linked work being done in the countryside immediately adjoining towns and cities (the urban fringe).

In comparing European work with that carried out in North America, it is important to appreciate that the conservation of game species is of virtually no significance in European urban programs and, indeed, that where nature conservation in general is concerned in Europe it is overwhelmingly involved with nongame vertebrates, invertebrates, and plants.

SCIENCE-BASED PROGRAMS

A useful summary of European urban research is given in Sukopp and Werner (1982). Although most countries have some contribution to make here, the Federal Republic of Germany, and, in particular, the Institut für Ökologie, Technische Universität Berlin, stand out as the main sources of recent research in urban ecology in Western Europe. This is not simply academic work, but also research applied to the development and re-development of German cities very directly, as the use of climatological data in the planning of Stuttgart (e.g., Hoffman 1976, Loessner 1978), and a broad spectrum of environmental data in the nature conservation plan for Berlin (West) illustrate. The USSR and other Council for Mutual Economic Aid (Com-Econ) countries, notably Poland, also have impressive programs of research in urban ecology. In the USSR, a special working group on urban ornithology was set up in 1980, and since then a great number of studies have been carried out. Poland, however, provides one of the most detailed investigations conducted, and this is outlined below.

In the early 1970s, a major residential extension to Warszawa was proposed on a site covering 5,000 acres (2,000 ha) to the north of the city center at Białołęka Dworska. A research program coordinated by the Institute of Environmental Management began in 1975, one part of which was zoological investigations by the Institute of Zoology, Polish Academy of Sciences. The purposes were to: (1) gather data on the species and population densities of species present on the site; (2) evaluate the fauna and determine its usefulness in planning new urban greenspace within the proposed development; and (3) forecast the species composition of animal communities and population densities of those species after development. The forecasts could be made for any number of scenarios and could be used to guide planners in achieving optimal designs. In this work, the invertebrate soil fauna, fauna of the herb layer, synanthropic

Integrating Man and Nature in the Metropolitan Environment. Proc. Natl. Symp. on Urban Wildl., Chevy Chase, Md., 4–7 November 1986, L.W. Adams and D.L. Leedy, eds. Published by Natl. Inst. for Urban Wildl., 10921 Trotting Ridge Way, Columbia, MD 21044, 1987.

and hematophagous flies, and birds were selected for particular attention as useful indicators, or as groups with a potential impact on human existence (Bańkowska et al. 1984). Detailed studies were made concurrently of the geology (Stala 1982), hydrology (Jaroszewski 1982), soils (Konecka-Betley et al. 1982), climatology (Stopa-Boryczka et al. 1982, Ostrowski and Sierputowski 1982), and botanical structure (Roo-Zielińska 1982) of the site. The forecasts were based to a large extent on studies of the fauna of Warszawa (Czechowski and Pisarski 1981; Czechowski et al. 1982a,b; Czechowski 1982), which continue to be added to (Czechowski and Pisarski 1986). A second major study concentrating on the effects of urbanization on agricultural land on the periphery of Warszawa, and the species changes this causes, also has been carried out (Pinowski et al. 1986). This body of research is probably the most detailed and impressive study of an urban fauna carried out in Europe and, in common with the equally detailed and impressive work on an urban flora carried out in Berlin (West), has been put to practical use. However, it will come as no surprise to those who have been involved in planning studies that, in the case of Białołęka Dworska, the planners have partially negated the work of the scientists by demanding substantially more housing on the site than the original brief suggested. In general, the practical application of environmental research to the design and management of urban areas remains a matter of considerable difficulty. This is due in part to lack of understanding between scientists, planners, and land managers, and in part to the economic and political constraints placed on planners and land managers.

PLANNING-BASED PROGRAMS

In spite of—perhaps because of—the problems referred to above, many countries are developing strategic plans for nature conservation in towns and cities. The concept that towns and cities should be designed to include a substantial number of natural elements and a high proportion of greenspace is not new. However, it was the perceived needs of the human population that were being served, for example, in the garden cities of the nineteenth century. Although human social needs are still the main focus of planning, the strategies for nature conservation introduce a new element—that of care for, and development of, features that encourage a rich and varied flora and fauna to coexist with the human population. Also, the ideal of a city in tune with the natural environment is sought, where impacts on natural systems and processes are minimized, and where these same systems and processes are harnessed to give a more economical and, in the longer term, more sustainable city.

All European countries are interested in these lines of thought, but, in the majority, there is no concerted attempt to translate the theory into practice. However, there are serious attempts in a number of cities to address at least some of the issues. In the Netherlands, for example, park structure plans have been or are being prepared for several cities. These may focus on management and economic issues, e.g., Delft; public use, energy consumption, and climate, e.g., the Hague; or visual aspects and quality of experience, e.g., Amsterdam (Deelstra 1986). There is no systematic inventory of the fauna or flora of inner cities in the Netherlands to give a basis for nature conservation strategies for whole cities. In the Federal Republic of Germany, a great deal of progress has been made towards achieving such inventories. Here the conflicts between prospective developers and those wishing to see wildlife habitats preserved, require evaluation of the sites under discussion. Objective evaluation requires a thorough knowledge of the ecological resources of the city in question. This has been based on botanical survey as described by Sukopp et al. (1980), although attempts have been made to simplify the methods (Wittig and Schreiber 1983). Over 80 cities and major towns in the Federal Republic have been surveyed to date (Sukopp and Weiler 1986) and the information used to develop nature conservation strategies, the first of which—for West Berlin—was published in 1984. Similar detailed surveys aimed at providing data useful in developing strategies for nature conservation have been carried out in several cities outside the Federal Republic of Germany, e.g., Basle (Blattner and Ritter 1985) and Nottingham (Rieley and Page 1985).

In England, it is the policy both of the Government's wildlife advisory agency—the Nature Conservancy Council—and of the voluntary nature conservation organizations to encourage and assist local authorities to prepare strategies for nature conservation in urban areas. These strategies attempt to combine ecological factors and social needs in relation to greenspace and the wildlife it contains (Barker 1984, 1986). The surveys on which they are based seek not only to identify, classify, and evaluate the ecological resource, but, also, to pinpoint areas of need where people have no access to wildspace. The policies generated in these strategies reflect both the requirements of wildlife and the needs of people to have ready access to it for enjoyment, education, and relaxation. The strategies also take into account some potential economic benefits that "a combination of careful planning and benign neglect," as Davis and Glick (1978) expressed it, bring. The areas most actively involved in developing this approach in England are the major conurbations where the urgent needs of inner city regeneration have combined with the aspirations of the UK response to the World Conservation Strategy (Davidson and MacEwen 1982), and the rising tide of public concern for the environment as expressed in direct community action to produce a shift in immediate planning objectives. None of the published strategies for the major conurbations are statutory planning documents. They do, however, give clear guidelines that can be built into statutory plans, present a basis from which detailed District strategies can be elaborated, and provide a framework within which everyone concerned with conservation, land management, and development can operate (West Midlands County Council 1984, Greater London Council 1986, Greater Manchester County Council 1986; Tyne and Wear County Council 1986).

Although there is more emphasis in these English strategies on social factors than in strategies for cities in the Federal Republic of Germany, the bias in this direction is not so great as that reported for some other countries, e.g., South Africa (Poynton and Roberts 1985). Cooperative work between planners and scientists in developing the English strategies has, as a by-product, revealed a number of areas requiring a great deal more research by scientists if the planners are to be given authoritative guidance. One of these is the field of biogeography referred to by Poynton and Roberts (1985).

The cost of implementing these strategies is by no means as great as might appear at first sight. The Green Plan for Cape Town indicated that, by switching the emphasis from formal to informal recreation facilities, no extra money would be needed by the executive department (City of Cape Town 1982). A detailed analysis of the costs of the more radical proposals of the wildlife program for Berlin (West) calculated costs of about four million DM a year for 10 years if the unnecessary costs of mowing and horticulture in the city's parks were switched to the wildlife program (Hampicke 1985).

LAND MANAGEMENT-BASED PROGRAMS

"Greening the City" programs, which many countries subscribe to, are concerned with increasing the proportion of land with some kind of plant cover and making use of the hard landscape to support plant-life. In addition, there are other distinct programs aimed at existing parks, derelict land, and temporarily vacant land.

Most of the existing parks in urban areas are managed as formal gardens or in the English Landscape Tradition with a mixture of grassland and trees. Unfortunately, the practicalities of land management in cities led to modifications of the traditional ways in which English-style parks were managed. Herb-rich fields grazed by animals and hay-meadows of the old country estates were replaced in towns by an urban savannah of close-mown grass with isolated standard trees. However, the rising costs of managing the formal landscapes, combined with a shift in public attitudes towards the conservation of nature, are now beginning to result in less intensive methods of management that benefit wildlife (Corder and Brooker 1981). Although the harmful effects of intensive management regimes on wildlife are well known (e.g., Schaefer 1982, Kühnelt 1982), these were largely ignored and the trend towards less intensive regimes has been for the pragmatic reasons stated.

The needs to economize have, however, also led to extreme simplification in management in some areas. For example, in two parks in Knowsley, England, the management input has fallen from 1,508 man-days in 1974 to 650 man-days in 1986, and a total of 70 landscape features (flower-beds, tennis courts, paddling pools, etc.) have been lost in that period. The visual impact is immense, and local residents are no longer supportive of the park management—and this in turn makes maintenance budgets politically vulnerable. By economizing in this way, the system has been laid open to further cuts in financial support. Over Knowsley as a whole, 1,892 acres (766 ha) of land are under park management, and, in 1986, the proportion of this that is mowed grass is 98.96% (Handley and Bulmer 1986). In this kind of situation, ways are now being sought to use more naturalistic approaches to effect reasonable economies, but at the same time, to create landscapes that are varied and interesting, and ones that will regain the public support that the extreme simplification of management has lost. In this, the assistance of ecologists is being sought.

In established parks, there is a built-in resistance to change, both among managers and users. In addition, many parks are historic landscapes in their own right and should, for that reason, have their essential features preserved. Although this does not mean the requirements of wildlife should be ignored in their management, there are considerations that may preclude purely wildlife-based management options. It would be a brave man indeed who suggested substantial changes to Guëll in Barcelona or to the gardens of Versailles! However, throughout Europe there are examples of changes in management of major open spaces that are designed to favor wildlife. Hampstead Heath in London (Bellamy et al. 1986) is one example. It has been found that the users are now sufficiently well informed to lend positive support to such changes so long as the public relations exercise, which preceeds change and which interprets it after the event, is good.

Where new parks or landscapes are being created, there are definite moves towards developing more natural systems. These have as their inspiration the Dutch experience in creating natural biotopes built up since the early part of this century and given added impetus by the pressure of voluntary groups in the late 1960s. This pressure gave opportunities for people such as Le Roy and Reh to develop their concepts in a practical way. Ruff (1979) presented an account of the Dutch landscape designs that are beginning to replace the English style parks. In Britain, the ecological parks movement and the landscaping of some of our New Towns have the Dutch examples as their inspiration. A similar trend is evident in the general landscaping associated with new buildings, roads, and other developments. In many countries, considerable pressure is being exerted on professional landscape architects and their clients to move away from formal planting, monocultures of exotic species, and close-mown grass towards more natural biotopes (e.g., Keller 1982).

The same trend is occurring for many of the small-scale projects undertaken by neighborhood groups either with or without help from the official or voluntary organizations.

The Rally Gardens project in Leicester, England, for example, was developed by a voluntary organization and local residents from a derelict and rubbish-strewn railway station. Although some small flower beds have been created, spontaneous herb and shrub vegetation has been preserved over most of the site. Native trees, shrubs, and herbs were planted where bare ground was left after clearance of eyesores. Even the flower beds are filled with species of plants chosen for their attractiveness to insects. There are many similar schemes in Europe, which are a testimony to major change in the approach to urban green space design and management. A considerable literature is building up that gives guidance to those wishing to create landscapes favoring wildlife, whether these landscapes be natural parks or private gardens (e.g., Emery 1986, Baines and Smart 1984, Baines 1985).

The philosophy underlying most of these land management programs is to bring people into contact with attractive plants and animals so that they can enjoy them. It applies equally in most countries to the more formal nature reserves in urban areas where the practice of encouraging people to visit and use the reserves has gained favor over the more traditional policies of extremely limited public access. The main management problems generated by encouraging access have been found capable of resolution by sensitive on-site wardening. However, conflict between the legal and moral duties of ensuring the safety of visitors and the requirements of wildlife for intrinsically dangerous places in which to live, e.g., dead standing timber, vertical river-banks, rock screes and cliffs, remains something of a problem in many countries. It is not as yet generally accepted that wildspace cannot by its nature be made absolutely safe and that the human users of it should take this into account—just as road users need to take care in their use of those dangerous places.

A greater danger perhaps in land management programs focusing on a series of discrete sites is that nature conservation is seen by planners and politicians simply as a competing land-use. Clearly it must be seen in that light, and in many countries it is now accepted as a valuable use of land in urban areas. However, it is just as important that environmental conservation—of which nature conservation is a vital part—pervades the whole design and management of cities. Until this is so, the "Livable City" envisaged by Davidson and MacEwen (1982) will have no substance in fact.

COMMUNITY-BASED PROGRAMS

One of the phenomena of the last 30 years has been the great increase in public understanding of, and interest in, environmental issues. As this interest extended to include not only global issues such as practical uses of nuclear physics, but, also, local questions such as the loss to development of a small piece of woodland or a pond, so the voices of inner city residents became increasingly heard in environmental lobbies. Even in countries such as Britain, where public interest in natural history has traditionally been high, the issue of nature conservation in urban areas has had considerable impact. In the past, the voluntary nature conservation organizations in Britain have, in very broad terms, concerned themselves with the acquisition and management of nature reserves, have attracted a membership of upper middle-class people with political allegiances to the right of center, and have kept a relatively low profile. Presently, the new urban wildlife groups tend to attract younger people with political leanings to the left of center. These groups operate through vigorous publicity and seek to influence the management of land rather than acquiring it to manage directly. This pattern is reflected throughout Western Europe.

Community-based action ranges from the whole city scale to the neighborhood or single street scale. It includes street tree care, defense of treasured sites against development, sensitive adjustment of development plans, biological survey, education, and almost every other aspect of nature conservation. It is by no means confined to Western Europe, although the political differences between Eastern and Western Europe make comparison difficult. In Poland, for example, it was public protest backed by scientists that achieved not only the diversion of a major new road around, rather than through, the Bielanski Forest in Warszawa, but, also, insisted that a considerable length of this road should be raised on piers so that the connection between the woodland and the river Wista could be kept (Baum and Trojan 1982).

Although community-based groups are often in conflict with the authorities over specific proposals—indeed they are frequently set up in response to a specific threat to a treasured local amenity—they also can work very fruitfully in concert with the local authorities and statutory agencies. In Britain, for example, most major towns and cities have some kind of urban wildlife group that has a core team of professional staff supported by various central Government schemes, by grants from the statutory agencies and local authorities, and by money or secondment of staff from the private sector. This professional staff in turn helps and advises the smaller community-based groups. The help and advice given includes direct management of land, training, education, publicity, biological survey, representation at Public Inquiries into planning decisions, preparation of site management plans, and so on (Emery 1986). It is clear that given guidance, encouragement, and a little help communities are prepared to spend a lot of time and effort on small-scale site improvements for nature conservation. This in turn eliminates eyesores, generates proprietorial interest in the sites concerned, and boosts community morale. This is amply illustrated by the Blackbrook Valley Project in Dudley, itself a product of the Council of Europe's Campaign for Urban Renaissance, where in less than 5 years a neglected and vandalized area of woodland has been changed into a cherished local asset by a combination of official and voluntary initiatives aimed at local communities. Although the key here has been sensitive wardening by local authority staff, the scheme has made the local community realize not only that it has something worth looking after, but, also, that it has the power to make things happen in the way it wants. The result has been both to bring a site of value to nature conservation under good management, and to empower the community to take direct action and to voice opinions on a wide range of other issues affecting that community. In the context of the social problems of many European cities, it is the last aspect that is of considerable interest to city authorities and central Governments when nature conservation in urban areas is discussed.

Although this wakening of communities to the realization that they have the power to alter the course of events affecting them can only be applauded, it carries risks with it. Put obliquely, the community may not have the necessary knowledge to define or achieve its objectives, and extensive educational programs must be mounted to ensure that objectives are clearly identified and that technical knowledge is made available so that these objectives can be achieved. Put more directly, the community may not decide to do what we want it to do and must be steered towards the paths of righteousness as we perceive them. The divide between education and brain-washing is a narrow one.

In the case of voluntary organizations, there are signs of a cycle of events not unlike the cycle of development—decay—dereliction—redevelopment in a city's structure. Organizations set up to challenge the establishment and to set new standards grow, if successful, into miniature bureaucracies and become seen as part of the establishment that they were set up to challenge. New organizations then need to be generated to begin the cycle again. The recent proliferation of urban wildlife groups in Britain can be seen in this light, with the voluntary nature conservation organizations set up in the 1960s looked upon as too conservative to meet the needs of the moment. What is often forgotten is that each turn of the cycle drives the establishment a small pace forward. The sensitivity of the establishment to popular opinion may also be underestimated. The analogy of driving pigs to market is not inappropriate, where one minute the animals are trying to turn back and the next have rushed off down the road leaving you trailing after them—or worse, wondering whether they have turned off the road into someone's field to cause damage. The constructive tensions generated between the establishment and the community can lead to unpredictable results and ecologists, while needing to react to current trends, should also define and follow systematic programs of their own.

EDUCATION-BASED PROGRAMS

Two inter-related types of education-based programs can be distinguished. One type is aimed at raising the interest in, and awareness of, urban wildlife among the population in general and/or special audiences such as politicians, local authority officers, industrialists, tourists, and so on. The second type involves young people through the formal education system. Both types are found in all European countries, although in some they are rudimentary.

The public media have been particularly effective in the broader educational sense. Television lends itself very well to items about wildlife as the popularity of well known work of the BBC's Natural History Unit illustrates. Not only do features about wildlife create a foundation of public interest on which the nature conservation organizations can build, but they also can and do increasingly show what can be seen in towns and cities, and they present local issues involving urban wildlife.

The nature conservation organizations have discovered that conservation issues, while of great interest to them, are unlikely to fire the public imagination. Wildlife itself, however, is something of very general interest and by getting people involved in an enjoyable way with wildlife, a large constituency of public support is available when nature conservation issues are addressed. Thus, most British urban wildlife groups organize Fox Watches, Owl Watches, Butterfly Weeks, and so on in collaboration with local radio and the local Press to generate this constituency. The same kind of approach is found in most European countries and in its simplest form consists of the publication of information leaflets about urban wildlife.

Programs involving the formal education system, although overlapping the more general programs, can be treated as separate. There is increasing concern that children in inner cities will have no real contact with nature in the important years when experience will shape adult perceptions. These children may, in adult life, be alienated from nature. There seems to be unspoken agreement that in a world where decisions with far-reaching consequences for the natural environment will need to be made, it will be dangerous if any substantial part of a population is alienated from nature. There is also general agreement that children should not be deprived of the obvious enjoyment and interest contact with plants and animals can bring. More pragmatically, study of nature provides teachers with limitless opportunities ranging from applied mathematics and use of language, to art and drama, as well as the more obvious biological sciences.

All European countries have some kind of active program here, and, in some countries, very considerable emphasis is placed on ensuring that wildlife is studied at school. Switzerland, for example, has a policy that every school should have an area of land for classwork out of doors. The USSR has been developing Children's Ecological Stations where the pupils can design and perform their own integrated environmental programs with guidance from research institutes where appropriate (Bukin 1982). Urban wildlife is given weight in many countries because it is the towns and cities that contain the majority of schools and rising travel costs, together with the demands of the school curriculum, preclude regular class visits to rural areas. In the Netherlands, for example, teacher training includes urban ecology (van Wingerden 1982). In Britain, the literature includes guidance to teachers on urban wildlife studies (e.g., Sames 1982), and local authorities and voluntary organizations have developed natural areas in most cities where students can study urban wildlife. Probably the best known of these was the William Curtis Ecological Park, which was developed as a temporary use of 2 acres (0.85 ha) of land near Tower Bridge in London (Ecological Parks Trust 1978–1986, Cotton 1982).

PROGRAMS BASED ON STUDIES OF PERCEPTIONS AND NEEDS

Because nature conservation in urban areas seeks to meet the needs of wildlife and people, it is logical that active programs of work be set up to study the perceptions of urban residents, their use of wildspace, and the human needs for wildlife and wildspace. The fact unfortunately remains that relatively little has yet been done in this field. Even elementary studies aimed simply at identifying the main constituencies being addressed by nature conservation organizations are generally lacking (Barker 1986).

In several European countries, there are studies that illuminate this subject area. It is usually the case that such work is carried out primarily as academic research. However, studies linked to objectives set by urban wildlife programs have produced useful results. Work in France (Leroy 1986), Spain (Gonzalez-Bernaldez 1984), and Britain (Harrison et al. 1986) illustrate this. In Britain, the Nature Conservancy Council has promoted a low-key program beginning in 1978 with an investigation of the impact of participation in urban wildlife projects on the people taking part (Mostyn 1979), and currently continuing with a study of public perceptions and uses of green space. There has been a tendency to move away from the standard questionnaire approach towards the in-depth group or individual discussion technique. This has been due to the fact that the underlying reasons for particular attitudes being held, or actions being taken, are seen as more important than the attitudes or actions are in themselves. The accumulation of politically helpful statistics that questionnaire surveys can generate has not been seen as essential in urban wildlife programs in Britain—although this view is being modified as the value of such surveys carried out mainly in the USA (e.g., U.S. Department of the Interior, Fish and Wildlife Service and U.S. Department of Commerce, Bureau of the Census 1982; Witter and Sheriff 1983) become better appreciated. There is of course the danger that, as Andrew Lang said, we use statistics as a drunken man uses lamp-posts—for support rather than illumination. It is probably legitimate to use their support so long as we profit from their illumination. At present, their absence relieves us of this decision.

DISCUSSION

Although a great deal of work has been done, and progress made, in urban wildlife programs in Europe, there are very real practical difficulties in bringing this work together. These include the multiplicity of languages, enormous political differences between countries, a wide range of socially accepted uses of land in urban areas, and differences in the degree to which countries are urbanized and the history of that urbanization. In spite of these problems, there is increasing interchange of ideas and information through official links, e.g., UNESCO MAB Project 11, Council of Europe, Com-Econ Conferences, and through informal links between individuals and institutions. This has helped towards a broad consensus view that environmental factors, including wildlife, should be taken fully into account in the design and management of cities. Scientific research has suggested ways in which this integration can be achieved. Also, it has been recognized that many cities are in urgent need of attention for social as well as environmental reasons, and that wildlife programs have a useful part to play in inner city regeneration (Deelstra 1985). Investigations into the needs of people for, and their perceptions of, urban wildlife have helped to define the reasons behind the values of wildlife programs in urban regeneration. The voluntary nature conservation organizations, where they exist, help by giving a focus for local initiatives and by giving a political edge to the topic. The whole has been given impetus by the economic need to find less costly ways of managing open space in urban areas; this in essence implies working closely with natural processes rather than perpetually fighting these processes.

The application of all this knowledge, political goodwill, and community action is, at first glance, disappointing. Research is still ignored by planners; social needs are still ignored by many developers; children are still deprived of wildspace; the cities still look much as they did 20 years ago. It took, after all, nearly two hundred years to make the mess, and it will take a long time to clear it up. However, what have changed dramatically are the attitudes that local residents, land managers, planners, and politicians hold. Ten years ago in Britain the idea of nature conservation programs in cities was so unusual that the publication of a document referring to the topic (Teagle 1978) attracted national media coverage. Now the concept is so much accepted that the recent publication of the Nature Conservation Strategy for London (Greater London Council 1986) was hardly mentioned, and the declaration of the country's first purpose-built statutory Local Nature Reserve in an urban area at Camley Street in London raised no eyebrows. This trend is evident in most, if not all, European countries, being perhaps most clearly seen in middle and northern Europe; and the Com-Econ giant is stirring. Reinforcing the trend is the universal acceptance of the value of educational programs directed both at schools in particular and at the public in general.

A momentum has been generated, which will be hard to stop. The imperative lies now with the official nature conservation organizations to ensure that the best possible technical and theoretical advice is available to the Government Departments, the local authorities, and the voluntary organizations to enable them to define and achieve worthwhile goals. The danger is that the speed of executive action will send the whole movement so far ahead that science will be left stumbling behind. This will inevitably be true in the detail of projects, but it is probably true to say that sufficient is known to ensure that sensible directions are taken—assuming that Action will listen to Reason.

REFERENCES CITED

Baines, C. 1985. How to make a wildlife garden. Elm Tree Books/ Hamish Hamilton, London, England. 192 pp.

Baines, C. and J. Smart. 1984. A guide to habitat creation. Ecology Handbook No. 2, Greater London Council, London, England. 44 pp.

Bańkowska, R., W. Czechowski, H. Garbarczyk, and P. Trojan. 1984. Present and prognosticated fauna of the housing estate Białołęka Dworska, Warsaw. Memorabilia Zoologica 40:1–166.

Barker, G. 1984. Urban nature conservation abroad. The Planner 70:21.

Barker; G. 1986. The links between ecological science, local authority action and community involvement in planning and land management for nature conservation in British cities. Paper given to International Seminar on the use, handling and management of urban green areas. Barcelona, 21–24 April. MAB-UNESCO Comite Espagnol.

Baum, T. and P. Trojan (eds). 1982. Las Bielański w Warszawie Rezerwat Przyrody. Polish Academy of Sciences, Warszawa. 311 pp.

Bellamy, J. et al. 1986. Hampstead Heath flora. Habitat Handbook No. 1, Greater London Council, London, England. 60 pp.

Blattner, M. and M. Ritter. 1985. Basler Natur-Atlas. Vols. 1–3. Basler Naturschutz.

Bukin, A. 1982. Children's Ecological Station. Ecology of a Small Town 11. Scientific Centre for Biological Research of the Academy of Sciences of the USSR, Pushchino, pp. 69–76. Synopsis also in E E Bozhukova and D N Kavtaradze (eds). Main Works on the Programme 'Ecopolis' (1979–1982). Ecology of a Small Town, 1983. S.C.B.R.A.S. of the USSR, Pushchino.

City of Cape Town. 1982. Greening the city: open space and recreation plan for Cape Town. Rep. No. 214/1982. City Engineer's Dep., Cape Town, South Africa. 121 pp.

Corder, M. and R. Brooker. 1981. Natural economy: an ecological approach to planting and management techniques in urban areas. Kirklees Metropolitan Council. 92 pp.

Cotton, J. 1982. The field teaching of ecology in central London—The William Curtis Ecological Park 1977–80. Pages 321–327 *in* R. Bornkamm, J.A. Lee, and M.R.D. Seaward, eds. Urban ecology. Blackwell Sci. Publ., Oxford.

Czechowski, W. 1982. Occurrence of Carabids (Coleoptera, Carabidea) in the urban greenery of Warsaw according to land utilization and cultivation. Memorabilia Zoologica 39:3–108.

Czechowski, W., H. Garbarczyk, B. Pisarski, and J. Sawoniewicz (eds). 1982a. Species composition and origin of the fauna of Warsaw (Part 2). Memorabila Zoologica 35:1–168.

Czechowski, W., H. Garbarczyk, B. Pisarski, and J. Sawoniewicz (eds). 1982b. Species composition and origin of the fauna of Warsaw (Part 3). Memorabilia Zoologica 36:1–262.

Czechowski, W. and B. Pisarski, (eds). 1981. Species composition and origin of the fauna of Warsaw (Part 1). Memorabilia Zoologica 34:1–259.

Czechowski, W. and B. Pisarski, (eds). 1986. Structure of the fauna of Warsaw: effects of urban pressure on animal communities (Part 1). Memorabilia Zoologica 41:1–230.

Davidson, J. and A. MacEwen. 1982. The livable city. Report No. 5 in Earth's survival: a conservation and development programme for the UK. Programme Organising Committee. 96 pp.

Davis, A. and T. Glick. 1978. Urban ecosystems and island biogeography. Environ. Conserv. 5:299–303.

Deelstra, T. 1985. Urban development and mental health: a planner's view. Paper presented at the conference "Health in towns: urban development, psycho-social disorders and mental health," Strasbourg, 3–5 December. Council of Europe, Strasbourg. 39 pp. (typescript)

Deelstra, T. 1986. National, regional and local planning strategies for urban green areas in the Netherlands: an ecological approach. Paper given to International Seminar on the use, handling and management of urban green areas. Barcelona, 21–24 April. MAB-UNESCO. Comite Espagnol.

Ecological Parks Trust. 1978–1986. The William Curtis Ecological Park, Annual Reports. The Linnean Society, Burlington House, London, England.

Emery, M. 1986. Promoting nature in cities and towns: a practical guide. Croom Helm, Beckenham, England. 400 pp.

Gonzalez-Bernaldez, F. 1984. The use of public perception of landscape in the planning process: the Spanish MAB experience. International Experts Meeting on Ecological Approaches to Urban Planning. Suzdal, Sept. MAB-UNESCO.

Greater London Council. 1986. A nature conservation strategy for London: woodland, wasteland, the tidal Thames and two London boroughs. Ecology Handbook No. 4, London, England. 92 pp.

Greater Manchester County Council. 1986. A nature conservation strategy for Greater Manchester. Manchester, England. 45 pp.

Hampicke, U. 1985. Die Volkswirtschaftlichen Riosten des Naturschutzes in Berlin. Landschaftsentwicklung und Umweltforschung 35. 545 pp.

Handley, J. and P. Bulmer. 1986. Making the most of greenspace: a guide to the management of vegetation around towns and cities. A report to the Department of the Environment (contract number (PECD7/2/013-1/83). 133 pp. (typescript).

Harrison, C., J. Burgess, and M. Limb. 1986. Popular values for the countryside. A report to the Countryside Commission on the Greenwich Open Space Project. 75 pp. (typescript).

Hoffman, U. 1976. Problems of the city climate of Stuttgart. *In* E. Franke, ed. City climate: data and aspects for city planning. Karl Kramer, Stuttgart.

Jaroszewski, T. 1982. Hydrological conditions in the region of a designed group of housing estates in Białołęka Dworska in Warsaw. Człowiek i Środowisko 6:311–344. (English summary).

Keller, H. 1982. Nature en milieu urbain. Ligue Suisse pour la Protection de la Nature, Bale. (Also published in German).

Konecka-Betley, K., K. Czarnowska, Z. Czerwinski, E. Janowska, E. Kepka, P. Pracz, and S. Russel. 1982. The issues concerning the soil in the design of the Białołęka Dworska residential area in Warsaw. Człowiek i Środowisko 6:371–402. (English summary).

Kühnelt, W. 1982. Free-living invertebrates within the major ecosystems of Vienna. Pages 83–87 *in* R. Bornkamm, J.A. Lee, and M.R.D. Seaward, eds. Urban ecology. Blackwell Sci. Publ., Oxford.

Leroy, C. 1986. Role des espaces verts urbains et peri-urbains dans le maintien de la sante et de l'identite de l'homme. Paper given to International Seminar on the use, handling and management of urban green areas. Barcelona, 21–24 April. MAB-UNESCO Comite Espagnol.

Loessner, F.A. 1978. An air quality program with visible results. Practicing Planner 9:35–37.

Mostyn, B. 1979. Personal benefits and satisfactions derived from participation in urban wildlife projects: a qualitative evaluation undertaken on behalf of the Nature Conservancy Council. Social and Community Planning Research, London, England. 66 pp.

Ostrowski, J. and P. Sierputowski. 1982. Model tests of flow phenomena at the built-up areas of housing estates based on the group of housing estates in Białołęka Dworska in Warsaw. Człowiek i Środowisko 6:351–370. (English summary).

Pinowski, J., T. Traezyk, Z. Czerwinski, and A. Kostrowicki. 1986. Habitat changes in suburban zones. Paper presented at IV International Congress of Ecology, Syracuse, New York, 10–16 August.

Poynton, J. and D. Roberts. 1985. Urban open space planning in South Africa: a biogeographical perspective. South African J. Sci. 81:33–37.

Rieley, J. and S. Page. 1985. Botanical and vegetation survey of the City of Nottingham. James Davies and Partners, Nottingham. 84 pp.

Roo-Zielinska, E. 1982. The geobotanical structure and its ecological conditions of a future housing estate area in Białołęka Dworska in Warsaw. Człowiek i Środowisko 6:403–422. (English summary).

Ruff, A. 1979. Holland and the ecological landscape. Deanwater Press, Stockport.

Sames, T. 1982. Wildlife in towns: a teacher's guide. Nature Conservancy Council, London, England. 23 pp.

Schaefer, M. 1982. Studies on the arthropod fauna of green urban ecosystems. Pages 65–73 *in* R. Bornkamm, J.A. Lee, and M.R.D. Seaward, eds. Urban ecology. Blackwell Sci. Publ., Oxford.

Stala, Z. 1982. Geomorphological and geological conditions in the design of housing settlements in Białołęka Dworska in Warsaw. Człowiek i Środowisko 6:289–309. (English summary).

Stopa-Boryczka, M., M. Kopacz-Lembowicz, E. Ryczywolska, J. Boryczka, and A. Górka. 1982. The assessment of a local climate in the design of housing estates in Białołęka Dworska in Warsaw. Człowiek i Środowisko 6:335–349. (English summary).

Sukopp, H., W. Kunick, and C. Schneider. 1980. Biotope mapping in the built-up areas of West Berlin. Garten & Landschaft 7:565–569.

Sukopp, H. and S. Weiler. 1986. Biotopkartierung im besiedelten Beriech der Bundesrepublik Deutschland. Landschaft & Stadt 18:25–38.

Sukopp, H. and P. Werner. 1982. Nature in cities. Council of Europe, Strasbourg. 94 pp.

Teagle, W. 1978. The endless village: the wildlife of Birmingham, Dudley, Sandwell, Walsall and Wolverhampton. Nature Conservancy Council, Shrewsbury. 58 pp.

Tyne and Wear County Council. 1986. Draft nature conservation strategy. Newcastle upon Tyne. 56 pp.

U.S. Dep. of the Inter., Fish and Wildl. Serv. and U.S. Dep. of Commerce, Bureau of the Census. 1982. 1980 national survey of fishing, hunting and wildlife-associated recreation. U.S. Gov. Printing Office, Washington, D.C. 20402. 156 pp.

van Wingerden, W. 1982. The teaching of urban ecology to future teachers. Pages 315–320 *in* R. Bornkamm, J.A. Lee, and M.R.D. Seaward, eds. Urban ecology. Blackwell Sci. Publ., Oxford.

West Midlands County Council. 1984. The nature conservation strategy for the County of West Midlands. Birmingham, England. 60 pp.

Witter, D. and S. Sheriff. 1983. Obtaining constituent feedback: implications for conservation programs. Trans. North Am. Wildl. and Nat. Resour. Conf. 48:42–48.

Wittig, R. and K. Schreiber. 1983. A quick method for assessing the importance of open spaces in towns for urban nature conservation. Biol. Conserv. 26:57–64.

Wildlife Conservation in Rapidly Expanding Metropolitan Areas: Informational, Institutional, and Economic Constraints and Solutions

William W. Shaw, *School of Renewable Natural Resources, University of Arizona, Tucson, AZ 85721*

Vashti Supplee, *Arizona Game and Fish Department, 555 N. Greasewood Rd., Tucson, AZ 85745*

INTRODUCTION

The historic role of state game and fish agencies has been the management of huntable wildlife species reflecting, in large part, the primary sources of funding (hunting and fishing licenses and surcharges on hunting and fishing equipment) (WMI 1975). The shift in the United States population from rural to urban centers has been accompanied by changes in public perceptions of wildlife resources, and in the ways the public enjoys wildlife–oriented recreation (Kellert 1979, 1980; Shaw and Mangun 1984). Although the primary emphasis of state wildlife departments remains with hunting and fishing recreation management, in recent years there has been a significant commitment of dollars and resources to non-hunted species.

Pressures upon wildlife habitats for commodities, such as minerals and timber, have caused state wildlife agencies to develop programs and expertise in wildlife habitats in addition to knowledge of species populations (Sikorowski and Bissell 1986). As the emphasis on habitat management has increased, it has become clear that many of the greatest losses in wildlife habitats are occurring as a consequence of the expansion of metropolitan areas. Furthermore, because of the concentration of people in cities and suburbs, these are also the areas where the potential for nonconsumptive wildlife appreciation is greatest. For all of these reasons, many state wildlife agencies are increasing their commitments to urban wildlife conservation and this change is requiring new and innovative approaches to wildlife management. Nowhere are the pressures for these changes greater than in the rapidly expanding sunbelt cities. This paper reviews the evolution of Arizona Game and Fish Department's (AGFD) urban wildlife program. It compares wildlife conservation in rural settings with wildlife management in metropolitan environments and identifies a number of constraints and problems that may limit the success of urban wildlife programs.

CONSERVATION OF URBAN WILDLIFE IN ARIZONA

AGFD's activities in metropolitan environments have evolved over a period of time. However, in retrospect there have been several critical steps in the process: creation of a habitat evaluation program (1979), creation of a nongame division (1983), and finally adoption of an urban wildlife policy (1986).

Habitat Evaluation in Metropolitan Environments

Although AGFD is responsible for the management and protection of wildlife species within the state, Arizona lands are primarily under federal management. Greater than 40% of the state is managed by the U.S. Forest Service, Bureau of Land Management, and National Park Service. Another 25% of Arizona lands is within Indian reservations. The remaining 30 to 35% is State Trust lands and private ownership. To facilitate land management that is consistent with wildlife habitat needs, AGFD created a statewide habitat evaluation program in July, 1979. A wildlife biologist, with the title of habitat evaluation specialist, was placed in each of six regional offices, with two program coordinators located in the Phoenix central office. The program has emphasized local cooperation with land management agencies and other governmental units with a management objective of incorporating wildlife habitat requirements into land management activities.

Integrating Man and Nature in the Metropolitan Environment. Proc. Natl. Symp. on Urban Wildl., Chevy Chase, Md., 4–7 November 1986, L.W. Adams and D.L. Leedy, eds. Published by Natl. Inst. for Urban Wildl., 10921 Trotting Ridge Way, Columbia, MD 21044, 1987.

The habitat specialists have primarily been oriented towards the development of Land Management Plans (USDA Forest Service) and Wildlife Habitat Management Plans (USDI Bureau of Land Management). However, in some regions, such as the one including Tucson, urban expansion is a major habitat issue. As a result, the habitat specialists in these regions spend a great deal of time reviewing development proposals for their impacts on wildlife resources. A major function of these habitat specialists is to provide information on wildlife values to local governments and developers. This urban habitat program has increased the visibility of the Department's nongame concerns and has enhanced the public image of AGFD as a concerned wildlife resource management agency with a comprehensive approach to wildlife conservation.

Nongame Wildlife Division and Metropolitan Environments

The formation of a nongame wildlife branch within AGFD in 1983 further expanded the agency's capability to be a knowledgeable source of information for all wildlife species. The backbone of the nongame program has been a data management system that was developed by The Nature Conservancy and was originally known as the Arizona Natural Heritage Program. The Natural Heritage Program data base includes location files of sensitive and threatened animal and plant species. Since its transfer to the Arizona Game and Fish Department in 1983, the data base has been called the Arizona Nongame Data Management System. The AGFD has made a commitment to integrate the information stored in this data base into agency habitat reviews. The regional habitat specialists are currently functioning as the local contacts for nongame information requests. A typical Department response for a project or site review will include nongame and threatened or endangered plant and animal information along with the more standard analysis of impacts to game species.

An Agency Policy on Urban Wildlife Management

Several Arizona cities are among the fastest growing communities in the country. As a result, habitat specialists in these areas are spending more and more of their time dealing with urban wildlife issues. In acknowledgment of this, the Arizona Game and Fish Commission approved a policy statement on urban wildlife in 1986 that recognized these activities as legitimate concerns of the agency. The statement reads:

> "The Commission recognizes that wildlife has both a positive economic and aesthetic value to the people of Arizona. Through uncontrolled and unplanned urbanization many of these values have been negatively impacted. In order to slow the degradation of wildlife benefits in urban areas and to develop an understanding of wildlife resources in urban areas, the Arizona Game and Fish Commission directs the Arizona Game and Fish Department to develop an urban wildlife management program which promotes habitat development and preservation. In addition, the Department is directed to further public awareness of urban wildlife management opportunities and to cooperate with the programs of governmental subdivisions of the State of Arizona in establishing and maintaining urban wildlife habitats." (Arizona Game and Fish Commission 1986).

Although this is a very general policy statement, it is a significant event in the evolution of this agency's role in metropolitan environments because it is an explicit acknowledgment of the agency's concern with this issue.

With over 20,000 new residents each year, Tucson is experiencing tremendous growth. For this reason, the emphasis of our urban wildlife management program has been on habitat. However, Arizona Game and Fish Department is only one of many entities with an interest in the management of urban lands. Therefore, it is absolutely essential that the wildlife agency work in concert with other private and public groups. For example, the existence of a habitat evaluation program provided a logical point for communication between the wildlife agency and the local planning and zoning department (Pima County Planning and Development Services). The local habitat specialist worked closely with the agency in developing site analysis procedures that integrate wildlife concerns into the development process. Using a model developed by Boulder County, Colorado, Tucson has adopted a procedure requiring developers and landowners to prepare a site analysis report that includes maps of vegetative communities and sensitive wildlife habitats. This information must be gathered prior to submitting a rezoning request to Pima County Planning and Development Services. Fig. 1 displays the county rezoning process and shows the sources for biological input into this process. The wildlife component specifically requires contacting the Tucson habitat specialist, and receiving a letter from AGFD that evaluates the wildlife and critical wildlife habitat values for the site. The wildlife section in the site ordinance reads as follows:

WILDLIFE

1. The petitioner shall provide a letter of confirmation from the habitat specialist in the Arizona Game and Fish Department Tucson Regional Office in regards to the following characteristics and any other topics of concern.
2. If Arizona Game and Fish states any concerns, describe and map wildlife habitats which support the following:
   a. State-listed threatened or endangered species (see Threatened Native Wildlife in Arizona—Ariz. Game and Fish Department Publication);
   b. High densities of a given species' population (based upon Arizona Game and Fish Department data) or an unusually high diversity of species; and

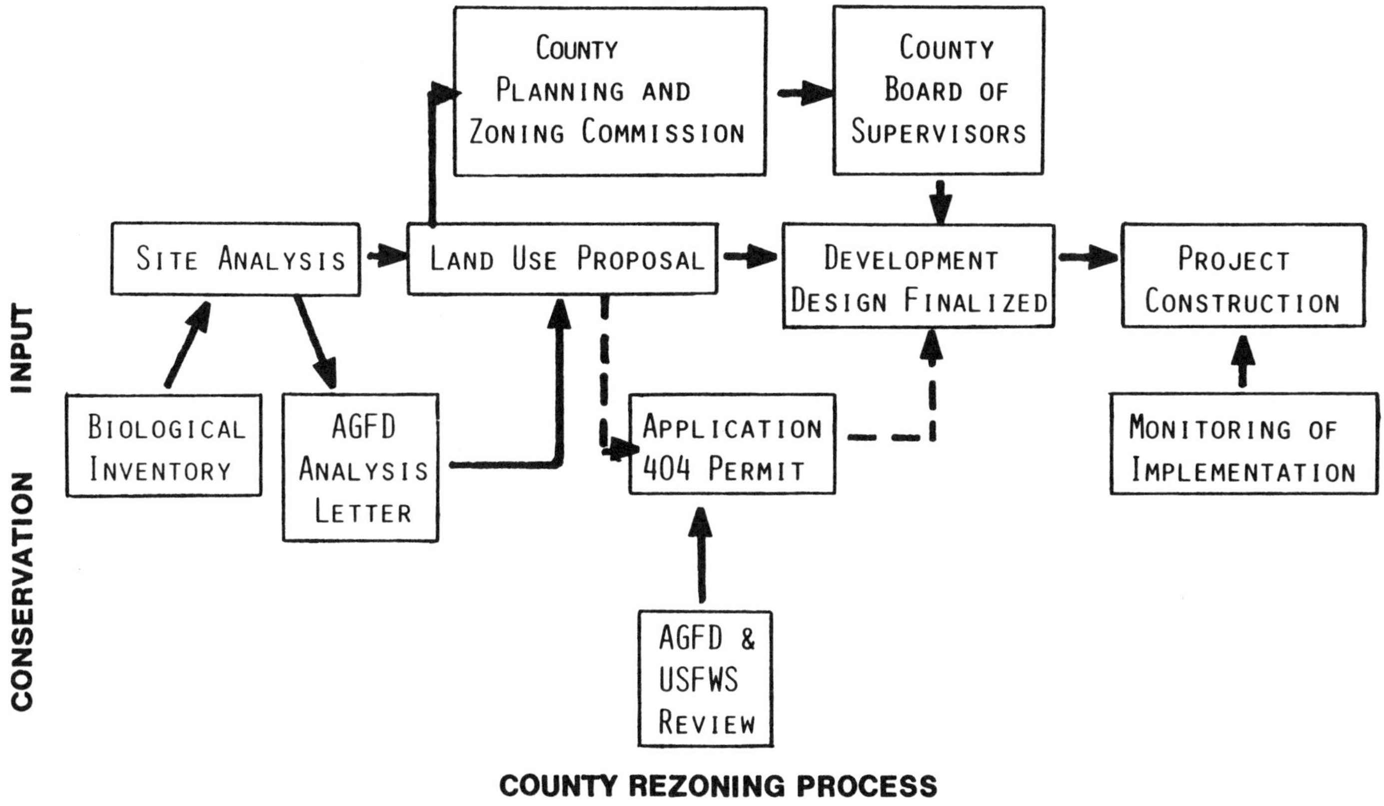

Fig. 1. Conservation input into the county rezoning process.

c. Aquatic or riparian ecosystems.

Following the preparation of a site analysis, the developer is required to prepare a land use proposal based, in part, upon site analysis information. The land use proposal enables the developer to set forth design concepts derived after the analysis of the site's characteristics. Importantly, this step in the process provides the developer with an opportunity to present sensitive design and mitigation techniques that respond to unique site characteristics and the character of the surrounding neighborhood.

Within the land use proposal is included a description of the appropriate steps to mitigate losses of wildlife habitat, or a rationale why none is necessary.

Finally, the crucial element that has enabled a significant urban wildlife program to evolve in Tucson has been the development of a coalition of interests, all fighting for complementary objectives. For example, at the same time AGFD was working to save riparian habitats, the Pima County Urban Design Commission was recommending protection of watercourses for aesthetics and recreation, and the Open Space Committee was promoting watercourses as a logical foundation for an interconnected open space system. Concurrently, the university was conducting new studies providing data on urban wildlife habitats. This, timed with an upsurge in public concern for comprehensive planning and a sympathetic Board of Supervisors has created a favorable climate for the integration of wildlife conservation into the planning and development processes of this community.

Our experience in Tucson has been encouraging but not without frustrations and concerns. There are several lessons from this experience that may be relevant for other communities.

WILDLIFE MANAGEMENT IN METROPOLITAN VERSUS RURAL ENVIRONMENTS

Although the basic principles of biology and wildlife management are the same regardless of whether they are applied in a rural or urban setting, there are some fundamental differences in terms of who manages the habitats and who uses the wildlife resources (Fig. 2). To be effective, in cities, wildlife biologists must recognize these differences and adjust their approaches accordingly.

Habitat Managers

Protection and enhancement of wildlife habitat is an essential ingredient in any wildlife conservation strategy—regardless of whether the habitat occurs in a rural or metropolitan setting. In rural environments, wildlife managers most often work through large landowners or public land

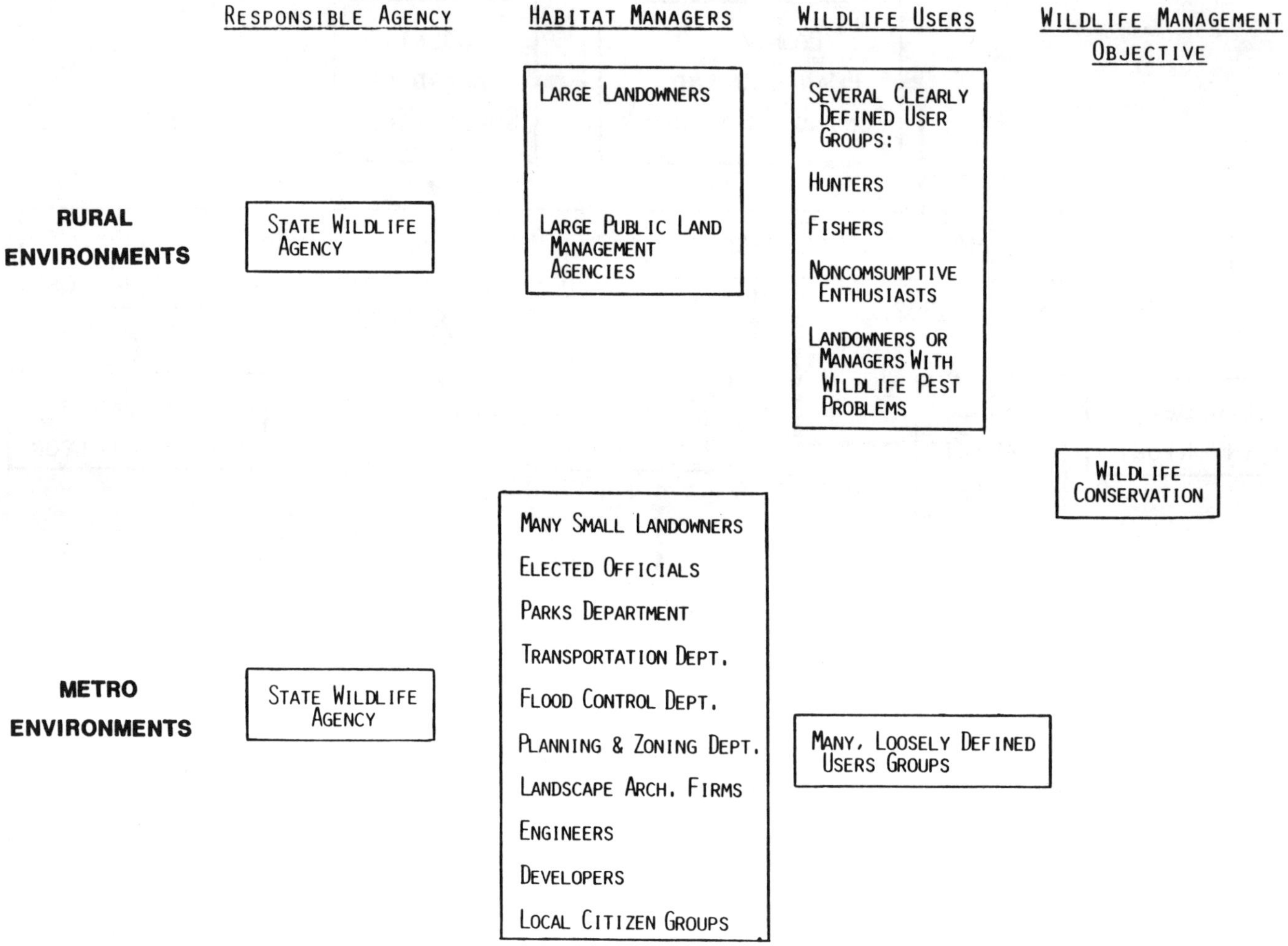

Fig. 2. Wildlife management in rural and metropolitan environments.

management agencies that control most of the wildlife habitat. In the metropolitan context, wildlife habitat is controlled by a much more diverse set of individuals and agencies (Fig. 2). Instead of a few large landowners, the habitat is spread through a large number of small property owners. Furthermore, there are many agencies and individuals representing many different professions making decisions about activities and developments on metropolitan lands. Cities are built on an infrastructure of flood control, transportation, land use zoning, and utility systems. The architects of these systems are engineers, planners, landscape architects, elected officials, and various citizen groups. Each of these entities has a significant impact on the wildlife habitat that remains in the metropolitan environment. Unfortunately, in most cases, land use decisions are made with little consideration of their implications for wildlife habitat. To be effective in a metropolitan context, wildlife managers must do a better job of working with and influencing those individuals whose decisions determine the existence and condition of urban wildlife habitats.

Wildlife Users

Another difference between rural and metropolitan environments involves the people who benefit from wildlife conservation (Fig. 2). In undeveloped areas, it is usually possible to identify the major user groups in terms of specific recreational activities such as hunting and fishing. In cities, the users are less easy to identify and they also represent a broader cross section of society. For example, many people enjoy the presence of wildlife near their homes. These wildlife "users" generally do not purchase licenses or join sportsmen's organizations and, as a consequence, they are not easy to identify. Nevertheless they are a large and significant group. Recent studies have revealed that 55% of the American public over 16 years old enjoy wildlife in their home environment (Shaw et al. 1985). A recent household survey in Tucson found that 57% of the households fed wild birds (Ruther 1986).

In metropolitan environments, a large and diverse group of people benefit from the presence of wildlife. Furthermore, these wildlife species are dependent on habitats that are owned and managed by an equally large and diverse group of individuals, private firms, and public agencies. To be effective in this context requires that wildlife managers assume some new and different roles that have not traditionally been emphasized in our training programs. For example, decisions made by planning and zoning authorities, transportation planners, flood control agencies, and private developers may have very significant implications for wildlife habitats. Habitat specialists must be involved in these processes by attending public hearings, participating in citizen committees, and providing written evaluations of various plans and proposals.

Even when the need for these kinds of activities are recognized, there are major constraints that may limit the ability of wildlife biologists to be effective in influencing metropolitan planning processes.

INFORMATIONAL CONSTRAINTS

A major impediment to incorporating wildlife conservation into the context of metropolitan planning is that we often do not have the basic biological information we need. An essential prerequisite for evaluating the biological implications of alternative development plans is information concerning the wildlife and habitat types that are found in the area of concern. In Tucson, this information need is being met through two systems. The first is the AGFD data base. This system is a computerized record of mapped locations for threatened and unique vertebrate and floral species in Arizona. Record sources include historic and current information. However, this data base is far from complete and lack of known species locations does not denote species absence.

A second source of information is a habitat map, which identifies those areas that are most valuable from a biological perspective in the metropolitan area. This map was developed as a "red flag" system to alert county officials, as well as developers and landowners, of those areas that are most sensitive and which warrant careful scrutiny when zoning changes and development plans are proposed.

A final note concerning information constraints concerns the basic naivety of the public concerning biological issues. Very often, the difference between a development that is environmentally sensitive and one that is a biological disaster is simply a matter of explaining basic biological principles to the decision-makers. As a profession, we have been woefully negligent in this regard. In Tucson, it became clear that one of the most powerful conservation strategies involves public education. To develop public concern and appreciation for wildlife and to explain the opportunities for integrating wildlife conservation into the urban setting, we developed a simple booklet describing how wildlife conservation can be integrated into the metropolitan planning process and recommending policies to be adopted by the local governmental agencies (Shaw et al. 1986). This booklet is accompanied by a regional habitat map prepared in an attractive poster format as an additional public education tool.

INSTITUTIONAL AND ECONOMIC CONSTRAINTS

Human organizations are invariably resistant to change. One important step toward integrating wildlife conservation into the planning of cities involves changes in the responsibilities of the organizations responsible for wildlife. Until recently, most state wildlife agencies ignored or attempted to ignore urban wildlife issues. It has only been in recent years that state agencies have developed funding for nongame wildlife and been in a position to develop and staff urban wildlife programs.

Fortunately, the evolution of urban wildlife programs within state agencies has not occurred in isolation. Important changes in laws and institutions at the federal and local levels and within our educational systems are also occurring (Fig. 3). For example, the state wildlife agency has assumed a significant role in conserving urban habitats largely due to new planning and zoning policies that mandate reviews by the wildlife agency. Furthermore, the authority for enforcement often comes from federal legislation such as the Endangered Species Act, NEPA, and 404 permits required by the Clean Water Act of 1972.

There are two basic strategies for integrating wildlife conservation into metropolitan planning. One is to expand the roles of the state wildlife agency towards greater emphasis on urban wildlife programs. However, it may be a mistake to assume that any one agency can adequately address all the issues involved in conservation of urban wildlife. A second strategy is to expand the concerns of other entities to include wildlife conservation. This second strategy can be accomplished in two ways. One is to place trained wildlife biologists within the organizations that have the greatest impacts on habitats. Wildlife biologists are needed in such nontraditional roles as with planning and zoning authorities, landscape firms, or even engineering firms. A second approach is to integrate wildlife conservation into the curricula of engineers, landscape architects, planners, etc. In both cases, university wildlife programs will need to make some major changes in their programs.

CONCLUSIONS

Although we have described some significant progress toward developing a meaningful urban wildlife conservation program, we would be remiss not to mention some of the limitations and problems we have encountered.

For example, in Tucson, we have seen some innovative approaches to integrating wildlife conservation into new developments. However, these examples are almost entirely in expensive, low density housing. A major challenge is to

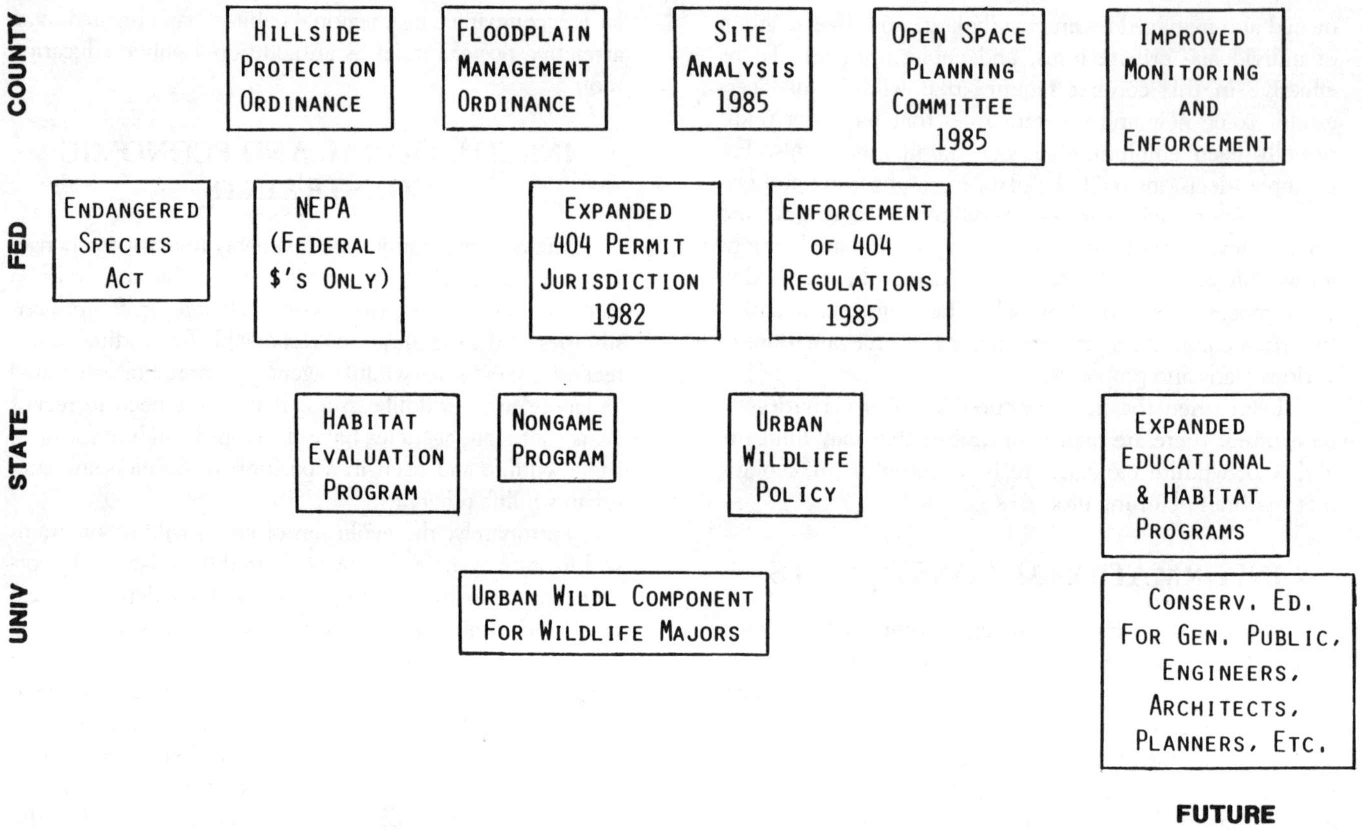

Fig. 3. County, federal, state, and university roles in urban wildlife conservation.

find ways to extend these conservation measures beyond the economically elite suburbs and into the middle and lower income housing that exists in much of the metropolitan area. We believe the best solution to this problem in Tucson is to develop an interconnected system of public open spaces that is built upon the riparian habitat associated with the watercourses that extend throughout the basin.

On paper, we are making significant progress towards incorporating wildlife habitat into the fabric and design of the community. Most major development proposals in Tucson now include significant open space and habitat components. However, nearly all conservation input occurs at the planning phases of development. We have some serious reservations concerning the actual implementation of conservation plans. It takes only one careless heavy equipment operator to obliterate valuable natural vegetation. In a desert environment, such damage is almost impossible to repair. What is needed is a mechanism for monitoring developments and enforcing the conservation elements called for in the development plans.

Finally, success in promoting wildlife conservation in metropolitan settings is entirely dependent upon public appreciation of wildlife and public understanding of the potential for enhancing wildlife in cities. To win support for these ideas, wildlife ecologists must come out of the wilderness and enter the urban arenas of public opinion formation. Fortunately, there are many compelling arguments for urban wildlife conservation programs. The preservation of critical habitats is often synonymous with environmental quality issues such as preserving recreational open space, aesthetics, and the regional character and identity of a community. Furthermore, practical concerns such as ground water recharge and appropriate uses of floodplains are usually consistent with habitat conservation programs. Because most people spend most of their lives in metropolitan settings, urban wildlife programs can be a powerful tool for developing public support for wildlife conservation in all kinds of environments.

REFERENCES CITED

Arizona Game and Fish Commission. 1986. Policy on urban wildlife. Adopted August, 1986.

Kellert, S.R. 1979. Public attitudes toward critical wildlife and natural habitat issues. USDI Fish and Wildl. Serv. and Yale School of For. and Environ. Studies.

Kellert, S.R. 1980. Activities of the American public relating to animals. Phase II Report. USDI Fish and Wild. Serv.

Ruther, S. 1986. Household survey of attitudes and beliefs of Tucsonans about wildlife and wildlife management. Personal communication of data to be published in 1987 M.Sc. Thesis.

Shaw, W.W. and W.R. Mangun. 1984. Nonconsumptive use of wildlife in the United States. USDI Fish and Wildl. Serv. Resour. Publ. 154.

Shaw, W.W., W.R. Mangun, and J.R. Lyons. 1985. Residential enjoyment of wildlife resources by Americans. Leisure Sci. 7: 361–375.

Shaw, W.W., J. Burns, and K. Stenberg. 1986. Wildlife habitats in Tucson: a strategy for conservation. Univ. of Arizona, School of Renewable Nat. Resour. 17pp + map.

Sikorowski, L. and S.J. Bissell, eds. 1986. County government and wildlife management: a guide to cooperative habitat development. Colorado Div. of Wildl. State Publ. Code DOW-R-M-1-86.

WMI. 1975. Current investments, projected needs and potential new sources of income for nongame fish and wildlife programs in the United States. Wildlife Management Institute, Washington, D.C. 93pp + Append.

Guidelines for Implementing Urban Wildlife Programs Under State Conservation Agency Administration

Report of the Urban Wildlife Committee of The Wildlife Society, prepared in collaboration with the Nongame Committee of the International Association of Fish and Wildlife Agencies[1]

DAVID L. TYLKA, *Missouri Department of Conservation, 1221 South Brentwood Blvd., St. Louis, MO 63117*

JOSEPH M. SCHAEFER, *Kansas Fish and Game Commission, P.O. Box 4750, Wichita, KS 67204*

LOWELL W. ADAMS, *National Institute for Urban Wildlife, 10921 Trotting Ridge Way, Columbia, MD 21044*

BACKGROUND

In July 1984, Dr. E. Charles Meslow, President, The Wildlife Society (TWS), charged the Urban Wildlife Committee with several assignments, one of which was to prepare a list of recommended urban wildlife program elements suitable for state wildlife agencies and a generalized job description of a state agency-employed urban wildlife biologist. The committee included two state agency urban biologists, two federal biologists, five university faculty members (two of whom were extension wildlife specialists), and four other practicing biologists, all with considerable urban wildlife-related experience. The committee's two state agency urban biologists, Joe Schaefer of Kansas, and David Tylka of Missouri, along with committee chairman Lowell Adams of the National Institute for Urban Wildlife, took the lead role in drafting these recommended guidelines. This report, prepared in collaboration with the Nongame Committee of the International Association of Fish and Wildlife Agencies (IAFWA), presents findings of the two committees and is in keeping with TWS's position statement on urban wildlife (adopted by Council on 11 October 1983) and the IAFWA's resolution, "Encouraging Management of Fish and Wildlife in Urban Environments," adopted 11 September 1984.

The suggested program elements outlined below are based in part on a report prepared by The Wildlife Society's Urban Affairs and Regional Planning Committee (predecessor to the Urban Wildlife Committee) and published in *The Wildlifer* (No. 180, May–June 1980). Also, state wildlife agencies with existing urban wildlife programs (as of 1983) were surveyed and asked to submit copies of job descriptions for their urban wildlife biologists. These were helpful in preparing the present report and copies of the job descriptions are on file at TWS headquarters in Bethesda, Maryland, and at IAFWA headquarters in Washington, D.C.

The objective of the present report is to provide guidance to state fish and wildlife agencies in establishing or modifying urban wildlife programs. Also, it is hoped the report will be useful to colleges and universities involved in wildlife training and research programs.

PROGRAM GOALS AND OBJECTIVES

The major goals of an urban wildlife program should be to establish and maintain diverse, self-sustaining urban wildlife populations at population levels in harmony with ecological, social, and economic values of the human community; to develop optimal levels of appreciation and use of urban wildlife and associated habitats; and to promote support for the state fish and wildlife agency. It is important that state conservation agencies understand who their urban clients are, what they want and will support, and how they perceive urban wildlife. We suggest that "urban wildlife" be construed to encompass non-domestic vertebrates and invertebrates of urban ecosystems.

[1]Adopted by Council of The Wildlife Society, 21 March 1986, and endorsed by the International Association of Fish and Wildlife Agencies, 16 September 1986.

Major objectives of state urban wildlife programs for meeting these goals might include:

1. conserving and managing the available fish and wildlife resources in such a way as to maintain, enhance, or create habitats for populations of desirable species,
2. enabling urban and suburban residents to enjoy to the fullest extent possible the fish and wildlife resources of their community,
3. educating residents so they can better appreciate the fish and wildlife resources and their ecological requirements and interrelationships, and
4. advocating sound, integrated wildlife control programs, including habitat alteration and/or removal of offending animals, to minimize conflicts between urban wildlife and people.

PROGRAM ELEMENTS AND JOB DESCRIPTION

As a first step in initiating an urban wildlife program, the agency may want to conduct or offer a training program for the existing professional staff designed to help them understand the importance, as well as other aspects, of the program. This could be accomplished through in-house training programs or by subsidizing the training of selected staff members at universities offering courses in urban-nongame wildlife management. In 1985, The Wildlife Society's Urban Wildlife Committee surveyed ninety-five North American colleges and universities with regard to teaching, and other activities related to urban wildlife. Results of that survey are available from the Society's headquarters in Bethesda, Maryland.

An efficient and effective urban wildlife program should be a key component of the state wildlife agency. Because the majority of the state's residents live in and around urban areas, urban wildlife has a great potential to be utilized, enjoyed, and appreciated. The urban-suburban environment is where most people interact and learn about wildlife and nature in general. A well-planned and operated urban wildlife program will enhance the public image of the state wildlife agency and will generate greater public support (including voter support) for all of the agency's activities.

An urban wildlife program should be tailored to blend with the existing programs of the wildlife agency as well as to fulfill the needs of urban residents and the urban resource. If an urban wildlife program is staffed by only one biologist, we recommend that the biologist function as a generalist by performing wildlife, fisheries, forestry, enforcement, information and education, and related duties. As urban programs grow and more personnel are assigned to metropolitan areas, a group of specialists can conduct their activities and operate more effectively as a team. For instance, if a wildlife agency has an education section whose people are the primary agency contacts with teachers, the urban wildlife biologists in that state would best serve as resource people for the agency's educational personnel. If the enforcement section of a wildlife agency has been given the primary responsibility of wildlife damage control, the urban biologists should again function in a resource capacity. If an agency lacks this organization or assignment of duties, the urban wildlife biologists may have to fill these roles.

Existing urban wildlife programs typically operate within the organizational structure of a nongame program. Therefore, we recommend that an urban wildlife component be part of a state's comprehensive conservation plan for fish and wildlife as defined by the Fish and Wildlife Conservation Act of 1980 (commonly referred to as the "Nongame Act"). It should be recognized that nongame programs (in rural and wilderness areas), rare and endangered species programs, and urban wildlife programs, though related, require quite different data collection and management activities and, therefore, should be recognized as different units in the organization of any conservation agency addressing these subjects. Nongame programs are commonly financed by state income tax check-offs, sales taxes, title fees, or other methods. Urban wildlife biologists are key persons to help stabilize or increase this funding (especially if the monies generated from state income tax check-offs are declining or the sales tax monies are in jeopardy of being lost). This point illustrates the need for urban wildlife biologists to be highly visible and proficient communicators.

To best address the needs of urban residents and the urban wildlife resource, states establishing urban wildlife programs are urged to set priorities for the activities of biologists. We recommend that urban wildlife biologists employed by state conservation agencies work closely with the Cooperative Extension Service, city and county recreation and planning departments, the local public school system, and citizen organizations. The most time-efficient methods should be stressed. Utilizing the media and addressing assemblages of leaders, teachers, etc. will facilitate dispensing information. Rather than spending valuable time personally alleviating wildlife conflicts and rescuing injured or orphaned animals, the urban wildlife biologists might well assist in the preparation of new materials and the distribution of existing materials that can be mailed to people. These materials should explain what is actually happening, why these situations occur, and what alternatives an individual himself can take to remedy these predicaments. Lists of live-trap sources, places to take injured wildlife, pest exterminators, and local organizations that offer on-site assistance should be made. It is especially important that the urban wildlife biologists not take on the label of the urban wildlife complaint officers who will individually solve every urban nuisance situation that arises. However, they should be available to assist with special or unique problems. Many routine nuisance calls can be remedied by receptionists and other trained and qualified agency personnel.

We recommend that an urban wildlife program incorporate four main elements as outlined below. Specific duties of urban wildlife biologists should reflect the challenges and opportunities available in a specific metropolitan area, as well as the personal abilities of the biologists assigned to that area.

I. Inventory and Research (5–25% of program budget)

Basic knowledge of urban wildlife species, populations, and habitats is limited. Results of investigations conducted in rural or wilderness areas often do not apply in urban areas. Information about urban wildlife is needed to develop appropriate management plans.

In order to satisfy public needs and effectively respond to requests for planning and management recommendations, an urban biologist should gather basic information on two levels.

A. Collect, organize, and interpret existing information obtained largely from the literature.
   1. Develop state and local lists of birds, mammals, fish, reptiles, amphibians, and some invertebrates, including rare, endangered, and threatened species found in urban and urbanizing areas.
   2. Obtain information on life history and habitat requirements of species found in urban and urbanizing areas, and where appropriate, recommended management methods. The National Institute for Urban Wildlife, in its quarterly newsletter, publishes a section entitled Current Research in Urban Wildlife Management designed to help inform others of ongoing or recently completed research in the area.
   3. Encourage publication of information relating to urban wildlife species, their habitat, and management potentials.

B. Conduct, either in-house or on a contract or other cooperative basis, research on wildlife in urban areas to obtain detailed knowledge on the characteristics of urban fish and wildlife populations and their habitats, and research of a socio-economic nature.
   1. Identify and map major habitat types in and around cities. For example, a St. Louis vegetative cover study was conducted with the aid of LANDSAT computer produced data that has application on regional, watershed, and municipal levels.
   2. Within each major habitat type, assess wildlife populations using accepted methodologies. Conduct life history and habitat studies for those species that are rare and endangered and for those species that studies have indicated are preferred by urban residents. Several permanent breeding bird transects have been established in city parks and different aged residential areas in Wichita, Kansas.
   3. Determine methods of reducing wildlife-related problems in urban and urbanizing areas.
   4. Survey public attitudes and perceptions about urban wildlife and associated habitats. Determine public preferences for various forms of wildlife. Studies of this sort may provide a vehicle for the development of ordinances to encourage establishment of urban wildlife habitat. States that have conducted surveys include Kansas, Missouri, New York, and Pennsylvania.
   5. Investigate how biotic and abiotic factors of the environment affect the populations of particular urban wildlife species. For example, Kansas is conducting an ongoing study to determine the effects of bird houses on urban cavity-nesting populations.
   6. Monitor any events that may adversely affect urban wildlife and habitat.
   7. Determine the value of urban wildlife and wildlife habitat to the physical and mental wellbeing of urban residents. Bird watching, nature walks, aesthetics, environmental education opportunities, and the economic and indirect benefits of wildlife habitat could be included. Concerns about wildlife, e.g., snake bites, transmission of diseases, and nuisance animals, should be dealt with objectively.
   8. Investigate the effectiveness of various existing planning and management measures, and develop improved techniques and approaches. Research is needed, for example, on the width of wildlife corridors, and on the size and configuration of wildlife sanctuaries in urban areas. Also, further research on the relative attractiveness to birds of various shrubs, trees, and herbaceous vegetation is needed. The effects on bird populations of extensive artificial feeding are poorly understood.

II. Wildlife Planning and Management (30–60% of program budget)

The urban biologist serves as the agency's lead representative in the management and enhancement of wildlife habitats in urban and urbanizing areas. The underlying objective focuses on maintaining or enhancing populations of desirable wildlife species and controlling populations of undesirable species.

The urban planning process is where major decisions are made and where there is a critical need for sound biological input to avoid or minimize impacts on wildlife. Special emphasis should be given to ensuring the input of wildlife biologists to planning groups because decisions concerning such things as dwelling unit densities, preservation of natural flowing streams and wetlands, and the distribution of open space are vital concerns.

A. Provide advisory services to city, county, regional, and federal governmental agencies; individuals; private developers; open space councils; civic groups, such as rotary clubs; sportsmen's groups, such as bass clubs; various organizations of planners, landscape architects, administrators, and park directors; and other groups, including nature organizations, such as Audubon and Sierra clubs. Wildlife management questions from individuals may be answered by telephone or by mail. The urban biologist should serve as a resource person by providing information that is not known or readily available to other office personnel.
   1. Furnish information on how to manipulate the biotic and abiotic components of the urban environment that affect the populations of various urban wildlife species. Examples include:
      a. Providing food plants for both adult and larval butterflies;
      b. Timing the mowing of a meadow to occur either in very early spring or immediately after ground nesting birds have finished nesting;
      c. Developing a nonmowing (or reduced mowing) policy for some meadows in public ownership, and burning fields to retard the growth of cool season grasses and encourage the growth of warm season grasses and forbs that tend to support more diverse wildlife communities;
      d. Applying soil amendments to enhance plant growth;
      e. Creating lizard habitat by providing rocks;
      f. Manipulating water levels to benefit shorebirds, waterfowl, and fish populations;
      g. Building multipurpose stormwater retention ponds;
      h. Controlling animals that are a nuisance or cause damage; and
      i. Planning construction work so that it will cause the least amount of environmental damage. This might include minimizing adverse environmental impacts by giving advice to government agencies concerning how such normally destructive activities as sewage disposal and road construction can be used in positive ways to enhance wildlife habitat. Although opportunities for guidance in effective urban-suburban wildlife management are greatest during the preplanning, planning, and construction stages of development, particularly in suburban and new town areas, opportunities still exist in areas already developed, including urban residential areas—even urban centers, especially in connection with redevelopment projects. State fish and wildlife agencies, in managing state-owned forests, parks, and refuges in urban areas, can set an example for managing other parts of a metropolitan area. In effect, these would be demonstration areas and, as such, be related to the states' role in wildlife extension and public education.
   2. Advocate the importance of recognizing wildlife in the planning process.

B. Stock or coordinate the stocking of desirable wildlife species into areas where they are lacking and conditions are favorable, and where stocking is a recommended management practice. For example, peregrine falcons have been hacked out on top of tall buildings in Baltimore, Maryland; New York City; and St. Louis, Missouri. Mississippi kites have been reintroduced into Memphis, Tennessee. Wild turkeys have been stocked in disjunct forested areas in Kansas City and St. Louis, Missouri. Chipmunks have been restored in Emporia, Kansas. Urban wildlife biologists should be in the forefront of these high-visibility projects.

III. Public Information, Education, and Extension Services (30–60% of program budget)

Public awareness and involvement are critical to the establishment and maintenance of a successful urban wildlife program. The program must be highly visible. Provisions should be made for public education at different age levels. Agencies might work with, and provide conservation education materials to, the state department of education and to schools at the elementary and secondary levels. In turn, school children and their teachers might provide valuable assistance on some types of wildlife conservation projects.

Public education can be enhanced through the use of demonstration areas to illustrate the effective management of wildlife. Natural areas should be established in or near large urban areas to provide these environmental education opportunities. Guidelines should be provided to ensure that natural areas afford optimum wildlife use and realize their full educational potential. Popularized publications that provide the public with information on urban wildlife management, and technical publications that acquaint other professionals with observations and findings, should be provided. Special emphasis should be given to publishing results of research on urban wildlife. Much of the management information available to date has been based on limited research.

An urban biologist should promote an appreciation of urban wildlife and wildlife habitat, urban wildlife recreational activities, nature and natural history, and the programs and activities of the agency that are designed to conserve and manage the wildlife resource. In this regard, an urban biologist should:

A. Develop a good rapport with, and furnish information through news releases or other means to, the newspaper, magazine, radio, and television media. Maintaining an annual phenological record of natural events will assist the urban biologist in preparing information-releases on a timely basis.

B. Write articles, organize slide presentations, conduct radio and television programs, and publish informational brochures, etc., on urban wildlife-nature topics. Information should be timely. Themes with a high human interest value will be given greater priority by the media. Work should be done with the assistance of (1) other agency personnel, and (2) local conservation groups and conservation authorities.

C. Maintain liaison with conservation, environmental, and other nature oriented organizations and coordinate agency programs with these groups.

D. Set up display booths and give programs at local flower, lawn, garden, and sport shows.

E. Present programs to school-teacher groups, nature organizations, garden clubs, homeowners' associations, senior citizen groups, civic organizations, and conservation groups.

F. Assist in developing interpretive-nature trails and nature centers (and their programs).

G. Organize public workshops, short courses, or conferences (backyard bird feeding, wildlife damage control, etc.).

H. Recognize individuals, groups, developers, or agencies for their efforts towards achieving the goals of the urban wildlife program. For example, Kansans who provide food, cover, and water for wildlife in their backyards can receive a free certificate and sign through the state urban wildlife program.

I. Communicate regularly with other urban conservation personnel and read the appropriate literature to stay informed of current information.

J. Implement educational programs to develop public understanding and acceptance of urban management practices, such as reduced mowing in some open space areas.

K. Work with existing educational networks such as the Cooperative Extension Service.

IV. Urban Habitat Acquisition, Development, Preservation, and Conservation (5–25% of program budget)

Significant habitat, including that harboring unique species, should be considered for purchase, especially if near urban areas or likely to be lost. Attention should be given to public access to acquired areas if such access is in keeping with the conservation objective and does not interfere with maintenance of desired fish and wildlife populations. Significant or critical urban habitat areas should be maintained and protected from development that would be detrimental to wildlife populations and to wildlife-recreational opportunities. We recommend that biologists work with city and regional planners in selecting areas for acquisition, and in devising best strategies for access.

Urban biologists should not overlook the potential for creating or developing wildlife habitat in urban or urbanizing areas. Cooperation with planners and landscape architects is recommended.

A. Investigate, evaluate, and recommend for purchase those tracts of land that are appropriate for urban wildlife-urbanite recreational usage, e.g., passive recreation such as birdwatching. The Missouri Department of Conservation gives priority to acquiring lands within 50 miles of metropolitan areas. Such lands in urban settings usually are designated "Urban Wild Acres" and are managed for maintenance and enhancement of wildlife habitat and for public use for birding, botanizing, hiking, and virtually any unstructured, non-destructive wildlife-related activity. In most cases, direct management is by a local governmental entity which provides police protection, litter clean-up, and, in some cases, interpretation. Leases are drafted so that wildlife values are fully protected and so that these tracts do not become parks. Missouri's experience has been quite successful; such tracts are heavily used and meet a need obviously felt by many urban residents, particularly those of limited mobility.

B. Develop methods and promote activities other than acquisition that would create, preserve, or conserve urban wildlife habitats and provide outdoor recreational opportunities like fishing on water supply reservoirs. Land acquisition in urban areas can be expensive, therefore alternatives to purchase, such as easements, sanctuary designation, zoning, or the dedication of permanent open space (with appropriate management), should be considered. For example, wetland wildlife habitat can be created or developed in many urban or urbanizing areas in conjunction with modern stormwater management practices. And, by promoting principles of land use planning such as cluster development that result in substantial open space areas in urban situations, significant wildlife habitat can be provided.

QUALIFICATIONS FOR AN URBAN WILDLIFE BIOLOGIST

Each urban area has its own identity. Therefore, the desired qualifications for an urban wildlife biologist should reflect the challenges and opportunities available in the metropolitan area(s) that will be serviced by the position. Although urban wildlife biologists rely heavily on their wildlife training and experience, they usually function as generalists. Therefore, an urban biologist should:

- Know the fundamental concepts of modern wildlife management (e.g., know how to manipulate the components of the environment to affect carrying capacity),
- Be familiar with the community approach to wildlife management,
- Be familiar with scientific methodologies (e.g., sampling and inventory techniques),
- Be able to recognize and evaluate the effects of urbanization on habitat (e.g., the effects of stream channelization, mowing practices, use of pesticides, construction of residential and commercial developments, etc.),
- Be able to integrate wildlife concerns into urban development and landscape design projects,
- Know identifying characteristics, life histories, and habitat requirements of highly visible and unique wildlife species (birds, butterflies, snakes, etc.),
- Be able to identify and relate wildlife utilization of local native flora and cultivated plant varieties (e.g., butterfly nectar sources, berry producing shrubs and trees, nesting cover, etc.),
- Have a basic understanding of nature interpretation techniques (e.g., selecting those natural subjects and presenting them in a way that appeals best to the human senses),
- Be a good communicator (written and oral) at both technical and popular levels,
- Have a good working knowledge of audio-visual equipment (e.g., cameras, projectors, etc.),
- Be willing and able to interview with mass media people,
- Have a pleasing personality and be able to effectively solicit intra- and inter-agency support for the urban wildlife program (i.e., able to work well with others),
- Have a basic understanding of municipal, county, state, and federal administration and planning operations, and environmental laws and regulations,
- Be willing and able to handle and solve urban wildlife damage and nuisance complaints, and
- Be able to evaluate public attitudes and execute a program of action to earn public understanding.

TRAINING AND EXPERIENCE FOR AN URBAN WILDLIFE BIOLOGIST

I. Experience

Preferences should be given to candidates with 3 or more years of experience as a wildlife biologist or other related position, and to candidates with work experience in urban areas. Graduate work at the masters or doctorate level on some aspect of urban wildlife may be substituted for 1 or 2 years, respectively, of professional work experience. Preferences also might be given to biologists who have been certified by The Wildlife Society or who have equivalent qualifications.

II. Education

Because of the potential impact of this position on the agency and the necessity of the urban wildlife biologist to work on a variety of unique wildlife problems with confidence and knowledge, a master's degree in a wildlife-related major and a diverse academic course background are recommended.

Required courses should cover the following subject areas:

Biology, vertebrate (including fishery), and invertebrate
Botany, dendrology, and forestry
Ecology
Entomology, herpetology, mammalogy, and ornithology
Public speaking
Taxonomy, plant and vertebrate-invertebrate
Techniques, vertebrate and invertebrate inventory
Wildlife management, principles and practices
Writing, technical and popular

Other preferred subject areas include:

Audio-visual techniques and operation
Chemistry, organic
Economics
Education
Environmental impact assessment
Extension, including animal damage control
Geology and soils
Horticulture and landscape architecture
Ichthyology
Lake and pond management
Nature interpretation
Psychology
Public administration and public relations
Urban sociology, government, and planning

Urban Wildlife Committee: A.D. Geis, F.F. Gilbert, W.P. Gorenzel, D.L. Leedy, J.R. Lyons, D.A. Manski, W.C. McComb, J.M. Schaefer, L.M. Talbot, D.L. Tylka, L.W. VanDruff, G.J. San Julian, and L.W. Adams, Chairman.

Nongame Committee: L.W. Adams, A. Brohn, B. Cowgill, D. DeCarli, P.S. Duncan, A. Egbert, T.M. Franklin, E. Hansen, J. Harn, W. Height, C. Henderson, P. Herig, J.L. Herring, R. Hess, K. Jackson, L.R. Jahn, T. Johnson, D.L. Leedy, J. Lipscomb, J.R. Lyons, P. McLain, J.M. Meyers, R. Miles, D. Miller, P. Myers, R. Nicotera, W.L. Pamplin, Jr., D. Paul, B. Radtkey, T.A. Reynolds, J. Smith, J. Sunderland, G. Swanson, G.J. Taylor, G. Tsukamoto, R. Turner, R.L. Wallenstrom, S.E. Wright, B. Zeedyk, and S. Wilson, Chairman.

Identifying and Targeting Urban Publics

JOSEPH M. SCHAEFER, *Kansas Fish and Game Commission, P.O. Box 4750, Wichita, KS 67204*

Wildlife biologists acquire many specialized skills through education, training, and experience. We know how to establish and maintain self-sustaining wildlife populations. Census techniques, habitat suitability indexes, and methods to improve environmental conditions for wildlife are familiar tools of our profession. But all of this knowledge is useless if our publics do not understand our rationale or accept our recommendations. Knowing whom to contact and how to gain their cooperation and support are key elements in any successful wildlife program.

In the past, our public relations efforts have targeted the needs and concerns of relatively homogeneous sportsmen's groups. Mutually beneficial relationships were easily developed between wildlife user groups and conservation agencies. Sportsmen paid the bills and in return were provided various services and recreational opportunities.

However, the old tools and approaches are not effective in our modern cities. Urban residents' life styles, attitudes, priorities, and opinions are diverse. Metropolitan environments are fast-paced and competitive. There are many recreational opportunities to exploit, and numerous causes to support. Multiple land-use strategies are a necessity. Time is of the essence.

Other successful service organizations, such as banks and insurance companies, have survived in competitive markets by effectively influencing public opinion. Marketing analysts, public relations officers, and sales departments identify potential publics or markets, find out their needs, and then develop services or deliver messages that meet the demands of each separate public. All of the technical knowledge of handling money and protecting investments is of no avail if these companies cannot convince the public to use their services.

Urban wildlife biology is an extremely people-oriented profession. We spend most of our time communicating with various publics rather than working directly with the wildlife resource or its habitat. Yet, ironically, we receive very little, if any, formal training in communications, public relations, and marketing. We have to learn through our own experiences. A few wildlife authors have addressed the general topic of public relations in the natural resources profession (Schoenfeld 1957, Chaplin 1971, Gilbert 1971). But no references specifically related to gaining public support for urban wildlife programs are available.

In this paper, I have suggested a philosophy and approach that integrate biological and human dimensions in establishing urban wildlife projects (Fig. 1). Appendix A provides a checklist to use when developing urban wildlife projects.

CONCERN

The first step is to identify a concern upon which to build a project. The concern may already be addressed in the overall plan for your urban wildlife program or it may be spontaneously introduced. Before any action is taken,

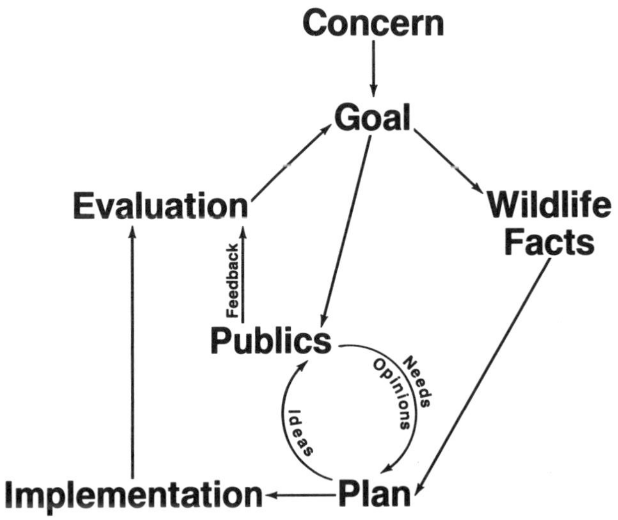

Fig. 1. Public relations model for urban wildlife projects.

Integrating Man and Nature in the Metropolitan Environment. Proc. Natl. Symp. on Urban Wildl., Chevy Chase, Md., 4–7 November 1986, L.W. Adams and D.L. Leedy, eds. Published by Natl. Inst. for Urban Wildl., 10921 Trotting Ridge Way, Columbia, MD 21044, 1987.

priorities must be examined. The concern must be put into the proper perspective. Is it addressed in the comprehensive urban plan? If not, does it belong? Will it help you to accomplish the primary objective of your urban program? If so, are you at a point where you can properly address this concern? Or, do some preliminary objectives have to be achieved first? For example, existing habitat should be evaluated before habitat improvement concerns are addressed.

A concern does not necessarily have to be a "problem." Perhaps a situation might simply be improved or a potential problem prevented. Sometimes it depends on your perspective. Is the lack of conservation easements a problem? Are trying to spend a $1 million corporate donation on urban wildlife and scheduling weekly radio spots on five different stations problems?

Several concerns may be closely related. Try to combine them into one statement. If this cannot be done satisfactorily, isolate and treat them separately.

Once the concern is identified, write it down. It may provide needed justification if the reason for your project is ever questioned.

GOAL

The next step is to transform the concern into a goal or primary objective. Again, write it down. This statement is like the title of a "how to" book. It tells what you would like to accomplish.

The goal must be feasible, acceptable to those involved, definable or clearly understood, and measurable. Are these criteria met in the following goals?

- To develop a breeding bird list for Montgomery County, Maryland, by 1 January 1987.
- To increase agency acceptance, support, and participation in the urban program.
- To increase and maintain attendance at the Pawnee Prairie Nature Trail to 500 people visits per week from 1 June to 1 September 1987.
- To establish native prairies at least one-half acre (0.2 ha) in size at 10 different open space sites in Memphis, Tennessee by 1 July 1988.

The goal statement provides direction for the rest of the planning process. From this statement, you can identify the types of wildlife and public information needed.

WILDLIFE FACTS

Collecting wildlife facts related to a goal is a familiar practice for wildlife biologists. However, there are a few precautions that I would like to point out.

Basic knowledge of urban wildlife species, populations, and habitats is limited. Results of investigations conducted in rural or wilderness areas and traditional wildlife techniques often do not apply in urban areas.

Be sure the facts are obtained from a competent source. Remember, this information will be used to convince your publics—so it had better be reliable.

Do not extrapolate data just to support your position. If you know of no incidents when Mississippi kites *(Ictinia mississippiensis)* have actually struck a passer-by in an attempt to protect their nestlings, do not state that they *never* will do so.

Collect factual information, not assumptions. If no data are available on a particular topic, it might be treated as a separate concern worth addressing through research.

PUBLICS

The next step is to identify publics and collect facts about each. Your publics are the people whose acceptance and support are necessary to achieve your goal. They include those who will be involved with planning, communication, or implementing the project, and those who will be affected by or merely concerned about it.

Do not overlook internal publics. If people within your agency are not advocates of your project, this potentially will have a negative impact on other publics with which they come into contact.

If I had a goal to provide a complete set of Wildlife Habitat Conservation Teacher's Pacs to 10 Wichita, Kansas, elementary schools during the 1986–87 school year, one internal public I would want to contact would be the Kansas Fish and Game Commission's Education Coordinator. Agency law enforcement personnel probably should be included in any projects relating to animal damage control.

External publics can be involved in projects for many reasons. Sometimes one public is needed to influence another one. For example, media sources might be included to provide information to the general urban public who, in turn, will be needed to express their support to elected government officials who have the authority to enact laws that will prevent development of floodplains.

You may need landowner permission, help from volunteers, and cooperation from local developers. National and local conservation organizations may be able to assist you.

When I developed a plan to establish an eastern chipmunk *(Tamias striatus)* population in Watson Park, Wichita, by releasing individuals obtained from Tennessee, I identified the following individuals and publics: coordinator of the Tennessee Nongame and Endangered Species Program, director of the Tennessee Wildlife Resources Agency, director of the Kansas Fish and Game Commission, Republic Airlines, my supervisor, Kansas Nongame Wildlife Advisory Council, Fish and Game staff working in the Wichita area, other Fish and Game personnel, Wichita State University Biology Department, Watson Park's manager and his staff, city naturalist, director of Wichita Park Board, Watson Park neighbors, Animal Damage Control supervisor, Wichita parks maintenance supervisor, Watson Park users, media sources, agency Information and Education staff, Wichita area residents, Nongame Tax Checkoff Contributors, and all Kansas taxpayers.

Publics will vary among projects and may differ for similar projects conducted at separate locations. Write down all of the publics for each project to help prevent overlooking anyone, especially those who expect to be involved.

After publics have been identified, facts about your audience should be collected. You have to find out their existing and potential needs, wants, current level of awareness and knowledge, attitudes, and opinions. Be a good listener and learn as much as you can about your publics. Conduct surveys, talk to representatives of various groups, organize facilitated discussion workshops and public meetings, and schedule appointments with individuals. Determine what motivates your public to action before you develop a communications strategy to enlist their support.

Facts about the important publics are inseparable from and equally as important as the wildlife facts you collect. Rational decisions can be made only after assessing available pertinent information. Intuitive decisions should be reserved for situations involving less important consequences. Again, you should not make assumptions or extrapolate data.

PLAN

Now you are ready to formulate a plan by organizing the information you have acquired about wildlife and your publics into objectives and action items. If you can relate your goal to the title of a book, then consider the objectives to be the table of contents, and the action items to be the words of each chapter.

The step-down planning technique described by Phenicie and Lyons (1973) is a method that uses logical reasoning to obtain precise statements of objectives. Briefly, the step-down plan involves reducing the primary objective or goal into less complex subordinate objectives until terminal items are reached. Terminal items are recognized as actions that can be performed or are candidates for solution by research, literature review, consultations, and experimentation. Each subordinate objective statement is included in the final plan only if it is necessary to accomplish the goal. An essential step in this process is to test for validity, using the conditional sentence, "If, and only if, (lower echelon objective) then (higher echelon objective)," each time a lower echelon of objectives is derived.

Plan development is from the top down, from the complex to the less complex. Execution of the plan is from the bottom up, from terminal items to the primary objective.

The step-down planning process is easy to follow and has provided good results for me. I strongly recommend that this or some other systematic approach be used to increase proficiency, to provide a well defined focus, and to assist in coordinating activities within a project.

If your goal is related to establishing or maintaining wildlife populations, plan development should start with objectives and action items that are biologically sound and based on the wildlife facts you have collected. Then incorporate the anticipated publics whose acceptance is needed to achieve your objectives. Follow this with a description of the proper messages and informational tools to be used for each public.

Your plan must be flexible enough to be revised if new information is gathered or if a different perspective is obtained. Ideas generated in the first draft then should be presented and discussed with your publics. Involve them in the planning process and let them know that their input is important. Show that you have listened to them and are addressing their concerns and needs. This two-way communication will be effective and appreciated.

This stage can be thought of as a pre-test. You are trying to get enough feedback on your proposed project to predict if your publics will accept it. If you receive strong opposition to any aspects, you have the options to leave it as is, to address the expressed opposition by changing the project, to negotiate a compromise, or to use a different type of communications approach in explaining your proposal.

When tentative ideas to establish chipmunks in Wichita were shared with park-user representatives, a concern was raised about the possibility of introducing diseases such as rabies. Neighbors and animal damage control personnel also questioned if the chipmunks could become a nuisance in the area surrounding the park. Aside from these concerns, the facts we collected from our publics indicated that this project will generate a great deal of support.

In your plan, the duties of participants should be clearly defined and expenses budgeted. Every aspect should be covered so there are no surprises. Poorly planned projects are responsible for many of the brush fires that conservation agencies are always trying to put out.

Once you are satisfied with your plan, you are ready to communicate it to all of your publics. Use the various planned communications methods to present the information about your project in a way that can be easily understood and accepted. Remember, you are trying to influence public opinion. Some communications strategies may only involve one telephone conversation or a short letter. Others will be more complex.

Explain how this project will benefit your public. Make your message appeal to their senses. Which of the following has the more effective message? "This new nature trail will provide more opportunities for area residents to observe wildlife and their natural habitats." "This new nature trail will give you an opportunity to watch a deer quietly feeding on native grasses, to hear a woodpecker drumming on a tree trunk, and to feel the rough,hard shell of a box turtle as it crosses the trail in front of you." Audio-visual tapes are extremely effective in relating realistic benefits.

Whenever you want to communicate a message to a large diverse group, networking techniques should be used. Networking involves selecting the most efficient means to spread the word. Commercial print and electronic news media are the most commonly used tools, but others also are available. Direct mailing, piggy-back mailings, employee newsletters, utility company inserts, organizational newsletters, tax preparers, community leaders, teachers, bird seed distributors, garden club and nurserymen's associations, and local extension agents can be helpful in certain situations. Presenting information to 50 school children is effective on a small scale, but not very efficient. Just as much time could be spent giving the same program to 50 teachers, but the eventual audience would be tremendously increased.

When working with the news media, do not expect reporters to cover every project. News directors try to gain support from their public by providing them with a broad array of newsworthy events. They might be more likely to cover one urban wildlife topic once a month rather than weekly. So plan your news releases accordingly. However, weekly scheduled radio or television programs are not out of the question, especially if you can find a sponsor.

Before implementing the actual project, allow enough lead time for your publics to understand and accept your goal. Soliciting public support is actually a continuous process. Gaining basic confidence and trust is certainly helpful before approval is needed for individual projects.

IMPLEMENTATION

The project should be implemented as planned. Any deviations may alter public opinion. If a last minute change is necessary, inform the publics why. The project coordinator is responsible for ensuring that all participants properly execute their jobs.

EVALUATION

Some project evaluation should occur continuously. If public opposition or other problems occur, they should be dealt with immediately. Feedback from publics is an important evaluation tool.

When the project is completed, a final evaluation should be made. This information should be recorded and used to improve your approach when addressing a similar concern in the future.

Because you originally identified a measurable goal, you can now determine if it was accomplished. If not, how close did you come? What problems did you encounter?

If the goal was achieved and the project is viewed as a success, the results should be publicized. Again, appropriate tools and messages should be planned. Telling publics when you did a good job helps to establish a credible image, which will help to sell future projects.

Hopefully, the process I have outlined will assist those working on urban wildlife projects to effectively use public opinion information during their planning phases. Too often, biologically sound projects fail because they are chosen for the wrong reasons and the appropriate publics are not properly targeted.

REFERENCES CITED

Chaplin, B.R. 1971. Public relations and the wildlife administrator. Pages 18–21 *in* R. Teague, ed. A manual of wildlife conservation. The Wildlife Society, Washington, D.C.

Gilbert, D.L. 1971. Natural resources and public relations. The Wildlife Society, Washington, D.C. 320 pp.

Phenicie, C.K. and J.R. Lyons. 1973. Tactical planning in fish and wildlife management and research. Bureau of Sport Fisheries and Wildlife, Res. Publ. 123.

Schoenfeld, C.A. 1957. Public relations aspects of wildlife management. J. Wildl. Manage. 21:70–74.

APPENDIX A

Checklist to Use When Developing Urban Wildlife Projects.

1. *Identify the Concern.*
   a. Is it already addressed in the comprehensive urban plan?
   b. If not, does it belong?
   c. Will it help you to accomplish the primary objective of your urban program?
   d. Do some preliminary objectives have to be addressed first?
   e. Did you combine closely related concerns?
   f. Did you write down the concern?
2. *Transform the Concern into a Goal.*
   a. Did you write down the goal?
   b. Is the goal statement like a title of a "how to" book?
   c. Is it feasible?
   d. Is it acceptable?
   e. Is it definable?
   f. Is it measurable?
3. *Collect Pertinent Wildlife Facts.*
   a. Are you using traditional wildlife information?
   b. If so, does it apply to urban areas?
   c. Did you extrapolate data?
   e. Did you collect facts or assumptions?
   f. Does it need more research?
4. *Identify Publics.*
   a. Is their support necessary to achieve your goal?
   b. Are they involved in planning, communicating, or implementing the project?
   c. Will they be affected by the project or merely concerned about it?

d. Did you list all of the internal publics?
e. Is anyone needed to influence another public?
f. Have you missed anyone who expects to be involved?
g. Did you write down all of your publics?

5. *Collect Facts About Publics.*
   a. Do you know their needs, wants, current level of awareness and knowledge, attitudes, and opinions?
   b. Are you a good listener?
   c. Are you using appropriate methods to collect your facts?
   d. Do you know what motivates your publics to action?
   e. Did you collect facts or assumptions?
   f. Did you extrapolate data?
   g. Are your data current and reliable?

6. *Develop a Plan.*
   a. Did you start with objectives and action items that were based on wildlife facts?
   b. Did you then incorporate anticipated publics and describe the proper messages and informational tools to use for each?
   c. Do you have a well-defined focus for your plan?
   d. Is your plan logical?
   e. Are your objectives related to your goal like a table of contents is related to the title of a book?
   f. Will it be easy to coordinate and execute this plan?
   g. Is your plan flexible enough to be revised if necessary?
   h. Are the duties of project participants clearly defined?
   i. Are expenses budgeted?

7. *Communicate Ideas to the Publics.*
   a. Did you communicate your tentative ideas to your publics?
   b. Did you involve publics in the planning process?
   c. Was opposition to any aspects expressed?
   d. If so, how did you address this opposition?
   e. Did you communicate the final plan to all of your publics before it was implemented?
   f. Did you explain how the project will benefit the publics?
   g. Did you use networking techniques wherever appropriate?

8. *Implement the Project.*
   a. Did you allow enough lead time after the communication phase?
   b. Was the project implemented as planned?
   c. Were any last minute changes made?
   d. If so, did you tell your publics why?

9. *Evaluate Success.*
   a. Have you been evaluating continuously?
   b. Did public opposition occur?
   c. If so, how was it dealt with?
   d. Was your goal accomplished?
   e. If not, how close did you come?
   f. What problems did you encounter?
   g. If done again, what would you change?
   h. If successful, did you publicize the results?

The Role of Wetland Regulation in Preserving Wildlife Habitat in Suburban Environments

MICHAEL A. AURELIA, *Inland Wetlands and Watercourses Agency, Town Hall, 101 Field Point Road, Greenwich, CT 06830*

Significant wildlife habitats can be protected and preserved through an effective wetland regulatory program. In Connecticut, there are two wetland regulatory programs that are implemented by three different levels of government. Tidal wetlands are regulated at the federal level by the U.S. Army Corps of Engineers (COE) and at the state level by the Connecticut Department of Environmental Protection (DEP). In certain restricted situations, tidal wetlands also can be regulated at the local, municipal level. Although inland wetlands and watercourses are primarily regulated at the local level by Connecticut municipalities, there also is a role for the COE and DEP.

As one might expect with any three-tiered regulatory program, the three levels of government sometimes work closely together in a coordinated manner and at other times act as a check and balance system. The final result usually is the preservation of significant wetland habitats.

TIDAL (COASTAL) WETLAND REGULATION

The Federal Role

The COE—New England division, regulates coastal wetlands in Connecticut under Section 10 of the Rivers and Harbors Act of 1899, and Section 404 of the Clean Water Act. Typically, the New England Division reviews 60 to 70 applications per year involving coastal resources of Connecticut. Only a handful of these applications involve the potential destruction of tidal wetlands. In most instances, the activities also are reviewed at the state level by the DEP. Most of the COE permit applications involve dredging of existing channels and alteration of private or public docks, piers, and bulkheads.

The public and concerned federal, state, and local officials may comment on specific applications by responding to "Public Notices" released by the COE. A comment period of 30 days is usually observed. Public hearings are sometimes held for the purpose of obtaining additional public input when a large number of people express concern about a specific application.

Application NEDOD-R-12-84-117 of the USM Corporation-Pop Fastener Division of Shelton, Connecticut, illustrates the COE involvement in tidal wetlands regulation. The USM Corporation proposed to undertake remedial action at a former metal hydroxide sludge lagoon site adjacent to the Housatonic River in Shelton, Connecticut. The project included:

1. the rehabilitation and extension of an existing access road along Ivy Brook,
2. the removal of observable sludge from tidal flats, wetlands and uplands,
3. the consolidation, capping, and reinforcing of sludge material at an adjacent upland, and
4. rehabilitation of wetlands.

The final result of COE involvement in this application will be the restoration of a 1.1-acre (1a = 0.405 ha) wetland area and a 0.6-acre tidal flat area. The Connecticut Tidal Wetland Act did not allow DEP involvement. DEP's Hazardous Waste Unit did, however, require the lagoon's cleanup, and its Water Resources Unit regulated those activities below mean high water on the tidal flat under Sections 22a-361 and 22a-98 of the Connecticut General Statutes and Section 401 of the Federal Water Pollution Control Act as amended. The lagoon area and adjacent river shoreline provided limited habitat for waterfowl, songbirds, and small mammals. The removal of a heavy metal contamination site, and the restoration of 1.1 acres of riverine wetland will significantly enhance wildlife habitat. Without COE involvement at this site, the 1.1-acre restoration project would not have been possible.

Integrating Man and Nature in the Metropolitan Environment. Proc. Natl. Symp. on Urban Wildl., Chevy Chase, Md., 4–7 November 1986, L.W. Adams and D.L. Leedy, eds. Published by Natl. Inst. for Urban Wildl., 10921 Trotting Ridge Way, Columbia, MD 21044, 1987.

The State Role

Tidal wetlands also are regulated by the DEP under Public Act 695 passed in 1969 (Sections 22a-28 through 22a-35 of the Connecticut General Statutes). "Tidal wetlands" are defined as "those areas which border on or lie beneath tidal waters, such as, but not limited to: banks, bogs, salt marsh, swamps, meadows, flats or other low lands subject to tidal action, including those areas now or formerly connected to tidal waters, and whose surface is at or below an elevation of one foot above local extreme high water; and upon which may grow or be capable of growing some but not necessarily all of the following:" (an extensive list of wetland plant species).

In order to be regulated, the "tidal wetlands" must be delineated on official tidal wetlands maps that are filed in the offices of the DEP Water Resources Unit, and municipal town clerks. More than 40 of Connecticut's 169 towns are affected by this wetland regulation.

Activities that are subject to regulation include dredging, excavating, draining, filling, or constructing structures within the bounds of designated tidal wetlands. Permits to perform regulated activities must be obtained from the DEP. The application process provides for the publication of a legal notice describing the proposed activities and a public comment period of 30 days. A public hearing can be scheduled on the application if the Commissioner of Environmental Protection concludes the activities are likely to have a significant impact on the affected tidal wetland. The hearing often is waived by the Commissioner when impacts are not significant. Twenty-five citizens can petition a public hearing on a specific application, however. Although the majority of DEP public hearings are scheduled in Hartford at 10:00 a.m. on weekdays, significant public concern often results in the scheduling of a public hearing in the affected community during evening hours. Local officials often play a critical role during the application review process. Public officials can comment directly about an application. Conservation commissions and/or inland wetlands agencies often provide an opportunity for public input at local public meetings.

As a result of Connecticut's public policy to preserve tidal wetlands and prevent their despoliation, very few tidal wetlands have been destroyed through the permit application process. The DEP reviews 40 to 50 applications per year dealing with tidal wetlands. Most applications are for the construction of pile timber piers over wetlands, the installation of stormwater or sanitary sewer lines, the replacement of existing bridges, and the installation of bulkheads or riprap. When applications involve the excavation or filling of tidal wetlands for marinas or condominiums, wetland creation or restoration at a ratio of 1.5 to 1 often is proposed. That is, 1.5 times the wetland area lost will be created or restored. Rarely are ecologically viable tidal wetland areas destroyed through this mitigation process.

Application TWSD-H-86-141 of WRG Limited Partnership—Guilford, Connecticut, illustrates the DEP's involvement in tidal wetlands regulation. WRG submitted an application to rehabilitate and expand marina facilities at the Guilford Yacht Club site on the West River in Guilford, Connecticut. The proposed activities included dredging, installation of bulkheads and riprap, and the construction of docks and floats within or adjacent to tidal wetlands. Three-tenths of an acre of designated wetlands were to be destroyed, 193 slips would be created, 173 slips would be sold to the general public as dockaminiums, and 20 slips would be rented to members of the Guilford Yacht Club. Dredging 112,500 cubic yards (86,062 m^3) of material from the West River channel also was part of the application and regulated under Sections 22a-361 and 22a-98 of the Connecticut General Statutes and Section 401 of the Federal Water Pollution Control Act as amended. Dredge spoil was to be disposed of in an approved site in Long Island Sound.

This application was the second one submitted by WRG for the project. The first application, TWSD-H-83-210, went through a lengthy review process that resulted in the denial of the application by DEP Commissioner Stanley Pac on 7 November 1985. The original application would have destroyed 36,000 square feet (3,344 m^2) of wetland and allowed for the creation of 52,000 square feet (4,830 m^2) of wetland. Additional impacts on tidal flats, shellfish resources, and an upstream aquaculture facility contributed to the denial.

The WRG—Guilford Yacht Club site consists of 23 acres surrounded by hundreds of acres of viable saltmarsh. Originally all 23 acres consisted of viable high and low saltmarsh communities. In the late 1950's, however, almost 14 acres were diked and filled, leaving 1 acre of open water and 8 acres of high and low *Spartina* marsh. The revised application addressed almost all of the significant environmental objections to the first application. The new proposal would:

- reduce the number of boat slips by 20,
- reduce dredging impacts on intertidal mud flats,
- reduce wetland impacts to 13,000 square feet (1,208 m^2),
- provide for the creation of 20,000 square feet (1,858 m^2) of salt marsh,
- provide an easement for public access to the West River,
- establish a detailed water quality monitoring program,
- create a habitat protection plan that included the creation of 25- to 30-foot (7.6–9.2 m) vegetated buffers adjacent to viable tidal wetland areas, and
- provide an alternate water source if necessary for the upstream aquaculture facility.

On 19 August 1986, Hearing Examiner William S. McGee recommended that the application for permit be approved, with 22 conditions. One significant condition required the posting of a performance bond or financial security to ensure the creation or restoration of the tidal wetlands. The application presently awaits action by Commissioner Stanley Pac.

Actions by concerned citizens, environmental groups, and local and state officials worked to protect the significant wildlife habitats associated with the West River salt marshes. This application was one in which activities associated with recreational boating activities could have significantly reduced wildlife habitat value in the vicinity of the WRG site.

The Connecticut Tidal Wetlands Act has undergone significant court challenges and so far has endured them all. One case involved the Stratford Land and Improvement Company that in 1970 proposed to fill and dredge 277 acres of salt marsh in Stratford, Connecticut. After a lengthy public hearing process, the application was denied and the denial appealed to the Connecticut Superior Court. The appeal process continued until 25 July 1986 when Judge Robert Satter issued a vague decision requiring the DEP staff to "work with and provide guidance for the Stratford Land and Improvement Company to indicate what development of the wetlands is likely to be acceptable." It should be noted that alternatives involving the destruction of between 131 and 277 acres of tidal wetland had already been rejected by the DEP Commissioner. It is anticipated that the applicant will submit a revised application, which, if denied, will return to the Superior Court. Although Public Act 695 has preserved the wildlife habitat value of 277 acres of tidal wetland for more than 16 years, Connecticut's tidal wetlands still are threatened.

FRESH WATER WETLAND REGULATION

Although inland wetlands and watercourses are regulated primarily by individual Connecticut municipalities under Public Act 155 passed in 1972, both the DEP and COE play a role as well. The DEP regulates inland wetlands and watercourses in those towns that chose not to regulate at the local level under Sections 22a-36 through 45 of the Connecticut General Statutes. The COE regulates freshwater wetlands primarily under Section 404 of the Clean Water Act. Presently, all but 13 of Connecticut's 169 towns regulate freshwater wetlands at the local level. If wetlands are regulated by the municipality, a citizen board or agency is the controlling authority. Special inland wetland agencies, conservation commissions, planning and zoning commissions, or environmental protection boards have been appointed the regulating authorities. Citizen membership on the board or commission varies between five and 11 individuals. Although most boards or commissions do not have staff, many have part-time clerical or professional help and a few have one or more full time professional staff members.

"Inland wetlands" are defined by soil type in Connecticut. Soil types designated as poorly drained, very poorly drained, alluvial, and floodplain by the National Cooperative Soils Survey of the Soil Conservation Service of the U.S. Department of Agriculture are wetland soils.

"Watercourses" are rivers, streams, waterways, lakes, ponds, marshes, bogs, and all other bodies of water natural or artificial, public or private, which are contained within, flow through, or border on this state or any portion thereof not regulated pursuant to Sections 22a-28 to 22a-35 of the Connecticut General Statutes.

The Municipal Role

All local wetland regulators and DEP officials are empowered by the same state statute, and all local regulations must be in conformance with DEP wetland regulations. There are variations in the implementation of the regulation from town to town, however. The variations are due in part to differences in individual philosophy, the availability of professional staff, and the pressures created by development in specific communities. Some municipal agencies, especially in those areas where development pressure is the greatest, set a very conservative policy and minimize wetland-watercourse encroachments through the use of setbacks and mitigation actions. Other agencies, especially in communities that encourage development, issue permits for activities in wetlands without detailed environmental assessments or evaluation of less destructive alternatives.

The Greenwich Inland Wetland and Watercourses Agency (GIW&WCA) is a municipal board with seven members and three alternates. It has a three-member professional staff—a director, senior wetland analyst, and a compliance officer—and use of a five-member clerical pool shared with the Conservation Commission and Planning and Zoning Commission. During the last two calendar years, the Agency has reviewed 200 applications per year. Although most applications are to construct single family residences, a substantial number involve tennis courts, swimming pools, residential additions, subdivision roadways, and stormwater detention structures.

Since 1973, when local wetland regulation took effect, the Agency has attempted to develop wetland protection standards that can be used by engineering and planning professionals in designing developments. Guideline setbacks are the heart of these standards (see Appendix A). Setbacks vary in different watersheds of the town. Minimum setbacks are greater in watersheds that are tributary to the town's drinkable surface water supply system. Setbacks also vary with the activity proposed, e.g., construction of a house, roadway, septic system, or animal stable. Minimum guideline setbacks vary between 25 feet and 200 feet (7.6–61.0 m). Unlike some other Connecticut municipal wetland agencies, the GIW&WCA requires a permit application for any activity *likely to affect* an inland wetland or watercourse. Some agencies and the DEP only require permit applications when activities are *within* the regulated areas. This difference in interpretation of the state statute has made a substantial difference in the preservation of critical wildlife habitats associated with wetlands throughout the town.

In addition, the GIW&WCA encourages alternative proposals that minimize the encroachments on wetlands wherever possible. Where wetland encroachments are unavoidable, mitigation proposals to minimize the wetland loss are required.

The Agency also requires, where appropriate, the control of stormwater runoff. Runoff from the site after development must be essentially the same as before development. As a result of this policy, wetland areas on many developments become an integral part of a stormwater management system.

The availability of development alternatives is critical to the protection of wetlands and watercourses in Greenwich, Connecticut. Fortunately, the Planning and Zoning Commission has recognized the need for flexibility to protect the town's natural resources and has two residential zones—Planned Residential and Conservation—that allow for clustering development. In the former, 60% of the land can be set aside as open space, in the latter 40%. In addition, there is flexibility on the width of roadways and driveways.

With pressure from the GIW&WCA to minimize impacts on wetlands, developers have been forced to concentrate development on upland areas. This pressure often results in a conservation zone subdivision. The Old Stone Bridge Subdivision is such a development. This development on 83 acres in a 2-acre residential zone could have resulted in 35 2-acre residential lots with only 15% or 13 acres set aside as open space. The developer, however, chose to submit a conservation zone proposal that ultimately resulted in 41 1-acre residential lots and 36 acres of open space. Two critical stream corridors and associated wetlands and ponds were preserved within the 36 acres of conservation land. The conservation land is permanently protected by a local land trust.

Although the 1976 Old Stone Bridge subdivision is an example of a successful conservation zone subdivision, the wetland review process was a complex one that involved numerous public hearings and the denial of the first subdivision proposal. In the new application, subdivision roadways were realigned to minimize wetland encroachments, and a roadway crossing was eliminated, as were two large ponds. A flood control structure was developed near the outlet of Strickland Brook and within a significant wetland area. Numerous lot boundaries also were changed to minimize wetland involvements.

Ten years after development, all wetland-watercourse corridors within the 36 acres of open space remain viable. Minor landscaping encroachments have occurred in six lots containing wetlands, but the main corridors remain undisturbed. The misplacement of a roadway culvert flooded a red maple swamp and eliminated 10 acres of trees. The old swamp is now an open water-emergent wetland that has attracted waterfowl and other species not normally associated with a forested wetland. This one early liability has turned into the most productive wildlife habitat on the subdivision.

Two of the four ponds excavated or enlarged during development regularly experience algal blooms and duckweed problems. Both eutrophic ponds are relatively shallow and experience direct runoff from roadway surfaces. One critical element in the conservation zone plan was to link the 36 acres of open space with the 20-acre Greenwich Audubon Caldwell Sanctuary immediately down stream. That Sanctuary is linked via a 2-acre open space parcel to the much larger 102-acre town-owned Montgomery Pinetum. Linkage with the Old Stone Bridge subdivision provides a stream belt corridor 6,000 feet (1,830 m) in length along Strickland Brook.

Quite often wetlands play a critical flood water storage function. Flooding of Strickland Brook has been a serious problem in the Cos Cob section of Greenwich, Connecticut, for years. Each private development on Strickland Brook—like the Old Stone Bridge subdivision—must not increase runoff after development for a specific design storm (usually 50 years). Because the Strickland Brook watershed was highly developed, flood water detention opportunities were limited. For this reason, the Greenwich Flood and Erosion Control Board evaluated numerous sites on town property and concluded in 1977 that the Mianus Park Pond was an ideal site for flood water detention. Actually, the Mianus Park Pond was a marsh developed on an old pond bed. After considerable analysis by the Engineering Division of the Department of Public Works, an application was made to the Wetland Agency to repair the Mianus Park Pond Dam and install a flood control weir. Because the Agency was anxious to preserve the Mianus Park Pond marsh and add almost 25 acre-feet of flood storage capacity to Strickland Brook, it carefully reviewed the floral and faunal communities associated with the marsh before approving the repair. The Agency decided its long-term goal was to maintain the marsh habitat (one of the few large herbaceous marshes on public property). Since issuing the permit to modify the dam, the Agency has monitored the floral community in the pond for more than 8 years. The monitoring program is designed to recommend necessary weir adjustments to maintain the marsh habitat.

Planned residential (RPR) developments have been used in Greenwich, Connecticut, to cluster development on 40% of a site, thus preserving the other 60% as open space. The RPR zone requires that half of the open space be deeded to the town. RPR's must be on sites of 100 acres or more. The 120-acre Lyon Farm property was developed as a planned residential development. Thirty-six acres were given to the town and added to Pemberwick Park. The 36 acres have been managed as a conservation area by the town's Parks and Recreation Department. Eight acres of the original park remain for active recreation whereas the 36-acre managed conservation area is for passive recreation.

All significant wetland and watercourse habitats were preserved within the public and private open space areas associated with the development. One hundred ninety-one condominium units were developed on the property—20% of the units were attached. As on other developments in urban areas, flood control structures were critical elements of all ponds developed within wetland areas. Except for an occasional road crossing and pond development, all significant wetland corridors were preserved on this tract. Wetland habitats support a variety of songbirds, small mammals, waterfowl, and other water birds. The presence of open water significantly diversified the wildlife habitat found on the original Lyon Farm.

On other developments where standard subdivisions were approved, the Agency has required the use of conservation easements and deeds or declarations of restrictions to protect significant wetland and watercourse resources. These easements and declarations become part of the land records of the town and serve as a notice to future purchasers that wetland and watercourses are located on a specific property, that these areas are subject to regulation by the GIW&WCA, and that a specific wetland permit limits activity within regulated areas. Deed restrictions and declarations may require the preservation of the wetlands or watercourses in an "undisturbed natural state."

Wetland regulation at the local level can be very effective in preserving and protecting wildlife habitat and other significant wetland functions. The necessary ingredients for a strong, local regulatory agency are:

1. a desire among individual agency members to preserve and protect significant wetlands and watercourses,
2. trained agency members and professional staff capable of evaluating environmental impacts associated with developments and issuing permits with conditions designed to minimize wetland impacts,
3. a strong permit compliance program to ensure the preservation of protected wetlands, and
4. the funding necessary to accomplish the above.

The State Role

The Water Resources Unit of the DEP plays the role of a local regulatory agency in 13 of Connecticut's 169 towns. In addition, the DEP regulates other state agencies that want to perform activities within inland wetlands and watercourses. The state's authority to regulate inland wetlands and watercourses is derived from Sections 22a-36 through 22a-45 of the Connecticut General Statutes and is more clearly defined in the administrative inland wetland and watercourses regulations of the DEP. All municipal regulations must be in conformance with the DEP regulations and the DEP Commissioner has the right to examine all local regulations to determine conformance with the state wetlands act and DEP regulations. This state oversight ensures that all communities meet the minimum wetland protection standards.

Permit application reviews for the 13 regulated towns are completed in Hartford, Connecticut, at the Water Resources offices in the State Office Building. The distance between Hartford and the regulated community can create substantial hardships for the applicant, concerned citizens, and the DEP's own professional staff. A 3-hour round trip from Hartford to the affected community is not unusual. This travel-time problem, when combined with small staff assigned to the program, severely limits the state's ability to establish adequate regulatory programs in each community. Applications are difficult to submit, the application review process is slow, and the public's ability to comment on specific applications is very limited. Citizens of the affected community learn of applications through a legal notice in the local newspaper. Often public hearings are waived on applications because state officials conclude impacts are not significant. In order to request a public hearing on an application, a petition with 25 signatures is required. Public hearings are usually held in Hartford at 10:00 a.m., further limiting input by the public.

Two hundred applications are evaluated by the DEP each year. Because the DEP only requires applications for activities *in* wetlands and watercourses, significant activities immediately adjacent to regulated areas are not evaluated. A review of recent applications and notices to waive public hearings indicated that the DEP routinely allows the destruction of wetlands in one-half to 1-acre increments. A general wetland protection policy seems to be absent in DEP's regulatory program. When large, significant wetlands are threatened, however, the state program seems to work. This was particularly evident in a recent proposal to excavate one million cubic yards (765,000 m^3) of peat from a 100-acre open water–wetland complex known as Mono Pond in Columbia, Connecticut. After an extensive DEP evaluation, public hearings, and citizen-conservation group pressure, a decision recommending the denial of the application was made by the DEP hearing officer. Although the final decision has yet to be made by the DEP Commissioner, the hearing officer's recommendations are normally implemented.

One major weakness in the state's regulatory program is the inability to ensure compliance with specific permit conditions. This weakness is in large part due to the distance separating the DEP and the regulated community, as well as the volume of applications reviewed and limited staffing.

Connecticut's wetland regulatory program also has had its difficulties with the Connecticut Department of Transportation's (DOT) new highway program. If large wetland areas are being destroyed with any regularity in Connecticut, it is by the DOT. Recently, however, a major emphasis has been placed on wetland mitigation. Many highway projects now include wetland creation elements designed to replace wetland lost on a one for one basis. Although this is a step in the right direction, quite often the new "wetland" or "open water" environment cannot replace the wildlife habitat value associated with the destroyed wetland.

The Federal Role

In Connecticut the COE's role in protecting inland wetlands and watercourses is very restricted but often quite important. The COE regulates freshwater wetlands under Section 404 of the Clean Water Act. Permit applications are required where significant filling of wetlands, lakes, rivers, and streams are proposed.

The application of Old Sugar Hollow Associates to fill 1.6 acres of Wolf's Pond and 8.7 acres of adjacent wooded and shrub swamp for the construction of an office park in Danbury, Connecticut, clearly illustrates the COE's role in protecting significant wildlife habitat. The office park would have destroyed a significant habitat for herons; American woodcock; black ducks, mallards, and other waterfowl; raptors; woodpeckers; songbirds; deer; fox, raccoon, skunk, muskrat, beaver, rabbit, and other small mammals; and finfish; and also would have eliminated a very important flood storage reservoir. The proposal was evaluated by the Danbury Wetland Agency and denied. The denial was appealed by the applicant to the Connecticut Superior Court and overturned by the Court. After a review of the application and public comment opposing the application, the New England District Engineer of the COE denied the permit. Without federal involvement at this site, a significant wetland habitat would have been destroyed.

DISCUSSION

Connecticut has two wetland regulatory programs. One protects tidal wetlands, the other inland freshwater wetlands. Each of these regulatory programs involves local, state, and federal levels of government. Although each program is working under different state or federal statutes, the goals are similar: to preserve and protect significant coastal and inland wetland habitats.

Since the implementation of Public Act 695, little additional tidal wetland acreage has been lost. Significant wildlife habitats have been protected in all 40 coastal communities. The law has been particularly successful in protecting 277 acres of high and low marsh in "Great Meadows" of Stratford, Connecticut. Although the statute has weathered numerous assaults, the Stratford Land and Development case has raised a significant cloud on the horizon.

The protection of significant freshwater wetland habitats is possible at the local level using Public Act 155. Communities with strong, local regulatory agencies and supporting staff have slowed the loss of inland wetland and watercourse habitat throughout the state. The weakness in the Act, however, is the variability in implementation from community to community. This weakness is due in part to political or developmental pressures, and the lack of adequate funding and professional expertise.

Although the DEP regulates only 13 of Connecticut's 169 towns, it plays an extremely important role in protecting wetlands threatened by super-highway construction. This role is often strengthened by the companion COE regulatory process. In some situations, the COE is the last "environmental safety net" for valuable wildlife habitats associated with Connecticut's freshwater wetlands.

APPENDIX A

GUIDELINES FOR *MINIMUM* SETBACKS *WITHOUT* SPECIAL ANALYSIS* REV. 10/5/81

INLAND WETLANDS & WATER COURSES
AGENCY—GREENWICH, CONNECTICUT

A / B

"A" = Setback (ft)
"B" = No Disturbance (ft)
("B" is included in "A")

	BODY TO BE PROTECTED	Construction Activity: Any part of sub-surface sewage disposal system	Construction Activity: Structures other than animal shelter A/B	Construction Activity: Pool & Tennis Court-Limit of Fill or Cut A/B	Construction Activity: Driveway edge of shoulder A/B	Construction Activity: Animal House (2) or animal run (3)
WETLAND	Does Not Feed Surface Drinking Water Supply	50	35/15	35/25	25/15	125
WETLAND	Feeds Surface Drinking Water Supply	100	50/30	50/40	25/15	200
WATERCOURSE (1)	Does Not Feed Surface Drinking Water Supply	50	35/15	35/25	25/15	125
WATERCOURSE (1)	Feeds Surface Drinking Water Supply	100	50/30	75/65	50/40	200
WATERCOURSE (1)	High Water Level of a Public Water Supply Reservoir	150	100/80	100/90	50/40	200

(1) Includes intermittent watercourse.
(2) Animal house is any structure that houses or boards one or more horses, ponies, donkeys, mules, burros, cows, sheep, swine, or goats; five or more dogs; or 10 or more cats.
(3) Animal run is a fenced in area to accommodate animals listed under (2), above.
*In evaluating deviation from these guidelines, the Agency will take into consideration the viability and importance of the wetland or watercourse and the effectiveness of the buffer strip.

APPENDIX A

Natural Resource Management Policy Constraints and Trade-offs in an Urban National Recreational Area

John T. Tanacredi, *National Park Service, Gateway National Recreation Area, Brooklyn, NY 11234*[1]

INTRODUCTION

The National Park Service (NPS) has an unique opportunity in the new Urban Park units to reverse and, in many instances, restore or revitalize those natural and cultural systems that have been degraded or stressed by the urban environment. However, the NPS must do more than just bring the national park ideals out of the "countryside" into the urban milieu. It must, additionally, be actively pursuing opportunities to demonstrate that abused natural resources can be regenerated, building a receptivity to man and the environment–"To help," as the late Rene Dubos put it, "urban people move progressively and with increasing understanding from the completely humanized world into the wilderness." (Mitchell 1978).

Gateway National Recreation Area (NRA), 26,645 acres (10,791 ha) of ocean beach, estuary, grasslands, forest and wildlife preserves in the New York/New Jersey area, is part of a program intended to bring the National Park System closer to the urban areas of the United States. The lands and waters now included in Gateway represent some of the last remnants of the original Hudson-Raritan estuarine system and are subject to delicate management decisions regarding the protection, preservation, and enhancement of these natural resources. Management at Gateway must strike a balance between resources and the park's stated mission to provide recreation.

Recreation is a broad category encompassing a variety of "passive" and "active" activities, and is one of the largest and fastest growing economic forces in the United States. Because fishing and wildlife observation are totally dependent upon the natural flora and fauna of Gateway's ecosystem, recreational activities will compete with the use of these areas for wildlife preservation or industrial development. Pollution, for example, stemming from industrial and municipal waste disposal, will seriously limit or preclude certain recreational uses. However, even with these severe environmental stresses, Gateway's barrier beaches, estuarine ecosystem, upland forest, grasslands, and bay provide an experience with a natural coastal system to over nine million visitors each year.

The park has been allocated into six management zones, each of which has specific planned management strategies and types of allowable use and development. The six zones are protection, use-by-reservation, beach, unstructured recreation, structured recreation, and development.

This paper will discuss some of the natural resource management approaches to the *Protection* and *Use-by-reservation* zones because it has been demonstrated that in these zones, ecosystems are more sensitive to human activities, and are not suitable in the sense of "active" (resource consumptive) recreation. Because these two areas encompass the majority of the Park's acreage, management cannot just provide "recreational spaces," but rather as the Second World Conference on National Parks in 1972 endorsed, must work toward shaping Gateway to be a place "where visitors are allowed to enter, under special conditions, for inspirational, educative and recreative purposes." (Wauer 1982, Natl. Park Serv. unpub. ms.).

This discussion will highlight the significance of these special areas in an urban context as well as emphasize those natural resource management activities and needs that will aid in increasing or maintaining desired levels of biological diversity in this unit of the U.S. National Park system.

QUALITY OF THE RESOURCE

Due in part to the impacts associated with its proximity to a major metropolitan system, and in part to the National Park Service inheriting already impaired natural resources,

[1]The author's comments are his own and do not necessarily reflect the position or policy of the United States Department of the Interior, National Park Service, or Gateway National Recreation Area.

Integrating Man and Nature in the Metropolitan Environment. Proc. Natl. Symp. on Urban Wildl., Chevy Chase, Md., 4–7 November 1986, L.W. Adams and D.L. Leedy, eds. Published by Natl. Inst. for Urban Wildl., 10921 Trotting Ridge Way, Columbia, MD 21044, 1987.

conserving the scenery at Gateway NRA in some cases may require manipulating these highly altered systems and then allowing nature to take its course. The basic premise to such activities is to mimic natural conditions by providing an atmosphere conducive to increasing habitat diversity and for increasing levels of species diversity approaching historical levels.

The U.S. Department of the Interior's Management Policies (1975) have recognized the need to determine the attributes and constraints of all land within the park system and to classify the resources accordingly. Management objectives have been developed by land class, and are applied to all units regardless of their administrative designation (natural, historical, or recreation park) (Stottlemyer 1981).

Due to urgently needed open spaces in the United States, particularly near metropolitan areas, recreation areas such as Gateway NRA, although created for use by the general public, also were envisioned to be free from exploitative practices for the protection of wildlife and its habitat. It was noted recently (Cahn 1982) that some of Gateway's natural resources.

> "do not clearly bespeak 'quality' much less national distinctiveness. To create quality here will require more dollars and more concensus than have been available so far. One target would be cleaning up Jamaica Bay."

The question presented here is how much of the resource should be manipulated to some level of environmental quality. There are clearly areas that, by allowing nature to take its course, would revitalize themselves to almost original levels of quality. A related question becomes one of sheer quantity. How much area is left to "non-use?" Perhaps the most important example in this regard is the condition of Jamaica Bay. Continued pollution loads limit the diversity and numbers of organisms in the Bay. If the pollution can be prevented, however, natural processes could certainly return the natural systems to the historically higher level of "quality" spoken for.

This reflects Rene Dubos' belief (Dubos 1978) that "an ecosystem that has been changed can be brought back to a good condition if you help nature to function with the natural repair systems that exist." The Bay, in addition to its ecological significance, therefore, provides for urban dwellers the "spirit of individual place" Rene Dubos spoke of (Dubos 1980).

Diversity

In his "The Folklore of Birds" E.A. Armstrong stated that "The ecologist knows that the most interesting, beautiful and efficiently integrated type of habitat is that in which there is great variety." In a major population area such as New York City where there is urban encroachment upon the few remnant natural areas that exist, fostering habitat preservation and enhancement becomes almost a monumental task. Those areas that have been despoiled by such human activities as landfilling are still subject to natural processes, and are forever subject to a myriad of "development"scenarios. Previously filled lands are not "natural" the argument goes, so that "preservation" of the overlaying developing natural system, no matter how diverse or close to the primitive habitat type, is best foregone, or at the minimum, prime for resource consumptive activities. Perhaps more importantly, the zeal to develop this type of habitat is expressed in such understated terms that, not until one observes the small encroachments added up over a long period of time, does one observe the loss. Likened to an ecological triage, management in response to user-demands must utilize the more "devastated" area first. This devastated area is highly subjective, and is usually measured by the area's level of accumulated knowledge or data (i.e., plant species composition or occasional use by waterfowl, etc.) or by a desire to not utilize another area, so that these "less desirable" spaces can be developed.

At Floyd Bennett Field, for example, from purely an ecological standpoint, management is plagued by the conflict and competition over the multi-use capacity concept of the area. Identifying Floyd Bennett Field as a "refuge" along the Atlantic Flyway becomes more a function of "visitor-use" rather than environmental reality, because it functions unabated as a refuge even in its present condition.

In urban areas, it has been taken for granted that species inventories would be easy to develop because urban systems support a low diversity of plant and animal life. Yet some recent evidence has exhibited the ecological resilience of ecosystems in urban areas (Venezia and Tanacredi 1982, unpub. rep.).

High diversity is of importance to scientists and urban natural resource managers because the potential carrying capacity of a system to support a high diversity of wildlife will be significant to visitor experiences as well as the particular ecosystem's stability. Greater habitat diversity will increase the biological carrying capacity of a system, yet greater diversity will not directly increase visitor carrying capacities for an area unless a particular vegetation is so unique (as in an arboretum) that visitors would be attracted to this area of the park just to be able to afford the experience. In order to increase visitor numbers (if this is a primary premise we go by), there must be a reduction of habitat diversity by keeping areas in "manageable" parcels so that these areas will be able to handle a greater variety of "recreational activities" of greater numbers. When the type of recreational activity is directed away from protection and preservation, then natural carrying capacities will be reduced. The expense is the loss of contiguous natural areas. Ultimately, because of these breaks in the overall parcel of open space available for use, there is a consumate reduction in natural habitat, biological carrying capacities and, in most instances, overall species diversity. As Dr. Dubos has pointed out (Dubos 1980), "From the point of view of human and environmental quality, it is probable that diversity and flexibility are more valuable than productivity and efficiency."

Natural Resource Base

The term "urban wildlife" has increasingly been utilized to connote those species that have adapted to urban encroachment and are somehow removed from their "wild" kin. Wildlife is wildlife, and without distracting from the fact that management of such organisms may, in some instance, require somewhat manipulated technologies in the urban setting, traditional wildlife management techniques continue to be applied. One very significant difference, but only in gradation, not in content, is the need for greater emphasis on effective educational programs evolving out of our focus on the natural resource base. Maintaining natural sites near metropolitan areas facilitates environmental education as well as provides for park managers an understanding that the research function, and its park role in decision-making, can create public support for conservation programs both within and without urban areas (MacMullan 1968).

What the resource manager becomes, therefore, has been described (Dolan et al. 1978) as being "the translator of scientific material into the language of the decision-makers. He must see that the research meets the needs of the decision-maker and that the decision-maker has the scientific data necessary to make reasonable decisions," when deciding on the use or non-use of a park's natural resources.

As R.H. Wauer has put it (Wauer 1980), "Today there is a growing acceptance of the fact that ignorance of science, like ignorance of the law, is an unjustifiable excuse for environmental abuse." Trial and error does not work when it comes to the National Park Service's primary responsibility of protecting the resource for future generations.

One of the primary roles of the urban park is to provide a National Park Service experience. At Gateway, there also is the added opportunity to remind the city dweller that there is a larger "nature" outside the city, and one should be aware of it and if possible explore it. Sax (1980) noted, "The growth of the National Park System is justified by a recognition that the symbolism of parks needs to be brought closer to the public, not that the symbol should be urbanized."

When the urban public thinks of, or is questioned about Gateway's wildlife, invariably one or two living species or plant or animal groups are recognizable: Norway rats, insects, and *Phragmites,* possibly fish, but generally little else. Ideally, inventory is the first step in determining a natural resource base and the suitability for a variety of potential uses or non-use. For example, some original vegetation work conducted at the Jamaica Bay Wildlife Refuge, in 1976, identified some 65 or so families of plants (Bridges 1976, Natl. Park Serv. unpub. rep.). This basic list was mapped on vegetative maps that were subsequently used as "planning" maps. The survey techniques included aerial photograph review and limited field verifications. Due to time constraints, little transect work was accomplished. During the summer of 1982, a detailed floral inventory covering only 10 acres (4.0 ha) of some 100 acres (40.5 ha) in the northern section of Floyd Bennett Field was conducted. A total of 350 species comprising over 85 families was identified for the parkwide herbarium reference files (Venezia and Tanacredi 1982, unpub. rep.). What is acknowledged here is that the level of detail and scope of work committed to species composition revealed an even greater plant species number than previously thought. The implication for management is that activities requiring major manipulations of the existing landscape may not be tenable based on already existing plant diversity level knowledge.

Biological Productivity and Natural Function

In unstressed ecosystems, it may be relatively easier to demonstrate the economic value of the system. For example, several investigations regarding economic analyses on wetlands have been conducted exhibiting the significance of these ecotypes (Thibodeau and Ostro 1981). Yet even in stressed estuarine systems, the ability of wetlands to continue to function naturally and provide relatively high biological productivity levels, is significant. Once an ecosystem is lost (i.e., through filling, development, etc.), its potential use in the form of biological productivity based upon its natural functioning may become irreversible. Remnant parcels must be allowed to function unimpaired and be reinitiated into the landscape of the original habitat types and forms, if the overall ecosystem is to have a chance to regenerate to some predetermined historical level.

In order to accomplish this, efficient management of renewable natural resources must depend on a knowledge of the inter-relations of organisms at various levels of activity and their relationships to abiotic subsystems. This interdependence of various strata of organisms with the same habitat, and their relationship to the environment, is well documented (Odum 1971). Manipulation of components must, therefore, be carefully in tune with the functioning of the system as a whole before management decisions are implemented.

Most work on terrestrial systems, for example, will be limited to the relationship of the dominant plant species or vegetation with its consumer. *Phragmites communis* has long been thought to be not only the dominant plant species at Gateway, but, also, to be of little wildlife support significance. Both of these points have been shown to be somewhat inappropriate. Depending on where you are in the park, *Phragmites* may very well be the dominant cover species. However, its frequency and abundance levels are about 23rd in the park. In addition, recent studies have shown *Phragmites* to contribute as much, if not more, organic material to detrital accumulations in estuarine systems as does *Spartina alterniflora. Phragmites* also provides excellent escape habitat for pheasant, meadow voles, etc., while acting to prepare soils for other plant species introduction (letter dated 10 November 1980 from U.S. Fish and Wildl. Serv.).

Preservation of the natural functioning of ecosystems has been a prime resource management goal of each national park. In 1963, the Leopold Committee, an advisory board to Interior Secretary Udall, recommended that natural processes such as fire, insect outbreaks, coastal geomorphologic phenomena and the like, be allowed to operate "with reasonable freedom" within the national parks. "Reasonable freedom" generally means freely within an ecosystem so long as no species or biotic community is exposed to the possibility of extinction, no unacceptable losses to other resources are anticipated, and there is no threat to human safety (Bonnicksen and Stone 1982).

It has been NPS policy to restore to natural conditions ecosystems that have undergone major European settler-induced changes. How closely the natural condition is approximated depends upon existing knowledge of that condition and to what degree the biological and physical processes molding that system presently can simulate or regenerate pre-settlement conditions. For example, at Floyd Bennett Field vegetated areas have been allowed to function unimpeded for a minimum of 15 to 20 years. The diversity of plant material has been shown to be good. Once a detailed inventory of all plants is made for the Field, the natural resource management option could be to leave these developing systems alone. Regardless of the decision or lack of decision, vegetative succession will continue. To return Floyd Bennett Field back to Barren Island (a part of the coastal outwash plain and a marsh island in Jamaica Bay) is impractical. Allowing natural marsh accretion along Floyd Bennett Field's periphery and planting indigenous species propagated from existing plants or their seeds from the area, are examples of providing for natural functioning of ecosystems to regenerate and revitalize themselves. Care must be taken, however, to preserve intact natural systems and not to allow, in the case of marsh restoration, a substitution for natural systems by man-recreated systems.

For example, it has been demonstrated that the benefit-cost ratio of preserving the Charles River Wetlands near Boston, Massachusetts, is 150:1 based upon a conservatively determined worth of $150,000 per acre if left undeveloped (Thibodeau and Ostro 1981). Their market value for construction is between $200 and $5,000 per acre. This ratio was projected as being a typical benefit-cost ratio for wetland preservation efforts near urban areas. Under the mitigative measures called for in environmental compliance procedures for U.S. Army Corp of Engineers projects, recreated marshes are viable substitutes for filling, ditching, and otherwise eliminating natural marsh areas. Such replacement marshes have been shown to be of lower quality and biological productivity than natural coastal marshes (Seluk-Race and Christie 1982). In some cases where marshes are planted to reduce shoreline erosion, or in cases where degraded tidal wetlands are replanted to be influenced again by tidal action, this technique has proven effective. A 2-acre (0.8 ha) area at the Jamaica Bay Wildlife Refuge threatened by erosion was replanted and has stabilized the shore excellently. The bottom line, however, must be the maintenance of natural functioning ecosystems with commensurate reduction in pollutional loads so as to allow the recruitment and increase of natural biological productivity and diversity levels. The value of natural ecosystems from an ecological and economic standpoint has been well documented (Hall and Day 1977, Farnworth et al. 1981).

Multi-Use Capacity

An area such as Floyd Bennett Field, which is planned for a variety of recreational uses on a macroscale level, requires microscale assessments in order to determine carrying capacities for wildlife. Variety in habitat components is essential for food, shelter, and visitor perceptions of wildlife. Planning wildlife habitat must be multidisciplinary in approach, and recognize that man is a biological component in the system under study.

Considering capacities of parcels of space within an overall unit poses problems that directly affect natural systems. For example, consideration of types of vegetation to support wildlife should include more than just food source, but rather suitable habitat. This involves escape cover, nesting space, alternative species (floral and faunal) interactions, continuity of habitat, and potential nuisance problems to and from man. Wildlife does not recognize boundary or jurisdictional lines. Few animals have small home ranges or territories that they will remain in. Contiguous systems, not potmarked sites within an entire district, must be maintained and monitored. As stated by Gold (1973, *Urban Recreation Planning*, p. 333), we should be . . . "emphasizing the fact that we over-groom our parks when most portions of them could be left more natural to benefit wildlife and also save money. Once the economic value of attractive natural areas is established, then development pressures, which would predictably reverse positive aspects of environmental quality, would decrease precipitously."

Traditionally, urban parks have emphasized lawn areas, and areas that contain only mature trees. Yet, other area types are important; shrubs, saplings, and a tall herbaceous ground cover will be productive to a variety of wildlife. Grey and Deneke (1978) noted the benefits of urban forests such as climate amelioration (temperature modification in cities, which are generally 0.5° to 1.5°C warmer during the day than the countryside), wind protection, water runoff control, noise abatement, air pollution abatement, and aesthetics.

Fragmented ecosystems affect migratory species, many of which have been characteristically dependent upon large tracts of forested areas. Long-distant migrant populations decrease when large tracts of land are broken into smaller tracts and isolated from a source of repopulation. Floyd

Bennett Field and Jamaica Bay Refuge are two of the remnant tracts and remaining coastal estuarine systems in New York that can support such a variety of species. Extirpated wildlife species now find the 17,000 plus acres of Jamaica Bay their last outpost.

It has been shown (Franklin 1981), that provision of freshwater habitat directly influences the variety of wildlife. Several activities have been suggested that can improve habitat conditions in urban areas:

1. Maintaining wetland habitat,
2. Creating additional impoundments where practical,
3. Erecting various types of nesting boxes, and
4. Providing brush (cut for road and trail maintenance) near woodland borders as valuable habitat for species ranging from bacterial decomposers, to fungi, wood-boring insects, amphibians, reptiles, birds, and mammals.

Without implementing long-term monitoring of carrying capacities in a multi-use area, the detection of alterations and their prime causes will be extremely difficult. Comprehensive monitoring programs covering habitat management activities must be in place prior to implementation of any planning scenarios (Gregg 1980). Critical thresholds of visitor demands must be acknowledged prior to placing ecosystems under their stress. In urban areas where systems are presently in danger of being irreversibly lost or irreparably damaged, biological carrying capacities must be compatible with visitor demand levels so that natural regenerative capacities of systems can work unchecked to restore or maintain equilibrium conditions for that ecosystem. The abiotic component of natural systems never changes in function no matter what the political, social, economic, or even developmental conditions are!

NATURAL RESOURCE MANAGEMENT CASE HISTORIES

Erosion, Shoreline Dynamics, and Marsh Restoration

Letting nature take its course is in concert with the conservation-preservation ethic of the National Park Service and, in many cases, is the most economical way to handle a particular ecological problem. However, application at Gateway has depended upon existing environmental conditions and the originally intended purpose of this "recreation area" (Psuty et al. 1976, Natl. Park Serv. unpub. rep.; Godfrey 1978; Leatherman et al. 1978). Natural resource management considerations are sometimes dependent on man's manipulation of the landscape.

An example is beach nourishment, where sand naturally accruing due to littoral drift is recycled back through the system to the eroding and high visitor use area (Niedoroda et al. 1975). Thus, natural tasks would be performed that have previously been rendered unworkable.

Several sites at Gateway have been determined to be ideal for applying breakwater technology to control erosion. Plumb Beach, an area of only 15 acres (6.1 ha), yet under intensive visitor use, has been subject to severe erosion impacts. Several marsh restoration-revitalization projects have been implemented (Gay and Enrico 1979) and are presently being monitored for long-term erosion prevention. Once the natural system (replanted with *Spartina alterniflora*) has been able to propagate, with help from man, nature can take its course to "develop" this marshland (Gay and Tanacredi 1982). Coupling the breakwater and marsh restoration approaches together will aid these environmentally-stressed areas. Ignoring past mistakes that have altered the barrier, and allowing the system to oscillate significantly is not appropriate where many factors must be considered, not the least of which is public access and usage of the seashore (Godfrey 1975).

Water Quality Monitoring

In the mid-1960's, public health officials studying the problems of sewer sludge disposal in the New York Bight noted that bottom sediment offshore had relative high populations of coliform bacteria. Marine biologists had been collecting information on the effects of sewage sludge, dredge spoils, and chemical wastes on living resources including plankton, bottom dwelling invertebrates, and finfish. Initial results from sampling stations through the Bight apex indicated that waste materials were not accumulating in a single restricted area, but rather, were spreading out over much of the New York Bight apex (Pearce 1976). During the summer of 1976, low dissolved oxygen levels in area coastal waters lasted from June through September. Millions of dollars worth of commercial shellfish were killed. Beaches were closed along Long Island and the Jersey shore. In response to this pollution episode, Gateway has incorporated monitoring of bacteriological water quality into its management activities. Presently, weekly samples are collected at some 28 sites within the waters of our jurisdictional boundaries. These samples provide water quality data for beaches at existing levels of use and for potential beaches. Because bathing and beachcombing are two of the primary uses of Gateway, and among the most enjoyed activities by the American public, water quality plays a critical role in acceptability of Gateway's use (Heatwole and West 1980). Water pollution within the New York coastal region, and particularly within the harbor area, is well known to the public. Such conditions can and do affect the quality of the beach environment and often result in negative user perceptions of local beaches (David 1971). Under the terms of the Federal Water Pollution Control Act, the New York harbor and estuary waters gradually are being cleaned up. Although much work still has to be done (i.e., reduce waste hydrocarbon contributions) (Tanacredi 1977), improvements are likely to continue to the extent that "closed areas" may become sites for aquatic contact-recreation type activities.

Landfill and Development

Considerable amounts of Gateway properties were created by previous landfill activities. Pennsylvania Avenue Landfill, for example, is a man-made peninsula of 110 acres (44.6 ha) located on the north shore of Jamaica Bay. Refuse was dumped from 1959 until 1962. Dried sewer sludge was deposited there from 1962 until 1972. From 1972 to 1985, construction debris was being placed to achieve contour lines of 75–100 feet (22.9–30.5 m) above mean sea level. As part of a cooperative agreement, a plan developed in 1974 by the City of New York would be considered for implementation. The plan used various disciplines in coordinating the creation of a recreational facility out of construction fill; from raw fill to finished terraced park (Anonymous 1974).

The implementation of the Pennsylvania Avenue Plan would be an attempt to echo nature and designers had sought to create an environment that functioned both as a recreational facility and as natural habitat. Vistas, terraced landscapes, public access, and energy (methane gas) generation are all advantages assigned this landfill scheme. The problems that have developed are basically hazardous material leachates into surrounding waters. As of 1981, it was found that upward of 30 million gallons (114 million liters) of hazardous wastes, including PCB contaminated waste oil had been routinely, yet illegally, deposited at the two north shore landfills. The National Park Service will, in response to potential public health hazards, direct long-term research efforts toward determining to what extent these contaminants are entering the Jamaica Bay ecosystem, as well as establishing a floral and faunal inventory to aid in the future reclamation of this land into the natural landscape.

CONCLUSION

Gateway has been noted as having a "significance of complexity;" that is, the National Park Service is to provide here, or has the opportunity to provide here, a creative leap in leadership and stewardship to translate past military, abandoned, and remnant pieces of open space and stressed-degraded coastal ecosystems into traditional Park Service purposes and mandates. We must certainly recognize that this urban park is interrelated with the myriad of public lands that surround it, yet Gateway provides one of the last spaces for many species of wildlife (both floral and faunal) remaining in the metropolitan area. Management must, therefore, focus on this latter concern. As Butcher (1969, *Exploring Our National Parks and Monuments*) noted, we must "keep (National Parks) free from artificial amusements, which have no rightful place in nature sanctuaries but defeat their purpose; and at all cost must prevent the deterioration of the National Park and monument system to the common level of playgrounds and commercialized resorts. . ."

The majority of Americans believe as the 1980 Public Opinion on Environmental Issues Report prepared by the Council on Environmental Quality stated,

> "All told if public opinion is any guide, it would seem that business continues to have little recourse but to learn to cope with the fact that environmental protection no longer is the exclusive domain of a handful of professional social critics and environmental activists, but the continuing concern of the public as a whole."

The true test for Gateway is to reverse the trends of "hundreds of little decisions" (Odum 1982), which have added up over the span of years to a conscious loss of habitat that may never had been planned for. It is certainly easier and politically more feasible to make decisions on a single tract of land or a single issue than to attempt a policy or plan of land-use on a large scale. I call this tyranny of small decisions, "nickel-dime ecology!" This is expedient decision-making based upon the most paultry of ecological datum or information.

Gateway, as well as the National Park Service in its urban context, cannot be short-changing ecological principles by anything less than a significant commitment to natural and cultural resource protection and management. What is occurring is that even within other National Park Units, there are pot-marked "islands of activities" surrounded by park boundaries that are not isolated from urban infringement. This insularization of activities cuts off the natural flow of species in an area, and similar to the isolation phenomenon being identified in larger Park Units there is an isolation of species with little natural recruitment within parks themselves. Man, in his traditional development and multi-use scenarios, simplifies ecosystems and reduces their diversity. Certain organisms are forced to move or adapt, or they die. The loss of some species endangers other species, and so on, until an entire ecosystem may be lost. Harwood (1982) has noted that as "we reduce biotic diversity in more and more habitat, we at the same time create islands of remaining natural habitat." The smaller an isolated habitat becomes, the fewer species it contains. When we maintain monocultures of cut grass, for example, it represents an imposed sterility and a negative example of diversified land management.

In sum, the natural resource management approaches within this urban National Park exhibit these significant restraints and trade-offs:

1. It is difficult to maintain multiple-use practices when respective uses are so close to one another. Management is, therefore, undermined by the conflict and competition over the multi-use capacity of an area.
2. Relatively unmodified, or recuperating portions of

the park must be closely guarded and maintained in as primitive a state as possible.

3. Visitor numbers increase and habitat diversity decreases because areas are kept in "manageable parcels" so as to handle overall greater types of recreational activities. At the expense of a loss of contiguous natural areas, large tracts of open space are parcelled out into activity zones to support greater visitor carrying capacities. Biological carrying capacities must determine visitor carrying capacities; not vice versa.
4. Extensive natural systems inventorying and establishing a detailed data base must be accomplished early in the planning of an urban park with an ongoing annual monitoring network established to note alterations imposed on systems by types of recreational activity. This must be accomplished through traditional biological and natural resource management survey and inventory techniques. This should not be a planning activity!
5. There must be a closer tie between natural resource management and traditional National Park Service interpretive skills and programs in order to make scientific data more palatable to the general public as well as to managers.
6. Reduction of pollutional loads to estuarine-coastal ecosystems, coupled with allowing natural processes to run unabated, will return degradated natural systems to historically higher levels of productivity and aesthetic quality.

REFERENCES CITED

Anonymous. 1974. From landfill to park. NYC DCP 21-74:80.

Bonnicksen, T.M. and E.C. Stone. 1982. Managing vegetation within U.S. national parks: a policy analysis. J. Environ. Manage. 6:109–122.

Cahn, R. 1982. Series on national parks, Christian Science Monitor, 14–18 June.

David, E.L. 1971. Public perceptions of water quality. Water Resour. Res. 7:453.

Dolan, R., B.P. Hayden, and G. Soucie. 1978. Environmental dynamics and resource management in the U.S. national parks. J. Environ. Manage. 2:249–258.

Dubos, R. 1978. Think globally, act locally—an interview with Dr. Rene Dubos. U.S. Environ. Protection Agency Journal, No. 5, Oct.

Dubos, R. 1980. The wooing of Earth. Charles Scribner and Sons Publ., New York.

Farnworth, E.G. et al. 1981. The value of natural ecosystems: an economic and ecological framework. Environ. Conserv. 8:275–282.

Franklin, T.M. 1981. Wildlife in city parks. Trends in Urban For. 18:14–18.

Gay, B.L. and J.T. Tanacredi. 1982. Shoreline stabilization through marsh restoration. Trends 19:14–17.

Gay, B.L. and J. Enrico. 1979. Transplanting the valuable marsh grass *Spartina alterniflora* in an environmentally stressed area. *In* Proc. 2nd conf. on res. in natl. parks, San Francisco, Ca.

Godfrey, P.J. 1975. Comments on present beach management philosophy in relation to Gateway NRA. Univ. of Mass./Natl. Park Serv. CRU Rep. No. 9.

Godfrey, P.J. 1978. Management guideline for parks on barrier beaches. Parks 2:5–10.

Gregg, W.P. 1980. Development alternative: new directions. Pages 43–53 *in* Barrier island forum and workshop proc., Cape Cod Natl. Seashore, May.

Grey, G.W. and F.J. Deneke. 1978. Urban forestry. John Wiley Press, New York.

Hall, C.A.S. and J.W. Day, Jr., eds. 1977. Ecosystem modeling in theory and practice: an introduction with case histories. John Wiley and Sons, Inc.

Harwood, M. 1982. Math of extinction. Audubon.

Heatwole, C.A. and N.C. West. 1980. Beach use and user constraints in the NYC coastal region. NYS Sea Grant Rep. Ser., NYSG-RS-80-01.

Leatherman, S.P., P.J. Godfrey, and P.A. Buckley. 1978. Management strategies for national seashores. Pages 322–377 *in* Proc. symp. of technical, environmental, socioeconomical and regulatory aspects of CZ planning and management, 14–16 March, San Francisco, Ca.

MacMullan, R.A. 1968. Meeting urban wildlife needs. Pages 31–37 *in* Man and nature in the city. Proc. of a symp. sponsored by the Bureau of Sport Fish. and Wildl., U.S. Dep. of the Inter., Washington, D.C.

Mitchell, J.G. 1978. The re-greening of urban America. Audubon 80:29–52.

Niedoroda, A.W., N. Coch, and P.J. Godfrey. 1975. Preliminary report on erosion problems at Great Kills Park and Sandy Hook, Gateway NRA. Univ. of Mass./Natl. Park Serv. CRU Rep. No. 8.

Odum, E.P. 1971. Fundamentals of ecology. (3rd ed.). W.B. Saunders Co., Philadelphia, Pa. 574 pp.

Odum, W.E. 1982. Environmental degradation and the tyranny of small decisions. BioScience 32:728–729.

Pearce, J.B. 1976. Our coastal waters: an endangered zone. The Science Teacher 43(9).

Sax, J.L. 1980. Mountains without handrails: reflections on the national parks. The Univ. of Michigan Press, Ann Arbor.

Seluk-Race, M. and D.R. Christie. 1982. Coastal zone development: mitigation, marsh creation, and decision making. J. Environ. Manage. 6:317–328.

Stottlemyer, J.R. 1981. Evolution of management policy and research in the national parks. J. For. 79:16–20.

Tanacredi, J.T. 1977. Petroleum hydrocarbons: contribution to the marine environment. J. Water Pollut. Control Fed. 2:216.

Thibodeau, F.R. and B.D. Ostro. 1981. An economic analysis of wetland protection. J. Environ. Manage. 12:19–30.

Wauer, R.H. 1980. The role of the National Park Service natural resources manager. Univ. of Washington/CPSU Rep. B-80-2.

Crane Aquaculture Facility: A Utility Company's Commitment to the Quality of Life in the Service Area

JOHN N. KRAEUTER, L. CURRY WOODS III, AND ELIZABETH I. BAUEREIS, *Baltimore Gas and Electric Co., P.O. Box 1475, Baltimore, MD 21203*

Baltimore Gas and Electric Company (BG&E) provides electric and gas service to over 2 million people in the greater Baltimore and central Maryland area. The region has a diverse economy including tourism, financial institutions, heavy industry, a major port, a number of internationally renowned institutions of higher learning, and a high concentration of scientists and engineers. These factors yield a high standard of living, but place a large demand on our natural systems. One of the most important of these natural resources is Chesapeake Bay. The bay serves many functions for the people of central Maryland. It is a major source of cooling water for industry, provides a conduit for shipping, acts as a recreational mecca for swimmers, boaters, fishermen and nature lovers, provides a living for the individuals harvesting seafood, and is a source of aesthetic beauty to all visitors and residents. What affects the bay affects the quality of life for BG&E employees and customers, and thus the company itself.

Human population growth in the BG&E service territory in the 1960s and 70s began to strain the means of disposing of waste products from an increasingly urban society. BG&E recognized a need to utilize waste by-products of energy production and looked for opportunities to utilize by-products of our increasing population. BG&E currently has four products from this effort: fly ash, refuse derived fuel, methane, and fish, highlighted below.

- Fly ash is a by-product of coal combustion and is collected from the flue gas streams at our plants. A BG&E subsidiary, Constellation Holdings, is using this ash as structural fill to convert marginal real-estate properties into prime business park sites. Several buildings constructed on the filled portions of these sites are already occupied.
- A joint agreement with Baltimore County allowed the construction of a facility to turn garbage into fuel for power plants. The use of this material extends the life of Baltimore County landfills and thus protects the environment and provides BG&E with a supplemental fuel for its C.P. Crane Power Plant.
- A plant was installed at the Back River Waste Treatment Plant to extract methane from raw sewer gas produced by the anaerobic digestion process. The processed gas is now pumped through BG&E's natural-gas pipeline to our customers. This gas was formerly flared at the waste treatment plant as an unwanted residue from processing Baltimore's sewage.
- Perhaps the most ambitious project was an aquaculture facility that would use power plant heated discharge water to raise striped bass *(Morone saxatilis)* fingerlings. The use of thermal discharges for rearing fish and shellfish has been the subject of a number of investigations (Guerra et al. 1976, Tennessee Valley Authority 1978, Godfriaux et al. 1979). The current project was designed at a pilot scale to determine if a larger production facility could be developed in conjunction with other power plants (Bauereis and Kraeuter 1984). Striped bass (usually called Rockfish or Rock, in Maryland) was selected for culture because it is well adapted to the estuarine conditions of Chesapeake Bay, it is the premier food and sport fish of the area, its population was suffering a precipitous decline, it is the state fish of Maryland, and it is a symbol of the quality of life in the bay region. The latter three items assured that the company would receive recognition for its efforts to restore the stocks in the bay while emphasizing company goals of utilizing waste resources and minimizing the impact of power production on the environment.

OPERATION CYCLE

The operation cycle of Crane Aquaculture Facility begins in spring (April–May) with the return of striped bass to the Chesapeake Bay spawning grounds. We purchase from private suppliers, or are given (by the State of Maryland), 1-

Integrating Man and Nature in the Metropolitan Environment. Proc. Natl. Symp. on Urban Wildl., Chevy Chase, Md., 4–7 November 1986, L.W. Adams and D.L. Leedy, eds. Published by Natl. Inst. for Urban Wildl., 10921 Trotting Ridge Way, Columbia, MD 21044, 1987.

day-old sac fry. These fish are transported in lots of 50,000 to 100,000 in plastic bags filled with oxygen-saturated water. Upon arrival, the fish are acclimated to the temperature, salinity, and pH of a 6-foot (1.8 m) diameter tank. Acclimation is accomplished by floating the plastic bag in the tank and gradually adding tank water to the bag. As soon as possible, the fish are released into the circulating water of the tank. Water is supplied from the power plant discharge canal to a head tank before it flows at 2 to 4 gal/min (7.6–15.2 l/min) to the circular tanks containing the fish. Water entering the head tank is filtered to 0.004 inches (100 μm) for the first 7 days and then filters are removed. Each head tank is supplied with a heater to maintain temperatures above 60°F (15.5°C) should the power plant require shutdown. Temperature, dissolved oxygen, salinity, and pH are monitored 24 hours/day.

Sac fry do not require feeding for the first 5–7 days, but are nourished by the oil and yolk found in their yolk sac. Once the oil and yolk are nearly gone, the small fish require a diet of live food. Brine shrimp are used to initiate feeding, and we hatch nearly 200 million per day for each one million striped bass. The hatched brine shrimp nauplii must be carefully cleaned because the hatching process incubates large numbers of potentially harmful bacteria. These brine shrimp are automatically fed to the fish every 15 minutes, 24 hours/day, for the next 2–3 weeks. The interval between 15 and 45 days of age appears to be the most critical for survival. It is during this period when the fish are first offered finely ground dry meal to acclimate them to dry foods. Then they are gradually trained to use a demand feeder. This period is when we experience the major mortalities associated with our intensive culture conditions. When the fish have reached approximately 1 inch (2.5 cm), they have accepted the dry diet, and disease and other sources of mortality recede or are treatable.

Once the fish have accepted dry food and are large enough to activate demand feeders, they are graded by size to remove larger, potentially cannibalistic siblings. These small fingerlings then are placed in 20-ft (6-m) diameter tanks. Water exchange in these larger tanks is increased as the fish grow so that by early fall all water in the 10,000 gal (37,800 l) tanks is exchanged three times per hour. Tanks are cleaned weekly to remove fouling (algae, hydroids, barnacles, and amphipod tubes) on the tank walls. This activity continues until late fall (October—November) when the State of Maryland transports the 6–10 in (15–25 cm) fingerlings to its Cedarville hatchery for marking. All fish are marked with micro-coded wire tags and then transported to their natal rivers for release.

RESULTS

The good publicity generated by striped bass aquaculture has been invaluable in amortizing the capital cost and the research and development expenses required to assure success of the project. The success of this project in meeting goals has encouraged two other public utilities to add striped bass culture facilities near their power plants. Because this project was started as a pilot scale facility, a large portion of the effort has been devoted to research and development. This program has led to ongoing cooperation between BG&E and many federal, state, and university research facilities. To date, we have provided fish to 21 governmental agencies or research facilities.

The major constraint to aquaculture of striped bass at the Crane facility has been the mortality of larvae 15 to 45 days old. Progress in determining the causes of this mortality has been slow. Nutritional deficiencies, genetic anomalies, disease, and toxic effects due to bacterial metabolites are potential sources of the mortality. The major inhibitor of progress is the dependence on spawning stocks in Chesapeake Bay to provide larvae. This restricts the time for experimentation to about 1 month each year. We are maintaining spawning stocks at the Crane facility in the hope that we can utilize the warmed effluent to extend the spawning season. This program is now in its fourth year, and the fish should be mature enough to spawn by the spring of 1987.

The tag and release program is part of a major initiative between the U.S. Fish and Wildlife Service and the State of Maryland to restore striped bass to its former importance as a sport and commercial fish in Chesapeake Bay. In 1985, 187,000 fish were tagged and released into the bay by this joint effort. BG&E supplied nearly 22% of these fish by number and nearly 49% by weight. Fish reared at Crane are nearly double the size of those expected in nature (Bauereis and Kraeuter 1984, Setzler et al. 1980). The added weight and size are due to the longer growing season provided by the warm water effluent of the power plant. Through the end of 1985, BG&E had released or donated nearly 479,000 fish.

Education and research are important components of the Crane Aquaculture Facility function. School tours, talks to community groups, papers given at scientific society meetings, and publications in scientific journals are all part of this effort. From 1983 through 1985, aquaculture facility personnel have given tours to 4,100 grade school students and 1,600 interested individuals. We have given 69 talks to civic and other groups, and 15 presentations have been made at professional society meetings. Eleven publications have been authored by Crane facility personnel.

All these efforts have been funded by BG&E from company profits. The board of directors has permitted BG&E to utilize a portion of the money that would be available for distribution to stockholders to fund this exploratory project. The aquaculture project has received enthusiastic support from company personnel and has been recognized as an important symbol of the company's commitment to the environment. Thus far, we have received recognition in the scientific community, notice by the local press, and were honored by receiving a national conservation award from the Issac Walton League/duPont Company. These rewards are partial payment for our efforts to maintain the natural environment in an increasingly urbanized Chesapeake Bay watershed while developing the techniques and expertise required to determine the feasibility of a larger aquaculture facility.

REFERENCES CITED

Bauereis, E.I., and J.N. Kraeuter. 1984. Power plants and striped bass: a partnership. Oceanus 27:40–45.

Godfriaux, B.L., A.F. Eble, A. Farmanfarmaian, C. Guerra, and C. Stephens. 1979. Power plant waste heat utilization in aquaculture. Allanheld Osmun and Co. Montclair, N.J. 266 pp.

Guerra, C., B.L. Godfriaux, and A.F. Eble. 1976. Power plant waste heat utilization in aquaculture. Workshop I Papers. Public Serv. Electric and Gas, Newark, N.J. 238 pp.

Setzler, E.M., et al. 1980. Synopsis of biological data on striped bass, *Morone saxatilis* (Walbaum). NOAA Tech. Rep. NMFS Circ. 433. U.S. Dep. Commerce. 69 pp.

Tennessee Valley Authority. 1978. State-of-the-art waste heat utilization for agriculture and aquaculture. Electric Power Res. Inst. Palo Alto, Calif. EPRI EA-922 Final Rep. 111 pp.

Poster Session

Chairman: WILLIAM BRIDGELAND, *Maryland Chapter, The Wildlife Society, Reisterstown*

Cochairman: JANET S. MCKEGG, *Maryland Chapter, The Wildlife Society, Woodbine*

Effects of Nest Boxes on Urban Bird Populations

GARY BLEVINS, *Natural Science Department/Biology, Hutchinson Community College, 1300 North Plum, Hutchinson, KS 67501*

JOSEPH M. SCHAEFER, *Kansas Fish and Game Commission, PO Box 4750, Wichita, KS 67204*

GARY CRESS, *1517 Floberta, Wichita, KS 67206*

The number of snags available to cavity-nesting birds in urban residential areas is extremely limited. During 1984, a study was initiated in Wichita, Kansas, to determine if nest boxes placed in residential areas would increase cavity-nesting bird populations. Experimental and control study areas were established. Both areas were adjacent to a riparian "parent area" containing ample habitat and relatively abundant populations of cavity-nesting birds. Preliminary censuses of cavity-nesting birds were conducted during the summer of 1984 in both parent and study areas. Approximately 130 wren-chickadee, 130 woodpecker-flicker, and 30 kestrel-screech owl nest boxes were placed in the 142-acre (57.5-ha) experimental area. Bird censuses were conducted in both parent and study areas during summers of 1985 and 1986. A significant increase in the house wren *(Troglodytes aedon)* population occurred in the experimental area. Census data were supplemented by a landowner survey of nest box usage during both 1985 and 1986. The survey indicated that nest boxes were most commonly used by house wren, European starling *(Sturnus vulgaris)*, house sparrow *(Passer domesticus)*, and fox squirrel *(Sciurus niger)*. Negative landowner response to the usage of nest boxes by starlings and sparrows indicated that a mechanism to prevent those birds from utilizing boxes needs to be developed; or woodpecker-flicker nest boxes should not be used in areas where European starlings and house sparrows present a problem.

Urban-Nesting Mississippi Kites: History, Problems, Management, and Benefits

JAMES W. PARKER, *Aerie East Environmental Education Programs, RFD 3, Box 3110, Farmington, ME 04938*

Because of little food limitation, and because of its use of shelterbelts and urban trees, the colonial Mississippi kite *(Ictinia mississippiensis)* is continuing its recent population expansion into urban areas in several Great Plains states, despite the bird's low reproductive potential. Urban breeding populations may prove more productive than rural populations.

With increasing frequency, urban kites, which often reuse nests, are involved in nest defense against humans. Diving usually does not involve more than one or two birds, although flocks often form when it begins. Diving is usually by females, it occurs at fewer than one of five nests, and it is most intense and frequent against women and children (small humans). Although actual injury of humans is usually minor, stitching of lacerations on the scalp and treatment for infection has been required in a few cases. Falls by older citizens, collisions between cars and children on bicycles as they dodge diving kites, etc. are not uncommon. The frequency of persons being hit by kites is increasing, and the perception of threat by people is major.

Both in large cities and small towns, diving incidents have produced major conflicts among fish and wildlife officials, environmentalists, and persons who want the offending kites removed. Common problem sites include city parks, golf courses, and residential areas. In some instances, numbers of kites have been illegally and needlessly killed. On a wide scale diving situations have generated negative public relations for many forms of urban and general wildlife.

Integrating Man and Nature in the Metropolitan Environment. Proc. Natl. Symp. on Urban Wildl., Chevy Chase, Md., 4–7 November 1986, L.W. Adams and D.L. Leedy, eds. Published by Natl. Inst. for Urban Wildl., 10921 Trotting Ridge Way, Columbia, MD 21044, 1987.

In four states, private research biologists (including myself), state and federal biologists, game managers, extension specialists, Audubon Society representatives, and nature center personnel have responded to complaints in a variety of ways. Responses to the problem have included: (1) public education at the site of the diving; (2) production of popular magazine articles; (3) efforts to depress media sensationalism; (4) preparation of educational posters and street signs to make the public aware of kites and their behavior; (5) the use of dummy nests and model kites to discourage offending kites from reuse of nests; and (6), as a final solution when needed, the removal and transplant of eggs and nestlings into the nests of rural kites. The last procedure in this list originated from my field experiments.

Most recently, Federal Animal Damage Control has accepted first responsibility (in close cooperation with State Fish and Game and private professionals) for response to complaints in Kansas and Oklahoma. This has greatly improved the quality and speed of official response to diving complaints and has significantly depressed public hostility to kites. It also has generated an increasing number of reports of nestling kites that have been "orphaned" by falls from their nests (commonly caused by storms), which reflects an improving human response to urban kites and other wildlife. I am now making plans for an expanded, region-wide effort to develop an educational program based on kites for use by all involved agencies.

Canada Goose Population Management at the Minneapolis-St. Paul International Airport

JAMES A. COOPER AND MARI SMABY, *Department of Fisheries and Wildlife, University of Minnesota, St. Paul, MN 55108*

Canada goose *(Branta canadensis)* strikes are a significant aircraft hazard at the Minneapolis-St. Paul International Airport. Canada geese have used the airport since 1975 when a 2-year-old female, hatched at a nearby park reserve, nested on the airport property. By 1981, goose flights through the operations (take-off and landing) airspace became sufficiently frequent to pose a hazard. Proposed goose control techniques included habitat modification on and near the airport, harassment to get the birds to move elsewhere, and goose population reduction. The present study was designed to test the effectiveness of reduction.

Breeding Canada goose groups within 10 miles (16 km) of the airport were located in May, 1984. Flightless goose concentrations of more than one family were captured by drive-trapping. Adult geese were marked with neckbands and immatures leg-banded. Goose use of the airport area was ascertained from 1 August until the birds left the area (20 December 1984 and 29 November 1985). Population counts and neckband readings were conducted four to five times per week within the airport area, and weekly at the other banding sites. Goose flights through the operations airspace were sampled during the peaks of goose movement, 1–2 hours after dawn and before dusk in 1984 and 1985. Observations were made from the airport air traffic control tower and the time, direction, altitude, and number of birds in each flock were recorded during 1- to 2-hour periods, three to six times per week.

Three hundred seven flightless geese were captured at 11 sites and 51 birds were caught at two sites in June, 1984, and 1985, respectively. One hundred thirty-four adults were neck-banded. Marked geese from seven of the 11 banding sites were observed in the airport area in 1984, and six of 12 in 1985. Breeding groups with more than one observation/neckband and geese breeding within the airport area were deemed problem birds. One hundred seventy-three geese from six sites were captured in June 1985 and translocated to Oklahoma (adults) and elsewhere in Minnesota (immatures). Based on pretrapping population counts, 90% of the birds at these locations were removed.

Weekly airport area populations ranged from 41 to 293 birds in 1984, and from 58 to 304 in 1985. The population was lowest in early August and highest from late October to late November, when migrant geese joined the local breeding groups. The airport area population was significantly ($P<0.05$) lower during 1985. The number of goose flights seen from the control tower declined by 48% in 1985, a significant ($P<0.05$) drop. The number of geese observed was even lower, 67%. Declines were greatest in September and November.

These preliminary findings suggest that airport concentrations of locally breeding Canada geese can be limited by identifying and removing problem subflocks. Additional research is needed to control migrant goose airport use.

Integrating Man and Nature in the Metropolitan Environment. Proc. Natl. Symp. on Urban Wildl., Chevy Chase, Md., 4–7 November 1986, L.W. Adams and D.L. Leedy, eds. Published by Natl. Inst. for Urban Wildl., 10921 Trotting Ridge Way, Columbia, MD 21044, 1987.

A Strategy for Managing Urban Waterfowl Populations

LOWELL W. ADAMS, *National Institute for Urban Wildlife, 10921 Trotting Ridge Way, Columbia, MD 21044*

CHARLES D. RHODEHAMEL, *The Columbia Park and Recreation Association Inc., 1 Knoll North Drive, Columbia, MD 21045*

JANET S. MCKEGG, *Maryland Forest, Park and Wildlife Service, Tawes State Office Building, Annapolis, MD 21401*

There is widespread need for improved management strategies of urban waterfowl populations. In the United States, the need is particularly acute for Canada goose *(Branta canadensis)* and mallard *(Anas platyrhynchos)* populations, which sometimes reach higher than desired densities. Recreational and locally-sanctioned supplemental feeding activities are recognized major factors contributing to the maintenance of high densities of these species in urban and suburban impoundments (Figley and VanDruff, 1982, Wildl. Monogr. 81; Heusmann and Burrell, 1984, J. Field Ornithol. 55:89–96). Survival rates of drake mallards are often higher than survival rates of hens (Heusmann, 1981, J. Field Ornithol. 52:214–221), resulting in sex ratios unnaturally weighted in favor of drakes.

Residents of Columbia, Maryland, enjoy seeing waterfowl on the city's impoundments, but high densities of mallards and mallard-domestic duck hybrids on two of the lakes in downtown Columbia have caused recent complaints. Objections have centered around excess algae in the lakes, caused in part by nutrient enrichment from duck droppings; messy sidewalks; and harassment (mostly rapes and rape attempts) of hens by groups of two or more unmated drakes, sometimes resulting in drownings to the hens. In response, we formulated a management goal of maintaining small populations of resident mallards on the city's three lakes for the benefit of Columbia residents and for reducing the nuisance problems resulting from dense populations.

Ninety-four mallards and mallard-domestic duck hybrids were live-trapped from two lakes during the winters of 1983–84 and 1984–85, resulting in a 44% reduction in the March–April duck population of 1985 compared to the average pretrap population of 1982 and 1983. All trapped birds were relocated outside Columbia. Mallard-domestic duck hybrids were moved to private ponds. Wild mallards were weighed, measured, sexed, banded with standard U.S. Fish and Wildlife Service leg bands, and released either on the Potomac River in Montgomery County or on the Monocacy River in Frederick County, Maryland.

The fact that supplemental feeding of waterfowl by people attracts and holds birds at urban impoundments, sometimes at unnaturally high densities, must be recognized and dealt with in management plans. Live capture and removal of excess birds can be effective in reducing populations, but the procedure is labor intensive and may be only a temporary solution if supplemental feeding is not curtailed or reduced. Nelson and Oetting (1982, Aquila 89:303–306) suggested that urban Canada goose flocks might best be managed primarily by the jurisdiction where the birds are located, with strong public input, together with U.S. Fish and Wildlife Service and state conservation agency technical and planning assistance. We recommend the same approach for other waterfowl species. In addition, local jurisdictions, with assistance from the U.S. Fish and Wildlife Service and state conservation agency, should establish a policy on supplemental winter feeding of waterfowl under emergency conditions, with detailed guidelines for implementing a feeding program only when needed. The guidelines should include a clear definition of conditions when feeding is permissable, types of feed to use, and responsibilities for the program. A well-prepared and implemented management plan for urban waterfowl will benefit both the resource and people residing in urban-suburban areas.

Heterogeneity of Avian Distribution in Residential Areas

STEPHEN PENLAND, *Washington Department of Game, 16018 Mill Creek Blvd., Mill Creek, WA 98012*

The degree of heterogeneity of avian distribution within a habitat influences the design of studies that involve censusing, i.e., greater heterogeneity requires either larger or a greater number of study areas. Residential neighborhoods often appear to be relatively uniform over a given area regarding conditions of vegetation and housing, and corresponding uniformity of avian distribution is often assumed. This assumption was examined by studying the distribution of birds in relatively similar residential areas.

Birds were censused in 16 pairs of 109-yard (100-m) segments in residential areas of Seattle during two winter and spring seasons between 1979 and 1982. The paired segments were located on adjacent blocks or were separated by one block, and therefore were very similar in amount,

Integrating Man and Nature in the Metropolitan Environment. Proc. Natl. Symp. on Urban Wildl., Chevy Chase, Md., 4–7 November 1986, L.W. Adams and D.L. Leedy, eds. Published by Natl. Inst. for Urban Wildl., 10921 Trotting Ridge Way, Columbia, MD 21044, 1987.

type, and condition of both vegetation and housing. The Ellenberg similarity index was used to compare the bird populations of the paired segments. The index during the winter averaged 63% ± 19%, with a range of 24% to 93%; during the spring it averaged 64% ± 17%, with a range of 37% to 90% among the paired plots.

If birds are responding to different environmental features, then these findings indicate that the urban environment is quite heterogeneous regarding the distribution of avian resources over relatively short distances. This can result from the actions of individual residents involving the feeding of birds, upkeep of the exterior of the house, or other resources used by birds. The use of a limited number and size of plots to characterize avian communities in urban areas may not be adequate. Also, studies of habitat associations of urban birds should include the same plot for sampling both birds and environmental features.

Reproductive Ecology of Two Heronries in New York City

KATHARINE C. PARSONS AND ALAN D. MACCARONE, *Manomet Bird Observatory, Box 936, Manomet, MA 02345*

We studied nest-site selection, hatching success, and chick survival of five wader species: black-crowned night heron *(Nycticorax nycticorax)*, great egret *(Casmerodius albus)*, snowy egret *(Egretta thula)*, cattle egret *(Bubulcus ibis)*, and glossy ibis *(Plegadis falcinellus)* nesting on two islands off Staten Island, Richmond County, New York. A total of 866 pairs of Ciconiiforms nested on Prall's and Shooter's Islands in 1986—a 33% increase in abundance from 1985. Both islands were colonized by waders within the past 10 years. Ninety percent of all nests occurred in gray birch *(Betula populifolia)* trees. Dates of first and last egg-laying were 30 March and 20 June, respectively. Great egrets and black-crowned night herons hatched approximately 70% of eggs laid, whereas cattle egrets hatched only 45%. Glossy ibises and snowy egrets showed intermediate hatching success. First and last dates of observed hatching for the colonies were 30 April and 11 July, respectively. Great egrets and black-crowned night herons showed greatest rates of chick survival with more than 90% of hatchlings surviving 20 days in the nest. Only 45% and 41% of glossy ibis and cattle egret hatchlings, respectively, survived 20 days. Sixty-three percent of snowy egret chicks survived 20 days in the nest. Predation and accidental egg loss accounted for most hatching failures. Eggs of some species were smaller than those recorded for an established heronry in Massachusetts, suggesting a younger breeding population in New York. Primary factors of chick mortality were predation, starvation, and accidental death. Reproductive failure in many nests might be explained by a relatively inexperienced breeding population. Ciconiiform nesting in lower Newark Bay is characterized by population demographics, patterns of reproductive success, and life history parameters that typify recent colonization of a marginal area.

Avian Mortality, Plate Glass, and Landscaping

DANIEL KLEM, JR., *Department of Biology, Muhlenberg College, Allentown, PA 18104*

Plate glass ranging in size from the smallest windows to those essentially covering multistory buildings pose a lethal hazard to flying birds. Conservative estimates of avian mortality resulting from collisions between birds and glass range into tens of millions of victims in the United States annually. A uniquely human concern is the guilt and anxiety expressed by a growing number of the general public upon discovering that the windows of their homes, and places of employment and recreation, are killing birds. Possibly, the recognition of this fact will have an increasing impact on the glass industry, architectural designers, and the conservation community as additional studies document the magnitude of this man-caused mortality factor on wild bird populations. My observations and experiments conducted over the past 12 years indicate that collisions will occur wherever birds and plate glass occupy the same environment. The hazard is most acute where glass panes create a see-through or reflective effect. Any feature that enhances the deceptive quality of glass or increases the density of birds near windows should be avoided. The popularized use of single objects such as a falcon silhouette sold by private institutions and government agencies, although well-intentioned, does not significantly prevent collisions. Architects and landscape designers are encouraged to recognize this hazard and attempt to reduce or eliminate the danger that glass poses to flying birds. Attention to the orientation of the glass and its relationship to the surrounding vegetation is most important. Alternatively, my experiments reveal that complete or partial covering of the glass surface will reduce or eliminate the hazard. Glass surfaces must be uniformly covered to significantly reduce or eliminate this source of man-caused mortality for birds.

Integrating Man and Nature in the Metropolitan Environment. Proc. Natl. Symp. on Urban Wildl., Chevy Chase, Md., 4–7 November 1986, L.W. Adams and D.L. Leedy, eds. Published by Natl. Inst. for Urban Wildl., 10921 Trotting Ridge Way, Columbia, MD 21044, 1987.

Raccoon Ecology in and Adjacent to an Urban National Park

DAVID A. MANSKI, *National Park Service, Aniakchak National Monument and Preserve, P.O. Box 7, King Salmon, AK 99613*

JOHN M. HADIDIAN, *National Park Service, Center for Urban Ecology, 1100 Ohio Dr., S.W., Washington, D.C. 20242*

Like many other national parks, Rock Creek Park (ROCR), located within Washington, D.C., is surrounded by man-altered habitats. In order to determine the effects and impacts of adjacent urban development on raccoons (*Procyon lotor*), we studied raccoon population dynamics, movements, and resource utilization along the boundary of this 1,754-acre (710-ha) park. Twenty-four radio-collared raccoons were located 8,995 times during 16 months between 1983 and 1984. Although data analysis is in progress, evaluation of raccoon denning patterns and food habits is complete. Both ROCR and the city provided raccoons with good denning habitat. Raccoons used six different types of den sites; approximately 30% were located in the city. Although most raccoons (64%) used dens in both ROCR and the adjacent residential community, some individuals denned almost exclusively in either area. Complaints from park neighbors implicating ROCR raccoons as the culprits in trash or house invasions may not be accurate. Tree cavities, virtually all located in ROCR, were the most common type of den used in spring, summer, and fall, whereas storm sewers, found primarily in the city, were the most frequented den in winter. Most of the foods eaten by raccoons were found in both ROCR and residential areas, including ornamental-landscape plants. Raccoons probably helped disseminate seeds of the many exotic plants found in ROCR. Garbage occurred in 31% and 22% of collected scats and in dead animals collected from roads, respectively. Raccoon feeding emphasized human refuse and vertebrate foods in winter and early spring, and plant food in summer and fall.

Creating Butterfly Habitat in the Gardens of Ontario

KATHERINE DUNSTER, *Graduate Programme, School of Landscape Architecture, University of Guelph, Guelph, Ontario, Canada, N1G 2W1*

Public interest and participation in recreational activities associated with urban wildlife were studied by Statistics Canada as part of a survey conducted in 1982 (Filion, et al., 1985, No. CW66-62/1983E, Canadian Wildlife Service, Ottawa, Ontario K1A OH3). The study reported that about 67% of Canadians participated in non-consumptive residential wildlife-related activities such as feeding, watching, photographing, studying, or maintaining plants or shrubs to provide food or shelter for wildlife. This recreational role of wildlife in cities has implications for the design and management of urban parks, residential gardens, and other urban open spaces.

Butterflies are among the most delightful wildlife visitors to gardens, and their presence can be encouraged through the design of habitat, and by planting associated adult and larval food plants. In Southern Ontario, over 100 species of butterflies have been recorded, including the West Virginia white (*Pieris virginiensis*), which is the only butterfly listed as rare and endangered in the province.

The food and habitat requirements of each of these butterfly species are very specialized, yet the large number of potential species that could inhabit an Ontario garden presents diverse clientele needs to the landscape architect who is attempting to create gardens for them. Easy access to a data base of information regarding butterfly life histories, habitat requirements, and food needs is vital to producing a design that is ecologically correct as well as aesthetically pleasing.

I incorporated butterfly habitat data and food requirements from many sources into a microcomputer data base. Information can be retrieved to assist in planning a garden design and selecting the appropriate plant material. I am currently testing the usefulness of the data base.

Integrating Man and Nature in the Metropolitan Environment. Proc. Natl. Symp. on Urban Wildl., Chevy Chase, Md., 4–7 November 1986, L.W. Adams and D.L. Leedy, eds. Published by Natl. Inst. for Urban Wildl., 10921 Trotting Ridge Way, Columbia, MD 21044, 1987.

An Assessment of Wildlife and Wildlife Habitat in Kane County, Illinois

STEVEN M. BYERS, ROBERT A. MONTGOMERY, AND GEORGE V. BURGER, *Max McGraw Wildlife Foundation, Box 9, Dundee, IL 60118*

Kane County is located in northeastern Illinois and has been subjected to increasing demands upon its remaining open spaces. The County Development Department was concerned with the loss of the County's high quality open spaces and, specifically, what impact continued development would have on the County's wildlife community. Consequently, the Max McGraw Wildlife Foundation was asked to assess the importance of the County's remaining open spaces to wildlife.

Wildlife surveys were conducted in nine major habitats to document the species composition, abundance, and distribution of wildlife in Kane County. An assessment procedure, utilizing avian species diversity and faunal point values (values from Graber and Graber, 1976, Ill. Nat. Hist. Surv. Biol. Notes 97), was developed to evaluate the relative importance (or basic wildlife value) to wildlife of each major habitat surveyed. Wetlands, and undisturbed upland and riverine woodlands proved most valuable to wildlife. Greenbelts and disturbed woodlands were of intermediate value, and cropfields were of relatively little value to wildlife.

Input from this assessment can be used to evaluate the importance of specific sites to wildlife by land-use planners and managers not schooled in wildlife biology. The land-use planner is required to be able to correctly identify the habitat in which a development is proposed (habitat keys were developed for this purpose) and further consider two additional factors—rarity of the habitat in the County, and the size or functional value of the habitat. Both of these factors are important to consider in evaluating specific sites. Scores for the basic wildlife value(s) of the habitat in which a development is proposed, size, and functional value are summed to provide wildlife values (specific wildlife values) for a specific site. Specific wildlife values for hypothetical sites in place of developments ranged from 46.8 for wetlands greater than 80 acres (32 ha) to 4.3 for croplands. Application of the assessment procedure to specific sites considered for development in Kane County was presented.

The Max McGraw Wildlife Foundation recommended to the Kane County Development Department that those areas within the County with specific wildlife values of 25 or higher (approximately 4% of the County) be preserved from further development. This recommendation serves to protect those still-remaining wetlands and undisturbed woodlands within the County. The Kane County Development Department and Kane County Land-Use Committee have formally adopted the results of this assessment procedure and have successfully used the assessment to halt or redirect planned development in habitats of particular importance to wildlife.

A Wildlife Survey and Management Plan for New York City's Central Park

JOHN D. HECKLAU, *Central Park Conservancy, 830 Fifth Avenue, New York, NY 10021*[1]

New York City's Central Park is an 840-acre (340-ha) green space in the center of the most solidly urbanized area of the United States. It is a multiple-use area that provides various forms of recreation for some 14 million visitors annually. In 1981, after years of neglect, a $100 million restoration effort was initiated. In 1982, as part of a comprehensive restoration and management plan, a survey of Central Park's wildlife was commissioned. The survey was undertaken in recognition of the importance of wildlife to many park users. It also represented a response to activist bird watchers and naturalists, who believed park administrators and planners were insensitive to wildlife.

The survey involved (1) an inventory of the wildlife species found in Central Park, (2) an inventory and evaluation of park habitats, and (3) management recommendations for the maintenance and improvement of park habitats. Survey results indicated that approximately 300 resident and migratory species can be found in Central Park. The existence of such species diversity is attributable to the wide variety of habitat types, e.g., deciduous forest, wetlands, meadows, ponds, and streams found within the park's boundaries. The survey revealed abundant opportunities for the incorporation of habitat management into ongoing park maintenance and restoration activities. Approaches for improving habitat diversity and quality that are both economical and compatible with other park uses and management goals, were suggested. Park planners and administrators, however, will accept such recommendations only when they are convinced that wildlife is an important part of the

[1]Present address: New York Power Authority, P.O. Box 191, Marcy, NY 13403.

Integrating Man and Nature in the Metropolitan Environment. Proc. Natl. Symp. on Urban Wildl., Chevy Chase, Md., 4–7 November 1986, L.W. Adams and D.L. Leedy, eds. Published by Natl. Inst. for Urban Wildl., 10921 Trotting Ridge Way, Columbia, MD 21044, 1987.

recreational experience of most park users. Implementation of wildlife management in an urban park, therefore, requires (1) education of park planners, administrators, and maintenance personnel; (2) resolution of conflicts among various park user groups; and (3) communication among those groups and park administrators and planners.

Wildlife Management in Natural Areas of New York City Parks

CHARLES H. NILON[1] AND ROWAN A. ROWNTREE, *USDA Forest Service, 5 Moon Library, SUNY CESF, Syracuse, NY 13210*

NATURAL RESOURCES GROUP, *New York City Department of Parks and Recreation, New York, NY 10021*

Since 1984, the Natural Resources Group of the New York City Parks Department, with assistance from the USDA Forest Service, has focused on developing management plans for natural areas within New York City's parks. Wildlife-related recreation and nature interpretation are important components of the plans.

The largest park in the city, 2,700-acre (1,092-ha) Pelham Bay, is the first park with a completed management plan. Areas for wildlife management and nature interpretation were located by determining the habitat potential of mapped vegetation units. Wildlife habitat appraisal guides were developed to measure the habitat suitability of wildlife management and interpretive areas for five species: ring-necked pheasant (*Phasianus colchicus*), black-capped chickadee (*Parus atricapillus*), yellow warbler (*Dendroica petechia*), eastern cottontail (*Sylvilagus floridanus*), and gray squirrel (*Sciurus carolinensis*). The appraisal guides were field-tested in November 1985 and modified to better reflect habitat conditions in the park. The guides also will be used to monitor the impact of park management activities on the five species.

The Pelham Bay management plan, and the procedures used to develop it, serve as a model for the procedures used to develop management plans for other natural areas in city parks. The habitat inventory procedures and appraisal guide will be incorporated into a handbook used by park managers and planners in all five boroughs of the city.

[1]Present address: Department of Biology, Morehouse College, Atlanta, GA 30314.

Wildlife and Landscape Architecture Students Plan Urban Wildlife Habitat

KERRY P. REESE, *College of Forestry, Wildlife and Range Sciences, University of Idaho, Moscow, ID 83843*

JAMES J. KUSKA, *College of Art and Architecture, University of Idaho, Moscow, ID 83843*

WAYNE E. MELQUIST, *Idaho Department of Fish and Game, P.O. Box 25, Boise, ID 83707*

In 1984, personnel of the Idaho Department of Fish and Game expressed interest in developing two plots of state-owned property into habitat expressly for nongame wildlife. The sites were to serve as public demonstrations of what can be accomplished on relatively small parcels of urban land [4 and 7 acres (1.6 and 2.8 ha)]. The first and second authors assembled four senior wildlife and four senior landscape architecture students to develop plans for each site as part of the students' undergraduate curriculum in 1985. The landscape architecture students contributed technical expertise in site preparation, trail design and placement, structures, visual impacts, and aesthetics. Wildlife students provided information on wildlife species likely to use the areas, vegetational and structural components of habitats required by specific species, and food habits of wildlife. The poster described the two areas, presented the goals for the areas and the constraints on each, summarized the design plans that incorporate both wildlife and human use of the areas, and provided a progress report on implementation of the plans.

Rallying Public Interest in Urban Wildlife Conservation

NANCY TANKERSLEY, *Nongame Wildlife Program, Alaska Department of Fish and Game, 333 Raspberry Road, Anchorage, AK 99518*

Many agencies are unable to accomplish their goals of urban wildlife conservation and public education about wildlife because of understaffing. Biologists could take better advantage of the high public interest in wildlife and wildlife watching in urban and suburban areas by recruiting volunteers to aid in meeting those goals. More than 100 volunteers

Integrating Man and Nature in the Metropolitan Environment. Proc. Natl. Symp. on Urban Wildl., Chevy Chase, Md., 4–7 November 1986, L.W. Adams and D.L. Leedy, eds. Published by Natl. Inst. for Urban Wildl., 10921 Trotting Ridge Way, Columbia, MD 21044, 1987.

were easily recruited during the summer of 1986 for a nesting loon study around Anchorage, Alaska. The success of the study in gathering data, educating the public about wildlife, and rallying support for urban wildlife conservation led to development of the following suggestions for others desiring to stimulate public support and awareness for urban wildlife conservation.

1. Initiate research projects in which volunteers can assist.
2. Target species that have high public interest and are relatively easy to collect information about.
3. Focus on species that have problems from human development or disturbance and that can be helped by increased public awareness and conservation measures.
4. Use species that are indicators of environmental quality.
5. Publicize and recruit volunteers through local media, and community and conservation groups.
6. Create sample designs and distribute data forms that are easy for the general public to use and return.
7. Communicate results of the study and plans for future conservation measures periodically to all volunteers and local media.
8. Reward research volunteers.

The Role of Private Conservation Organizations in Improving Habitat for Urban Wildlife

ALBERT M. MANVILLE II, *Wildlife Management Program, Defenders of Wildlife, 1244 19th Street, N.W., Washington, DC 20036*

A 1980 U.S. Fish and Wildlife Service (FWS) survey indicated that 83 million Americans engaged in watching, photographing, or feeding birds or other wildlife. A 1986 FWS poll, now being compiled, will almost certainly indicate further public interest in nongame wildlife. A 1986 survey for the President's Commission on Americans Outdoors (PCAO) indicated that 81% of adult Americans "strongly agreed" that government should act to preserve natural areas for use by future generations. PCAO also indicated that 75% of the American population now lives in an "urbanizing" environment where development tends to outpace and overcome efforts to retain adequate open space. For the wildlife enthusiast, this can provide a real quandary. Although nonconsumptive interest in wildlife continues to increase, many people in the urban community do not know how to attract, manage, or provide critical habitat for urban wildlife species. This presentation briefly addressed these needs and illustrated the role wildlife conservation organizations can play through their activist and public education networks.

Loss of habitat is wildlife's greatest threat, but care in urban planning and development can provide sufficient food, water, and cover—wildlife's essential elements for survival—for many species. Careful planning and management can be beneficial to wildlife. Columbia, Maryland, and Reston, Virginia, are two local cases in point. Private conservation organizations can and do play a significant role in educating the public about urban wildlife. Articles in wildlife conservation magazines have proved useful in the past, including "The Wildlife in Your Life" (1976), "Wildlife Downtown" (1978), and "Let's Build a Bat House" (1984), which appeared in *Defenders* magazine. Articles such as these not only help to educate the public, but also help interested individuals to design and build "wildlife gardens," plant proper wildlife food and cover crops, attract butterflies and hummingbirds, house and feed songbirds, and even provide shelters for bats. Field trips, workshops, and training programs conducted by conservation organizations also can help to educate and involve the public.

In growing residential and commercial areas, urbanization typically results in declines of some species, but increases in others. In Columbia, Maryland, chipping sparrows, song sparrows, mockingbirds, and the less desired house sparrows, pigeons, and starlings increased substantially with development of the city. White-tailed deer and red fox have expanded their range into some urbanized areas. With a little imagination, professional advice, plant species selection, and habitat improvement, virtually everyone can attract desired invertebrates like butterflies; and bird, mammal, amphibian, and reptilian species.

Kansas Backyard Wildlife Certification Program

JOSEPH M. SCHAEFER, *Kansas Fish and Game Commission, P.O. Box 4750, Wichita, KS 67204*

In 1985, the Kansas Fish and Game Commission initiated a free Backyard Wildlife Certification Program to develop a mutually beneficial relationship with a large, mostly urban, wildlife user group. To apply for certification, Kansans are required to provide a sketch of their property, some

Integrating Man and Nature in the Metropolitan Environment. Proc. Natl. Symp. on Urban Wildl., Chevy Chase, Md., 4–7 November 1986, L.W. Adams and D.L. Leedy, eds. Published by Natl. Inst. for Urban Wildl., 10921 Trotting Ridge Way, Columbia, MD 21044, 1987.

photographs or slides, and a short description of how they supply food, cover, and water for wildlife. This program is not restricted to homeowners as wildlife habitat can be maintained at many types of rental residences and businesses.

The Kansas Backyard Wildlife Certification Program is rapidly growing in popularity because of cooperation and support from the National Wildlife Federation, The Kansas Nurserymen's Association, Kansas Associated Garden Clubs, Extension Service horticulturists, and homeowners' associations. To date, about 50 backyards, including the Governor's Mansion, have been certified. Participants in the program receive a personalized congratulations letter, an illustrated certificate, a colorful sign with the inscription, "I DID SOMETHING WILD IN MY BACKYARD," and several booklets and pamphlets containing information on how to meet the needs of wildlife.

The Urban Wildlife Program of the Washington Department of Game

STEPHEN PENLAND, *Washington Department of Game, 16018 Mill Creek Blvd., Mill Creek, WA 98012*

Washington State, the smallest and second most populated of the 11 western states, has 640 recognized vertebrate species, 536 of which are classified as nongame. A nongame program, funded through revenues from the sale of personalized motor vehicle license plates, was established in 1973 for research and management of these non-hunted species. The urban wildlife program was initiated in 1981 as a regional position in the nongame program to serve the greater Puget Sound area. This most urbanized area of the state has a human population of some 2.2 million and includes the metropolitan centers of Seattle and Tacoma. Overall functions of the urban program include:

(1) Urban habitat management—habitat protection and restoration projects, EIS reviews, and consultation with planning–development authorities;
(2) Urban species management—permit reviews, field surveys, and species protection–enhancement projects; and
(3) Information & education—public education courses, backyard wildlife sanctuary program and enhancement of urban open spaces for wildlife habitat, and lecture–slide programs.

The National Wildlife Federation's Urban Wildlife Programs . . . Working for the Nature of Tomorrow™

CRAIG TUFTS, *National Wildlife Federation, 1412 16th Street, NW, Washington, DC 20036*

The Backyard Wildlife Habitat Program . . . Keystone of the National Wildlife Federation's Urban Wildlife Efforts

The National Wildlife Federation's (NWF) Backyard Wildlife Habitat Program began in 1973, with publication of "Invite Wildlife To Your Backyard" and initiation of the certification program. The Program provides information about improving urban wildlife habitat and acknowledges the individual's habitat improvement efforts as detailed on an application. Applicants meeting criteria are awarded a personalized certificate and receive periodic program updates. To date, 4,700 habitats have been certified. The program goal is to educate and motivate the public to develop and maintain suitable habitat for a diversity of native animal and plant species. Program objectives are to: (1) *provide* the public with information and direction so they understand the whys and hows of habitat improvement and maintenance; (2) *motivate* the public to produce new or modify existing habitat by providing them with a hands-on process for habitat improvement on their own property; (3) *acknowledge* the efforts of those who have improved habitat through this process by awarding a certificate and publicizing their efforts; and (4) *maintain and strengthen* their commitment to habitat conservation by offering them updated information, contacts with other program participants, and direction as to how they might become involved in habitat issues beyond the borders of their own property.

Promoting The Urban Wildlife Habitat Idea

The NWF contacts well over 2 million people annually with urban wildlife habitat information through its publications. How does the NWF access the additional tens of millions who have some interest in the wildlife around them?

- Since 1984, the NWF has worked with *The Victory Garden*, the top-rated PBS gardening program. In 1986, five wildlife-oriented segments will each reach four million television viewers.
- "The Backyard Naturalist," a twice monthly, wildlife-oriented newspaper column, now appears in 48 states and over 300 diverse publications.

Integrating Man and Nature in the Metropolitan Environment. Proc. Natl. Symp. on Urban Wildl., Chevy Chase, Md., 4–7 November 1986, L.W. Adams and D.L. Leedy, eds. Published by Natl. Inst. for Urban Wildl., 10921 Trotting Ridge Way, Columbia, MD 21044, 1987.

- "Garden for Wildlife," a nationwide marketing campaign of The Planting Council and the NWF, provides wildlife landscaping information to garden centers and nurseries.
- With help from Program staff, three major magazines, with a combined readership in excess of 11 million, produced backyard wildlife habitat articles in 1986.

Putting Words Into Action

New programs and directions promise greatly expanded urban wildlife educational and outreach initiatives in the next year. Recent developments include:

- The opening at the NWF's Laurel Ridge Center in Vienna, Virginia, of an interpreted eighth-acre demonstration Backyard Wildlife Habitat and a half-mile-long model handicapped-accessible trail. The trail's interpretive theme is property owner management of woodlots for urban wildlife.
- Initiation of a Corporate Habitat Program to promote and acknowledge private sector efforts to improve and maintain wildlife habitat.
- Initiation of two pilot projects introducing the Backyard Wildlife Habitat concept to 4-H members in 10 states and to teachers throughout the public school system in South Carolina.

Ecology and Nature Conservation in London

DAVID A. GOODE, *Greater London Ecology Unit, The County Hall, London SE1 7PB, England*

The past 5 years has seen a dramatic growth of interest in urban wildlife, with the development of entirely new approaches to nature conservation in urban areas. In London, there have been pioneering developments in the public sector, and the rapid growth of several new voluntary organizations also has resulted in considerable progress.

In July, 1982, the Greater London Council (GLC) appointed an ecologist at a senior level in the planning department to develop an ecological dimension to the Council's work. A small team of ecologists and planners worked together to develop appropriate policies and to promote the adoption of such policies in planning and land management. The GLC's program can be divided into eight areas of activity, extending from policy planning and the development of appropriate data systems to the provision of demonstration areas and establishment of a new Ecology Centre for London. A series of handbooks was published to make such information more widely available, and throughout the whole operation considerable emphasis was placed on forging links between the local government and voluntary conservation organizations.

Details of the ecological policies for strategic planning are contained in Ecology Handbook No. 1. These deal with the need to conserve the best examples of natural habitats, especially those such as ancient woodlands, which cannot be recreated. Also, the policies place considerable emphasis on the need to have examples of wild nature throughout the urban environment. Conserving the best examples is not enough, nor is it necessarily the most important approach. The need for people to have ready access to wild areas, even though such places may be very ordinary with no special features such as rare species or habitats, is something that has gradually gained acceptance. Policies also include the need to protect the floodplains of rivers within the urban area to reverse the trend towards canalization of these rivers. Other policies advocate the creation of new habitats in built-up areas where there are at present no examples of naturally occurring vegetation. Throughout the whole approach, maximum use is made of all the habitats occurring within the urban environment, including vestiges of the original countryside caught up within the urban sprawl, and the variety of unintentionally created wild places such as railway sides, reservoirs, old cemeteries, derelict docklands, abandoned sand and gravel quarries, and other areas of industrial dereliction. The variety of wildlife in London is dependent on this range of habitats, including suburban gardens, and conservation policies need to take all the opportunities into account.

As a basis for decisions, a survey was conducted in 1984 of about 2,000 sites totalling 20% of the land area of London. Data collected on the habitats and species are stored in a comprehensive ecological data-bank that is used daily as a basis for advice in planning and management of land. The way in which such data can be used in the application of policies for local planning is described in Ecology Handbook No. 3.

Since 1982, advice has been given on nearly 400 planning cases, and staff of the Ecology Unit have given evidence at 10 public inquiries. As a result of the new initiatives, local borough councils in many parts of London have now adopted a more enlightened approach to nature conservation and there are currently plans for a substantial number of new nature reserves in the capital.

A series of demonstration areas for urban wildlife conservation were developed by the GLC including the creation of a new ecology park near King's Cross Station. The creation of wetland habitats at Camley Street Park has been one of the notable success stories of urban nature conservation in London and demonstrates forcibly the possibilities that exist elsewhere.

Integrating Man and Nature in the Metropolitan Environment. Proc. Natl. Symp. on Urban Wildl., Chevy Chase, Md., 4–7 November 1986, L.W. Adams and D.L. Leedy, eds. Published by Natl. Inst. for Urban Wildl., 10921 Trotting Ridge Way, Columbia, MD 21044, 1987.

The GLC also set up a new London Ecology Centre with buildings in Covent Garden and King's Cross, which acts as a public focus for ecological activities in London. It provides a venue for exhibitions and events and also a base for many of the voluntary organizations. The centre is now independent of local government and is run by a charitable trust. Over a 4-year period, 1982–1986, the GLC provided grant-aid to voluntary organizations for ecological projects totalling over £700,000. This was regarded as an essential element in forging links and ensuring that the voluntary conservation movement had a proper basis to grow and prosper.

Since April, 1985, when the GLC was abolished by central government, the work of its ecology unit has continued and grown. This unit, known as the Greater London Ecology Unit, is responsible to a new joint committee of the London Boroughs.

Urban ecology has become firmly established in local government in London and there is no doubt that it will continue to develop in both the official and voluntary sectors.

Public Attitudes and Response to Wildlife and Wildlife Problems in an Urban-Suburban Area

MICHAEL A. O'DONNELL[1] AND LARRY W. VANDRUFF, *Faculty of Environmental and Forest Biology, State University of New York, College of Environmental Science and Forestry, Syracuse, NY 13210*

A telephone survey of Syracuse, New York, metropolitan area households was conducted over a period of 4 months. Thirty percent of the contacted households had experienced a problem with local wildlife during the 2 years preceding the survey. Respondents who had experienced a wildlife-related problem were asked about the types of problems they had, what they did to solve the problem, and their attitudes toward certain local species of wildlife. In addition, some information about the household itself was obtained. Actual occurrence of wildlife conflicts was determined on a city- and suburb-wide basis. Contingency tables were constructed, and frequency distributions of the categorical data were compared by cross tabulation analysis.

Species that caused the most problems in the city were the gray squirrel (*Sciurus carolinensis*) and pigeon (*Columbia livia*) (23% and 20% of all problems, respectively). Most suburban problems were attributed to the gray squirrel and cottontail rabbit (*Sylvilagus floridanus*) (23% and 19% of all problems, respectively). The most common type of problem reported in the city was general nuisance (39% of all problems); but in the suburbs, the most frequently reported problem involved damage being done in the yard (41% of all problems). Yard damage usually involved the lawn or vegetable garden. General nuisance accounted for 25% of all reported problems in the suburbs. The distribution of wildlife-related problems and responses to those problems were independent of the measured socioeconomic factors (household income, lot value, age of household members).

Only half of all respondents attempted to solve their problems. Of those who did try, only 45% were successful. The majority of residents who did not attempt a solution cited lack of knowledge of suitable control methods as the reason for inaction. Twenty-five percent of the respondents tried to call someone for help with the problem, though most respondents did not know whom to call in dealing with nuisance wildlife.

Measurement of respondents' preferences showed common songbirds to be the most-liked animals, followed by squirrels and rabbits. There was a significant correlation between reports of problems with a species and the respondents' attitudes toward that species. Respondents' species preference strongly correlated with their preferred management goal for that species (gamma $>$ 0.60 for all species), and the experience of a previous problem with the species made the preference rating an even stronger predictor of the preferred management goal for that species (gamma $>$ 0.70). The ability to use the preference (likeability) rating as a predictor of management preference, however, varied from neighborhood to neighborhood, because the types of offending animals varied among neighborhoods. This correlation also depended upon the background of the respondent. Residents with a non-rural background had a stronger correlation between likeability of a species and desired management goal for that species than respondents with rural backgrounds (gamma = 0.722 vs. 0.561). Urban respondents were more tolerant of the problems caused by well-liked animals than were respondents with a rural background, and urbanites were less tolerant of the problems caused by the least-liked animals. Urban residents were more emotionally attached to animals, and did not respond to wildlife problems and control in the same manner as rural residents. Public attitudes toward, and perceptions of problem-causing wildlife will affect public perception of any urban wildlife management program. The knowledge of what characteristics affect occurrence of wildlife conflicts and how those problems affect residents' attitudes toward wildlife are important considerations in urban wildlife management.

[1]Present address: Department of Biology, Trinity College, Hartford, CT 06106.

Integrating Man and Nature in the Metropolitan Environment. Proc. Natl. Symp. on Urban Wildl., Chevy Chase, Md., 4–7 November 1986, L.W. Adams and D.L. Leedy, eds. Published by Natl. Inst. for Urban Wildl., 10921 Trotting Ridge Way, Columbia, MD 21044, 1987.

Symposium Summary

Daniel L. Leedy, *National Institute for Urban Wildlife, 10921 Trotting Ridge Way, Columbia, MD 21044*

HISTORICAL PERSPECTIVE

Before commenting on this symposium, I think it is appropriate to present a brief historical perspective on urban wildlife conservation. Little attention was given to urban wildlife 50 years ago. The emphasis was on game, then in short supply, rather than on wildlife as we think of it today. It was in 1929 that Aldo Leopold introduced the important American Game Policy to the American Game Conference. In a section of that policy (adopted in 1930) concerned with how game could be protected, Leopold stated that cessation of hunting might be considered as a last resort. Although a hunter himself, he concluded that ". . . The opportunity to see and study game is just as valuable as the opportunity to shoot it, and half a loaf is better than none." In his classic book, *Game Management,* published in 1933, Leopold commented, "A pair of wood thrushes is more valuable to a village than a Saturday evening band concert and costs less," showing that he appreciated songbirds, too.

By 1937, the term "wildlife" often was used in place of "game," and in that year, The Wildlife Society was founded. The first issue of the *Journal of Wildlife Management* carried a statement of policy. The gist of that policy was that wildlife management is not restricted to game management, but it embraces the practical ecology of all vertebrates and their plant and animal associates.

Professor Rudolf Bennitt, University of Missouri, was the first President of The Wildlife Society and principal author of that policy statement. He summarized the North American Wildlife Conference in 1946. In doing so, he stated ". . . I still look forward to the day when we shall hear men discuss the management of songbirds, wildflowers, and the biota of a city, a tropical rainforest, or the eroded wastelands of China . . . We shall not play our part if we concern ourselves only with sport and only with North America."

Most of the things that Professor Bennitt envisioned have happened, but it took time. During the 1960s and 1970s, especially, there was a growing public awareness of the value of wildlife resources. Demands for cleaner water and air, and protection of threatened and endangered species resulted in the enactment of many environmental laws at both federal and state levels. Many more trained professionals entered the wildlife field, and more papers relating to urban wildlife began to appear in the proceedings of the North American Wildlife and related natural resources conferences. Raymond Dasmann, in his 1966 book, *Wildlife and the New Conservation,* urged more wildlifers to get out of the woods and into the cities to work with planners, landscape architects, and others in making the urban environment more livable for people and wildlife alike. In 1968, the U.S. Department of the Interior sponsored a symposium, "Man and Nature in the City." Since then, several other symposia focusing on urban wildlife have been held. Most of these meetings have been organized by universities where a few professors and some of their students have been giving increased attention to urban wildlife conservation. Though, in many cases, instruction relative to urban wildlife is included as a part of typical wildlife courses, a few institutions, like Utah State, the University of Arizona, the State University of New York (Syracuse campus), and West Virginia University now offer more specialized urban wildlife courses. A new program in urban wildlife involving extension, education, and research is being developed at the University of Florida. Also, Colorado State University expects to offer in the spring of 1987, a new senior-level course in urban wildlife to meet the needs of students in fishery and wildlife and other natural resources areas. Working citizens, e.g., planners, developers, landscape architects, and civic leaders will be permitted to register in this experimental course through the University's Division of Continuing Education, making it possible for them to obtain a kind of on-the-job training in wildlife planning and management.

Private conservation organizations should not be overlooked in this historical perspective. The National Institute for Urban Wildlife (previously the Urban Wildlife Research Center) was created in 1973. This Institute, which organized the present symposium, is dedicated to promoting

Integrating Man and Nature in the Metropolitan Environment. Proc. Natl. Symp. on Urban Wildl., Chevy Chase, Md., 4–7 November 1986, L.W. Adams and D.L. Leedy, eds. Published by Natl. Inst. for Urban Wildl., 10921 Trotting Ridge Way, Columbia, MD 21044, 1987.

research, planning, and education related to wildlife in urban and other developed areas. Those of you who viewed the posters on exhibit in the poster session of this symposium gained some idea of what the National Wildlife Federation and Defenders of Wildlife are doing to promote urban wildlife conservation. Others like the National Audubon Society and Nature Conservancy consider urban wildlife in their respective programs.

Professional societies, also, have become involved. The Wildlife Society, one of the sponsors of the present symposium, has had a very active urban wildlife committee, has helped NIUW stage informal information exchange sessions on urban wildlife at the annual North American Wildlife and Natural Resources Conferences sponsored by the Wildlife Management Institute, and has issued a helpful position statement on urban wildlife. Other societies that have helped promote urban fish and wildlife conservation include the American Fisheries Society, the Ecological Society of America, and the American Association for the Advancement of Science.

At the international level, the International Association for Ecology (INTECOL) has sponsored symposia on urban ecology as a part of the programs of the International Congress of Ecology, the most recent one being held at Syracuse University in August, 1986; the Second European Ecological Symposium, held in West Berlin, 1980, addressed the theme, "urban ecology"; the American Association for the Advancement of Science (AAAS) had a session on urban ecology at its meeting in May, 1985; and the General Assembly of the International Union for the Conservation of Nature and Natural Resources (IUCN) passed a resolution at a 1984 meeting in Madrid, Spain entitled "Human Settlements and Conservation Action." This assembly called on all nations to take action to bring about a more sustainable approach to the management of human settlement systems in such a way that local people can participate in programs to reduce the damaging impacts of human settlements and improve the quality of life for urban dwellers. Programs of the World Wildlife Fund concerning endangered species and some of the international programs of the Fish and Wildlife Service and of other federal agencies would probably please Professor Bennitt, if he were living.

In general, however, progress in urban wildlife conservation has been slow and actions to promote such conservation efforts, particularly by federal and state agencies, have been somewhat disappointing. Though some substantial research on urban wildlife has been done by federal agencies, current efforts are minimal in the U.S. Fish and Wildlife Service and the U.S. Forest Service; and though state fish and wildlife agencies—mostly in their nongame programs—are devoting increased attention to urban wildlife, only seven or eight states have programs specifically designated as urban wildlife programs. Lack of adequate funding is the chief obstacle to further participation. The Fish and Wildlife Conservation Act of 1980 (P.L. 96-366) authorized the federal government to provide financial and technical assistance to the states to plan and implement programs for fish and wildlife (including nongame and urban wildlife), but to date no federal funds have been appropriated under this Act. It is encouraging, however, that more than 30 states have, through income tax check-off or other systems, developed means of providing some funds for nongame and urban wildlife. To date, most of these funds have been used for nongame programs.

Despite all of the activities I have mentioned and the sizable body of knowledge on urban wildlife that has been developed, we have barely scratched the surface on the mountain of work that needs to be done. I think our success in getting on top of the mountain, i.e., in reaching our goals of maintaining, improving, and creating an urban environment of high quality for humans and wildlife depends largely on obtaining more adequate funding and more effective participation from the public. This, in turn, depends on leadership, education, and how well scientists, educators, planners, developers, landscape architects, builders, engineers, government and city officials, and the public can learn to work together. One of the objectives of this symposium was to bring these people together, identify problems, relate what is known and what is being done about urban wildlife, and suggest what can be done to improve the situation.

THE SYMPOSIUM

There is considerable interest in urban wildlife conservation as indicated by this symposium. More than 250 people, including most of the recognized leaders in this field, attended the symposium. There were registrants from over 30 states, the District of Columbia, Canada, England, and Japan. I believe Professor Bennitt would have been impressed, as I was, at the number of women participants. Some of the outstanding papers were presented by women. All but one of the papers in the five technical sessions were contributed papers, and about one-third of those submitted had to be declined. All 20 of the poster session papers were voluntarily contributed. Can you imagine such a response as recently as 10 or 15 years ago?

In the time allotted, I cannot comment on all of the papers or mention the names of all the authors and session chairmen who made the symposium successful. Also, my comments will not necessarily follow the order in which the papers were presented; and they will include references to several of the poster presentations which, in my opinion, constituted an excellent session.

We were privileged, in the opening session, to have talks from busy administrators and officials representing the U.S. Fish and Wildlife Service, the American Institute of Certified Planners, the Conservation Fund, a real estate development company, the American Society of Landscape Architects, and a university, the latter representative being a biologist, author, and educator. These types of organizations and institutions are all intimately concerned with urban wildlife conservation.

Director Frank Dunkle observed that the Fish and Wildlife Service has a mission ". . . to conserve, protect, and enhance fish and wildlife and their habitats for the American people." For nongame species and urban wildlife, he envisioned the Service having a small specialized staff to help coordinate and advise others in their conservation efforts.

Melvin Levin presented an informative paper on planning. He stated that planners, although they are more or less straight-jacketed by the market, have made headway in the past 20 years in planning for people and in developing a sensitivity to ecology. Both he and Paul Faraca, a real estate developer, indicated that if the public, environmentalists, whoever, can show the value or feasibility of doing something for wildlife and people in a given way, planners and developers probably can do it. John Wacker, landscape architect, questioned whether we—presumably wildlife biologists and the public—have demonstrated wildlife values sufficiently well to decision makers. He expressed the need to educate young people regarding nature and said that landscape architects are in the education business. Also, he said that landscape architects should have a policy on wildlife, and offered to work with wildlifers in developing such a policy. Wildlifers should accept this invitation. David Bird demonstrated, through a rather unique use of cartoons and slides, one method of educating the public about "City Critters." Patrick Noonan, in a stimulating address, presented the symposium participants with a preview of what was then scheduled for early publication in reports of the President's Commission on Americans Outdoors. He pointed out the need for more funding and cooperation at federal, state, and local levels and greater participation of the private sector in conservation efforts; and he outlined a proposal for establishing a nationwide network of greenways to link together the open spaces of the American landscape. This recommended system of greenways for wildlife and recreation was elaborated on by Hal Salwasser of the USDA Forest Service in a later session of the symposium.

Until recently, wildlifers displayed more interest in animal damage-nuisance control than in other aspects of urban wildlife. It still is of concern, as evidenced by six papers presented on this subject. We learned that the trapping and translocation to Oklahoma of adult Minneapolis-St. Paul Canada geese was not an effective long-term method for reducing the goose population in the Twin Cities. Too many of the geese did not like being "Okies" and came back home. The procedure worked better for young birds, however, and in the new city of Columbia, Maryland, the trapping and removal of resident mallards and mallard-domestic duck hybrids was rather effective.

I would not have thought it physically and biologically possible, or economically feasible to trap, vaccinate against rabies, and release enough skunks and raccoons in a metropolitan area to be effective in rabies control. However, researchers in Toronto, Canada, believe this approach will work *if* the residents will support the program and not interfere with the traps. Wildlife research and management in urban areas often are more difficult than in rural or wilderness areas because of people's reactions—in this case to trapping. People's attitudes will be important, also, in the implementation of a well designed project on deer control in the Greater Chicago metropolitan area. As pointed out by the authors in reporting on a research phase of the project, solution to the urban deer problem—and it is one of growing importance—involves interagency cooperation, an equitable dispersion of political liability and responsibility, and public awareness and participation. Another example of how wildlife can create problems in an urban area was described by James W. Parker in a poster session paper dealing in part with the diving attacks on people of urban-nesting Mississippi kites.

Though not emphasized in the symposium, many aspects of urbanization are, on the other hand, detrimental to wildlife—air, water, and noise pollution could be mentioned in addition to highway/street mortality, elimination of vegetation and other factors. In this connection, Daniel Klem, in a poster session paper, described how plate glass windows in urban buildings resulted in large losses of birds. More research on preventing such undesirable impacts is needed.

Some planners, developers, architects, landscape architects, and builders still fail to recognize that through their planning and work, wildlife habitat is destroyed, modified, or created. By working together and in cooperation with fish and wildlife biologists, they can ensure developments of higher environmental quality than most developments exhibit currently. Some developers are beginning to realize that such a cooperative endeavor may pay off financially and also be good from the standpoint of public relations and responsible citizenship. Shaw and Supplee, for example, described approaches to urban wildlife conservation in the rapidly growing Tucson, Arizona area in which the development community itself has supported conservation because of its value to marketing strategy.

Habitat and other resource inventories are needed for planning, and several papers in the symposium dealt with this subject. Tylka and Cook described a system for mapping vegetation types and providing St. Louis City and County officials with maps and other pertinent information for planning. Houch described a wildlife habitat inventory method used by the Audubon Society of Portland and the Portland Planning Bureau to document all significant wildlife habitat in the Portland area. Hench and others described how valuable wildlife habitat is being protected through a process of resource planning and management used by the Montgomery County, Maryland park system. A good example of the use of local zoning ordinances for protecting and developing urban wildlife habitat was described by Kathi Demarest of the Colorado Division of Wildlife. Also relevant to planners was the assessment of wildlife and wildlife habitat in Kane County, Illinois, made by the Max McGraw Wildlife Foundation. This Foundation recommended to the Kane County Development Department that about 4% of the county, including many of the remaining wetland areas, be preserved from further development.

Landscape architecture goes hand in hand with planning and development and, again, there is need for landscape architects and wildlife biologists to work together, especially in the selection and siting of plant species that satisfy both aesthetic and wildlife needs. I thought Lyle, as a landscape architect, showed that he has a good understanding of ecology and is doing his part to bridge the gap between his profession and wildlife biologists. He may be exceptional, however. Katherine Dunster found, in a survey of members of the Canadian Society of Landscape Architects, that only 13.5% of the responding members considered the requirements of wildlife in 76–100% of their projects—this, despite another survey by Filion that showed that more than two-thirds of Canadians participated in residential wildlife-related activities. The Idaho project described in a poster session paper by Reese, Kuska, and Melquist may be an innovative way of getting landscape architects, foresters, and wildlife biologists to work together. In this project, senior students in forestry and landscape architecture at the University of Idaho were asked to prepare plans for developing two small state-owned urban land parcels as demonstration areas for nongame management. Perhaps, if they learn as students that each other's discipline has important techniques and know-how to contribute, they will continue to collaborate later, when employed in their respective fields.

The home ranges, food habits, and behavior of wildlife species in urban areas have been found to differ somewhat from those in rural or wilderness areas. Wildlife biologists have much to learn before they can describe, in detail, urban habitats that satisfy the requirements of various species. Richard DeGraaf suggested that, in the planted environment of developments, maximizing the crown volumes of trees and shrubs is likely the one management practice that will yield the greatest increases in breeding bird species richness. Roland Roth observed that in the Newark, Delaware area, there is better than a 50% chance of providing nesting habitat for the wood thrush if you have a minimum of 0.2 acres (0.08 ha) of tree canopy, preferably contiguous, with a canopy that blocks 70% or more of the sky, and under which one maintains natural leaf litter, native shrubs, and moist soil. The type of conclusions reached in these two papers, it seems to me, is the kind of specific information that planners and landscape architects can use.

To implement urban wildlife planning and management, it is necessary to know something about people's perceptions and knowledge of wildlife, what people like and what they do not like, what urban residents will support, and what they will not support. Lisa Schicker presented some most interesting information on what children like to do in the out-of-doors and suggested design criteria for children and wildlife in residential developments. Marilyn Freeman and her associates learned that Seattle, Washington, residents have the visual ability to recognize habitat diversity, perhaps intuitively. They also discovered that preference for such habitat, valuable for wildlife, particularly if it consisted of an overgrown "left-over" site, tended to decrease as its location moved closer to one's home. These researchers suggested that, through education, a more informed public might have clearer conservation goals and support management of remnant urban habitats currently unmanaged for wildlife.

Clark Adams and others found that urban high school students in Houston, Texas, knew very little about the mammals of that area. The students were least knowledgable about the opossum. Can you believe that 60% of the students identified the opossum as a rat? And in Seattle, based upon responses of 274 residents to a questionnaire, Stephen Penland found that only 2% could name more than 10 bird species that frequented their neighborhood. I was not surprised that the American robin was the most frequently identified bird, but I was surprised that the house sparrow was perceived to be one of the more desirable species.

In Syracuse, New York, O'Donnell and VanDruff learned that common songbirds were the most liked species, followed by squirrels and rabbits—this despite the fact that the gray squirrel caused the most problems, both in the city and in the suburbs.

These and other studies have shown that urban residents, in general, have little knowledge of wildlife and that there is great need for education. Extension Service personnel, though traditionally operating in rural areas, can play an important role as educators in urban areas, also, as described by Wayne Marion. Robert Kent and others of New York State gave an interesting account of how knowledgable volunteers can be enlisted and trained to help educate and train others to work in fish and wildlife conservation programs, and, among other things, serve as 4-H Club leaders. The cooperation involved in this program, and in the one described by Matthews and Lewandowski for training New York City park rangers, is commendable.

Extension specialists, educators, planners, landscape architects, developers—all the people we have been talking about—need more usable information and techniques that can best be produced by research. In addition to the reports of research projects already mentioned, several others were presented at this symposium on topics as diverse as butterfly gardening and effects of nest boxes on urban bird populations. One of the few papers dealing with effects of urbanization on wildlife was that of Wesemann and Rowe conducted in Cape Coral, Florida. They concluded that land clearing and the development of prairie-like habitat in connection with residential development were favorable for the burrowing owl until development exceeded 60% of the area, after which the owl population declined with further urbanization. The researchers attributed the increased population of owls to increases in their primary foods—insects and lizards. The burrowing owl is a species of special concern in Florida and the information developed through this study will be useful to the Florida Game and Fresh Water Fish Commission in its program planning.

In connection with management, I found interesting and encouraging the National Park Service's efforts to preserve and protect natural sites in urban areas and to recreate a greatly deteriorated community of reptiles and amphibians on the Jamaica Bay Wildlife Refuge in the Gateway National Recreation Area in New York. Similarly, I would like to recognize the efforts of Chevron USA to protect and manage remnants of habitat needed for the survival of the endangered El Segundo blue butterfly in California; also, the conservation programs of the Baltimore Gas and Electric Company, including the Company's cooperation with the State of Maryland and the U.S. Fish and Wildlife Service in its efforts to improve the status of the striped bass in Chesapeake Bay.

As demonstrated in the final session of the symposium, federal, state, and local agencies, industry, private conservation agencies, and professional societies all have a role to play in urban wildlife conservation, along with individuals in a community. Michael Aurelia described how, with local initiative and cooperation with state and federal agencies, wetland regulations have been effective in preserving wetland habitat in suburban Connecticut. The Wildlife Society has developed guidelines and other information that should be useful to state conservation agencies in implementing urban wildlife programs. Joe Schaefer gave good advice on identifying and working with urban publics. George Barker, Nature Conservancy Council, England, gave an excellent overview of urban wildlife programs in Europe, and the poster paper presented by David A. Goode of London also was very informative. There is much we can learn about urban conservation and ecology from Europe. I have been particularly impressed in recent years with what the British have been able to accomplish in urban nature conservation through community-based programs involving volunteer services of citizens and students, and the cooperation of public and private agencies. Several papers in this symposium suggest that we Americans may be catching on and learning to work together in the face of scarce public funds. Implementation of the greenways program discussed by Noonan and Salwasser will be a good test as to how successful we shall be in such cooperation.

I think you will agree that this symposium has demonstrated a growing interest in urban wildlife conservation. It brought together people from many disciplines, and with varied interests in urban wildlife, for a useful exchange of information and ideas. The papers presented here added much to our knowledge of this area of conservation. They described action programs at various levels that may serve as models for other agencies, organizations, and industries; described useful techniques for inventorying wildlife and wildlife habitats and for educating the public; and identified a host of things that need to be done. We still have a mountain of work to get on top of, as suggested earlier, but I believe, as a result of this symposium, the scratches on its surface are a little deeper.